T0313284

Development and the Politics of Human Rights

PUBLIC ADMINISTRATION AND PUBLIC POLICY
A Comprehensive Publication Program

EDITOR-IN-CHIEF

DAVID H. ROSENBLOOM

Distinguished Professor of Public Administration
American University, Washington, DC

Founding Editor

JACK RABIN

RECENTLY PUBLISHED BOOKS

Development and the Politics of Human Rights, Scott Nicholas Romaniuk and Marguerite Marlin

Public Administration and Policy in the Caribbean, Indianna D. Minto-Coy and Evan Berman

The Economic Survival of America's Isolated Small Towns, Gerald L. Gordon

Public Administration and Policy in the Caribbean, Indianna D. Minto-Coy and Evan Berman

Sustainable Development and Human Security in Africa: Governance as the Missing Link, Louis A. Picard, Terry F. Buss, Taylor B. Seybolt, and Macrina C. Lelei

Information and Communication Technologies in Public Administration: Innovations from Developed Countries, Christopher G. Reddick and Leonidas Anthopoulos

Creating Public Value in Practice: Advancing the Common Good in a Multi-Sector, Shared-Power, No-One-Wholly-in-Charge World, edited by John M. Bryson, Barbara C. Crosby, and Laura Bloomberg

Digital Divides: The New Challenges and Opportunities of e-Inclusion, Kim Andreasson

Living Legends and Full Agency: Implications of Repealing the Combat Exclusion Policy, G.L.A. Harris

Politics of Preference: India, United States, and South Africa, Krishna K. Tummala

Crisis and Emergency Management: Theory and Practice, Second Edition, Ali Farazmand

Labor Relations in the Public Sector, Fifth Edition, Richard C. Kearney and Patrice M. Mareschal

Democracy and Public Administration in Pakistan, Amna Imam and Eazaz A. Dar

The Economic Viability of Micropolitan America, Gerald L. Gordon

Available Electronically
PublicADMINISTRATION*netBASE*
http://www.crcnetbase.com/page/public_administration_ebooks

Development and the Politics of Human Rights

Edited by
Scott Nicholas Romaniuk
Marguerite Marlin

Routledge
Taylor & Francis Group
New York London

First published 2016 by CRC Press

Published 2019 by Routledge
711 Third Avenue, New York, NY, 10017
2 Park Square, Milton Park, Abingdon, Oxon OX14 4RN

International Standard Book Number-13: 978-1-4987-0706-0 (Hardback)

Library of Congress Cataloging-in-Publication Data

Development and the politics of human rights / editors, Scott Nicholas Romaniuk and Marguerite Marlin.
    pages cm. -- (Public administration and public policy ; 198)
    Includes bibliographical references and index.
    ISBN 978-1-4987-0706-0 (alk. paper)
    1. Human rights. 2. Human rights--Political aspects. I. Romaniuk, Scott Nicholas. II. Marlin, Marguerite.

JC571.D476 2015
323--dc23
          2015023689

Visit the Taylor & Francis Web site at
http://www.taylorandfrancis.com

Contents

SECTION II HUMAN RIGHTS

Abstracts

Revisiting World-Systems Analysis in Understanding Development

Marinko Bobić

This chapter presents a reevaluation of critiques of Immanuel Wallerstein's World-Systems Analysis (WSA) in light of the recent financial crisis that has had a tremendous impact on countries around the world. The analysis and discussions are guided by the overarching question: *Is WSA experiencing a legitimacy crisis?* In asking this question, the chapter seeks to revisit and engage with an "old" theory by using recent events in the world with the aim of justifying WSA as an approach to studying development and inequality. While one has to certainly acknowledge some value in the critiques of WSA, they should not significantly shake WSA's theoretical foundations. This chapter argues in favor of WSA as still a positive and therefore fruitful approach to discerning inequalities in a globalized world. Rather than accepting WSA at face-value—simply because it has attracted so much attention over many years—there is a need to reengage in this debate while taking into account some of the most pressing matters of a globalized world. Doing so not only helps to reinforce the usefulness of WSA, but also enables us to shed light on the most salient issues facing politics of development.

Does the Primary Condition for a Sustainable Human Development Meet the Feasibility Condition of Cost–Benefit Analysis?

Hasnat Dewan

The primary condition for sustainable human development (SHD) uses both monetary and non-monetary indicators to determine the sustainable level of human development. As defined, this condition can be expressed in terms of the damage elasticity of human development, where damage is defined based on the nonmonetary cost to the natural and social environments (NSE). A comparison between this sustainability condition and the feasibility condition of cost–benefit analysis (CBA) is useful for determining the sustainability premium or the deadweight loss. Since the cost–benefit methodology uses monetary estimates of all impacts and the primary condition for sustainable human development uses both monetary and nonmonetary indicators, the two methodologies are unlikely to yield the same outcome—unless there is a one-to-one relationship between monetary and nonmonetary benefits and costs. Unlike the feasibility condition of CBA, the primary condition for a sustainable human development varies based on the level of human development and the damage to the NSE in any locality/country.

Crossing Borders: Academe and Cultural Agency in Agricultural Research

Robert W. Blake, Elvira E. Sánchez-Blake, and Debra A. Castillo

This chapter explores social educator actions by academe as cultural agency's natural partner in ways that echo, connect, and create plural discourse among the many dimensions and disciplines of society. Based on collaborations with Mexican partners, we argue this goal is achieved with multiplicative effects when students and faculty, key agents themselves and trainers of intercultural agents learn first-hand by crossing borders to frame issues and work together to articulate collaborative research problems. In so doing, a more inclusive worldview becomes integral context in needs assessments. This has been our long-standing pedagogical approach in leading students—undergraduates and graduates—and faculty from around the world on a multidisciplinary, intergenerational examination of rural and urban development in tropical Latin America. Greater academic agency through more alliances of this kind is needed to better achieve equity goals supported by greater investments targeting community engagement and applied problem solving. We illustrate this learning framework and provide specific livestock research cases in southern Mexico that reveal potentials realized by bringing academe to the field and the field to academe, as part of a reinforcing educational process that promotes understanding and social transformation.

Subordinated Inclusion: The Developmental State and the Dalit Colonies of Southern Kerala

K. M. Pramod

This chapter focuses on the Dalit colonies—or the Dalits residing in distinct parts of India—and problematizes the subject position of "colony-Dalits." For the purpose of the empirical investigation, there is a focus on four Dalit colonies in Southern Kerala/Thiruvithamkur. Through this investigation, the author explores varied dimensions of the process of subordination—including social, historical, economic, and political dimensions—in addition to the process of subordinate inclusion in the larger context of the developmental discourse of modern Kerala, India.

Impact of Labor Law Enhancement in China on Development and Its Implications for Global Development Theory

Marguerite Marlin and Scott Nicholas Romaniuk

This chapter examines the significance of labor reforms in the People's Republic of China (PRC) in terms of their contribution to upholding human rights, and situates the resulting analysis in the context of global development theory. After providing historical context on labor laws previously introduced in the PRC, three key labor reforms (*Labor Contract Law* [2007], *Labor Disputes Mediation and Arbitration Law* [2008], and *Employment Promotion Law* [2008]) are discussed with a view to highlighting criticisms and praise of the reforms from various local and global actors. While the complexity involved in establishing causal linkages is acknowledged, statistical and substantive connections are then made between these reforms and various indicators of development in China in the years following their enactment. The result of the analysis is one that challenges orthodoxies of development theory by neoliberal institutions, such as the prioritization of commodities over rights-based development and standpoints that demonstrably have presented the strengthening of labor rights against development objectives. By extension, WTO current policy on labor rights is called into question and key policy prescriptions are articulated in order to provide greater impetus for rights-based development.

Persistence of Italian Mafia: Violent Entrepreneurs in Developed States

Marinko Bobić

Why does the Mafia persist in a state that stands in strong contradiction to the existence of such organizations? This chapter analyzes the existence and persistence of the Mafia in the Italian state in an era of globalization by taking into account several independent variables. In this vein, three independent variables are proposed: (1) the availability of violent entrepreneurs, (2) the existence of a market for private protection, and (3) the Mafia's transformation to serve and depend on a state. All three variables cause the Mafia's resiliency. This research is divided into the following sections: The first section provides alternative explanations for persistence of the Mafia in southern Italy; the second section begins with process tracing, dealing with a historical role of the Mafia; the third section deals with a transformation of the Mafia into its modern role. The fourth section addresses the symbiotic relationship that exists between Mafia and the Italian state. Prospects for further research are presented after the conclusion.

Bridging Worlds: Academe and Cultural Agency in Southern Mexico

Robert W. Blake, Elvira E. Sánchez-Blake, and Debra A. Castillo

The pedagogical portfolio presented in this chapter contains cultural agency and performance studies in addressing some of the main challenges facing the peoples of Chiapas, Mexico. It is designed to share and to build knowledge on a foundation of respect and solidarity. Human rights and other issues are rooted in tolerance, inclusion, and value enhancement deriving from the celebration of cultural difference. We briefly describe a series of encounters between Chiapanecan social realities and academe. Concerned about the limited political and social power of the groups with whom our students interacted, they committed to finding an appropriate artistic response that would supplement other forms of activism in the area. Accordingly, a devised script—*Kan Balaam*—was co-written with students to elicit awareness and understanding about socio-cultural issues. Presented in a complexly staged performance, *Kan Balaam* integrates Maya myths and cosmology with contemporary issues facing Chiapanecan communities as interpreted by students.

By remembering, reenacting, and transmitting these stories, we hope to contribute to a stronger voice with greater understanding and visibility for the forgotten people of our hemisphere. We also analyze the power of performance as an engine of cultural agency that naturally connects with community and reinforces academe. Thus, cultural attitudes and perceptions are transformed, knowledge is created through research and disseminated, and social awareness and respect are raised. The performing culture theatrical experience described in this chapter condenses into a clear example of the adoption of cultural agency by academe.

A New Index to Measure Group Inequalities in Human Development for Sustainability

Hasnat Dewan

Different types of inequality exist among different groups in a society. Inequality in terms of capabilities or end goals of life may lead to unrest, and is against the spirit of sustainability. When the goal of sustainability is to optimize resource allocation between generations, it cannot ignore the rights of the deprived people on resources within the current generation. This chapter proposes a new equity index that measures group inequality in terms of human development or end goals of life. The proposed index meets the Pigou–Dalton condition of transfer and is consistent with Rawlsian justice. This chapter shows how the equity index can be used to compute gender inequality and regional disparity. A nonpositive change in the value of the equity index over time is desirable for national integrity and social sustainability. This index can be used to evaluate the effectiveness of any affirmative action or equity program.

Coordination Failure in Global Common Pool Governance?

Jan-Erik Lane

As we may recall, Marx argued that capitalist society suffered from in-built contradictions that would lead to its demise in time. Today, the globe faces another major kind of contradiction: rapid economic development against ecological sustainability. The relationships between economic growth and environmental sustainability have been much debated: Can they be combined to give both prosperity and environmental protection? On the micro level, many projects show that this is indeed possible. However, on the macro level, global emissions of greenhouse gases follow the advancement of country affluence closely. The link is the constantly increasing need for more energy provided by fossil fuels.

Bernard Stiegler on Agricultural Innovation

Pieter Lemmens

According to Bernard Stiegler's theory of techno-evolution, technologies have an intrinsically pharmacological nature. This means that they are simultaneously supportive and destructive for sociotechnical practices based on them. Technological innovations always first disrupt existing sociotechnical practices, but can and should then always be appropriated by the social system to be turned into a new technical system upon which new sociotechnical practices are based. As constituted and conditioned by a technical system, agriculture is necessarily a system of care. Current deployment of transgenic technologies under capitalist conditions induces processes of proletarianization in agriculture, which has led to their widespread rejection. However, they can and should become the basis of a new system of care—but only under the condition that they are wrought from corporate control and redeployed to initiate a process of deproletarianization.

Foreign Aid and Human Rights: Putting Investment into Perspective

Sebastian D. T. Jedicke and Scott Nicholas Romaniuk

Does foreign aid work? The World Bank, United States, and European Union are the major players pumping billions of USD into foreign economies in order to improve their infrastructure, military, education, combat disasters, and aid in other ways. *How do we decide on which country will be the recipient of aid and why?* Scholars such as Sachs, Moyo, and Easterly all present a different opinion regarding the approach and if it can effectively achieve desired aims. *Foreign aid should be an investment in the future, but does investing in a faulty political system benefit the people or does it benefit the foreign policy objectives of the donor countries?* Foreign aid could be an effective weapon for human rights, but rewarding countries that violate human rights with aid packages does not contribute toward the achievement of the Millennium Development Goals (MDGs) and Human Rights by the target date of 2015 as outlined by the United Nations. While some rights steps were made toward the achievement of the MDGs, it is clear that aid is often wasted and does not link human rights, good governance, and development as the United Nations intended. This chapter outlines why it does not matter if foreign aid is effective or not, as long as it is an effective foreign policy tool.

Discrimination and Hate: Overcriminalization or New Normativity?

Charis Papacharalambous

Criminal legislation against hate speech is controversial. The main objections against such legislation refer to primacy of freedom of speech, the disproportion of the penal reaction, and reservations as to the effectiveness of penal control. On the other hand, repression of hate speech seems well-founded since a serious harm or at least a significant offense can be traced in such conduct. This chapter argues in favor of an extensive and holistic incrimination of hate speech. Points of departure are a normative rather than naturalistic conception of harm, the connection to democratic militancy as legitimacy base of the respective criminal law control, and the abandonment of a fully-fledged liberalism, as it is displayed through the United States paradigm. It is also argued that this standpoint fits better in a proper doctrinal frame concerning hate speech and discriminatory conduct. Certain traits of a proper criminal reaction to hate speech are discerned: The group-based legal nature of the insulting behavior, the preventive orientation of the criminal law system (especially the conception of hate speech acts as inchoate offenses) the limitations as to accepting error of facts of the defendant, and the criminal significance of the perpetrator's "animus," from which the very harmfulness of the conduct cannot be separated. As a conclusion, it is submitted that a "maximum" criminal law against hate is needed expressing the normative primacy of democracy over abstract and negative "freedom."

Work Discrimination against Women Employees in Malaysia

Zaiton Othman and Nooraini Othman

The Malaysian government has been highly committed to achieving gender equality by providing education parity, equal employment opportunities and antidiscriminatory tools, and regulations. Despite these efforts, discrimination against women persists in the workplace, especially at the managerial level. This chapter aims to discuss the nature and forms of discrimination faced by female employees in Malaysia. It also discusses how the government, employers, and educational institutions can better enhance their roles in addressing and possibly curbing work discrimination and, finally, positively enhance women's mental health levels.

Employee Rights: The Equity–Equality Conflict as a Dilemma in the Management of Reward Systems

Steen Scheuer

This chapter investigates the factors that determine workplace actors' appeal to social norms of fairness in some situations and what "fairness" is perceived as consisting of. *When is a pay level considered relativity fair, and when is it not? When are contingent pay systems (i.e., pay-for-performance systems) perceived as fair and when are they not? When can differences in contribution (equity) overrule the social norm of equality? Which contingent reward structure should be applied for teamwork members, if any? Which reward structure should be utilized to motivate employees to a continuous search for smarter working procedures and solutions?* These are central concerns of motivation theory in which rational choice decisions are counterbalanced by endowment effects or other fairness concerns. Management is placed in a dilemma between what is, for example, an economically rational structure of incentives on the one hand, and, on the other, what is considered equitable in accordance with employment rights by employees. Since equality in reward counts for more among a considerable fraction of employees—while equity in contribution counts more for most employers—this is an inherent dilemma, constantly having to be negotiated and solved but never reaching any decisive solution in any company. On the basis of this dilemma, implications for management are described and recommendations for the utilization of and limitations for pay variance among peers are given.

Securing the Future of the Community: Child Protection in ASEAN

Palapan Kampan and Adam R. Tanielian

This chapter reflects upon effects of the Convention on the Rights of the Child and related treaties since their inception, with a focus on the ASEAN group. Literature, legal, and statistical review and analyses show successes and failures on several points: nutrition, child soldiers, child sexual exploitation, HIV/AIDS, substance abuse, child labor, violence, and education. The research found abuse of children's rights is high enough to warrant serious concern. Violations of rights both come from and lead to deep poverty, leaving the ASEAN community vulnerable in the present and future. Creative, aggressive policy changes are promoted while universal acceptance and enforcement of children's rights—like any human rights—are likely to succeed or fail due to actions or inactions in smaller social segments and communities.

Researching International Humanitarian Law: A Decision-Making Process Model for Operationalizing State Practice

Matthew T. Zommer

A methodological challenge confronting scholars of international law (IL) and international relations (IR) is operationalizing customary international law and state practice. This challenge is compounded when the subject has given rise to extensive primary source material, as is the case with international humanitarian law (IHL). This chapter develops a comprehensive research model that examines state practice of IHL as a decision-making process and employs diverse source material, involving multiple levels and types of government agencies, officials, military practitioners, and non-state actors. One of the advantages of the process perspective is that it helps to organize the large body of IHL material that often goes overlooked and underutilized. This chapter offers an alternative to prevailing methodologies and advances an approach that is both exploratory and structured. This "foundational" perspective can potentially serve as a bridge between IL and IR, providing the raw material for interdisciplinary dialogue and theory development. Finally, this chapter introduces the argument that both disciplines would benefit from including a historical perspective when writing on this controversial and emotive subject.

Gender Conjectures and Politics of Land Right Deprivation in South-Eastern Nigeria

Amaka Theresa Oriaku Emordi and Emeka Thaddues Njoku

This chapter examines how various gender conjectures reflected in the narrative *nwanyi adighi enwe ala* aids in the continued denial of the rights of women to inherit, acquire, or sell land in Igbo, Southeastern Nigeria. It posits that these conjectures have survived over time due to a systematic process of socialization, where male children learn early in life the subservient roles of women and their very limited rights in the family. Although the Land Rights Act of 1978 was introduced to replace the customary land laws, the Act did nothing to correct the limited land rights of Igbo women as it recognizes many provisions of the customary law. Thus, the chapter concludes that many urban and rural Igbo women's responses to these cultural practices demonstrate frustration and acceptance, respectively. These have significant implications for the socioeconomic development of Igbo women in Nigeria.

Monitoring the Right to Health: The Political, Social, and Ethical Impact of Patient Satisfaction

Emmanuel Kabengele Mpinga and Philippe Chastonay

The concept of patient satisfaction has a long history of controversy and debate, yet it remains a topic of scientific investigation that is of great importance to the improvement of health in communities around the world. Although little is known about its importance as a tool for monitoring the right to health, a nonexhaustive review of scientific articles reported in *Medline* was undertaken for this study in order to better understand how patient satisfaction can be investigated and what it indicates. In recent years, the concept of patient satisfaction has shown an evolution toward complexity while becoming increasingly operational. Patient satisfaction studies have proven to be of value as a health indicator, enabling the implementation of improvement strategies in the health sector based on "the voice of the patient"; therefore, becoming a potential right to health indicator. In spite of the inherent limitations, these studies remain of interest as a health indicator and should be considered such within public health agendas in communities across the globe.

European Models of Citizenship and the Fight against Female Genital Mutilation

Renée Kool and Sohail Wahedi

Today, many Western countries face the consequences of an "open admission policy" of immigrants from all over the world. One of these consequences concerns the application of cultural practices that are generally considered harmful within modern liberal democracies. It seems that female circumcision (better known as female genital mutilation or FGM), in particular, appeals to a broad sense of injustice, as this practice is considered a gross violation of human rights. The debate on FGM culminated provisionally after the adoption of the resolution 67/146 by the General Assembly of the United Nations, which calls upon its member states to eliminate this practice by the use of "punitive measures" (among other means). Although 10 Western European countries have specific criminal law provisions on FGM, the global calls for the elimination of this practice as well as the political and academic consensus that FGM is a criminal practice have not resulted in a broad criminal enforcement in banning this practice. In contrast, the criminal prosecution hereof diverges widely. This is remarkable, as prosecution of FGM fits the human rights-based approach to eliminate this practice by restoring the violated standards. Therefore, the question arises whether national views on citizenship and multiculturalism may offer an explanation for the differences in outcome in the criminal prosecution of FGM. This study pays particular attention to the way France, England, and the Netherlands have criminalized FGM, and whether the results of their legal approaches in banning this practice by using criminal law can be declared by the particular notions of citizenship that are leading in the studied states.

"You Just Don't See Us": The Influence of Public Schema on Constructions of Sexuality by People with Cerebral Palsy

Tinashe M. Dune

This study investigated how people with cerebral palsy (CP) perceived the influence of public sexual schema on their construction of sexuality. In-depth, semi-structured interviews were conducted with five men and two women with moderate-to-severe CP from Australia and Canada. The interview discourse focused on how, if at all, public constructions of sexuality influenced the way in which respondents understood and negotiated their sexuality. Interview data were thematically analyzed using NVivo and manual line-by-line analysis. Findings suggest that people living with CP found the media to be informative, albeit skewed in favor of typical others. As such, they perceive themselves to be asexualized by the public media and popular culture. They also believed the general public to share popular media's regard of persons with CP as unlikely sexual partners due to their inability to meet normative expectations of physical movement and functioning. The respondents also believed public perception was linked to the range of access to services, resources, sexual opportunities, and privacy for people with disabilities. Participants preferred typical others as their ideal partners regardless of being devalued as sexual beings by popular culture and its manifestations. For people with CP, inclusion in public presentations of sexuality and intimacy is necessary in order to reinforce people with disabilities as sexual (candidates).

The contributions in this volume represent the seeds of a growing culture of resistance against those who wish to persecute the ideas and practices of freedom and enlightenment. Although countries differ markedly when it comes to quality of life, a spirit of promise and determination in its populace is ubiquitous. These elements are the critical conditions for directing development and the establishment of human rights, even amid waves of conflict, economic instability, and arrested social and political progression.

Preface

The growth and management of the state (including institutions, government and governance, democracy, and civil society and social movements) and human rights have always been, and promise to continue to be, a hazardous and emotive affair. As this book emphasizes, the domain of human rights and its related theoretical principles can be fully explored in all global jurisdictions, in ways not merely limited to basic principles of liberty and survival, but also in a manner that encompasses all aspects of human freedom and quality of life. Each chapter of this book presents a different context in which a set of unique challenges to the establishment, maintenance, and strengthening of human rights is examined.

There are significant socioeconomic and political dimensions to the definition, public acceptance, and upholding of the practice of human rights. The manner and state of worldwide political and socioeconomic development provide a dynamic perspective from which to view the symbiotic relationship between development and human rights. By providing holistic perspectives that help the reader to understand the state of play in these select regions and their linkages to communities experiencing similar issues in other global corridors, the relationship of development to both "positive" and "negative" human rights* is evident. This is an important contribution to the understanding of these issues, for while development is more readily associated with positive human rights such as the right to food, water, and shelter, so too is the correlation between development and negative human rights, such as the right to be free from oppression, persecution, and abuse, a substantial one. That development has a role to play in this range of contexts and is a central tenant of this work as it underscores the utility of an approach to upholding human rights that does not solely consist of a legal focus.

Many who realize that greater value exists in a right granted rather than in a right taken away would also see the major themes presented in this book as more than mere rights. To a significant degree, there is a great divide between those who are right-receivers and right-granters. So strong is this divide, that the lives of more than half the world's population are enshrined in a Dickensian horror—the major themes of which are poverty and social injustice. In spite of the fact that the uniqueness and difference of peoples around the world are overtly apparent, a common theme links every human being whether he or she is living in excess or surviving in poverty: We are all peoples deserving the same sense of security, freedom, respect, opportunity, and fair treatment. Human rights extends beyond these fields to include the right to education, to participate in democratic processes and participatory governance, to practice religion or religions so desired by

---

* A positive right is a right *to* something, requiring action to be upheld; conversely, a negative right consists of the freedom *from* something, requiring inaction to be upheld.

any individual or group of individuals, and to receive fair pay for honest work in places of employment where the safety of those laboring is ensured and protected.

The unique challenges related to the struggle for human rights explored in this book are also addressed with a view to answering pivotal questions of capacity for change. *Are current human rights enforcement regimes equitable in their practice? How do responses to conflict and humanitarian crises affect questions of and the practice of human rights?* These questions vary according to the topics presented in the following chapters, but they share one consistent feature: a demonstrable focus on determining best practices for ensuring that human rights are recognized, protected, and upheld in the various contexts presented.

The ensuing pages also paint a portrait of the significant impact that abandonment of the struggle for the maintenance and strengthening of the above three themes would have on the future of free and open societies. Ultimately, organizations big and small, social awareness groups, advocacy groups, active citizens, professionals, and academics should continue to interact, advise, pressure, and act as the critical forum that will ideally facilitate the development of a cooperative and involved network of communities around the world. Through the consideration of a variety of interregional perspectives and cases, this volume engages with questions of liberal restraint and limitations as well as how advocates respond and should respond in their policy choices. Even after decades of addressing and confronting some of the most egregious issues afflicting states, the extent of atrocities—particularly in terms of attacks on democratic practice, social movements, and the rights of human beings—remain tremendously chaotic, controversial, and confusing.

One instance of this caustic mixture was seen in the pugnacity that characterized much of the Arab world, beginning in early 2011 with the so-called "Arab Spring." A testament to the strength of feeling experienced by humanity everywhere when citizens stand up for their democratic and human rights is the extent to which this movement captured the attention and sympathy across the globe. Dynamics of change in all parts of the world, however, become less captivating when they do not follow a simplified narrative of teleological change without interruption—as the aftermath of the "Arab Spring" showed. Indeed, the unfolding and recurrence of complex obstacles requiring contextual knowledge are confounding specters for a public that had viewed these developments through a more simplified (politicized) lens.

To foment a truly civilized discourse, those viewing these movements from a Western perspective must be wary of relegating these issues to other areas of the world; indeed, if those in developed countries are serious about the pursuit of democratic and human ideals at a global level, it is all the more important to subject the systems in one's own sphere to the same kind of vigorous scrutiny. This principle is what forms the basis of "practice what you preach," and renders it a crucial element in this body of work.

The chapters in this book touch on the fundamental tenants of human rights theory and practice in a global context, at all multiple levels of development. The book's focus moves inwardly from global to local, beginning with a structural examination of human rights policy and practice in international governmental institutions, and following with analyses of human rights-related dynamics operating within various localities and states. Freedom from hardship, persecution, and abuse, and the right to be treated equally in relation to the rest of society are the overarching motivators driving the analysis found in the following chapters.

As a result, a reader will be able to sense a certain imperative for profound understanding and means for change that are the subtexts of each work of research, and will be able to piece together a patchwork of blueprints and emancipatory pedagogy for a better world—a world in which human rights flourish alongside development and are championed effectively and thoroughly in all corridors of global society. Though the resulting work is a heady mixture of diverse elements—and by no means does it cover all existing ground within the field—the microcosmic approach in each study allows for both an on-the-ground perspective and an adequate representation of the broader picture bringing these elements together.

Scott Nicholas Romaniuk and Marguerite Marlin

Editors

Scott Nicholas Romaniuk is a PhD student in international studies (University of Trento, Italy). He has an MRes in political research (University of Aberdeen), a BA with a double major in history, and German language and literature (University of Alberta), and Certificates in Conditions of War and Peace (University of Tokyo), Understanding Terrorism and the Terrorist Threat (University of Maryland), Terrorism and Counterterrorism: Comparing Theory and Practice (Leiden University), and Terrorism Studies (University of St. Andrews). His research focuses on asymmetric warfare, counterterrorism, international security, and the use of force. He is a native speaker of English, and is proficient in German and French.

Marguerite Marlin is a PhD candidate in political science (comparative public policy) at McMaster University in Hamilton, Ontario. She specializes in comparative legislatures, nongovernmental influence on public policy, and Arctic affairs. She previously completed an MA in European, Russian, and Eurasian Studies at Carleton University in Ottawa and continues to provide analysis on Canadian–Russian relations and Ukrainian constitutional reform at speaking engagements associated with the Canadian International Council and others. She was a young researcher at the Northern Research Forum's Open Assembly in 2014 and has had written works featured in a variety of academic and nonacademic publications.

Contributors

Robert W. Blake is professor of animal science and from 2009 to 2014, director of the Center for Latin American and Caribbean Studies, Michigan State University, East Lansing, and professor emeritus at Cornell University, where he directed the Latin American Studies Program and the graduate field of International Agriculture and Rural Development. His international program emphasizes economic, nutritional, and genetic issues of management of livestock and mixed farming systems. Foci include management of livestock systems, especially dual-purpose ruminants, and economic evaluation and decision-making, especially matching animal genetic potentials to environmental constraints in alternative agroecosystems. Outreach and development are integral activities with information disseminated to international collaborators and other decision makers.

Marinko Bobić is a PhD student in international studies at the University of Trento, Italy. His areas of expertise are geopolitics and international security. His dissertation focuses on asymmetric conflicts between great powers and smaller states. He earned an MSc in international relations and diplomacy (Leiden University, Netherlands) and a BA in political science (Simon Fraser University, Canada). Marinko is a contributing analyst for Wikistrat, a private consulting firm, and he has also worked for the Citizenship and Immigration Canada and several NGOs. He has published a book, chapters, and academic as well as media articles.

Debra A. Castillo is Stephen H. Weiss Presidential Fellow, Emerson Hinchliff Professor of Hispanic studies, and professor of comparative literature at Cornell University. She was appointed president of the international Latin American Studies Association from 2014 to 2015. She specializes in contemporary narrative from the Spanish-speaking world (including the United States), gender studies, and cultural theory. Her most recent books are *Cartographies of Affect: Across Borders in South Asia and the Americas* (with Kavita Panjabi), *Hybrid Storyspaces* (with Christine Henseler), *Mexican Public Intellectuals* (with Stuart Day), and the forthcoming *Despite All Adversities: Spanish American Queer Cinema* (with Andrés Lema Hincapié).

Philippe Chastonay is former professor of public health at the University of Geneva. With his primary interest in pedagogy and andragogy, he was responsible for reorganizing and renewing the teaching of public health at the Faculty of Medicine. He is currently deputy director of the Swiss School of Public Health.

Hasnat Dewan has more than 20 years of experience teaching economics at universities in the United States, Canada, China, and Bangladesh, and he is currently chair of economics at Thompson Rivers University, Canada. Dewan earned an MA in international and development economics from Yale University, and a PhD in economics from the University of Texas at Austin. A Fulbright scholar, Dewan was awarded the highest university-wide academic honor—the Asadul

Kabir Gold Medal—for his outstanding results in his BSc (honors) examination at Jahangirnagar University, Bangladesh. He also ranked first among more than 32,000 students in the Secondary School Certificate Examination in Bangladesh. Dewan specializes in environmental and natural resource economics, urban and regional economics, and sustainable development. He has received 16 awards from government agencies and universities in three countries for academic teaching, research, and service excellence.

Tinashe M. Dune's research, teaching, and publications focus on sexual marginalization and health inequities. She explores the phenomenological experiences of sexuality, sexual health, sexual well-being, and cross-cultural understandings of sexuality in marginalized populations (i.e., GLBTIQ people, aging populations, people with disabilities, women's health, African women, and indigenous women). Her academic pursuits and interests are supported by several years of hands-on community outreach work. She has dedicated herself to the Sex Worker Outreach Program (SWOP) in Sydney and made trips to Western Australia and Queensland to provide support to sex workers of various backgrounds. Dune has also been a Disability Support Worker for several years in Canada for Carleton University students with physical disabilities. Tinashe has interned at the World Health Organization in Geneva, Switzerland with the Violence, Injury, and Disability and Reproductive Health Research Units. She also functions as an honorary research associate for the Collaborative Research Network Mental Health and Well-Being (funded by the Department of Education Employment and Workplace Relations) at the University of New England and has been an honorary research associate for the Australian ICF Disability and Rehabilitation Research Program (AIDARRP) at the University of Sydney. Dune cofounded and acted as Collaborative Research Liaison Officer for the *Regional Research in Intersexuality, Gender, Human Rights, Transissues and Sexualities (RRIGHTS)* at the University of New England. In her role as vice-chair, Research and Development for African Women Australia, she actively seeks funding, and conducts and disseminates findings from research undertaken by AWAU and its collaborators.

Amaka Theresa Oriaku Emordi earned a PhD in political science from the University of Ibadan, Nigeria, where she serves as an academic advisor. She is a 2015 short-term scholar at Brown International Advance Research Institutes (BIARI), Watson Institute for International Development, Brown University. She is a gender expert who is passionate about gender equality, committed to building a viril and full society, and acts in the interests of women's education and engagement through all levels of governance. Emordi has played a role in the multinational manufacturing industry where she worked in senior human resources personnel for seven years.

Sebastian D. T. Jedicke is a politics and international relations (MA) student at the University of Aberdeen, Department of Politics and International Relations, UK. He is a South African national educated in Germany and the Netherlands. Collecting military experience as part of the University Officer Training Corps during his studies, his research focuses on terrorism and counterterrorism. He has a keen interest in energy security, analyzing the impact of energy demands on the political relationship of Russia and the European Union. He holds multiple junior powerlifting records in Scotland and was awarded Full-Blues in 2015 by the University of Aberdeen in recognition of his athletic achievements.

Palapan Kampan, a Thai national, is an expert researcher at the National Institute for Development Administration in Bangkok, Thailand. He earned bachelor's degrees in psychology and law, and master's degrees in business, finance, and law. He also earned a PhD in population and environmental studies, and is currently working toward an LLD in international law.

Renée Kool is an associate professor at the Willem Pompe Institute for Criminal Law and Criminology and the Utrecht Center for Accountability and Liability Law (UCALL), Utrecht University. She focuses mainly on liability-related themes and conducts research on the convergence of criminal and private law. She publishes regularly on criteria for criminalization and procedural justice, cultural offenses, discrimination, and victim rights. Renée Kool is a deputy judge at the criminal division of the regional court of Midden-Nederland, Utrecht.

Jan-Erik Lane has taught politics and economics at many universities around the world. He has been a member of many editorial boards of political and social science journals. He has published roughly 300 books and articles. In 1996 and 2009, he received the Alexander von Humboldt-Foundation's Humboldt Award, a Lady Davis Fellowship at the Hebrew University in 2006 and 2012, and honorary medals from Cairo University and the University of Qatar. He is a permanent resident of Switzerland and lives part-time in Myanmar. He has been a full professor at three universities and a visiting professor at many more.

Pieter Lemmens is both a philosopher and a biologist. He wrote his philosophy thesis on the intimate relationship between humans and technology entitled, "Driven by Technology: The Human Condition and the Biotechnology Revolution," and earned a PhD in 2008 from the Radboud University in Nijmegen, Netherlands. He currently teaches philosophy and ethics at Radboud University. He has published on themes in the philosophy of technology and innovation, and on the works of Martin Heidegger, Peter Sloterdijk, Bernard Stiegler, Michael Hardt, and Antonio Negri, and in other fields. He is currently interested in the political potential of new digital IC-technologies, politics of human (cognitive) enhancement technologies, and the philosophy of technology in the age of the Anthropocene.

Emmanuel Kabengele Mpinga is a keen human rights defender in the Democratic Republic of Congo. He is currently Professor of Health and Human Rights in the Faculty of Medicine at the University of Geneva, where he teaches the importance of the link between health and human rights. His research focuses on the epistemology of health and human rights, the understanding of human rights by health personnel, and the impact of violations of basic human rights on the health of individuals and communities. He also acts as an expert in several international organizations.

Emeka Thaddues Njoku holds a BSc in political science from Enugu State University of Science and Technology, Nigeria and an MSc in political science from the University of Ibadan, Nigeria. He is currently a PhD candidate in the department of political science, University of Ibadan. His research foci include terrorism and counterterrorism, civil society, and development. He has researched and written extensively on terrorism in Nigeria, examining the success rates of terrorist attacks and the Nigerian government's capabilities to curb the growing trend. He is a fellow of the Social Science Research Council in New York and the Institute of French and African Studies (IFRA) in Ibadan. Njoku is a contributing analyst with Wikistrat, Washington, DC, and academic advisor in the Department of Political Science, University of Ibadan, Distance Learning Center.

Nooraini Othman is an associate professor at the Perdana School of Science, Technology and Innovation Policy, Universiti Teknologi Malaysia. Her areas of study include psychology, education, and policy studies. She specializes in Islamic psychology. Her research and publications as well as postgraduate supervisions are related to her main study areas. Her major publications include *Exploring the Ummatic Personality Dimensions from the Psycho-Spiritual Paradigm*

(2011), *A Comparative Study Between Western and Islamic Perspectives on Human Development and Life-Friendly Environment* (2014), and *Integrated System in the Malaysian Education Paradigm: A Catalyst for a Holistic Personality Development* (2014). She currently leads a research project entitled, "An Intervention and Psychological Module to Strengthen the Affective and Cognitive Domains of the Muscular Dystrophy Patients in Malaysia."

Zaiton Othman is currently a lecturer at the School of Management, Institut Profesional Baitulmal, Kuala Lumpur. She is a business graduate of Idaho State University and holds an MBA from University Putra Malaysia. Her area of specialization is human resource management and she is a certified professional trainer.

Charis Papacharalambous is an associate professor of criminal law, Department of Law, University of Cyprus. He holds a PhD in Criminal Law and Law Theory from Goethe University, Germany, and is a lawyer at the Greek Supreme Court. He formerly served as a legal advisor to the Greek Minister of Justice, Senior Investigator at the Greek Ombudsman. He is the author of two books on criminal law, and numerous articles and remarks on court judgments in Greek, Cypriot, and international legal journals. His areas of interest include imputation theories, complicity theories, international criminal law, critical legal studies, and the theory of criminal law discourse.

K. M. Pramod earned his PhD in education from the University of Calicut, India. His PhD thesis is titled, "Education and Development among Tribals in Kerala: A Study with Special Reference to Wayanad District." He previously earned an MEd in education from the University of Calicut, and an MPhil in interdisciplinary social sciences and economics from Mahatma Gandhi University, School of Social Science. His MPhil thesis is titled, "Spaces of Subordination: The Making of Dalit Colonies in Kerala." He also holds an MA in development economics with specializations in agriculture, economics, rural development, and international economics from Mahatma Gandhi University, Dr. John Mathai Center, Department of Economics, and an MA in sociology from the University of Calicut, School of Distance Education. He completed the National Eligibility Test (NET) in economics and education, and a Junior Research Fellowship (JRF) in education, conducted by the University Grants Commission (India) in 2006. He currently works at Devaki Amma Memorial Teacher Education College, Chelembra, Kerala, India.

Elvira E. Sánchez-Blake is an associate professor of Latin American literature and culture at Michigan State University. She is the author of *Patria se escribe con sangre* (Anthropos, 2000), a collection of testimonials from women in the Colombian conflict. She is the coauthor of the anthology, *Voces Hispanas Siglo XXI: Entrevistas con Autores en DVD* (Yale University Press, 2005); the critical collection of essays, *El Universo Literario de Laura Restrepo* (Taurus, 2007); and *The Literature of Madness by Latin American Women* (McFarland, coauthor with Laura Kanost, forthcoming, 2015). As a creative writer, she has published the novel, *Espiral de Silencios* (Beaumont, 2009), short stories, theater plays, and poetry.

Steen Scheuer earned an MA in sociology from the University of Copenhagen, a PhD in business economics, and a DSC from the Copenhagen Business School. He is currently a professor at the Department of Leadership and Corporate Strategy, University of Southern Denmark, where he teaches sociology of work and management and supervises graduate and PhD students. He has published articles in *Acta Sociologica, British Journal of Industrial Relations, European Journal of Industrial Relations, Industrial Relations Journal, Journal of Labor Research,* and *Thunderbird*

International Business Review, and the books, *Social and Economic Motivation at Work: Theories of Motivation Reassessed* (2000) and *The Anatomy of Change: A Neo-Institutionalist Perspective* (2008).

Adam R. Tanielian is an American working as a foreign English lecturer at King Faisal University in Hofuf, Saudi Arabia. He has 10 years of experience as a certified math and business studies secondary school teacher. Tanielian earned his bachelor's degree from Michigan Technological University, where he studied international business, electrical engineering, psychology, and Japanese. He completed an MBA and an LLD in international law at the Institute of International Studies at Ramkhamhaeng University, Thailand.

Sohail Wahedi is a doctoral researcher at the *Erasmus School of Law*. He has successfully completed the prestigious Legal Research Master (LLM) at Utrecht University. His doctoral research focuses on the dynamics of religious manifestations and the contemporary constitutional value of religion within liberal democracies.

Matthew T. Zommer, PhD, studied at the City University of New York (CUNY), Graduate Center and John Jay College of Criminal Justice. His academic expertise is in the laws of war, where he utilizes an interdisciplinary approach—including perspectives found in the fields of international criminal justice, international law, and international relations. Zommer is currently writing on the role of reciprocity in military training and the theoretical application of the English School of international relations on the laws of war. As a professor at The Citadel, he teaches courses in international humanitarian law, comparative counterterrorism, and international crime.

DEVELOPMENT

I

Chapter 1

Revisiting World-Systems Analysis in Understanding Development

Marinko Bobić

Contents

Introduction

After the September 11, 2001 (9/11) terrorist attacks in the United States , the seemingly strengthening focus on human security, and human rights, gave way to renewed focus on state security, the main protagonist of which became terrorism. Hopes that humanitarian imperatives would overcome traditional views on conflict quickly faded away. Further, the global financial crisis of 2008 exposed growing global inequalities, which fueled conflict, including terrorism. Indeed, as though a can of worms had been opened, the closer we approached to 2015, the more we saw the return of revolutions, revolts, instability, and conflict of various types. Development, in other words, apparently failed to adequately address growing global inequalities and the subsequent necessity to protect human rights. While these renewed trajectories were tackled from many different angles, it is those of the world-systems analysis (WSA) that specifically focused on development's inherent inability to overcome growing inequalities. Any discussion of development will face severe challenges, as long it does not recognize growing inequalities in a capitalist system. The idea of uneven development is worth revisiting as the globe faces very similar challenges that Immanuel Wallerstein raised a few decades ago.

Wallerstein analysis left an important legacy in social sciences broadly, development studies specifically. It has been derived from neo-Marxism, the French Annales School with Fernand Braudel, and dependency theory (Sanderson, 2005: 180). Although it is not an official theory, it proposes to be an approach to studying social issues and/or international relations, especially socioeconomic particularities. As much as many authors embrace WSA as an approach, there are those who reject it, some partially though critically enough question the value of its basic concepts. This chapter seeks to reevaluate several critiques of WSA in light of the recent financial crisis. Thus, guided by the question whether WSA is experiencing a legitimacy crisis, the purpose here is to revisit an "old" theory through a fresh lens in order to justify WSA as an approach to studying development and inequality. While one has to certainly acknowledge some value in the critiques of WSA, they should not significantly shake WSA's theoretical foundations. On the contrary, I propose that WSA offers much usefulness in discerning inequalities in the globalized world of today. Perhaps the observation that WSA has attracted so many disciples should speak for itself as to its attractiveness. Yet, engaging debate in light of the recent crisis can perhaps shed much more light on the most salient (if regrettably egregious) issues facing politics of development.

Main Concepts of WSA

The most fundamental concept of WSA is its basic unit of analysis: the world-system. As Wallerstein illustrates, the world-system is meant to replace the nation state as the unit of analysis because the nation state has proved an inadequate unit in understanding the processes that cut across spatial/temporal zones. On the same note, he states that key to his approach is understanding that the world-system represents, "an integrated zone of activity and institutions that obey certain systemic rules" (Wallerstein, 2004: 16–7). Historically, there were three world systems. We should be concerned only with the current one, which he calls the modern world-system, or the capitalist world-economy. The current world-system contains an extensive division of labor, multiple political units, and no overreaching centralization or unification (Sanderson, 2005: 180). Indeed, the ultimate goal of the world-system as a unit of analysis is to put forward a grand narrative, which reflects reality more closely than other grand narratives (Wallerstein, 2004: 21). Essentially, this basic concept is important to understand how other concepts fit in.

As previously mentioned, WSA has been largely influenced by the dependency theory, which sought to explain the historical aspect of unequal economic exchange between countries. This is where the concept of core–periphery relations becomes relevant to explain that surplus value tends to flow from the weaker, peripheral countries, to the stronger core countries (Wallerstein, 2004: 12). WSA utilized this concept to explain relational differences between countries in terms of their production process. More specifically, a process that is relatively monopolized (what Wallerstein calls "oligopoly") is relatively more profitable in comparison to the free market process that is characteristic of peripheral and semiperipheral countries. The end result is that a monopolized process in exchange with a free market peripheral process would carry off larger profits (Wallerstein, 2004: 18). This creates an unequal exchange, and thus, capital moves from the weak regions to strong regions. Two items, in particular, are important to mention. First, the role of the state is ensuring the protection of these quasi-monopolies or in the case of semiperipheral and peripheral countries, to compete for industries, which have left core-like processes (such as textiles in the modern day). Second, production processes change. What was core-production yesterday would eventually become a peripheral-production tomorrow (Wallerstein, 2004: 29).

The concept of core–periphery is related to another important concept of WSA, the occurrence of evolutionary, or cyclical, trends in history. There are two types of cycles essential to WSA, the Kondratieff cycle and hegemony cycle (Sanderson, 2005: 182). The former refers to the occurrence of economic growth/decline phases every 40–60 years. Specifically, growth and decline refer to, "the expansion of the world-economy when there are quasi-monopolistic leading industries and contraction in the world-economy when there is a lowering of the intensity of quasi-monopoly" (Wallerstein, 2004: 30). Essentially, this trend repeats itself throughout history with industries and technology changing their roles. The latter cycle—hegemony cycle—refers to the historical domination of a single political authority over the world economy, in other words, possessing most of the core-like processes. According to Wallerstein, every strong state has an interest to become a hegemonic power because it reduces interstate competition, thereby creating stability for its capitalist enterprises (Wallerstein, 2004: 58). Both of these cycles are important for WSA because they demonstrate the dynamic nature of the interstate system and world-economy. Different industries rise and fall, as do countries, but not necessarily simultaneously.

The fourth important concept of WSA is that which is considered geoculture of the modern world-system. This concept is defined as, "the normality of political change and the refashioning of the concept of sovereignty, now vested in the people who were 'citizens'" (Wallerstein, 2004: 60). The French Revolution and the birth of liberalism opposed traditional hierarchies (conservatism) and revolutionary movements (radicalism) influencing the acceptance of societal change as an inevitable social condition, yet, at the same time they retained order and hierarchy. Thus, liberalism is a defining feature of geoculture, an ideology encompassing nearly all political participants. Wallerstein claims that the social sciences supplied intellectual basis of the moral justifications used for operation of modern world-system through liberalism, until the cultural revolution of 1968, which shook liberal geoculture (Wallerstein, 2004: 75). The importance of 1968 is related to the fifth and central concept of this chapter.

After the revolution of 1968, the liberal supremacy, the ideology of geoculture, became dislocated, "unhinged the underpinnings of the capitalist world-economy" (Wallerstein, 2004: 77). In other words, the capitalist world-economy was begging to reach its threshold, or what Wallerstein calls, a truly systemic crisis. Essentially, this crisis ought to occur due to many inherent contradictions of the capitalist system, one of them, for example, is that capitalism is based on endless capital accumulation in an environment that cannot sustain it. These contradictions, according to Wallerstein, will lead to a complete demise of the capitalist world-system although it is uncertain in which direction. During early phases of his theory, Wallerstein claimed that it would be replaced by a global socialist world-system, which will be more humane and rational (Sanderson, 2005: 182). However, Wallerstein has recently acknowledged that the current world-system could be replaced by what he calls "rightist forces," essentially being led by the neoliberal ideology as seen in policies of Ronald Reagan and Margaret Thatcher (Wallerstein, 2004: 86). It is clear that this last concept is the overall conclusion of Wallerstein's realization that capitalist world-economy cannot be sustained, and, therefore, must change.

Critiques of WSA

Just like WSA has evolved over time, so have the critiques. Here, we look at two authors who critiqued WSA—one having been written during the midevolution of Wallerstein's writing on WSA, and the other having been written recently. The purpose here is to measure the consistency of critiques aimed at WSA, and also to more easily identify changes or clarifications that Wallerstein has adopted in response.

The older concern with WSA has been its most basic concept: the world-system. The idea of "one economy" or "one social system" has come under heavy attack. "[E]conomic interdependence carries consequences, of course," according to Pieterse (1988: 253), "but it is obvious as well that it can go together with enormous diversity; hence to speak of 'one economy' and a 'social system' introduces an element of arbitrariness." It appears that Pieterse is attacking the assumed homogeneity that exists within WSA. Indeed, he speaks of the fact that we have different autonomies of subsystems, different spheres, levels, and dimensions of social existence. Thus, according to Pieterse, in reality, we see many different social and economic organizations that would be impossible to categorize as "one economy." On the other hand, Wallerstein claims that two systems cannot exist within one (Pieterse, 1988: 256). In other words, this critique puts forward the argument that Nazi Germany, North Korea, and the European Union (EU) would simply not show significant differences in Wallerstein's approach. To summarize, Pieterse believes that in WSA, "the parts are not granted autonomy and the whole [...] predominates as a totalizing principle" (Pieterse, 1988: 256). It appears that from this critique we ought to question the supremacy of the system over its parts.

The second, more recent critique has challenged the validity of the hierarchy of the system, the core peripheral relations. According to Sanderson (2005), the tripartite hierarchy of the system is the most serious weakness of WSA because Wallerstein's hierarchy ends up reifying itself. More specifically, the system assigns roles to the core, semiperipheral, and peripheral countries. The role of one of these depends on the roles of the other two, and they all act in a relationship, which has a consciousness of its own. As Sanderson (2005: 186) states, "it seems to me that all the WSA talk of cores or peripheries as actual structures that have larger roles to play is an illogical theoretical construction that ought to be abandoned." He goes further than this, claiming that the idea that exploitation of the periphery is necessary for capitalism has been disproven; as has the idea that the periphery is a creation of the core. Indeed, the best evidence for this is the claim that the world functions according to a positive-sum formula, where everyone can benefit, and the best example of this is Latin America and most of Asia's recent economic growth (Sachs, 2005: 27–28). Moreover, Sanderson believes that the semiperiphery has become a dumping ground category, "a place to put those societies that don't fit very well in one of the other categories" (Sanderson, 2005: 187). As such, we find in this category countries such as the Soviet Union, Saudi Arabia, Iran, India, China, Canada, Australia, Cuba, and Israel, among others. It would be pretty strange to lump the Soviet Union and Israel together, Canada and Cuba, or all of them. In essence, this critique focuses on the fact that vast differences in processes and organization of countries cannot fit neatly into three categories or adequately explain the relationship between those categories.

The concept of the occurrence of evolutionary, or cyclical, trends in history has also not escaped criticism. While the concept of hegemonic cycles is less critiqued, it was the concept of the Kondratieff cycle that received much attention from critics. Sanderson claims that such cycles have existed for the past 500 years, but the recent world-economy has failed to display traditional signs of a Kondratieff cycle. Namely, the world economy has not entered a new expansionary phase, which it should have (Sanderson, 2005: 184). It is new leading industries, which stimulate a new expansionary phase. However, new leading industries have not emerged, leaving the Kondratieff cycle broken, and thus, an unreliable tool for the future.

Finally, the predictive nature of WSA has received substantial attention. The initial WSA has predicted an emergence of a global socialist world-system, one that will be more rational and humane (Sanderson, 2005: 184). This concept is borrowed from Marxism and applied on a global scale. However, the prediction of socialism as a future scenario is critiqued because it depends on a single factor, an anticipated global economic downturn (Pieterse, 1988: 262). Downturns, according to Pieterse, are unlikely because many have occurred without undermining the system. As such, Wallerstein's claim is questioned because he does not explain what would separate the crucial future downturn from the rest. In more recent works, Wallerstein shifts his original claim of socialism as a future scenario, instead focusing on a struggle between centrist and rightist forces (or "the establishment") and socialist counterrevolutionaries. In this new trajectory, either scenario is possible; therefore, socialism is not inevitable (Wallerstein, 2004: 86). By changing his initial prediction, Wallerstein removes the label "economically deterministic" from WSA. He claims that an emergence of a future system depends on our current and future actions.

Cases

A number of critiques have demonstrated weaknesses of WSA as an approach within the social sciences. While critiques are able to demonstrate the fallibility of some of the assumptions behind WSA, it is my intention in the following part of this chapter to demonstrate strengths of WSA through a discussion of four cases. By the end of this section, it should be clear that certain inter-state relations or processes cannot be adequately explained without looking at the bigger picture: the system. Indeed, globalization is a phenomenon attached to capitalist abilities to undermine the state, forming an important focus of analysis. For this reason, processes such as globalization and hierarchical shifting of state capacities best remain within a framework such as WSA.

Sweden

Sweden is a concrete example because it addresses the first two critiques against WSA mentioned earlier. First, the case of Swedish economic development cannot be adequately understood without a system as a unit of analysis. Second, a hierarchical framework helps us understand the importance of Swedish accession into the most prosperous category. To understand this, Swedish developmental history is important. Prior to the seventeenth century, Sweden found itself in a peripheral position, exporting raw ore to core countries, who would then process it. It had a harsh climate and no agricultural surplus, which led to centralization and militarization to conquer more fertile lands. During that time, Sweden expanded militarily, becoming a regional empire, which led to Swedish control of Baltic trade. This, in turn, led to trade surplus, which was used by Sweden to establish an iron and steel industrial. This was the point when Sweden joined semiperipheral nations (Leckband, 2008). After the failed attempt to invade Russia, the Swedish empire fell apart, causing Sweden to fall back into peripheral status. However, industries established during the empire phase remained in full production, although international demand was featured relatively low. However, of crucial importance was the industrial revolution in Britain and Germany, especially latter phases, when demand for Swedish iron, steel, and timber skyrocketed, catapulting Swedish export earnings and bringing Sweden to core status (Leckband, 2008: 11–12). The implication of this was clear. Sweden caught up to Western Europe only because it was able to apply technology from core countries, and because core countries demanded a growth of Swedish industry to satisfy their needs. Wallerstein's concepts of "system" and its hierarchy help us understand regional effects of industrial capitalism and the profitability of particular processes. It is necessary to be reminded that core processes are ones that contain relatively monopolized leading industries. It would be imprudent to overlook the importance of Swedish steel and iron industries in case of Swedish accession into the core.

Iraq

The example of Iraq reaffirms the necessity of looking at the system and establishing the hierarchical order to bring about a better understanding of global economic processes. The last 40 years in Iraq have been marked by initial economic growth from an impoverished country to a prosperous semiperipheral position, and eventually back into the periphery. As Siemsen (1995/1996: 24) states, "[t]he outcome of Iraq's attempts at semiperipheral mobility is also determined by the global petroleum hunger and geopolitical situation." In essence, after 1973, Organization of the Petroleum Exporting Countries (OPEC) oil price increase, Iraq state revenues grew phenomenally, and, thus, Iraq was able to purchase high-wage goods, services, and technologies from the core. To understand Iraq's phenomenal growth during 1980, just prior to the Iran-Iraq War (1980–1988), it is worth noting that the national income from oil stood at approximately USD $30 billion with import between 1979 and 1980 having grown over 55%. Trade with the United States grew eight-fold between 1971 and 1974 (Siemsen, 1995/1996: 32). Formerly, an unstable Iraq was ruled by Saddam Hussein, who gave away generous subsidies and contracts to secure loyalty from the parts of the population. It is clear that oil was one of the leading industries of the time, and by having large reserves of it Iraq was able to monopolize this industry (nationalizing it in 1971) (Siemsen, 1995/1996: 31). This step marked Iraq's ability to utilize the oil industry for economic growth, something that is characteristic of only core and semiperipheral countries. Thus, Wallerstein's concept of hierarchy does help us understand how a global economic process shaped Iraq's world standing, and consequently, the importance of oil industry for Iraq has a global framework. Of course, geopolitical interests between Iraq and the United States did not match, which led to subsequent warfare and Iraq's fall back into the periphery.

Jamaica

The case of Jamaica supports Wallerstein's claim that peripheral countries can be hindered in terms of growth. This is so, given that core countries can exploit peripheral countries, or prevent them from doing so. In other words, "strong states relate to weak states by pressuring them to keep their frontiers open to those flows of factors of production that are useful and profitable to firms located in the strong states, while resisting any demands for reciprocity in this regard" (Wallerstein, 2004: 55). Since Jamaica's independence in 1962, it has lost its traditional role in the international division of labor—exporting sugar and bananas to the United Kingdom. Thus, it was necessary for Jamaica to restructure its economy through the International Monetary Fund (IMF) and World Bank loans. However, Jamaica was not allowed to spend that money on development, being pressured instead to adopt "structural adjustment" policies that subsequently indebted the country with no economic progress. Moreover, Jamaica had no industry that would compete with powerful U.S. exports, which were subsidized by the U.S. government. According to Black (2001), these were the reasons behind Jamaica's poverty. This conclusion can be further supported by a general critique of neoliberal institutions such as the IMF, which is often described as upholding the interests of its biggest financiers, the United States, the EU and Europe, and Japan (Brouillette, 2008). Therefore, the case of Jamaica illustrates the importance of periphery as a concept. It is in peripheral countries where we *do not* find monopolistic or quasi-monopolistic control over the leading industries. Instead, we find only industries under intense competition, leaving countries like Jamaica with no successful industry to export.

Yugoslavia

The last example addresses the critique aimed at WSA as regards its socialist vision. Some claim that history teaches us that socialism has been economically inefficient and politically repressive in almost every case (Sanderson, 2005: 203). That is certainly true, however, this fact overlooks Wallerstein's claim that, "states governed by old antisystemic movements found it extremely difficult to resist the pressures for 'structural adjustment' and opening frontiers" (Wallerstein, 2004: 84–6). Because of this, they have failed to implement truly socialist policies, turning into some kind of perverse capitalism. Rojek and Wilson have illustrated the best example of this in the context of the former Yugoslavia. While in theory it was practicing self-management, in reality self-management was a myth. Yugoslavia was heavily tied into the Western system of finance (especially debt), which created inflationary tendencies within the domestic market. Moreover, Yugoslav firms were working exclusively for the needs of the Western customer, and most of them had Western licenses and shareholders (Rojek and Wilson, 1987: 305). Thus, although theoretically workers held the power to make decisions, in reality management had real power and deep connections to the Western capitalist system. Indeed, a similar system today exists in modern Cuba, which utilizes capitalist currencies and largely relies on tourists from capitalist countries. These cases support Wallerstein's claim that old socialism in practice has failed because it was intrinsically linked to capitalism. Although it is debatable whether such phenomena are natural or imposed, their occurrence is significant.

Capitalist Contradictions and Crisis

Finally, a discussion about WSA's socialist vision, or at least, its vision of capitalist crisis, ought to be made. It is credible to claim that Wallerstein's analysis of capitalist contradictions has certain validity for several reasons. First, the globalization debate is largely focused on transnational capital in which the claim is made that, "productive forces within national spaces can only mature if and when they comply with the rules of the global capitalist system and that eventually, the state itself will disappear" (Taylor, 2005: 1029). Clearly, capitalist global perspective is becoming increasingly important. Second, inequality on a global level has grown while living standards have dropped (Taylor, 2005: 1029). Third, globalization is creating a debt-driven expansion of the privatized financial markets. In essence, this means that credit expansion will create debt burdens, a factor often cited as responsible for recent financial crises (Nesvetailova, 2005: 415–417). Fourth, countries like China and India are increasingly developing insatiable appetites for resources like oil (Corkery, 2009; Moyo, 2009: 108). This means that the earth's sustainability in providing a high level of consumerism to newly emerging global powers should certainly be questioned. All these factors combined signal that capitalism is experiencing an increase in almost all costs of production, resulting in capital movement to avoid state taxation, increasing wage dissatisfaction by low-wage workers, and increasing public costs of infrastructure, as well as dealing with externalities from industries (Wallerstein, 2004: 80–82). We can, therefore, expect a greater, not a lesser, need to look at a global level of capitalism and access its contradictions because many socioeconomic problems are on the rise globally. This ought to be a concern for any discussion on development and how it will affect human security as well as human rights.

Conclusion

The critique of the Kondratieff cycle in WSA remains the only unaddressed critique in this chapter. Let that critique serve as one of many examples where WSA riddles us with, as Pieterse (1988: 264) calls them, "illogical axioms." However, this does not undermine the final assertion that some processes, like globalization and development, require different levels of analysis. One cannot understand development, globalization, or global neoliberalism, without looking at certain systematic patterns, which transcend countries. Certainly, WSA should never be the only level of analysis for many social phenomena; yet, the cases illustrated in this chapter—Sweden, Iraq, Jamaica, and Yugoslavia—demonstrate that WSA, which utilizes concepts of a system, hierarchical structure, and crisis evaluation, can certainly be fruitful. Because of the practicality of WSA in explaining global capitalist processes, it remains a strong tool for understanding global inequalities and possibly future challenges. It can only contribute to our understanding of the lack of development and security that many semiperipheral and peripheral populations increasingly feel and export to core countries, further permeating any debate on how to safeguard human rights in an increasingly stressed system.

References

Black, S. 2001. *Life and Debt*. DVD. Directed by Stephanie Black. Kingston, Jamaica: Tuff Gong International.

Brouillette, R. 2008. *Encirclement: Neoliberalism Ensnares Democracy*. DVD. Directed by Richard Brouilette. Saint-Paulin, Canada: Les films du passeur.

Corkery, J. 2009. *India Reborn*. DVD. Directed by Jacqueline Corkery. Toronto, Canada: CBC Documentaries.

Leckband, C. 2008. Sweden's ascent in the world-system: A historical case study, *Paper Presented at the Annual Meeting of the ASA Annual Meeting*, Sheraton Boston and the Boston Marriott Copley Place, Boston, USA.

Moyo, D. 2009. *Dead Aid: Why Aid is Not Working and How There is a Better Way for Africa*. New York: Farrar, Straus, and Giroux.

Nesvetailova, A. 2005. United in debt: Towards a global crisis of debt-driven finance? *Science and Society*, 69(3): 396–419.

Pieterse, J. N. 1988. A critique of world system theory, *International Sociology*, 3(3): 251–66.

Rojek, C. and Wilson, D. 1987. Workers' self-management in the world system: The Yugoslav case, *Organization Studies*, 8: 297–308.

Sachs, J. D. 2005. *The End of Poverty: Economic Possibilities for Our Time*. New York, NY: Penguin.

Sanderson, S. K. 2005. World-systems analysis after thirty years: Should it rest in peace? *International Journal of Comparative Sociology*, 46: 179–213.

Siemsen, C. 1995/1996. Oil, war, and semiperipheral mobility: The case of Iraq, *Studies in Comparative International Development*, 30(4): 23–44.

Taylor, I. 2005. Globalization studies and the developing world: Making international political economy truly global, *Third World Quarterly*, 26(7): 1025–42.

Wallerstein, I. 2004. *World-Systems Analysis: An Introduction*. Durham, UK: Duke University Press.

Chapter 2

Does the Primary Condition for a Sustainable Human Development Meet the Feasibility Condition of Cost–Benefit Analysis?*

Hasnat Dewan

Contents

---

* This chapter is a revised version of the author's published article: Dewan, H. 2011. Does the primary condition for a sustainable human development meet the feasibility condition of cost-benefit analysis? *Journal of Sustainable Development*, 4(2): 3–15.

Introduction

Different variations of cost–benefit analysis (CBA) are used for project or policy evaluations by economists.[*] Assessing the sustainability of a human development policy, or any policy for that matter, with the CBA brings up many thorny issues (Gowdy and Howarth, 2007). A number of different sustainability indices and conditions have been developed in the recent years through global, national, regional, and individual initiatives for sustainability assessment. This chapter compares such a condition defined by Dewan (2009) for a sustainable human development (SHD) with the feasibility condition (FC) of CBA, and attempts to determine the deadweight loss associated with it. Though there are many definitions of SHD available in the literature, to our knowledge, no other study has attempted to find a condition for SHD. A comparison between the sustainability and the FC is useful for determining the sustainability premium, or the cost of making human development sustainable. The cost–benefit methodology compares the present values (PVs) of benefits and costs to evaluate a project or a policy. The term "sustainability" recognizes future generations' rights in the calculation of benefits and costs. Therefore, a sustainability condition (SC) is expected to include marginal present and future benefits and costs, where costs must account for all damages to the natural and social environments (NSE) that may possibly restrain future wellbeing.[†]

In welfare economics, benefits are measured in terms of consumption (or Hicksian income) whereas, in a nonwelfarist approach, economic development or benefits are measured in terms of capabilities and freedom, among others (Sen, 1999; Nussbaum, 2000). For sustainability assessments, it is also common among natural scientists and environmentalists to ignore benefits altogether and focus only on damages to the environment (environmental sustainability). Furthermore, economists and natural scientists are often at odds in evaluating damages to the natural environment. Mainstream economists prefer monetary valuation simply because it represents the scarcity value of resources while natural scientists prefer indices or policies that use methodologies such as physical accounting of the stocks of natural resources (Alfsen et al., 1987; Theys, 1989; Bojö et al., 1990), maximum sustained utilization rate for elements of the environment, or critical loads (Hall, 1993). Most economists find policies based on any such mechanism arbitrary and inefficient (Dubourg and Pearce, 1996), though many international agreements such as the Kyoto Protocol, the Helsinki Protocol, etc., have used these mechanisms to ensure, in their words, sustainable use of natural resources and the environment.

The well-publicized *Stern Review* (Stern, 2006) on climate change, which has used somewhat compromising economic models to estimate the benefits of climate change intervention (1% of global gross domestic product [GDP] loss per year) and the costs of inaction (5%–20% of global GDP loss per year) has drawn criticisms from all sides. Not only have the scientific evidences used in the *Stern Review* been challenged, questions have also been raised about the

---

[*] Some prefer the term Benefit–Cost Analysis (BCA) to Cost–Benefit Analysis (CBA), because historically, the term BCA was used when analyzing economic, ethical, and philosophical issues, and CBA was used for evaluating more mechanical issues, by engineers and scientists, for example (see Swartzman et al., 1982; Zerbe and Dively, 1994). That distinction in a multidisciplinary study like this is rather unnecessary.

[†] The NSE includes environment, natural resources, natural amenities, and sociocultural, political, and institutional conditions. Therefore, *natural and social capital* and what sociologists call *cultural capital* are part of the NSE. Some may argue that (environmental) sustainability issue is not about computing benefits and costs; it is about ensuring sustainable levels of ecological resources. Our argument is that in addition to ascertaining critical levels of the NSE, a benefit–cost comparison is important for minimizing the deadweight loss or the sustainability premium.

appropriateness of using a cost–benefit methodology with the positive discount rate (Beckerman, 2007). Mainstream economists point out that the "radical" conclusions of the *Stern Review* are mainly due to "a near-zero time discount rate combined with a specific utility function" (Nordhaus, 2007) and believe that spending on climate change issue is about "how much insurance to buy to offset the small change of a ruinous catastrophe that is difficult to compensate by ordinary savings" (Weitzman, 2007). This approach to the environment is unacceptable to many noneconomists (and some economists). The use of CBA in dealing with sustainability issues has been extensively analyzed in a special issue of *Ecological Economics* (2007) on sustainability and CBA. Beckerman (2007) has rightfully observed that there may be a temptation to, "discard traditional economic methods and established ethical systems and replace them by the concept of sustainable development" due to discount rate controversy. However, "vagueness" of the concept of sustainable development and inadequacy of standard CBA to intergenerational policy decisions have forced him to believe that the society needs "new ideas about justice" to address intergenerational issues.

To improve the human development index (HDI), changes may have to be made to the NSE, which includes climate conditions and much more.* Therefore, for an SHD, it is essential to guarantee that life sustaining conditions on earth remain above their *critical levels* forever.† The condition for an SHD is expected to do that. The condition for SHD, as defined in Dewan (2009) and described in this chapter, is essentially a condition based on nonmonetary benefit–cost ratio (BCR) that includes environmental and social impact assessment into the benefit–cost calculation. Its strength is that it is immune to many of the criticisms outlined above. The computation of benefits in this methodology is consistent with a nonwelfarist developmental policy. Instead of using market valuation, contingent valuation (CV) and/or deliberative monetary valuation (DMV) to monetize all indicators, the condition for SHD uses both monetary and physical indicators to measure present and future benefits and costs.

SC, as defined, ensures that each element (or subsystem) of NSE will always remain above the *critical level*, which the mainstream economic approach or the conventional CBA cannot guarantee, and which is the main concern of ecologists, environmentalists, and many others about pure economic approach to sustainability. Since the conventional cost–benefit methodology uses monetary estimates of all impacts, the primary condition for SHD uses both monetary and nonmonetary indicators, the two methodologies are unlikely to yield the same outcome unless there is a one-to-one relationship between monetary and nonmonetary benefits and costs. The following section defines the cost–benefit methodology and the concept of SHD. It also explains Dewan's (2009) primary condition for an SHD. The chapter then turns to comparing the primary condition for an SHD with the FC of CBA, and computes the deadweight loss. A brief note on project evaluations with sustainability and FCs is also presented. A concluding section follows.

---

* The UNDP's Human Development Index is a measure of the level of human development. It is a composite index based upon equal weights on income, level of education, and longevity. In this chapter, I use the Human Development Index to measure progress in human development. Therefore, an improvement in human development and an improvement in the Human Development Index are used indistinguishably throughout the chapter.

† *Critical levels* for different environmental elements are defined in many scientific studies. For exhaustible natural resources, the development plans in many countries consider certain quantity of reserve as critical. For social conditions index, ethnocentric values as well as globally accepted human rights along with other pertinent factors need to be weighed and compared against the "baseline profiles." Dewan (1998) also proposed some methodologies to define such critical levels.

Methodology

Cost–Benefit Analysis

Though some of the basic concepts of CBA were developed during the eighteenth and nineteenth centuries (Franklin, 1772; Dupuit, 1844; Marshall, 1890), it was the U.S. Corps of Engineers that first used a formalized CBA in 1936. Since the 1950s, the works of many economists have refined the CBA methodology and have made it much more rigorous. Variations of the basic CBA accounting framework are used in different disciplines. The CBA decision rule or the FC is: discounted flow of benefits from a project greater or equal to discounted flow of costs from the project. This condition can be rearranged to find: the ratio of discounted flow of benefits to costs from a project greater or equal to 1. The CBA decision rule appears to be very simple. It compares the discounted flow of benefits from and the discounted flow of costs of a project to determine its feasibility. However, in practice, the valuation of all impacts extended over a period of time is not so simple. Different valuation methods based upon option price, existence value, shadow price, CV, and so on, have been used to find monetary values of benefits and costs where no direct valuation is available.

Time horizon and discounting are two critical factors in the monetary evaluation of any project. Based on average capital depreciation rate and approximate length of generations, it is argued that projects with considerable impacts beyond 50 years should be considered truly intergenerational (Greenberg et al., 2006). A distinguishing factor between intra and intergenerational projects is the use of different discount rates. From fixed interest rates to various forms of time-declining discount rates are proposed as probable discount rates for CBA analysis in the economics literature. Behavioral studies show hyperbolic discount rate for human preference (Laibson, 1997; Gowdy, 2007). Weitzman's (2001) gamma discounting is another popular nonlinear method of discounting. For a single project evaluation, the FC of CBA is a nonnegative net present value (NPV) or a discounted BCR of greater than or at least equal to one. The decision outcome is the same irrespective of the method used. However, NPV criterion is often preferred to BCR criterion when choosing between alternate projects (Greenberg et al., 2006).

Ex ante CBA is used for determining the feasibility of a project or policy. *Ex post* CBA is used to find the efficacy of CBA. Flyvbjerg et al. (2002, 2005) evaluated a number of transportation projects and showed that cost estimates were consistently understated and benefit estimates were overstated. For road and rail projects, they found that *ex post* costs were 20.4%–44.7% higher, and riderships were 20%–51.4% lower. In another study by Harrington et al. (2000), it was found that U.S. regulatory cost estimates were overstated. Due to the uncertainty in expected impacts and appropriateness of monetary valuation, often the researchers perform sensitivity analysis for *ex ante* CBA. Yet, it may be prone to "omission errors, forecasting errors, measurement errors, and valuation errors" (Greenberg et al., 2006).

Gowdy and Howarth (2007) wrote in the preface of the special issue of Ecological Economics: "When BCA is applied to evaluate questions of 'sustainability,' thorny issues such as intra and intergenerational equity, interpersonal utility comparisons, ecological complexity, and ethics toward the non-human world come to the forefront." Howarth (2007) states that CBA can be modified to incorporate sustainability issues while Norton (2005) who questions the concept of "pricing nature," recommends replacing CBA with "adaptive management" (Iovanna and Newbold, 2007). Spash (2007) demonstrates how various methods and concepts, such as willingness-to-pay (WTP), CV, and DMV, might "relate to existing value theory in economics and numbers used in CBA" is unclear, and they might be "incommensurable" (Sagoff, 1998). Dovers and Norton (1996) criticize CBA for not explicitly accounting for uncertainty. Knetsch (2007) is concerned about the disparity between WTP and willingness-to-accept measures of environmental elements in CBA. Gowdy (2007) contends that CBA is considerably improved when nonmarket sources of wellbeing are incorporated into CBA estimates.

SHD

The term sustainable human development has been used since 1991 with different meanings. Jolly (1991) defines SHD as protecting our children's wellbeing with an "integrated, human approach to environment."* Speth (1994) defines SHD as development that is pro-poor, pro-nature, pro-jobs, pro-democracy, pro-women, and pro-children. Hasegawa (2001) considers SHD and environmental sustainability as two components of sustainable development. According to the United Nations Educational, Scientific, and Cultural Organization (UNESCO) (2010)

> the interdependent links between environment and development are not simply about conservation and economics, but also include a concern for issues such as human rights, population, housing, food security, and gender that are important parts of sustainable human development.

Each of these definitions of SHD brings up different dimensions of human development policy goals to the forefront. Environmental sustainability is not the focal point in any of these definitions of SHD. Most researchers within the human development paradigm consider sustainability as just another dimension of the human development policy goals whereas many researchers in the sustainability paradigm believe it to be the critical issue for our future existence. Dewan (2009) defines SHD by integrating sociocultural and environmental sustainability and human development policy goals in the definition. He states that SHD means finding the optimum level of human development with minimum damage to the NSE to promote the welfare of a maximum number of people in present and future generations. This definition comes from his earlier work (Dewan, 1998), and is consistent with the triple bottom line methodology (Elkington, 1998), which is now consensually applied in different sectors for full cost accounting.

A set of SHD indicators, similar to a set of sustainable development indicators, can be defined to assess the sustainability of human development. The HDI, constructed by Haq, Sen, and others for the United Nations Development Program (UNDP) in 1990, is a measure of the level of human development. It is a composite index based upon equal weights on income, the level of education, and longevity. The methodology of the HDI has many limitations, but it still is a popular index to measure the level of human development. However, the HDI alone cannot be an index for SHD because it cannot guarantee sustainability.

For human development to be sustainable, it must be ensured that it is achieved with sustainable means and the growth path of human development is nonnegative. Climate change, deteriorated quality of the environment, depletion of nonrenewable natural resources, and so on, are seen as potential threats to future sustainability. Therefore, all these are real concerns for an SHD. In addition to these, sociocultural changes need to be monitored as well. Dewan (2009) defines a

---

* Jolly's statement to the Third Session of UNCED Preparatory Committee, 1991. Quoted in Taylor and Taylor (1995).

damage index (*D*) to account for changes in all these conditions.* He also defines a set of indicators for the necessary and the sufficient conditions for SHD. The rest of this section defines Dewan's (2009) necessary or primary condition for SHD.

In the primary SC, benefits are measured in terms of changes in the UNDP's HDI (*H hence-forth*) and costs in terms of changes in the damage index (*D henceforth*). Therefore, any activity is viable, if $\Delta H \geq \Delta D$ (for an improvement in *H*) or $\Delta H \leq \Delta D$ (for an improvement in the quality of the NSE or a decrease in the damage index), where Δ stands for absolute change, and both *H* and *D* are measured on the same scale. The UNDP measures *H* on a one-point scale, where its components are occasionally revised upward by the UNDP based on higher expectations. $(1 - H)$ measures the difference between actual and expected (targeted) *H*. *D* is also measured on a one-point scale, where $D = 1$ means the exhaustion of a subcomponent of the NSE or the falling of a component of the NSE below the critical level where the ecology or the human life is not sustainable.

As innovation, technological progress, and advancement of knowledge change our under-standing of those critical levels, we must continuously revise the damage index. It will minimize errors in decision making under uncertainty. In other words, it will lower the uncertainty or sus-tainability premium.† Since *D* is the damage index, $(1 - D)$ is a measure of the quality of the NSE. Meeting the above condition, $\Delta H \geq \Delta D$ (for an improvement in *H*) or $\Delta H \leq \Delta D$ (for an improve-ment in the quality of the NSE or a decrease in the damage index), makes an activity viable; but it cannot guarantee that the quality of the NSE or $(1 - D)$ will always remain above the critical level as required for sustainability.

Instead of using $\Delta H \geq \Delta D$ or $(\Delta H / \Delta D) \geq 1$, if we use $(\Delta H / (1 - H)) / (\Delta D / (1 - D)) \geq 1$ or $\Delta H / (1 - H) \geq \Delta D / (1 - D)$ or $\Delta H / \Delta D \geq (1 - H) / (1 - D)$, as the SC, improving the same amount of human development at the equivalent cost of the NSE may not be sustainable, when the quality of the NSE is low as opposed to when it is high. This condition will also ensure the certain minimum quality of the NSE because when *D* is large, virtually no human development policy at the cost of the NSE will meet this condition. Rather, an environmental cleanup ($\Delta D < 0$) may become a sustainable activity based on $\Delta H / \Delta D \leq (1 - H) / (1 - D)$.

These conditions compare percentage gap closure of *H* (benefits) and percentage damage of the existing quality of the NSE (costs). Meeting the above condition (for $\Delta D > 0$) can safeguard against a "ruinous catastrophe." As there is no unique SHD path, by using policy parameters and choice variables, both conditions (for $\Delta D > 0$ or $\Delta D < 0$) can be customized to meet the needs of a nation or a community at a particular time. Once the SC is met, the goal should be to minimize the deadweight loss. In the following, we see the primary SC under two different scenarios.

---

* The damage index is defined as $D = \text{Max } \{\text{ENV, NAT, AMN, SOC}\}$, where ENV = an index for environmental degradation, NAT = an index for natural resource depletion, AMN = an index for the destruction of natural amenities, and SOC = an index for the change or degradation of socio-cultural-political and institutional con-ditions. All indices are in [0, 1]. Since maximum damage to a subsystem of the NSE is used to calculate *D*, the coefficient of variation (*V*) of various damage indices also needs to be monitored. The computational details of the subindices are beyond the scope of this chapter. The justification for using the worst condition of a sub-system of the NSE as the damage index is because each subsystem "has to have the capability to maintain its capability to survive and evolve" (Spangenberg, 2005).

† Since the sustainability condition may cause an economy to deviate from the optimum level of economic activ-ity, the resulting loss can be called the sustainability premium. Because of the nonavailability of full informa-tion and the uncertainty about the future, over or under conservation due to meeting a sustainability-condition is a very real possibility. By continuous correction of the indices based on available information, the errors in decision can be minimized. That will minimize the uncertainty or sustainability premium.

Scenario 1: Improvement in Human Development at the Cost of the NSE

If the NSE deteriorates due to developmental activities the resulting increase in human develop-ment has to be such that the ratio of ΔH to ΔD is greater than or at least equal to a minimum threshold value, which will rule out the possibility of the NSE, or natural and social capital, to ever fall below their *critical levels* until targeted H is reached. The targeted H can continuously be revised upward, as the UNDP does, to guarantee a livable environment forever. One of the advan-tages of this methodology is that it does not require macroplanning over an infinite time horizon.[*] As more data and information become available, they can be used to revise the parameter values in the SC to evaluate incremental human development.

Perceived risk parameter and discount factor can be added to the above condition to allow flexibility as may be needed in development planning depending on current states of H and D. Hence, the basic SC is

$$\left(\frac{\Delta H}{\Delta D}\right) \geq \frac{1}{1+\delta}\left(\frac{1-H}{1-D}\right)^{(\gamma/1-\gamma)} \tag{2.1}$$

where
H = the Human Development Index
D = the damage index of the NSE
Δ = positive or negative change
δ = the discount factor[†] and
γ = the risk-aversion parameter[‡]

H, δ, and γ are in [0, 1] and D is in [0, 1).
Rearranging the terms, the SC can be written as

$$(1+\delta)\frac{(\Delta H)/(1-H)^{(\gamma/1-\gamma)}}{(\Delta D)/(1-D)^{(\gamma/1-\gamma)}} \geq 1 \tag{2.2}$$

or

$$(1+\delta)\left(\frac{\Delta H}{\Delta D}\right)\left(\frac{1-D}{1-H}\right)^{(\gamma/1-\gamma)} \geq 1 \tag{2.3}$$

The main distinction between the SC and the FC of CBA is that the SC does not require the monetary valuation of all impacts. The numerical value of the left hand side of the expression (2.2)

---

[*] Macroplanning may be required for other purposes.

[†] An improvement in the present Human Development Index (H) may have some positive effect on the future H. Many economic development studies show that better opportunities exist for children from more educated and rich parents. This spill over benefit is captured by the nonnegative fraction δ.

[‡] The sustainability condition requires that the ratio of a change in H to a change in D be not less than $(\gamma/1 - \gamma)$ order of the ratio of a difference between targeted and actual H to the quality of the NSE. The value of γ determines the "degree of bias" toward further human development or conservation of resources and environ-ment. Bias toward conservation means taking less risk about the future. Therefore, γ can be interpreted as the "risk-aversion" parameter. $\gamma = 0.5$ implies risk-neutrality.

or (2.3) can be called the *Sustainable Human Development Index (SHDI henceforth)*, which can be used to assess and compare country performance or the performance of alternative projects in terms of SHD. To learn about the actual magnitude of change in human development (benefits) and damages to the NSE (costs), we must look at the values of the numerator and the denominator respectively in the left hand side of expression (2.1).[*]

Scenario 2: Environmental Cleanup or any Improvement in the NSE

Assume that $\Delta D < 0$, which implies an improvement in the quality of the NSE. Since an improvement in the NSE is expected to increase present and future wellbeing, any activity that improves the NSE with some loss in human development can still be considered a sustainable activity. Therefore, the basic SC is defined as

$$\left(\frac{\Delta H}{\Delta D}\right) \le \frac{1}{1+\delta}\left(\frac{1-H}{1-D}\right)^{(\gamma/1-\gamma)} \tag{2.4}$$

Rearranging the terms, the SC can be written as

$$(1+\delta)\frac{(\Delta H)/(1-H)^{(\gamma/1-\gamma)}}{(\Delta D)/(1-D)^{(\gamma/1-\gamma)}} \le 1 \tag{2.5}$$

or

$$(1+\delta)\left(\frac{\Delta H}{\Delta D}\right)\left(\frac{1-D}{1-H}\right)^{(\gamma/1-\gamma)} \le 1 \tag{2.6}$$

In the sustainability index, the risk-perception parameter γ is a policy instrument, which is partly determined by the current level of development and the quality of the NSE. A note of caution is that too high or too low γ can cause a high level of inefficiency.

Results

Primary Condition for SHD and FC of CBA

The primary condition for an SHD and the FC of CBA may not be synonymous due to methodological differences. If the Kaldor–Hicks criterion, which is the basis of CBA, is extended to include the future generations' rights, Dewan's (2009) SC will meet the criterion.[†] Besides separate environmental impact assessments (EIA), in practice, many CBAs strive for incorporating monetary values of externalities. However, they fall short of ensuring "sustainability" as envisioned by many outside the mainstream economics paradigm.

According to CBA, a project is viable if Discounted flow of benefits ≥ Discounted flow of costs

---

[*] The human development indices of different nations of the world are published annually by the UNDP in its Human Development Report;

[†] Kaldor (1939) and Hicks (1940). Greenberg et al. (2006) states the criterion as, "[a] policy should be adopted if and only if those who gain could fully compensate those who will lose and still be better off."

$$\Rightarrow \Delta Y_m \geq \Delta D_m$$

$$\Rightarrow \frac{\Delta Y_m}{\Delta D_m} \geq 1$$

where ΔY_m = the discounted flow of benefits or the PV of the income generated from the project and ΔD_m = the discounted flow of costs or the PV of the monetary costs of the project.

On the other hand, the proposed condition for SHD is

$$\frac{\Delta H}{\Delta D} \geq \frac{1}{1+\delta}\left(\frac{1-H}{1-D}\right)^{(\gamma/1-\gamma)} \quad \text{or} \quad \text{SHDI} \geq 1$$

for any positive damage to the NSE. One of the advantages of the SC or the SHDI over CBA is that unlike CBA, SC or SHDI is not prone to valuation error. To compare CBA and SHDI,[*] several cases require consideration:

Case 1
Assume that $H = D$,[†] $\Delta D \geq 0$, $\delta = 0$, and $\gamma = 0.5$, then

$$\text{SHDI} \geq 1 \Rightarrow \frac{\Delta H}{\Delta D} \geq 1$$

$$\Rightarrow \frac{1}{3}\left(\frac{\Delta y^i + \Delta E_d + \Delta L}{\Delta D}\right) \geq 1$$

where
  y^i = adjusted per capita real income (PPP$) index
  E_d = educational attainment index and
  L = longevity index

All variables are in [0, 1]

In general, the changes in E_d and L are much slower than the change in y^i (UNDP, 1991). Therefore, $(\Delta E_d + \Delta L) < 2\Delta y^i$.

$$\Rightarrow \frac{\Delta H}{\Delta D} < \frac{\Delta y^i}{\Delta D} \tag{2.7}$$

According to Atkinson's formula for the utility of income, which the UNDP initially used to calculate adjusted real GDP for the HDI, for a nation with per capita real income (PPP$) less than the world average income, $\Delta y = \Delta y_m$, and for a nation with per capita real income (PPP$) greater

---

[*] It is evident that the feasibility condition of CBA uses the PV of aggregate benefits and aggregate costs of a project, whereas the sustainability condition or the SHDI uses per capita benefits as measured by the human development index. Therefore, the same amount of environmental damage if benefits a few people or a large number of people will have differential effects on the value of SHDI.

[†] $H = D$ (measured on a one-point scale) means that the nation is on the "critical path of sustainable development" (Dewan, 1998). If the damage elasticity of H, $E_{dh} = 1$, a nation on the critical path will exhaust the quality of the NSE to reach $H = 1$.

than the world average income, $\Delta y < \Delta y_m$, where Δy and Δy_m are changes in adjusted and actual per capita real income respectively.[*] The UNDP's current methodology uses the log of *per capita* income to calculate the GDP index.[†]

Therefore

$$\Delta y < \Delta y_m \qquad (2.8)$$

The inequalities, (2.7) and (2.8), are significant for deriving relationships between the growth rates of human development (H); adjusted per capita real income (PPP\$) index (y^i); adjusted and actual per capita real income, y and y_m respectively; and adjusted and actual real income, Y and Y_m, respectively. For any positive population growth rate (n), the growth rate of y_m is smaller than the growth rate of Y_m. Therefore

$$\%\Delta H < \%\Delta y^i < \%\Delta y < \%\Delta y_m < \%\Delta Y_m \,\forall\, n > 0 \qquad (2.9)$$

Multiplying both sides of Equation 2.8 by the population, we find that

$$\Delta Y < \Delta Y_m \qquad (2.10)$$

$$\Rightarrow \frac{\Delta Y}{\Delta D_m} \prec \frac{\Delta Y_m}{\Delta D_m} \,\forall\, D_m > 0$$

$$\Rightarrow \mathrm{SHDI} \prec \mathrm{BCR}\left(\frac{\Delta D_m}{\Delta Y}\right)\left(\frac{\Delta H}{\Delta D}\right) \qquad (2.11)$$

In Equation 2.11, the numerical value of SHDI is smaller than the numerical value of the BCR, if

$$\left(\frac{\Delta D_m}{\Delta Y}\right)\left(\frac{\Delta H}{\Delta D}\right) \le 1 \quad \text{or} \quad \mathrm{SHDI} \le \frac{\Delta Y}{\Delta D_m} \qquad (2.12)$$

In other words, if the monetary cost of a project times SHDI is not greater than the log-adjusted income generated from the project, the SC is certainly more stringent than the FC of CBA in project evaluation. Expression (2.12) can be rearranged to find the condition

$$\Delta Y_m \ge e^{\mathrm{SHDI}^*\Delta D_m} \qquad (2.13)$$

If this condition holds, a project may be *feasible* in terms of CBA, but the resulting human development may not be *sustainable*. As showed in Equation 2.10, it is impossible for a change in income (ΔY_m) to be smaller than or equal to a change in the log of income (ΔY); therefore, the SC is always more conservative than the FC of CBA in this case.

---

[*] See UNDP (1997).
[†] See UNDP (2009).

From expression (2.9), we can derive another relationship between SHDI and BCR.

$$\%\Delta H < \%\Delta Y_m \,\forall\, n > 0$$

$$\Rightarrow \frac{\Delta H}{H} \prec \frac{\Delta Y_m}{Y_m}$$

$$\Rightarrow \left(\frac{\Delta H}{\Delta D}\right)\left(\frac{\Delta D}{H}\right) \prec \left(\frac{\Delta Y_m}{\Delta D_m}\right)\left(\frac{\Delta D_m}{Y_m}\right) \tag{2.14}$$

$$\Rightarrow \text{SHDI} \prec \text{BCR}\left(\frac{\Delta D_m}{\Delta D}\right)\left(\frac{H}{Y_m}\right) \tag{2.15}$$

In Equation 2.15, the numerical value of SHDI is smaller than the numerical value of BCR, if

$$\left(\frac{\Delta D_m}{\Delta D}\right)\left(\frac{H}{Y_m}\right) \le 1 \quad \text{or} \quad \Delta D_m \le \left(\frac{Y_m}{H}\right)(\Delta D) \tag{2.16}$$

Accordingly, if the monetary damage is not greater than Y_m/H multiple of the physical damage index, the SC is more conservative than the FC of CBA. In other words, if the ratio of monetary to physical damage index is not greater than Y_m/H, the numerical value of SHDI is smaller than the numerical value of BCR. If the opposite is true, SHDI $\gtreqless$ BCR.

Case 2
Assume that $H > D,^*$ $\Delta D \ge 0$, $\delta = 0$, and $\gamma = 0.5$, then

$$\text{SHDI} \ge 1 \Rightarrow \frac{\Delta H}{\Delta D} \ge \left(\frac{1-H}{1-D}\right)$$

$$\Rightarrow \frac{\Delta H}{\Delta D} \ge 1 - X, \quad \text{where } X = \left(\frac{H-D}{1-D}\right) > 0 \tag{2.17}$$

The SC, in this case, is more stringent than the FC of CBA, but it is not as stringent as the SC in the first case presented.

From inequality (2.14), we can find that

$$\left(\frac{\Delta H}{\Delta D}\right)\left(\frac{\Delta D}{H}\right)\left(\frac{1-D}{1-H}\right) \prec \left(\frac{\Delta Y_m}{\Delta D_m}\right)\left(\frac{\Delta D_m}{Y_m}\right)\left(\frac{1-D}{1-H}\right)$$

$$\Rightarrow \text{SHDI} \prec \text{BCR}\left(\frac{\Delta D_m}{\Delta D}\right)\left(\frac{H}{Y_m}\right)\left(\frac{1-D}{1-H}\right) \tag{2.18}$$

---

* $H > D$ means that the nation is in the "sustainable development region" (Dewan, 1998). A nation in the sustainable development region can always reach $H = 1$ without exhausting the quality of NSE, if the damage elasticity of H, $E_{dh} = 1$.

In Equation 2.18, the numerical value of SHDI is smaller than the numerical value of BCR, if

$$\left(\frac{\Delta D_m}{\Delta D}\right)\left(\frac{H}{Y_m}\right)\left(\frac{1-D}{1-H}\right)\leq 1$$

$$\Rightarrow\left(\frac{\Delta D_m}{\Delta D}\right)\left(\frac{H}{Y_m}\right)\leq 1-X \tag{2.19}$$

Case 3
Assume that $H < D,^{*}$ $\Delta D \geq 0$, $\delta = 0$, and $\gamma = 0.5$, then

$$\text{SHDI} \geq 1 \Rightarrow \frac{\Delta H}{\Delta D} \geq \left(\frac{1-H}{1-D}\right)$$

$$\Rightarrow \frac{\Delta H}{\Delta D} \geq 1+Z, \quad \text{where} \quad Z = \left(\frac{D-H}{1-D}\right) > 0$$

$$\Rightarrow \frac{\Delta H}{\Delta D} \gg 1$$

The SC, in this case, is not only more stringent than the FC of CBA, it is also more stringent than the SCs in the other two cases.

From expression (2.19), it is known that

$$\left(\frac{\Delta D_m}{\Delta D}\right)\left(\frac{H}{Y_m}\right)\leq 1+Z \tag{2.20}$$

If condition (2.20) holds, the numerical value of SHDI is smaller than the numerical value of BCR.

The above conditions lead to the following propositions:

Proposition 1

If SHDI $\leq (\Delta Y/\Delta D_m)$ or $\Delta Y_m \geq e^{\text{SHDI}^*\Delta D_m}$, the SC is more conservative than the FC of CBA.

Proposition 2

Unlike the FC of CBA, the SC is different in different sustainable development regions. The SC is the most stringent in the unsustainable development region and the least stringent in the sustainable development region.

Proposition 3

The SC is more conservative than the FC of CBA, if

---

* $H < D$ means that the nation is in the "unsustainable development region" (Dewan, 1998). If the damage elasticity of H, $E_{dh} = 1$, a nation in the unsustainable development region will never reach $H = 1$.

$$\left(\frac{\Delta D_m}{\Delta D}\right)\left(\frac{H}{Y_m}\right) \leq 1 + K$$

where $K = 0$, $-X$, or Z depending on whether the economy is on the critical path of sustainable development, in the sustainable development region or in the unsustainable development region, respectively.

The reasons for the SC to be different from the FC is due to the fact that there may not be a one-to-one relationship between monetary and physical damage, and also changes to the human development index may not be proportional to the incomes generated from a project. To be more conservative or risk-averse, one may suggest that a project be undertaken if, and only if, it meets both the FC of CBA and the SC in local, national and also in global sense. If that means a sub-optimal choice based on CBA, the deadweight loss can be calculated, and that can be deemed as uncertainty or sustainability premium.[*]

Deadweight Loss

Since the SC may require the more restrictive use of resources than what the FC of CBA would require, the sustainable level of human development is likely to be lower than the optimum level of human development. Hence, there is a potential for efficiency loss.[†] In Figure 2.1, SEL amounts to the deadweight loss when $H = D$ and marginal human development (MH) to marginal damage (MD) curve and marginal benefit (MB) to marginal cost (MC) curve are as shown. Since the ratio of marginal gains (MH or MB) to marginal losses (MD or MC) may not decline at the same rate for all developmental activities, the two curves may very well be nonlinear.

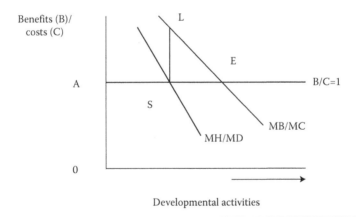

Figure 2.1   Optimum and sustainable levels of development.

---

[*] "The expected value of benefits under uncertainty is less than the value of benefits under certainty [...] Therefore, we should err on the side of under investment, rather than over investment, *since development is irreversible*" (Arrow and Fisher, 1974).

[†] In the Solow (1974) and Hartwick (1978) framework, sustainable growth path is different from the optimal growth path, which means that sustainability can be achieved at the cost of efficiency. Norgaard (1992) asserts that efficiency is not the objective in sustainable development.

Project Evaluations with Sustainability and FCs

CBA determines the feasibility of a project based on monetary estimates of the impact. The application of CBA diverges greatly from the textbook version of CBA, which can be seen in many case studies in Brouwer and Pearce (2005). When it comes to evaluating the effects of a project on SHD, neither the monetary CBA nor the EIA can be adequate. Canada, for example, uses 11 EIA techniques[*] , as well as the inclusion of SC as a project evaluation method would help measure additional dimensions of sustainability. It is possible for a project to meet the basic SC from a national perspective, but not from the local perspective. That is why sometimes the central government's plans are found to trigger unrest in the project area. To be conservative, a project should be carried on only if all necessary conditions for CBA and EIA along with local, regional, national, and global SCs are met. These additional constraints will likely cause deadweight loss, but they will ensure an SHD.

Conclusion

The FC of the CBA uses monetary estimates of the impact for project or policy evaluations. It can be used to find an optimum level of economic activity, but it cannot guarantee the sustainability of the outcome of such activity. Therefore, the FC alone cannot be used to determine the sustainable level of human development. The primary condition for an SHD, on the other hand, uses a composite index, called the Sustainable Human Development Index, to determine the sustainability of human development policy. The SHDI is an index based on the HDI and a damage index. By including both monetary and nonmonetary indicators, the computational methodology of SHDI combines both economic and scientific approaches to sustainability. Since the FC of CBA and the primary condition for an SHD are usually not synonymous, there will be a deadweight loss due to meeting the primary condition for SHD.

By redefining SHDI and/or by using appropriate policy parameters, the primary condition for SHD can be customized for the needs of any nation or region. That is appropriate because the level of economic development, the nature of damage to the NSE, and social perceptions are not the same everywhere. Since the value of SHDI is a function of the level of human development and the level of damage to the NSE, equal changes in the HDI and the NSE will yield different values for SHDI in different nations or regions. This is a significant difference between the static methodology of CBA and a more robust methodology of SHDI. The primary condition for an SHD, in general, does not meet the FC of CBA, but it is a useful tool to determine the sustainable level of human development.

References

Alfsen, K. H., Bye, T., and Lorentsen, L. 1987. *Natural Resource Accounting and Analysis: The Norwegian Experience 1978–1986*. Oslo, Norway: Central Bureau of Statistics of Norway.

Arrow, K. and Fisher, A. 1974. Environmental preservation, uncertainty, and irreversibility, *Quarterly Journal of Economics*, 88(2): 312–319.

---

[*] The President of the International Institute for Sustainable Development (IISD), David Runnalls, stated it in his speech at the Globe 2008 Conference on Business and the Environment.

Beckerman, W. 2007. The chimera of "sustainable development," *Electronic Journal of Sustainable Development*, 1(1): 17–26.

Bojö, J., Maler, K-G., and Unemo, L. 1990. *Environment and Development: An Economic Approach*. Kluwer Boston, MA: Academic Publishers.

Brouwer, R. and Pearce, D. (eds.), 2005. *Cost-Benefit Analysis and Water Resources Management*. Cheltenham, Camberley, and Northampton, UK: Edward Elgar.

Dewan, A. H. 1998. *Measuring Sustainable Development: Problems and Prospects*, PhD dissertation, Austin, TX, The University of Texas.

Dewan, A. H. 2009. Re-defining sustainable human development to integrate sustainability and human development goals, *The International Journal of Environmental, Cultural, Economic and Social Sustainability*, 5(4): 147–62, Victoria, Australia: Common Ground.

Dovers, S. R. and Norton, T. W. 1996. Uncertainty, sustainability, ecology and policy, *Biodiversity and Conservation*, 5: 1143–67.

Dubourg, R. and Pearce, D. 1996. Paradigms for environmental choice: Sustainability versus optimality, in Faucheux, S. (ed.), *Models of Sustainable Development*. UK: Edward Elgar, pp. 21–36.

Dupuit, A. J. E. J. 1844. De la mesure de l'utilité des travaux publics, *Annales des ponts et chaussées*, 2nd series, 8, On the Measurement of the Utility of Public Works (Barback, R. H. [trans.]), *International Economic Papers*, 2 (1952): 83–110.

Elkington, J. 1998. *Cannibals with Forks: The Triple Bottom Line of 21st Century Business*. Gabriola Island, Canada: New Society.

Flyvbjerg, B., Holm, S., Mette, K., and Buhl, S. L. 2002. Underestimating costs in public works projects: Error or lie? *Journal of the American Planning Association*, 68(3): 279–95.

Flyvbjerg, B., Skamris Holm, M. K., and Buhl, S. L. 2005. How (In)accurate are demand forecasts in public works projects? The case of transportation, *Journal of the American Planning Association*, 71(2): 131–46.

Franklin 1772. Letter to Joseph Priestley, in Mott, F., Jorgenson, C., and Franklin, B. (eds.), *Representative Selections, with Introduction, Bibliography and Notes*. New York, NY: American Book Company.

Gowdy, J. 2007. Toward an experimental foundation for benefit-cost analysis, *Ecological Economics*, 63: 649–55.

Gowdy, J. and Howarth, R. 2007. Sustainability and benefit-cost analysis: Theoretical assessments and policy options, *Preface in Ecological Economics*, 63: 637–8.

Greenberg, D., Vining, A., and Boardman, D. W. A. 2006. *Cost-Benefit Analysis: Concepts and Practice* (3rd ed.). Englewood Cliffs, NY: Prentice Hall.

Hall, J. 1993. Critical load maps: Europe and the UK, *Paper Presented to the Conference, Acid Rain and Its Impacts: The Critical Loads Debate*. University College London, UK.

Harrington, W., Morgenstern, R. D., and Nelson, P. 2000. On the accuracy of regulatory cost estimates, *Journal of Policy Analysis and Management*, 19(2): 297–322.

Hartwick, J. M. 1978. Substitution among exhaustible resources and intergenerational equity, *Review of Economic Studies*, 45(2): 347–54

Hasegawa, S. 2001. Development cooperation, presented in the *UNU Global Seminar on Global Issues and the United Nations*, Nov. 20, 2001, New York, US.

Hicks, J. R. 1940. The valuation of the social income, *Economica*, 7(26): 105–24.

Howarth, R. 2007. Towards an operational sustainability criterion, *Ecological Economics*, 63(4): 656–63.

Iovanna, R. and Newbold, S. 2007. Ecological sustainability in policy assessments: A wide-angle view and a close watch, *Ecological Economics*, 63: 639–48.

Jolly, R. 1991. Statement to the Third Session of UNCED Preparatory Committee, 1991.

Kaldor, N. 1939. Welfare propositions of economics and interpersonal comparisons of utility, *Economic Journal*, 49(195): 549–52.

Knetsch, J. 2007. Biased valuations, damage assessments, and policy choices: The choice of measure matters, *Ecological Economics*, 63: 684–9.

Laibson, D. 1997. Golden eggs and hyperbolic discounting, *Quarterly Journal of Economics*, 112: 443–7.

Marshall, A. 1890. *Principles of Economics: An Introductory Volume*. New York, NY: Cosimo.

Nordhaus, W. 2007. A review of the stern review of the economics of climate change, *Journal of Economic Literature*, 45(3): 686–702.

Norgaard, R. 1992. UNEP, *Summary Record: Workshop on Environmental and Natural Resource Accounting*, Feb. 24–6, Nairobi, Kenya.

Norton, B. 2005. *Sustainability: A Philosophy of Adaptive Ecosystem Management*. Chicago, IL: University of Chicago Press.

Nussbaum, M. 2000. *Women and Human Development*. Chicago, IL: University of Chicago Press.

Runnalls, D. 2008. *Speech at the Globe 2008 Conference on Business and the Environment*, Mar. 12–14, Vancouver, Canada.

Sagoff, M. 1998. Aggregation and deliberation in valuing environmental public goods: A look beyond contingent pricing, *Ecological Economics*, 24(2/3): 213–30.

Sen, A. K. 1999. *Development as Freedom*. New York, NY: Anchor.

Solow, R. 1974. Intergenerational equity and exhaustible resources, *Review of Economic Studies*, 41: 29–45.

Spangenberg, J. H. 2005. Economic sustainability of the economy: Concepts and indicators, *International Journal of Sustainable Development*, 8(1/2): 47–64.

Spash, C. 2007. Deliberative monetary valuation (DMV): Issues in combining economic and political processes to value environmental change, *Ecological Economics*, 63: 690–9.

Speth, J. G. 1994. The Foreword to the 1994 *Human Development Report*, UNDP.

Stern, N. 2006. *Stern Review on the Economics of Climate Change*. London, UK: Government Economic Service.

Swartzman, D., Liroff, R. A., and Croke, K. G. (eds.), 1982. *Cost-Benefit Analysis and Environmental Regulations: Politics, Ethics and Methods*. Washington, DC: Conservation Foundation.

Taylor, D. and Taylor, C. E. 1995. Community based sustainable human development, PEC Discussion Papers on *Children, Environment and Sustainable Development*.

Theys, J. 1989. Environmental accounting in development policy: The French experience, in Ahmad, Y. J., Serafy, S. E., and Lutz, E. (eds.), *Environmental Accounting for Sustainable Development*. Washington, DC: World Bank, pp. 40–53.

UNDP 1991/1997/2009. *Human Development Report*.

UNESCO 2010. *Sustainable Development*.

Weitzman, M. 2001. Gamma discounting, *The American Economic Review*, 91(1): 260–71.

Weitzman, M. 2007. A review of the stern review on the economics of climate change, *Journal of Economic Literature*, 45(3): 703–24.

Zerbe, R. and Dively, D. 1994. *Benefit-Cost Analysis: In Theory and Practice*. New York, NY: HarperCollins.

Chapter 3

Crossing Borders: Academe and Cultural Agency in Agricultural Research[*]

Robert W. Blake, Elvira E. Sánchez-Blake, and Debra A. Castillo

Contents

Introduction

Ours is a story of encounters and problems needing solutions. Different worlds reach out to one another on a transformative life-stage obtained by crossing borders. For more than four decades, Cornell University has led annual groups of 25–35 participants totaling about 2000 students—undergraduates and graduates—and faculty from around the world on a two-course multidisciplinary, intergenerational examination of rural and urban development in tropical Latin America.

---

[*] This chapter is a revised version of the authors' published article: Blake, R. W., Sánchez-Blake, E. E. and Castillo, D. A. Jan., 2015. Crossing borders: Academe and cultural agency in agricultural research, *Journal of Agricultural Science*, 7(2): 9–17.

The field component of these courses has been conducted in Puerto Rico, Dominican Republic, Costa Rica, Honduras, Ecuador, and Mexico. With library and lecture traded in the second course for mountaintops and mangrove swamps, aspiring intercultural scholars learn first-hand from real-world knowledge providers, some who are exceptionally marginalized.

This yearlong experience, which is training ground also for participating faculty, includes a preparatory course[*] followed by an intense research experience[†] that includes at least two weeks in the field and a subsequent on-campus agenda of distillation, analysis, and reporting. Preparation for informed and respectful dialog in the field by our constituency, including students and faculty from collaborating institutions through video conferencing, begins with the on-campus course in the preceding semester. This initial course is designed to introduce participants to basic cultural, historical, sociopolitical, literary, anthropological, linguistic, health, agricultural and food system, and social and family welfare issues that they are likely to observe. Inequality, possibly the key global social issue of our time, especially in the Americas, constitutes a dominant underlying theme. Besides a gap in income, social inequality also stems from unequal access to food, land, education at all levels, health services, markets, credit, capital, and justice.

A complementary section on Spanish for students with basic language skill was devoted to further discussion of topics from lectures and supported by additional readings in Spanish. In the field, recognizing the authority of "other" voices is crucial. Especially valuable are personal interactions "in culturally authentic and acceptable ways" (Meredith, 2010). Some of our hosts are indigenous peoples whose mother tongue is not Spanish, and so they too are learners of a second language and culture. We see this step toward intercultural practice, made more democratic by plural discourse, as obligatory in a world perceived by some to be increasingly dominated by a "globalization that flattens everything in its path" (Godenzzi, 2006). This platform, where academe learns from cultural agents—those whose actions affect collective change[‡]—evolved into a shared, live, video-streamed seminar during 2008–2011 involving our universities as well as Mexican collaborators. Sandwiched between the two campus-based courses was the field experience itself, where we strengthened our ties to individuals and host institutions, including El Colegio de la Frontera Sur (ECOSUR), El Centro de Investigaciones y Estudios Superiores en Antropología Social (CIESAS), and Instituto Nacional de Investigaciones Forestales, Agrícolas y Pecuarias (INIFAP).[§]

This chapter demonstrates how encounters during our field explorations helped students and faculty members alike to articulate problems, establish contacts, and develop subsequent research investigations based on these contextualized settings and inputs by our hosts. We illustrate how this consolidated pedagogical and problem-framing approach contributes to the intellectual growth of students and faculty alike with a sample of agricultural research outcomes built upon

---

[*] This cross-college course was entitled "Bridging Worlds: Rural and Urban Realities."

[†] This course was entitled "Experience Latin America: Through another Lens."

[‡] Practitioners of cultural agency, as defined by Sommer (2006), exploit vehicles that promote agency via thoughts and actions furthering the impetus for change in a collective sense. Other variants affecting collective action and change may include political agency and community agency.

[§] Chiapas field coordinators were Dr. Carlos Riqué Flores and Blanca Concepción (Conchita) Guzmán de Riqué. Host institutions in 2005–2008 were the Universidad Autónoma de Yucatán, Universidad Veracruzana and INIFAP, also with student and faculty participation partially supported through a Training, Internships, Exchanges, and Scholarships project funded by USAID-Mexico through Higher Education for Development.

issues initiated by immersed field experiences. William B. Lacy* summarized the achievement of this living laboratory undertaking†

> *Experience Latin America* is one of the richest learning experiences I have seen in higher education. The dynamic international learning environment is greatly enhanced by bringing together undergraduates and graduates with diverse backgrounds and international experiences with a multidisciplinary, intergenerational group of faculty, administrators, and extension educators. Each of the participants becomes an active learner and teacher (Blake, 2001).

Correspondingly, our learning forum is designed to share and to build knowledge, responding to what Godenzzi (2006) calls the great challenge of the twenty-first century, "the construction of an ethic of respect and solidarity." It strives to demonstrate tolerance, inclusion, and value enhancement through a celebration of cultural difference. Students and faculty typically represent Africa, Asia, and Europe as well as half a dozen countries from the Americas (including other regions in the host country). Accordingly, the program objectives are to explore equity-gap challenges, acknowledging rural-urban disparities and aspects of cultural heritage, improving intercultural dialog, and fostering greater contact and communication among the players—in-country hosts, students from afar as well as the host country, faculty, and other professionals. Acknowledged gaps include access to food, to education at all levels, to health services, land and water, justice, markets, credit, capital, and income.

It is not possible in a mere two weeks to thoroughly examine the many facets of the many problems faced by families in many settings. Nevertheless, the field laboratory provides a valuable opportunity to see first-hand how they live, to see their crops and animals, to speak with and learn from them, to visit projects of various institutions designed to serve them, and to listen to professionals who have devoted careers to these challenges. As Professor H. David Thurston (2001), a leader in this enterprise summarized

> I feel the essence of the field trip … is that the students … have had the chance to 'touch it, feel it and smell it.' The course brings a vast array of experiences into focus in settings that cannot be equaled in a classroom.

Correspondingly, we follow a beacon similar to the one provided to painter Georgia O'Keefe by her mentor, Professor Arthur W. Dow‡—structure one's work in better comprehending nature, landscapes, people and their livelihood systems "by not (only) mastering particular facts, but by seeing, experiencing, and creating (your) own systems or structures."

Course Organization

A hallmark of Cornell University's study abroad options, "Agriculture in Developing Nations" evolved with our understanding of agriculture and development primarily from graduate students

---

* Vice Provost, University Outreach and International Programs, University of California, Davis. Dr. Lacy was the Director of Cornell Cooperative Extension and Associate Dean of the Colleges of Agriculture and Life Sciences, and Human Ecology at Cornell University, 1994–1998.

† Personal communication appearing in Blake (2001).

‡ Professor Dow's advice was part of the 1999 exhibition of Georgia O'Keefe's work at the Phillips Museum in Washington, D.C. Thereafter, it was added to our course strategy materials.

in the agricultural sciences in the early years to a gender, disciplinary and culturally equitable mix of both undergraduate and graduate students from across the university and the globe, now branded *Experience Latin America*. Enrichments to this learning forum included participation also by extension educators, field activities designed to better grasp the major issues, and thematic teams to assess complex issues based on observation, consultation with hosts, and relevant literature.

Students are challenged to reconcile multiple facets with potentially competing goals to grasp pragmatically, and in ways witnessed to have touched our hosts, the complex issues of rural development. Jason Ingram summed up the experience of many others (Blake, 2001)

> I cannot stress the impact that this class had on me. It was one of the rare times when I felt that, having seen a well-rounded example of an issue, I could form an opinion based on my own observations, not just on what I had been shown in a classroom.

The relationships among the sometimes competing goals of poverty alleviation, economic growth, and the sustainable use of the environment and its natural resources help define a basic learning framework. Participants grapple for balance among them—and corresponding impacts on human welfare—within the context of the host nation's complex food, environmental, economic, and social systems. Culturally and experientially diverse participants also learn to debate effectively and to negotiate better disparate or conflicting viewpoints into collaboration, aided by hands-on opportunities and guidance in choosing effective criteria to better figure things out for themselves.

From the outset of the field component, participants are organized into multidisciplinary theme groups with faculty facilitators. Each group comprises undergraduate and graduate students in several disciplines, international and U.S. students, and Spanish-language competency. In addition to class discussions to daily process our observations, theme groups continue to deliberate throughout the field trip and subsequently in preparing written projects and their oral team presentations. Findings from rapid appraisals during the field study are also reported using this mechanism. Rapid appraisal exercises include mapping farm resources, mapping community transects, constructing a multilayer annual calendar of agricultural, household and community activities, and outlining a community and family history of agriculture as well as resource use. The expectation is that farm visits provide a powerful thread for connecting one's own experiential learning with the learning that comes from reading and discussions also involving our hosts, which may immediately help students to formulate their own projects, including potential return for thesis work.

Themes groups vary with the expertise held by the participating faculty as well as the interests of students. For example, themes in one *Experience Latin America* edition were, "Rural Realities: Livelihood Systems in Chiapas," "Politics, Identity, and Society," and "Indigenous Cultural Expression and Performance." Another edition focused on complementary livelihoods-related issues: "Livelihood Systems in Mexico's Gulf Region: Which are the Priority Information Needs, Policies, and Programs?" and "Livelihood Systems in Mexico's Gulf Region: How to Make Research and Extension Relevant?" Associated considerations were the potential "action plans" to increase the impact of research and extension, understanding better how information needs, interests, and knowledge systems of resource-limited farmers differ from those with greater endowments, and the roles of farmer organizations, and alliances with universities and government and nongovernmental organizations.

Research Aim: Agrarian Vulnerability

These living laboratory experiences provided opportunities for our participants to gain awareness and to learn about some of the rural realities that encompass many issues separately addressed by the academy. Farm visits initiated learning and insight about real-world issues concerning food production, land and water, climate change, biodiversity, family and community welfare, and the economic challenges faced by agrarian society. Conversations with farmers, indigenous folks, and other hosts helped articulate needs and contemporary challenges. Recognizing that valuable intellectual work and analysis take place in all disciplines, cultural agency and performance studies were also integrated into our portfolio of pedagogical interactions and the process of articulating researchable problems. Consequently, graduate and undergraduate student researchers developed projects and publications with the dual purposes of pursuing real-world issues and giving something back to our hosts and others with similar needs and interests.

We now illustrate our approach by describing an encounter with the Génesis farmers' organization, which subsequently led to the multi-institutional research collaboration by Absalon-Medina et al. (2012a,b). Our group had been invited to the Génesis annual meeting and *barbacoa* (barbecue) at Rancho El Yualito, on the central coastal plain near Cotaxtla, Veracruz. Dozens of these cooperative members, owners of farms with dual-purpose cattle systems to produce milk and beef gathered with their families for business meetings, reporting, and festivities. Reports included on-farm technology testing (and viewing of livestock), hearing from INIFAP advisors on technical and financial matters, and reviewing collaborative work plans for the coming year.

The Génesis encounter was graciously arranged and co-hosted by Dr. Francisco Juárez Lagunes, a Cornell University alumnus, a research scientist for INIFAP, and a professor at Universidad Veracruzana, along with Génesis farmers. Our El Yualito arrival was like finding a bustling, sunny-day county fair—a parking area for vehicles, streams of people along with the unloading of cattle from trucks, multicolored banners, lively music booming from loudspeakers, Génesis men all in red shirts like twins *requete* multiplied (galore), smiling wives, mothers, and daughters assuring order over chaos, organizing tables, chairs, projectors and screens, cauldrons of *carnitas* (savory pork) on open fires, and easels displaying posters reporting on-farm research with figures and photographs. This was a celebration of successful cooperative action. Upon arrival, our international delegation was warmly received by José Ausencio Muñíz Morales, owner of El Yualito, and his nephew, José Miguel Ruíz Espinoza. José Miguel, a former high school exchange student in the United States, was urged to address our group on equal ground as Génesis' bilingual spokesperson. Greetings and introductory remarks led to a farm tour, presentations, questions and many individual conversations, and ample opportunities to observe Génesis men and women in action with INIFAP advisors.

During the visit, our attention seized on a key organizational principle tied to their work ethic: Génesis insists on a membership comprising only committed, active participants. Subsequent discussions in our small groups highlighted radical differences in agency and voice between the active chorus of Génesis *socios* (members) and, the comparatively muted encounters in a previous visit with other farmers just a few hours away. This issue emerged again when visiting the Veracruz highland community of Micoxtla, above the city of Coatepec, where families struggle with seasonal food insecurity and economic instability. Micoxtla residents expressed the desire to be helped to organize cooperatively in order to enter higher-value local and regional markets. This expression and subsequent interaction eventually led to McRoberts' thesis project (2009) and research collaboration with INIFAP (McRoberts et al., 2013).

These and other field encounters helped bring to life the need to help communities and families to better secure their futures, a priority for the Government of Mexico that was emphasized by the United Nations (UN) Special Rapporteur (de Schutter, 2011). Despite gains in reducing the percentage of underweight children under five years of age (i.e., Millennium Development Goal #1), the Special Rapporteur emphasized the unacceptable uneven progress between rural and urban populaces. About 80% of the 18 million Mexicans living in municipalities characterized by high marginalization are in rural areas. Consequently, the Government of Mexico was urged to improve self-determination in rural communities through greater community participation and capacity building. Recommended actions included implementing mutually reinforcing environmental, agricultural, and social protections, among the priorities to improve public policy, education, diets, health care, and family incomes. Calling for a "Third Agrarian Reform" the rapporteur cited a growing income inequality fostered partly by the insufficient public support of agriculture. This reform was charged to provide greater public good expenditures, among them greater access to credit and financial services, agricultural technical assistance, and support to producer organizations and cooperatives.

In harmony with de Schutter's recommendations, many students subsequently formulated thesis research projects aimed at helping rural communities diminish their own vulnerability. These projects, typically considered multiple goals aligned with the resources and opportunity horizons already dealt to families and communities. In the following sections, we summarize outcomes from research endeavors that were initially based on exchanges with families owning livestock. We present results from a set of projects led by five graduate student *Experience Latin America* alumni—Australian, Japanese, American, and two Mexican students—who examined some of the nutrient constraints and farming system dynamics at the root of agrarian vulnerability in Mexico's Gulf region. In every case, coalitions with farmers, farmer organizations, communities, local researchers, and students enabled problem definition and project fieldwork. Key institutional partners were INIFAP, Universidad Autónoma de Yucatán (UADY), Unión Ganadera Regional de Yucatán, Unión Ganadera Regional del Oriente de Yucatán, Universidad Veracruzana, and Génesis and Tepetzintla farmer organizations in Veracruz.[*] Thus, these collaborations[†] constituted a kind of international consortium of its own making.

Cattle Systems

Animal agriculture is fundamental to the economy of Mexico's Gulf region. Cattle herds, like those owned by Génesis farmers constitute an important livelihood in rural Veracruz, a major supplier of Mexico's beef and milk. However, information for improving the productivity, profitability, and sustainability of dual-purpose cattle systems is scarce in tropical Latin America, including Mexico, and likely in tropical agro-ecosystems around the world, especially regarding the benefits and costs of alternative management strategies (Blake and Nicholson, 2004; Blake, 2008). Assisted by INIFAP Génesis members sought to improve farming performance by substituting traditional forages with more nutritious species to increase milk sales from their herds.

Therefore, working together with INIFAP and Génesis herd owners in what are probably the first published tropical case studies to systematically examine complex energetic interactions,[‡]

---

[*] These organizations are widely known as a Grupo Ganadero de Validación y Transferencia de Tecnología (GGAVATT), or GGAVATT Génesis and GGAVATT Tepetzintla.

[†] Decision Support of Ruminant Livestock Systems.

[‡] These interactions involve dietary energy balance, milk production, and expected growth (and indirectly, their potential effects on herd reproduction).

Absalon-Medina et al. (2012a,b) evaluated the limitations and potential improvements in milk production and profitability from alternative nutritional management. Other students similarly evaluated approaches to overcome productivity bottlenecks in Yucatan beef cattle herds (Baba, 2007) and juvenile female replacements in Tepetzintla herds of the low Huasteca region of Veracruz (Cristóbal-Carballo, 2009). These projects revealed a consistent pattern of key biological (energy) and management constraints on animal performance, which portends broader potential application for improving cattle system performance.

Heretofore, unrecognized vulnerabilities were revealed through a study designed to evaluate herd performance limitations parsed by the age of cow, physiological status, and forage season of the year. The most susceptible management groups were nonlactating cows of all ages and forage seasons, and young cows and herd replacements (heifers) suffering growth retardations. Energy deficits signify repeated opportunity losses across an animal's lifetime, which are manifested in delayed puberty of heifers, fewer offspring born, and less total milk per cow over expected lifetimes. Like past efforts by Génesis farmers, these impediments could be ameliorated by investing in nutritional management and improved forage quality. As a result, diets formulated with better quality grass and legume forages were predicted to increase milk sales by up to 74% with large economic incentives, about USD $600 to $1100 greater predicted net margin per cow. This increase in net margin is large, equaling, or exceeding in value the total milk from an additional full lactation per cow lifetime. A similar dietary strategy to assure normal growth also based on low-cost, locally produced feeds, especially available forages (i.e., grass hay, sugarcane, and legumes), resulted in heifers that were 20% younger at first parturition (signifying earlier commencement of milk sales) with lower rearing costs, heavier body weights, and greater adipose tissue reserves (Cristóbal-Carballo, 2009).

Large marginal rates of return, the change in net margin per unit increase in variable costs, indicated clear economic incentives to alleviate inherent energy deficits and impaired growth. However, alternative management options may be difficult to implement if they are little practiced, thus generating little knowledge among farmers about potential profitability, and if options are perceived riskier than status quo practices. *Ex ante* economic assessment of strategies, requiring greater nutrient inputs is important because higher production per animal is not always more profitable (Absalon-Medina et al., 2012b).

Crop-Livestock Systems

Another set of studies examined the nutrient dynamics underlying smallholder systems and the potential of small ruminants to their sustainability. For more than three millennia, the shifting cultivation *milpa* system in the Yucatán Peninsula has involved the cutting of forest after a fallow period, burning, and planting of maize mixed with squash and beans. *Milpa* (maize, often multi-cropped with beans) cultivation has been purported to be the only food production method available to farmers in forested areas without draft animals. Slashing and burning clears rocky soils for planting, releases nutrients from slashed vegetation for crop growth, and controls the population of weed seed. A major limitation to the productivity of *milpa* systems, indeed to food production in the developing world, is soil nutrient depletion. Nutrients and organic matter from animal manure—the world's oldest fertilizer—is a vital input for growing food. Agricultural systems of Yucatán have long comprised multiple species of livestock; and the incorporation of hair sheep, a recent practice, is likely driven by market demand for lamb and mutton in the central region around Mexico City. While all adopters of this practice let manure accumulate by corralling animals, only one-third of them fertilize with it. Most of these smallholder producers also cultivate a *milpa*, but cannot bear the expense of commercial fertilizer. Parsons et al. (2011a) summarized, "Farmers have only recently added sheep to their systems to increase household income, and opportunities may exist to develop greater complementarities between these two farming system components, particularly through manure use." Thus, a prime research objective was to evaluate the effectiveness of sheep manure fertilization rates combined with weed control in sustaining the productivity of *milpa* cultivation. A study of nutrient fluxes in the *milpa* system of Yucatán with continual maize cultivation and stover removal to feed animals showed that manuring with four metric tons of dry matter per hectare would sustain the soil stock of phosphorus, but not nitrogen or potassium, indicating threats to sustainability from lost fertility (Parsons et al., 2011a).

A companion study suggested that fertility losses and higher weed pressure were important causes of falling maize yields in *milpas*. Chemical control required much less labor than hand weeding, and fewer weeds mean greater maize production. Manure fertilization also increased grain and biomass yields. By third and fourth years of cultivation, high maize yields could be achieved only through a combination of manuring and weed control. "Small sheep flocks could theoretically provide a sufficient quantity of manure to fertilize a *milpa*, potentially allowing fertility to be maintained beyond the normal two years. Technologies that increase yield and maintain plots for a longer period have the potential to change elements of the current *milpa* system. The success of such practices ultimately depends on livelihood needs and aspirations of the households and the communities in which they live" (Parsons et al., 2009).

Mixed farming systems are enterprises where animal husbandry and crop cultivation are integrated components of one farming system: livestock are fed crop byproducts or residues (i.e., stubble) and significant income is earned by cropping. These systems provide many benefits to low-resource families and although smallholder households produce a large proportion of the food in the tropics, our understanding of the functioning of their farming systems is limited. To address the gap that he previously identified, Parsons et al. (2011c) developed an integrated crop-livestock model to assess biophysical and economic consequences of farming practices incorporated into sheep systems in Yucatán. The resulting dynamic model comprising stocks, flows, and feedbacks integrates scientific and practical knowledge of management, flock dynamics, sheep production, nutrient partitioning, labor, and economic components. It also accesses information about sheep performance (productivity and manure quantity) and cropping (weather, crop, and soil dynamics) obtained from other simulation models.

Thus, this simulation model embodies some of the complex interactions occurring between smallholder farmers, crops and livestock; it is a tool for examining selected suites of integrated crop-livestock practices compared to specialized cropping. Studies using this tool revealed that mixed farming scenarios with sheep provide more family income than specialized enterprises. This outcome capitalized on a lower on-farm price of maize grain, efficient utilization of surplus labor, and exploiting the availability of common land. However, more was not always better. It was most profitable to sell excess grain and maize stover, and instead of stover to use common land to feed livestock, thus warning that more integration may not always improve economic outcomes (Parsons et al., 2011b). This systems-oriented approach drew upon local knowledge, synthesizing it in a manner that added value. Humans often have a limited ability to predict outcomes in dynamically complex systems, such as agriculture, where short-term and long-term behaviors may differ.

Collective Action: Value-Added Agricultural Products

Another project embodied a response to rural community interest to organize cooperatively to increase family incomes by accessing higher-value local markets. Communities like Micoxtla in the Veracruz highlands, where most inhabitants work in agriculture, confront multiple livelihood challenges. These include food insecurity, unemployment, and low and variable family incomes, which may be surmounted by the creation of income-generating opportunities. Value-added agricultural products are a potential strategy for earning higher incomes. However, biological and economic uncertainties often must be reduced, especially for this strategy to benefit smallholders. Households may be unable to enter or to compete in high-value agricultural product markets because of low access to market information, seasonal production shortfalls, inconsistent product quality, costly market access and poor infrastructure, all of which increase transaction costs (Holloway et al., 2000). Collective action may help overcome these barriers. Value-added products manufactured and marketed by farmer groups or cooperatives might reduce uncertainty by improving rural livelihoods through collective bargaining, smaller transaction costs, and higher average net incomes.

Most Micoxtla families struggle with seasonal food and economic insecurity. After meeting household needs, the principal sources of cash family income are sales of goat's milk, young goats for meat (*cabrito*), and eggs. Community members identified growing demand for specialty products for the tourist trade in the nearby city of Xico, including aged cheeses made from goat's milk, as one potential component of a rural development project assisted by INIFAP. The community wanted to explore this option to increase incomes, which would require initial funds beyond the capacity of individual families. Further risks from producing and marketing premium cheeses stem from dynamic biological, economic, and social processes like weather patterns, market access, and available land to produce forages. Founding an agrarian cooperative supported with startup technical services and training by INIFAP could help reduce these risks.

Consequently, McRoberts (2009; McRoberts et al., 2013) worked with the community and INIFAP advisors to assess the *ex ante* potential of cheese production and marketing through a dairy cooperative comprising 25 families. This assessment was enabled by participatory group action to develop a dynamic mathematical simulation tool. With caveats acknowledged, the resulting analysis indicated that a cooperative has substantial potential to improve community incomes while controlling risk under a broad range of environmental and market conditions (McRoberts et al., 2013). Furthermore, this Micoxtla case supports de Schutter's (2011) admonishment to help foster community self-determination using participatory approaches, in this case through both identification and *ex ante* assessment of potential development interventions. Undertaken with a leading Mexican research and development institution, this case importantly demonstrates a methodological contribution to research and development programing. This approach could be applied more broadly to understand the potential behaviors over time resulting from proposed interventions, to determine their benefits and pitfalls, and to better inform decisions about potential investments by governments, donors, communities, and families.

Intellectual Gains from Cultural Context

Although these projects cover a limited disciplinary footprint compared to the many needs that were identified, they clearly exemplify learning from cultural agents with efforts to return the favor. Collectively they respond to de Schutter's (2011) criteria by providing technical assistance, better understanding of food system function and with methodology and action plans to support local communities' escape from poverty and growth of social capital through collective action. In addition to research publications to inform global audiences, project results were shared with local communities and farmer organizations through our collaborators. On an invited presentation,[*] Yucatán farmers generously expressed gratitude for the thought-provoking results about cattle system opportunities across the Gulf region. Thus, these agrarian research cases illustrate academe's role in transferring information from the community context to a broader public audience, creating discourse and analysis, and abetting social change along the way.

Our integrative curricular approach, incorporating both formal and communal knowledge producers, has co-evolved in ways that parallel the challenge laid down by Godenzzi (2006)

> to communicate research results, discourse analysis, and critical reflections with the agents of that education so that these may enrich curricula and pedagogical interactions. In this way, these disciplines will be contributing to the formation of intercultural agents capable of reinventing our life in society.

Taking up this challenge, we submit that academe is cultural agency's natural partner. To fulfill better its social educator role academe must provide curricula and pedagogy in ways that echo, connect, and create plural discourse among multiple dimensions and disciplines of society. Multiplicative effects may be achieved when students and faculty, key agents themselves and trainers of intercultural agents, learn first-hand by crossing borders. In so doing, a more inclusive worldview about life in society is found through another lens, thus providing critical context for needs assessments.

Conclusion

We have illustrated ways in which academe has employed intercultural agency to embrace a more inclusive worldview that helps to frame and effectively address the challenges of agrarian vulnerability and rural life. By allying with hosts from other walks of life who became key professors, students and faculty become colearners and collaborators charged with social responsibility in delivering voice, knowledge, and understanding to extended audiences. We contend that greater academic agency through more alliances like those demonstrated here, and the necessary education investment to foster them, is needed to achieve equity goals through effective community engagement and applied problem-solving. It also helps ensure that all can participate in public policy decisions, which is part of "reinventing our life in society," Godenzzi's challenge to education. Exposed to an enabling cultural landscape, the one carrying messages about the substantive contexts surrounding technical intervention and implementation, students winnow and amplify them through their own engagements, lenses and reflections, and finally delivering them through an egalitarian process to academe and society writ large.

Acknowledgments

We thank Emily Holley and Charles Nicholson for their helpful feedback on drafts of this chapter.

---

[*] "Limitaciones y Manejo Alternativo para la Producción de Carne en los Trópicos" (Limitations and Alternative Management for Beef Production in the Tropics) invited presentation by R. W. Blake (2010) at *Día del Ganadero 2010* (Cattleman's Field Day 2010), INIFAP Sitio Experimental Tizimín, Tizimín, Yucatán, México.

Appendix: Images from Southern Mexico

What is a Mangrove Forest? Students and faculty visit the Pantanos de Centla Biosphere Reserve wetlands ecosystem to learn about mangrove forests and the wildlife they support. (Centla, Tabasco, México, January 2006.)

A closer view—living laboratory students observe wetlands biodiversity. (Centla, Tabasco, México, January 2006.)

Multinational synthesis—a theme group studies information needs, policies, and programs to better support rural livelihoods in the Gulf region of Mexico. (Hotel parking lot, Paraiso, Tabasco, México, January 2006.)

Hosts José Miguel Ruíz Espinoza (foreground) and José Ausencio Muñiz Morales (right) welcome our international delegation and explain GGAVATT Génesis activities. (Rancho El Yualito, Veracruz, México, January 2008.)

Land used for cattle pasture, copra, and fuel collection. (Rural Tabasco, México, January 2006.)

Cow and calf—zebu-based herds produce beef in the Gulf region of Mexico. (Southern Veracruz, México, January 2007.)

Dr. Francisco Juárez Lagunes (leftmost) and Víctor Absalón Medina (second from right) report research findings to the Génesis membership. (Rancho El Yualito, Veracruz, México, January 2007.)

Hair sheep from the Gulf region partly supply Mexico's domestic barbacoa market. (Leonardo Cocom's farm, Xmatkuil, Yucatán, México, May 2005.)

Sale of goat's milk (in cans) provides important income to Micoxtla families. (Micoxtla, Veracruz, México, January 2007.)

Keenan McRoberts (center left) and Victor Absalón (center right) assist INIFAP at a Micoxtla field day. (Micoxtla, Veracruz, México, January 2007.)

Living laboratory students join the 2008 annual meeting of the Génesis farmer organization. (Rancho El Yualito, Veracruz, México, January 2008.)

References

Absalon-Medina, V. A., Blake, R. W., Fox, D. G., Juárez-Lagunes, F. I., Nicholson, C. F., Canudas-Lara, E. G., and Rueda-Maldonado, B. L. 2012a. Limitations and potentials of dual-purpose cow herds in Central Coastal Veracruz, Mexico, *Tropical Animal Health and Production*, 44(6): 1131–1142.

Absalon-Medina, V. A., Nicholson, C. F., Blake, R. W., Fox, D. G., Juárez-Lagunes, F. I., Canudas-Lara, E. G., and Rueda-Maldonado, B. L. 2012b. Economic analysis of alternative nutritional management of dual-purpose cow herds in Central Coastal Veracruz, Mexico, *Tropical Animal Health and Production*, 44(6): 1143–1150.

Baba, K. 2007. *Analysis of Productivity, Nutritional Constraints and Management Options in Beef Cattle Systems of Eastern Yucatan, Mexico: A Case Study of Cow-Calf Productivity in the Herds of Tizimin, Yucatan*, unpublished Master's thesis, Cornell University, Ithaca, NY, USA.

Blake, R. W. 2001. Tradition and transition: INTAG 602 and the graduate field of International Agriculture and Rural Development, *International Agriculture 602 Millennium Conference on Agricultural Development in the 21st Century, International Programs*, College of Agriculture and Life Sciences, Cornell University, Ithaca, NY, pp. 36–40.

Blake, R. W. 2008. Perspectivas de la investigación pecuaria en el mundo tropical: Utilización de recursos genéticos de ganado bovino, in Durán, C. V. and Campos, R. (eds.), *Perspectivas de Conservación, Mejoramiento y Utilización de Recursos Genéticos Criollos y Colombianos en los Nuevos Escenarios del Mejoramiento Animal*. Valle, Colombia: Universidad Nacional de Colombia, pp. 1–17.

Blake, R. W. and Nicholson, C. F. 2004. Livestock, land use change, and environmental outcomes in the developing world, in Owen, E. (ed.), *Responding to the Livestock Revolution—The Role of Globalization and Implications for Poverty Alleviation*. Nottingham, UK: Nottingham University Press, pp. 133–153.

Cristóbal-Carballo, O. 2009. *Management of Heifer Growth in Dual-Purpose Cattle Systems in the Low Huasteca Region of Veracruz, Mexico*, unpublished Master's thesis, Cornell University, Ithaca, NY.

de Schutter, O. 2011. End of mission to Mexico: Mexico requires a new strategy to overcome the twin challenges of 'Food Poverty' and obesity, says UN food expert. Geneva, Switzerland: Office of the High Commissioner for Human Rights (OHCHR).

Godenzzi, J. C. 2006. The discourses of diversity: Language, ethnicity, and interculturality in Latin America, in Sommer, D. (ed.), *Cultural Agency in the Americas*. Durham, NC: Duke University Press, pp. 146–166.

Holloway, G., Nicholson, C. F., Delgado, C., Stall, S., and Ehui, S. 2000. Agroindustrialization through institutional innovation, transaction costs, cooperatives and milk-market development in the East-African Highlands, *Agricultural Economics*, 23: 279–288.

McRoberts, K. 2009. *Rural Development Challenges: System Dynamics Ex Ante Decision Support for Agricultural Initiatives in Southern Mexico*, unpublished Master's thesis, Cornell University, Ithaca, NY.

McRoberts, K. C., Nicholson, C. F., Blake, R. W., Tucker, T. W., and Díaz-Padilla, G. 2013. Group Model Building to Assess Rural Dairy Cooperative Feasibility in South-Central Mexico, *International Food and Agribusiness Management Review*, 16(3): 55–98.

Meredith, R. A. 2010. Acquiring cultural perceptions during study abroad: The influence of youthful associates, *Hispania*, 93(4): 686–702.

Parsons, D., Ketterings, Q. M., Cherney, J. H., Blake, R. W., Ramírez-Aviles, L., and Nicholson, C. F. 2011a. Effects of weed control and manure application on nutrient fluxes in the shifting cultivation milpa system of Yucatán, *Archives of Agronomy and Soil Science*, 57(3): 273–292.

Parsons, D., Nicholson, C. F., Blake, R. W., Ketterings, Q. M., Ramírez-Aviles, L., Cherney, J. H., and Fox, D. G. 2011b. Application of a simulation model for assessing integration of smallholder shifting cultivation and sheep production in Yucatán, Mexico, *Agricultural Systems*, 104: 13–19.

Parsons, D., Nicholson, C. F., Blake, R. W., Ketterings, Q. M., Ramírez-Aviles, L., Fox, D. G., Tedeschi, L. O., and Cherney, J. H. 2011c. Development and evaluation of an integrated simulation model for assessing smallholder crop-livestock production in Yucatán, Mexico, *Agricultural Systems*, 104: 1–12.

Parsons, D., Ramírez-Aviles, L., Cherney, J. H., Ketterings, Q. M., Blake, R. W., and Nicholson, C. F. 2009. Managing maize production in shifting cultivation milpa systems in Yucatán through weed control and manure application," *Agriculture Ecosystems and Environment*, 133(1–2): 123–134.

Sommer, D. 2006. Introduction: Wiggle room, in Sommer, D. (ed.), *Cultural Agency in the Americas*. Durham, NC: Duke University Press, pp. 1–28.

Thurston, H. D. 2001. A living laboratory: Field study in agriculture and agricultural development, *International Agriculture 602 Millennium Conference on Agricultural Development in the 21st Century*, International Programs, College of Agriculture and Life Sciences, Cornell University, Ithaca, NY, pp. 33–35.

Chapter 4

Subordinated Inclusion: The Developmental State and the Dalit Colonies of Southern Kerala*

K. M. Pramod

Contents

* I would like to acknowledge my research supervisor, Dr. K. T. Rammohan, Associate Professor, School of Social Sciences, Mahatma Gandhi University, Kottayam (DT), Kerala, India. His guidance was critical for the completion of this project and I am very grateful for his ongoing support.

Introduction

This chapter focuses on the relationship between the developmental state, specifically the Indian state of Kerala and Dalits.[*] The state's affirmative action regarding Dalits dates back to India's colonial period. One of the important policy measures, among many, adopted by the state of Kerala during colonial times sought to "ameliorate the conditions of the depressed communities" through the establishment of colonies.[†] Dalits, who were rehabilitated in the colonies, were laborers attached to paddy and garden cultivation. The term "colony" in this context can be understood as an area of land that was designated for habitation by Dalits, sometimes with a supportive resource base as land for cultivation. In this chapter, the term "colony" refers to a social space—a space of subordinated inclusion. These colonies have received a great deal of attention from the governments and, therefore, have functioned as a site of state development operations. However, an interesting contrast can be seen between colony-Dalits and noncolony-Dalits. Simply put, they appear to have very different positions as subjects. That is, colony-Dalits are seen as having a lower social standing both in terms of self-perception as well as in the eyes of "outsiders" including Dalits living outside the colonies and elsewhere in India. In this chapter, I seek to problematize the subject position of "colony-Dalits" by focusing on Dalit colonies or Dalits residing in distinct parts of India. In doing so, I focus on four Dalit colonies in southern Kerala, Thiruvithamkur[‡] in particular, and explore varied dimensions of the process of subordination including social, historical, economic, and political dimensions, in addition to the process of subordinate inclusion in the larger context of the developmental discourse of modern Kerala, India.

The Problem and Its Significance: Objectives and Methodology

This study explores the relationship between the developmental state and Dalits within the colonies. Some of the colonies have been established by the state for Dalits to provide living space for them. Within the colony, there are differentials in terms of economic status and employment. Generally, however, and in relation to social groups beyond the colonies, colony-Dalits can be characterized as dispossessed peoples. Accordingly, this study problematizes the current socioeconomic subject position of "colony-Dalits."[§] The significance of this study is located in its conceptual understanding of the process of subordination as well as the strategy of subordinate inclusion of a particular social group in the sociopolitical structure of Indian society. Moreover, it provides an historical understanding of the making of the subordinate social space through the interventions of the modern state and society, and offers an account of the lives of Dalit in the aforementioned subordinate social space. Subsequently, and an understanding of the sociohistorical context of the making of Dalit colonies in Kerala is developed, specifically in the context of the state of Thiruvithamkur. Moving beyond this, the chapter

---

[*] Dalits: traditional lower caste peoples in India; those social groups who have been called as the "Scheduled Castes."

[†] Dalit colonies: communities of Dalits that have been marked as geographical spaces of dwelling, and sometimes, associated economic activities like cultivation, where all or the majority of the inhabitants are Dalits, but where there are also a few non-Dalits. The non-Dalits include the backward castes such as artisanal castes, Ezhavas, and Muslims. Importantly, however, it is very rare to see a single *Savarna* (higher caste) Hindu living in these colonies. The number of dwellings varies from colony to colony.

[‡] Thiruvithamkur/Travancore: a princely state of preindependent southern Kerala.

[§] Colony Dalits: Dalits who were rehabilitated within colonies.

explores the following question: *How do developmental state policies and initiatives create socially and economically subordinated and distinctive social spaces called "colonies" or "Dalit colonies?"* Finally, the chapter comments on the socioeconomic attributes of colonies.

In combining historiographical and fieldwork methods, this study draws upon a variety of data sources. The print sources on colonies are almost entirely governmental in origin. They include administration reports and evaluation reports of colonization schemes. They provide a pool of information regarding the state's departments and schemes involved in the welfare of Dalits or the ex-slave communities within the region. However, these reports merely document governmental activities and do not necessarily portray the perceptions of Dalits or other targeted groups. Therefore, these reports have been used as part of this study to provide a general understanding of the state's initiatives for the establishment of the colonies as subordinated communities. Information collected from the field/colonies, thus, represents the central pillar of the research conducted and presented in the page that follows, and was gathered through direct interaction and sample surveys.

Conceptual Premises: Subordinated Inclusion and Spaces of Subordination

Dalit subordination could hardly be seen as "marginalization" or "exclusion," nor could the social groups in question be perceived as "outliers." Rather, their position within Indian society can be more accurately described as one of subordinated inclusion. Such a description carries greater analytical value given the fact that it emphasizes the relational aspects of social positioning. *Subordinated inclusion* is an outcome of a definite mode of distribution of social space. This distribution corresponds to the requirements of the caste system found throughout India. The distribution of the social space was initiated and controlled by the *Savarna* castes, pushing the lower social groups into spaces of subordination. Such spaces are "real" in both geographical and nongeographical terms. For example, the dwellings of the Pulaya agrestic slaves were located at the far end of paddy fields, for reasons that were not merely economic—to maintain vigil over water flows crucial to reclaimed, wetland cultivation—but also social, as *Savarna* lords sought to keep them away from their own personal living space. Today, there are colonies in urban and rural communities comprised almost entirely of subordinated social groups. Spaces of subordination may also have a nongeographical dimension. For example, a Dalit girl might find herself trapped in a space of subordination within a university classroom, even today. In such a situation, she is locked in an unequal engagement in terms of her relationship with other students and teachers, most of whom are *Savarnas* and, therefore, she is seen as some type of social "other."

Dalit Colonies

While the colony is a valid conceptual category, it does not exist as a monolithic entity. In fact, a number of different types of colonies exist. These variations could be explained by the origin of the individual colony, the recognition of the colony by the state, the composition of the community, its power of negotiation, and even by its geographical attributes. Traditional settlements of some of the referred social groups have been recast as colonies. Some colonies and settlements, directly established by the state, have subsequently gained recognition by that state. These colonies are entitled to the assistance of the welfare state with the majority of colony-Dalits retaining the legal right to vote.

The community composition may vary across the colonies. Colonies with a more cosmopolitan/secular community composition tend to experience fewer social disadvantages than colonies that are primarily comprised of Dalits. Likewise, a colony in the Kerala highlands faces considerable geographical constraints regarding access to development resources such as education and health care. Emerging colonies may be seen as victims of development exercises such as large infrastructure projects related to transport, communication, irrigation, forest conservation, and power generation. This is so, given that colonies are often forced to move and resettle beyond the reach of such development projects. Some of these might cut across caste lines, as is the case with Kerala. The fate and survival of a colony might be more dependent upon economic and political variables since they do not retain "rights to land, to the availability of food, or the right to vote." Unlike Dalits within the colonies, they may belong to different castes or even different religions, and be denied rights to land, to the availability of food, and to the right to vote. Therefore, with respect to the possibilities of negotiation with the state and agencies like mainstream political organizations, such colonies are tremendously disadvantaged.

Dalit colonies are clearly marked as geographical spaces of living—and are sometimes associated with economic activities such as cultivation—where all or the majority of inhabitants are Dalits but where there non-Dalits are also residing. Non-Dalits are comprised of artisanal castes, *Ezhavas,* and even Muslims. However, very seldom are *Savarna* Hindus living within colonies of such composition. Regardless of ethnic and religious classification, the colonies are powerful instruments of segregation both socially and geographically. The establishment of colonies by the state has divided Dalits and cultivated a two-level understanding: (1) the colonies may be understood as having been shaped by external forces and (2) they may be understood as having been shaped by their own internal forces. Both perspectives are indeed demonstrative of the many factors that have impacted and continue to impact the overall development of these colonies, and both form part of the overall debate surrounding their existence.

Debating the Colonies: Thiruvithamkur and the Princely State of Pre-Independent Southern Kerala

Dalit colonies have a long and rich history. Their origins can be traced back to the monarchical period. However, the first Dalit colonies of Thiruvithamkur date back to the 1930s. These were conceived of as economically self-reliant geographical clusters of socially and economically disadvantaged groups within the region. The establishment of Dalit colonies in Thiruvithamkur during previous periods was done so while taking natural resources into account. In the post-state formation period, however, colonies began to be conceived of more as housing projects, that is, to provide housing in a specified area for Dalits without the means to obtain housing on their own. In certain cases, Dalits demanded the establishment of colonies as a result of their diminutive economic status and basic inability to afford their own housing. Although far from providing Dalits with ideal living conditions, the colonies, at the very least, provided them with basic shelter. The creation of the colonies might also be understood as having also served the purpose of assisting Dalits in becoming landowners. Those owning land and who granted Dalit agricultural laborers permission to build a hut on a corner of the land were key players in an important leap forward that saw the Dalits being provided with accommodations that Dalits themselves often considered favorable. This achievement, it should be remembered, was the result of a special arrangement between landowners and Dalits. Though an arrangement had been made, it was on an informal basis with—no formal contracts ever existed to support the construction of such accommodations. Consequently, the lord could evict Dalits whenever he or she decided to do so.

Dalits in the Sree Mulam Popular Assembly of Thiruvithamkur pleaded with the government to grant them land at concessional prices.* Given the continuing caste-based division of geographical space, expecting the government to allow Dalits land adjoining the dwellings of the *Savarna* (upper-caste) Hindus and Syrian Christians was an impossibility. These upper-castes and communities, moreover, would have resisted such a move on the part of the government if Dalits had been accommodated in their request.† It is also possible that given their sense of community bonding, the Pulayas (a Dalit caste in Kerala) might have shown interest in living together in a cluster of houses; however, this could also have been prompted by the hostile and *Savarna* dominated social environment in which they lived. One of the earliest references in the Sri Mulam Popular Assembly of Travancore to Dalits demanding the

---

* Access to productive land was a major demand of the depressed communities, raised in the assembly by their representatives. Even though they were tied to the land for generations, they were landless. They were allowed to work and live on the land, but they had no rights of ownership to it. Land was the most important productive asset at that time, and agriculture was the prominent productive sector of the economy. The government was forced to consider the demands of the landless communities for land. Dewan Bahadur T. Raghaviah, in his presidential address of 20 session of the Sri Mulam Popular Assembly in 1924, recognized the necessity of giving land at concessional rates to the depressed classes. He noted that these classes, namely Pulayas, Parayas, Kuravas, Vedas, and hill-men, comprising about 8.7% of the state's population, were entirely landless. Again in 1928, in his opening address of the 24th session of the Sri Mulam Popular Assembly of Travancore in 1928 (pp. 2–3), the Dewan emphasized the fact that in the context of the partition of property, Pulayas were to be provided with land for cultivation.

Pulayas are tillers of the land. The majority of them lived on the land they tilled and for many generations were cared for by the landlords. Following recent social legislation concerning the partition of property, estates were split up and many holdings became so small that in many cases the proprietor found himself unable to house and maintain the Pulaya field laborers. The result was that many Pulaya were made homeless and left to fend for themselves. The needs of these poor but indispensable people had to be met. Consequently, new guidelines were drawn up to assign them lands on concessional terms. A maximum limit of three acres per family was fixed. "Land for landless" therefore became state policy and the Land Revenue Commissioner and the Protector of Depressed Classes were asked to initiate implementation of the policy by earmarking the lands for distribution to the depressed classes. The total area of land registered in the names of members of depressed classes during the year was 394 acres in 1100 ME (Malayalam Era) [1924–1925]. In 1101 ME [1925–1926] 523 acres were allotted. By 1927 the total area assigned to the landless had reached 2995 acres.

† The governmental measures could not prevent the encroachments by the powerful Savarna castes over the registered land of the lower castes. The upper-caste officials also put obstacles in the way of land being distributing. The representatives of lower castes brought the problem to the attention of the state on numerous occasions. For instance, during the 23rd session of the Sri Mulam Popular assembly of Travancore held in 1927, Ayyankali complained that, "the portion of lands assigned to the Pulayas in the Vilappil pakuthi, Neyyattinkara taluk, in the year 1094 M. E., were still in the possession of the wealthy and influential people of the locality, though tax was being paid by the Pulaya registry-holders." Nor were the Pulayas able to sue the occupants in civil courts, because of their poverty.

The representatives also complained about the poor quality of the land granted to the depressed castes. Paradi Abraham Isaac, a nominated member in Sri Mulam Popular Assembly, quoting from the Proceedings of the Twenty-third Session of the Sri Mulam Assembly of the Travancore in 1927 (p. 24), noted: "The rule regarding the assignment of three acres of land under concessional terms to every family of the depressed classes failed to have the desired effect, mainly because of the lands earmarked for such assignment were quite unfit either for human habitation or cultivation." All the good land was in the possession of others. The unsympathetic attitude of the subordinates of the Revenue Department was another reason that the rules did not have the desired effect.

establishment of their own colonies can be traced back to 1919. The statement of Kurumban Daivathan, a member of the Sri Mulam Popular Assembly of Travancore, representing the Pulayas, commented as follows:

> [t]he member observed that lots of fifty or hundred acres of land may be set apart for *Pulayas* to live together that would help them to profitably cultivate their land and set up schools to educate their children. The experience of other countries confirms this. The "other country," Daivathan was referring to the Princely State of Mysore. The member pointed out, the revenue divisions in which the colonies could come up. Even the specific sites were pointed out complete with the survey numbers of the plots. Clearly, he must have been also trying to reassure the Savarna members of the Assembly that the land requested for would be now here near their dwellings (The Proceedings of the Sri Mulam Popular Assembly of Travancore, 1919).

In 1937, during the budget discussion in the Assembly, the Financial Secretary Rao Bahadur A. Rengaswami Aiyar announced that the government proposed to establish an "experimental rural colony." The site chosen for the project was called Enadimangalam in Kunnathur taluk[*] but the establishment of colonies in that location was not feasible due to officials who refused to facilitate any such development.[†] Within two years, however, the government developed three colonies at Narikulam, Kulathur, and Meenamkulam. During the same year, the Sachivothamapuram colony was established as a model colony at Kurichi in Changanachery taluk of Thiruvithamkur (Travancore Administration Report, 1937–1938: 142–143 and 1938–1939: 146). In 1938, the government granted 10,000 Indian Rupees (INR) for the colony at Kurichi (Proceedings of the Travancore Sri Mulam Assembly, Second Assembly, Second Session, 1938: 526). The Travancore Administration Reports for the late 1930s claim that "efforts were well on way" for the establishment of colonies at Anchamada, Venganoor, and Veliyathunad. Furthermore, preliminary arrangements were made for the establishment of colonies at Pacode, Kunnathur, and Kulakada Pakuthies (Travancore Administration Report, 1937–1938: 142–143 and 1938–1939: 146). Over time, the number of colonies increased. By the early 1950s, the state of Thiru-Kochi (a state that was independent of India and that formed by merging the princely states of Thiruvithamkur and Kochi) had 187 colonies (Report of the Administration of Travancore–Cochin, 1953–1954: 215–216).

The establishment of these colonies was welcomed by most of the representatives of the depressed castes within the Assembly, but there were also strong critics. N. John Joseph, for instance, denounced the establishment of these and other colonies, stating as follows:

> [t]he establishment of colonies would not provide any sort of socio-economic upward mobility to the depressed communities. A colony is like a cage that arrests the members of the depressed communities and does not permit them to grow. The inhabitants in a colony will only get 10 to 25 cents of land, which may not make any kind of benefits and future developments (Proceedings of Sri Mulam Popular Assembly, 3rd Session of the Second Assembly, 1938: 560).

---

[*] See the Presidential speech of Diwan, in Proceedings of the Travancore Sri Chitra State Council, Second Council, First Session—1937, Vol. 10, No. 1, Travancore: Government Press, 1938: 40.

[†] See the Assembly speech of Mr Adichan, nominated member from the lower castes. The Proceedings of the Travancore Sri Mulam Assembly, Second Assembly, Third Session, 1938: 567.

Other Dalits, including T. T. Kesavan Sastri, welcomed the idea of the colony. Sastri considered the establishment of the colony as an important ameliorative measure for the depressed social groups. His demands focused on the creation of facilities for education within the colonies.*

The Democratic State and the Colony

Resettlement schemes were planned and implemented throughout various regions of India long before India gained its independence from the United Kingdom in 1947. Such schemes were formulated with a simple aim in mind: to provide housing for the homeless. During the period of the Third Five Year Plan, colonization projects for "backward" communities were introduced. The Colonization Schemes introduced by the Government of Kerala, with the intention of "rehabilitating" Dalits and a*divasi* (tribal) landless/homeless, include the High Range Colonization Scheme, Cooperative Colonization Scheme, Wayanad Colonization Scheme, and Attapady Valley development Scheme.† Several further colonies were established for Dalits under the Special Component

---

* See the Speech of T. T. Kesavan Sastri, nominated member in Sri Mulam Popular Assembly, in Proceedings of the Third Session of the Second Assembly of Sri Mulam Popular Assembly of Travancore, 1938: 571.

‡ In Kerala a Department of Colonization was established under the administrative control of the Director of Colonization. This was to implement the rehabilitation programs of the state for the benefit of the landless poor. The department operated until November 1, 1956. Subsequently, the schemes undertaken by the department were transferred to the District Collectors. Settlement Scheme, Cooperative Colonization, Poor Housing Scheme, Low Income Group Housing Scheme, and Subsidized Industrial Housing Scheme were some of the projects overseen by this department (Kerala State Administration Report 1956–1957, 1958). In the following years the scope of the projects widened. During the year 1962–1963 a large number of housing and colonization schemes were implemented. These include settlement, poor housing, low income group housing, land development and acquisition, employees' housing, subsidized industrial housing, middle income group housing, village housing, High Range colonization, cooperative, Wayanad colonization, Attapady Valley development, plantation labor housing, and cooperation housing schemes (*Administration Report of the Housing and Colonization Scheme for the Year 1962–1963*, 1964; *Administration Report of the Housing and Colonization Scheme for the Year 1963–1964*, 1965). From 1964–1965 the colonization schemes were separated from the mixed plan of housing and colonization. These colonization schemes were under the administrative control of the Board of Revenue. The schemes were implemented under the authority of the District Collectors. Among the colonization schemes, the following ones were important: High Range Colonization Scheme, Cooperative Colonization Scheme, Wynad Colonization Scheme, and Attapady Valley Development Scheme (*Government of Kerala Administration Report for the year 1964–1965*, 1966).

High Range Colonization Scheme: This scheme was established and put into operation toward the end of 1954. The scheme envisaged the settlement of 8000 families of the landless agricultural laborers in an area of 40,000 acres of land. The estimated expenditure on the scheme was Rs. 233.50 lakhs and out of this a sum of Rs. 76 lakhs was estimated to be an outright expenditure, on roads, irrigation, water supply, buildings, and so on. Each inhabitant in the colony was given 5 acres for cultivation and habitation. A committee consisting of officials and nonofficials was responsible for the selection of inhabitants. There were four colonies in the High Ranges. These were respectively at Kallar, Marayoor, Kanthalloor, and Devicolam (*Government of Kerala Administration Report for the year 1964–1965*, 1966).

Cooperative Colonization Scheme: This was intended to provide cultivable lands to the actual cultivators who had no lands of their own and to encourage cooperative farming. Forest areas available and suitable for cultivation and habitation were utilized for the scheme. Cooperative colonies were to be organized in the areas set apart for the scheme. The area of a colony was conceived as ranging from 75 to 600 acres and consisting of 25–200 inhabitants. There was to be a paid secretary for each colony. Each colony was given a grant during the first five years to cover organizational and administrative expense (*Government of Kerala Administration Report for the year 1964–1965*, 1966). Seven Cooperative colonies were organized. Three of these were in Thiruvananthapuram district: Sasthavattam Cooperative colony, Puthuveettumuri Cooperative colony, and

Plan for Scheduled Castes* and *Harijan* (lower caste) Welfare Department.[†] A series of land reform schemes was also introduced with the intention of gathering surplus land for its eventual redistribution. There were also schemes aimed at reclaiming cultivable wastelands. Alongside these initiatives were movements such as *Bhoodan* (gift of land), which called for magnanimity on the part of landlords to provide land for redistribution among the landless.[‡]

Colony and Society

Colonies are often known by the name of the specific government scheme under which they were conceived of and created. Thus, there is the Lakshamveedu colony, Nalucent colony, and Harijan colony. Lakshamveedu colonies have double-dwelling houses with a maximum of eight cents of land for both families (four cents for each colony-Dalit). The Dalit of the Nalucent colony has four cents of land and a house. Harijan colonies are mainly for homeless Dalits. People living in these types of colonies are provided with a maximum of 10–14 cents of land and enough financial

---

Kallar Cooperative colony. Two were in Kollam district: The Kulathupuzha Agriculture Cooperative colony and the Kollamula Cooperative colony. Two were in Ernamkulam district: Vengola Cooperative colony and Neriamangalam. There were also Cooperative colonies to settle former soldiers ("ex-servicemen") at Vechuchira and Ranni in Pathanamthitta District.

Wayanad Colonization Scheme: The Wynad colony, with its headquarters at Ambalavayal, extends over an area of 33,802 acres or 53 square miles—comprising forest and uncultivated land—within the villages of Sultan's Battery, Ambalavayal and Nenmeni in South Wynad taluk. The scheme was meant to rehabilitate former soldiers, tribals, and other landless sections. The colony is administered by the District Collector, Kozhikode, assisted by the Administrative Officer and his staff consisting of two Special Deputy Thahasildars and other executive and ministerial staff at Ambalavayal and Sultan's Battery (*Government of Kerala Administration Report for the year 1964–1965*, 1966).

Attapady Valley Development Scheme: The object of this scheme was to further the development of the Attapady Village, situated in Mannarkkad taluk of Palakkad district. The extent of the valley is about 280 square miles, including reserve forests, and is inhabited by "tribes" such as Irulas, Muduvas, and Kurumbas. They have no economic security, hence the necessity of developing the valley by providing adequate facilities like irrigation and roads, and by improving the educational, social, and economic conditions of these social groups, who form the bulk of the population of the valley (*Government of Kerala Administration Report for the year 1964–1965*, 1966).

* Special Component Plan for Scheduled Castes: The special component plan was introduced in the state during the Fifth Plan period. This was with a view to enabling the Scheduled Caste population to cross the poverty line within as short a period as possible with the effort of economic development departments and agencies. A special cell was formed in the Government secretariat to review the flow of funds from the general sector to these schemes benefiting Scheduled Castes and Tribes (*Government of Kerala, Special Component Plan for Scheduled Castes, 1982–1983*, 1982). Under the special component plan for Scheduled Castes Rs. 8.71 crores (the total fund was Rs. 9.39 crores) were spent during the year 1981–1982. Colonization is one of the many schemes introduced by the Government for the benefit of the Harijans/Dalits. Reasonable financial assistance was also provided in the Annual and Five Year Plans (*Government of Kerala, Thonnakal Colonization Scheme, an Evaluation Study*, 1982).

† Harijan Welfare Department: Kerala, since its formation in 1956, has a Harijan Welfare Department. The department was established to provide economic opportunities for lower castes/Dalits, to make effective use of their skill, knowledge, and other abilities and to provide funds and equipment. The department saw the setting up of colonies as an important welfare measure for the socially disadvantaged groups. By 1982, the department had established 475 Harijan colonies. Five of these were considered major colonies. For each person, they provided two acres of land for cultivation and a site for a house (*Government of Kerala, Thonnakal Colonization Scheme an Evaluation Study*, 1982).

‡ See the Program Evaluation Organization Report, 1968: 1–3.

assistance to build a house. The four colonies dealt with in this study include Ayyankudi Nalu Cent colony, Appuzha Lakshamveedu colony, Mathuravely Harijan colony, and Mathuravely Lakshamveedu colony. These colonies are situated within the Upper Kuttanadu region, in the administrative area of present Muttuchira village, in Kottayam District of Kerala. Fieldwork experience from the four colonies has allowed for a greater understanding of the contemporary socio-economic positions of colony-Dalits.

Field Survey

Almost all the inhabitants of the colonies belong to Dalit communities particularly, the Pulayas and Christian Dalits. Out of the total households surveyed, 91.14% of the inhabitants belong to Dalit communities such as Hindu/Christian Pulaya, Velan, Sambhava, Ulladar, and Dheerava. Among the non-Dalit households, 85.71% are from the Ezhava community (an intermediate caste group in Kerala) and the rest are from other communities (Table 4.1).

The subject of this study (colony-Dalits) occupies the lowest position within the caste structure/hierarchy. Within the colonies, the subordinate caste status, coupled with low economic conditions, is a binding factor. When Dalits interact with the outside world, however, their caste identity becomes somewhat problematic. The so-called outsiders, overall, consider the colony-Dalits social outcasts and seen as people ranking even lower than Dalits residing beyond the colonies.

On one hand, colonies are a creation of the state as well as the social order. In the internal development of the colonies, the self-perception of the colony-Dalits is crucial. They perceive themselves as the lowest beings living their lives within the social and economic hierarchy. Unfulfilled ambitions and fruitless protests have led them to engage in and lead very self-destructive lives and to endure an exceptional degree of despair and hopelessness. Dalit youth often become addicted to alcohol and drugs or become *goondas* (criminal activists) of political parties, and *blade mafia* (gangs taking part in illicit business operations or lending money at high interest rates in an attempt to develop some sort of income base). Although the existing stereotypes of the colonies

Table 4.1   Caste Composition of Population in the Surveyed Colonies

Castes	Number of Households	% of Share Households
Hindu/Christian *Pulaya*	135	85.44
Velan	3	1.90
Sambhava	1	0.63
Ulladar	4	2.53
Dheerava	1	0.63
Ezhava	12	7.59
Kollan (blacksmiths)	1	0.63
Muslim	1	0.63
Total households	158	100

Source: Field Survey.

are of a place that is difficult to live in, positive aspects of life within these colonies can also be observed. Colony-Dalits, at the very least, live with their own people. Thus, there is a cultural component to the colonies that is both unifying and positively reinforcing. These positive aspects of the colonies and of how Dalits feel within them are quickly tempered when they venture beyond the colonies, at which point, there is a tendency for them to feel socially and economically inferior, and shamed.

Irrespective of the perceptions of others, these feelings come from the historically, politically, and economically constituted self-perception of colony-Dalits themselves. Most of the respondents spoken to and included within the study presented within this chapter expressed a desire to move out of their respective colonies. The colonies are perceived of as infamous spaces, notorious for disgracing their inhabitants and leaving them feeling both helpless and hopeless. When an inhabitant of the colony acquires a reasonable degree of education, employment, and income, they typically attempt to break free of the confines of the colony and integrate themselves into society beyond the colony. "Outsiders" tend to think of the colony as a labor pool, a hotspot of criminals, *goondas*, and prostitutes as well as a site for the distribution and use of drugs and narcotics. Moreover, the outsiders consider the youth in the colonies to be wasting their lives and see them as little more than troublesome. Activists of mainstream political organizations even see Dalit colonies primarily as vote-banks. Not only have the families of the middle- and upper-classes, but also those of the lower classes preferred to build their houses as far away from colonies as possible so as to disassociate themselves from the inhabitants. As one "outsider" expressed, "people in the colony are sexually anarchic and even have incestuous relationships." Usually, "outsiders" are reluctant to attend social functions, such as marriage ceremonies and funerals within the colonies, even if they attend they do so briefly and merely to offer money as a gift.

The lack of sufficient social networks (with individuals and institutions) reinforces the subordination of Dalits. While this is a problem faced by Dalits more generally, the problem is even acuter in the case of colony-Dalits. The absence of social networks restricts their socioeconomic opportunity usually resulting in their inability to break free from the colonies. As such, Dalits find themselves confined to their immediate surrounding and often remain trapped within the colonies for either long periods of time or for their entire lives. Not only are they unable to liaison with external organizations and institutions (sociocultural, governmental, and nongovernmental organizations [NGOs]), but also they are restricted from enhancing their socioeconomic and political position within society. The lack of network/social linkage denies them access to various opportunities and facilities provided by the state. Contrary to this, a *Nayar, Ezhava,* or Christian, through the large social networks available to them, is able to exploit the socioeconomic opportunities and resources. Through their strong community organizations, they are also able to apply pressure to and influence political parties. While community organizations of upper social groups, including *Savarna* Hindus, Syrian Christians, Muslims, and even lower-caste *Ezhavas*, own and control land, property, buildings, schools and colleges, technical training institutions, and hospitals, the community organizations of Dalits rarely enjoy their own office space.

The educational profiles of respondents within the surveyed colonies are depicted in Tables 4.2 and 4.3. Colony-Dalits are poorly educated. Those who are educated have usually achieved primary level education and most of the students from the colony study in nearby government schools. The nongovernment schools—often seen as providing quality education—are too expensive and, therefore, access to such educational opportunities is beyond their reach. For a Dalit student, being availed of state financial assistance may be relatively easier when he or she plans to attend a government school—distance coupled with the expenses associated with traveling serve as other deterrents. The "good" private schools are often located in larger cities than in rural

Table 4.2 Status of Students among Respondents

Status	Total Number of Students	Number of Girls	Number of Boys
Below high school (up to 7th standard)	18	5	13
High school (up to 10th standard)	4	2	2
Pre-degree/plus two (11th and 12th standard)	3	3	N/A
Bachelor's degree	2	2	N/A
Postgraduate Degree	1	1	N/A
Professional education	N/A	N/A	N/A
Total	28	12	16

Source: Field Survey.

Table 4.3 Educational Status of Mature Respondents

Status	Number of Persons	Number of Women	Number of Men
Below high school (up to 7th standard)	19	8	11
High school (up to 10th standard)	33	10	23
Pre-degree/plus two (11th and 12th standard)	13	4	9
Bachelor's degree	4	1	3
Postgraduate degree	N/A	N/A	N/A
Professional degree	1	1	N/A
Education diploma/I.T.C.	3	2	1
Persons without formal education	38	18	20
Total	111	44	67

Source: Field Survey.

areas. However, schools located within the cities are often seen as providing Dalits with some opportunity bring with them further challenges such as discrimination toward Dalits in terms of admission—just trying to get into the school presents almost an insurmountable challenge. One of the major perceptions that schools have of Dalits is their potentially poor academic performance once they are admitted, which would ultimately negatively affect the school's overall prestige and status.

Infrastructure facilities and academic standards within government schools are also extremely meager. As children of less-educated parents, Dalits often lack the initial advantages that their classmates and other children of other social groups possess. There are numerous factors that discriminate a Dalit child within the school's everyday life. Moreover, the economic necessity of supplementing the low income of a Dalit family prompts students who actually make it into these schools to look for part-time work or even leave school completely to assume full-time work instead of pursuing their educational goals. There are, consequently, a large number of school dropouts among the youth population of the colonies. Women within the colonies express a greater interest than men do in education (Table 4.2). This is most likely as a result of their desire to move away from the colony and possibly to marry an "outsider."

The economic life of the colony revolves mostly around agriculture and construction. The economic positions of colony-Dalits are more-or-less homogeneous, with very slight inequalities. There is no elite, no dominant economic class. Since colony-Dalits do not own the productive assets of the agricultural and construction sectors in which they primarily work, they are engaged in wage-based labor mainly in paddy fields and construction sites (Table 4.4). Some are active in such areas as fishing and domestic services. The absence of land and other productive assets, and the inconsistent nature of employment make their economic condition unstable.

So far, this chapter has shown one of the main if regrettable, characteristics of colony-Dalits is that they possess either very little or essentially nothing at all (Tables 4.5 and 4.6). Historically, Dalit communities were landless, and as previously stated, they were attached laborers and eventually became wage-based laborers. Thus, being landless and homeless were two key features that led to Dalits becoming a permanent part of the colonies with absolutely no assets beyond them. Out of 36 households, only six responded that they have land-holdings beyond their colony (Table 4.6). Among these, four households purchased low-cost land because they viewed the purchase of land beyond the colony as a way of escaping the colony. Three out of these four households have members with government jobs. Some of the inhabitants own land, from 11 cents to one acre, from the government as *michabhumi* (a program that oversaw the distribution of government-owned land—excess land—to landless/homeless people). According to colony-Dalits who received land under this program, the land is of poor quality and not suitable for cultivation or even habitation. Faced with an unhelpful state and an even less helpful market, inhabitants view the ownership of poor quality lands as nothing more than a burden.

Table 4.4   Details of Wage-Labor among Respondents

Description	Number of Laborers	Number of Total Respondents (Excluding Students)
Male	31	43
Female	18	40
Total	49	83

Source: Field Survey.

Table 4.5   Land Ownership within the Colony

Extent of holdings	$0.04	$0.10	$0.14
No. of households	26	6	4
Purpose of the land	House	House	House
Mode of acquisition	State assistance	State assistance	State assistance

Source: Field Survey.

Table 4.6 Land Ownership beyond the Colony

Extent of holdings	$0.10	$0.40	$0.80
No. of households	3	2	1
Purpose of the land	Site for house	Cultivation	Cultivation
Mode of accumulation	Purchase from other individual(s)	From government (*Michabhumi*)	From family property of the husband's family

Source: Field Survey.

Only a few inhabitants hold government/public sector jobs or other skilled or trained vocations. Among the respondents surveyed, only four—three men and one woman—were engaged in government jobs. Despite the fact that Dalits are entitled to positive discrimination, Dalit inhabitants are grossly underrepresented in government jobs. As noted earlier, this may be due to the lack of a wider social network and the lack of educationally qualified persons. The absence of a wider social network, which includes receiving recommendations, prevents them from seizing job opportunities (i.e., private and governmental) outside their locale. Educationally qualified persons are very few among the inhabitants. Thus, the number of older people who could guide younger generations in matters such as education and employment is limited.

Interestingly, no single person/household engaged in substantive business or other commercial activities was found within the surveyed colonies. This could be attributed to the fact that financial endowments or support of any kind is received, so business initiatives are rare if any actually exist at all. It is also possible to attribute this to their economic rationality, which is strikingly different from the modern economic rationality. Almost all of them are indebted and hold little-to-no savings/investments. Financial saving/planning as many Westerners understand these concepts are not prevalent among Dalits. Looking to the future in financial terms, and saving/planning strategically is nearly impossible given that Dalits already find meeting their day-to-day needs with their very limited employment and low income a constant struggle. Because most of their finances cater to their daily needs, little room is left for accruing money for future endeavors. According to the wage laborers who acted as respondents, they work on average only two or three days each week. Owing to the absence of any considerable savings, Dalits are forced further into debt by unforeseen expenses caused by diseases, heavy expenses such as marriage and having to seek credit from unauthorized lenders.

In economic terms, the "unnecessary expenditure" of Dalits is greater than their "necessary expenditure," on a daily basis.* Youths commonly engage in card games as a means of passing the time on any given day in the colonies. This is a typical daytime activity while, during the evenings, most of the male inhabitants visit nearby shops. Despite having their own rational explanations for this lifestyle, they do not easily appeal to others with more economic-conscious individuals who might consider it irresponsible to spend precious time in this manner. Some could consider the prevalence of leisure activities as carrying a high opportunity cost, resulting in less profit, investment, and savings than could be achieved if hours devoted to more income-oriented tasks. Although inhabitants live within the existing rational economic system and have

---

* Necessary expenditure refers to expenditure incurred in satisfying the basic requirements and unforeseen necessities of life of a person and his family, including food, shelter, dress, and hospital expenses. Unnecessary expenditure refers to expenditure incurred in purchasing nonessential items (drinking, playing cards, and smoking cigarettes).

notions of profit, loss, and income, they distance themselves from modern economic rationality in its most brutal forms.

Conclusion

Dalits in the modern period reflect many elements inherited from the past. At the same time, these elements are coupled with more recently generated elements forming the basis of Dalit colony lifestyle and thinking. Thus, inherited elements of Dalit colony culture are not recreated without being transformed by more recent cultural phenomena. This chapter has addressed these elements and the various transformations to provide a more nuanced understanding of the current social positioning of Dalits in Southern Kerala. While viewing Dalits as subordinate but still included within society, it describes their social dwelling as a space of subordination. The use of "subordinate inclusion" rather than the more commonly used "marginalization" is deliberate. These are not merely descriptive labels; both carry definitive conceptual and, therefore, analytical implications. Looking at the history of Dalits in Kerala, it is clear that their economic agency has been vital to the economy of the entire region. They have worked in the wetlands growing rice, the staple of Keralites of all castes and classes, for several centuries. In the new commodity economy shaped by colonialism, Dalit labor was crucial.

As agriculture increasingly shifted toward the cultivation of cash crops, the region became deficient in rice production, and new lands had to be developed by reclaiming backwaters. Dalit labor made this possible. In the new industries (under the initiative of the colonial capital and metropolitan demand) such as the cashew industry, female labor was preponderant. Dalits were also crucial in social terms. An upper-caste could be an upper-caste in any real sense of the term only if the lower-caste and outcasts continued to exist, at least conceptually. The caste system itself, moreover, was only possible because it included Dalits, albeit as outcasts. Indeed, Dalit colonies are a concentrated form of subordination, and colony-Dalits face far more political, social, and economic uncertainty, fear, and danger than Dalits living outside the colony. The early colonies were conceived of in a manner that included a self-supporting resource base. By contrast, inhabitants were provided land and sometimes, financial assistance to enable them to appropriately cultivate that land. Their status was identical to that of small peasants and small cultivators. Many of the inhabitants of the early colonies were also able to educate their children, which helped them to secure government employment, even if in lower positions.

Dalit colonies of the more recent period, however, appear to have been conceived of primarily as schemes of the settlement. The land provided was just enough to build a small house or hut-like structure. New inhabitants are not small cultivators or semiworkers, like the inhabitants of the earlier colonies, but pure wage-workers. With such a low resource base that they were rarely able to finance their children's education and even if, the latter were admitted to schools, they eventually dropped out due to economic constraints. Overall, geographic and social segregation denied Dalits within the colonies access to vital networks that could improve their social mobility.

Dalits within the colonies are subjected to the social constructions of others that play a major role in their subordination. In addition to being seen as "outcasts," they are labeled "immoral," "lazy," "troublesome," "incestuous," "antisocial," and "abusers of alcohol and drug addicts." Such social constructions have considerably influenced the self-image of the many Dalits. Many have internalized this social construction and tend to view themselves as conforming to the description provided by outsiders. Therefore, the Dalits themselves tend to contribute to the reproduction of a negative and a very damaging social stigmatization.

Affirmative action by the state has been vital for the upward mobility of many sections of Dalits. However, this has also created a situation of "state-dependence" among them. This often tends to destroy not only individual economic initiatives but also collective political initiatives in Dalit communities. In the case of the colony-Dalits, state-dependence is even greater, partly because colonies of this sort are a direct product of the state. Inhabitants depend upon the financial assistance of the state to build their houses, to secure drinking water, and to construct roads leading to the colony. Although Dalits within colonies look to the state for varied means of support, and negotiate with local political organizations and the bodies of local self-government that comprise representatives of these organizations, everyday life within these colonies takes place through an assortment of relational (social) support systems. Without such support, life in the colony, according to this model, would be simply unsustainable, representing a fundamental failing of the state to address basic human rights and security. For the "outside" that acts as the recruiter and employer of colony-Dalits, the support systems within the colonies may help to maintain wages paid at a low level. Capital, therefore, reinforces the social norms of the community by relying on them to make such low wages possible.

While Dalit colonies are not spaces of *confinement* in the sense that their inhabitants are prevented from "reaching-out" or that outsiders are prevented from "reaching-in." The limited social networks of their inhabitants, their social construction, and the self-image of colony-Dalits mean they are socially *enclosed* spaces. In a way, they are reminiscent of the enclosed spaces associated with lepers in Europe during the Middle Ages, the *hôpital général* in France during the seventeenth century, and the Poor Houses of England during the nineteenth century. This comparison may appear slightly stark, but it should be kept in mind that the purpose of confinement in Europe was not to *exclude*, but rather to *include*. Confinement was a specific device of the state employed to control different types of "problem populations" within the framework of "total institutional" society. As with the Poor Houses of Europe, the aim was correction—although it was never achieved. This chapter does not suggest that colony-Dalits are hapless. Attempts are made to break away from their own social *Savarna* construction. Moreover, efforts to disengage from the self-image of subordination are also visible. While mainstream political organizations tend to view colony-Dalits as a mere vote-pool, colony-Dalits attempt to negotiate with these organizations. Colony-Dalits may have an affiliation with any political party—most of them, however, have leanings toward leftist parties—but the colonies generally adopt a diplomatic and neutral stance in political terms. As the political power changes hands between representatives of the various parties, colony-Dalits cannot afford to alienate any one party. While new political and community organizations, including a Dalit tribal organization with the slogan "from colonies to farms," have formed, attempts to make inroads into the colonies have so far been unsuccessful.

References

Administration Report of the Housing and Colonization Scheme for the Year 1962–1963. 1964. Eranamkulam, India: Government of Kerala, Government Press.

Administration Report of the Housing and Colonization Scheme for the Year 1963–1964. 1965. Eranamkulam, India: Government of Kerala, Government Press.

Government of Kerala Administration Report, 1964-1965, Colonization Scheme. 1966. Eranamkulam, India: Government Press.

Government of Kerala, Special Component Plan for Scheduled Castes, 1982–1983. (June 1982). Thiruvananthapuram, India: State Planning Board, Government of Kerala.

Government of Kerala, Thonnakal Colonization Scheme an Evaluation Study. (December 1982). Thiruvananthapuram, India: Evaluation Division, State Planning Board.

Kerala State Administration Report 1956–1957. 1958. Thiruvananthapuram, India: Government Press.

Proceedings of the Travancore Sri Chitra State Council, 1937. 1938. 2nd Council, 10(1), First Session. Trivandrum, India: The Travancore Government Press.

Proceedings of the Travancore Sri Mulam Assembly, 1938. 1938. Second Assembly, Second Session, Trivandrum, India: The Travancore Government Press.

Proceedings of the Travancore Sri Mulam Assembly, 1938. 1938. Second Assembly, 3rd Session. Trivandrum, India: The Travancore Government Press.

Proceedings of the Travancore Sri Mulam Popular Assembly, 1919. 1919. Trivandrum, India: The Travancore Government Press.

Proceedings of the Twenty-Fourth session of the Sri Mulam Popular Assembly of Travancore, 1928. 1928. Trivandrum, India: The Travancore Government Press.

Proceedings of Twenty-Third session of the Sri Mulam Popular Assembly of the Travancore, 1927. 1927. Trivandrum, India: The Travancore Government Press.

Program Evaluation Organization Report 1968. New Delhi, India: Planning Commission.

Report of the Administration of Travancore—Cochin for the Year 1953–1954. 1956. Trivandrum, India: Government Central Press.

Travancore Administration Report, 1113 ME/1937-1938 AD (82nd Annual Report). 1939. Trivandrum, India: Travancore Government Press.

Travancore Administration Report, 1114 ME/1938-1939 AD (83rd Annual Report). 1940. Trivandrum, India: Travancore Government Press.

Chapter 5

Impact of Labor Law Enhancement in China on Development and Its Implications for Global Development Theory

Marguerite Marlin and Scott Nicholas Romaniuk

Contents

Introduction

Rights-based development is often espoused by the global nongovernmental organizations (NGOs), but it has yet to rise to prominence in the discourse of global trade institutions. While public interest has long been defined by many global institutions as connected to market outcomes as opposed to more principle-based definitions (Berger, 1996), the widening and deepening of certain categories of rights (i.e., labor rights) is conceptualized by neoliberal thinkers as analogous to the competitive advantage that draws multinational corporations (MNCs) to developing countries: low labor costs and less liability to be punished for rights infractions against workers. Despite this general aversion to embrace more substantial labor laws along the path to further economic development evidenced by the discourses and policies of technocratic global institutions such as the World Trade Organization (WTO), developing nations have not always followed suit. In the late 2000s, the Chinese government explicitly linked initiatives aimed at bolstering wages and increasing equality with a vision to further economic development. These initiatives took the form of three important Chinese labor laws introduced in 2007–2008 (namely, the Labor Contract Law, 2007, the Law of the People's Republic of China on Labor-Dispute Mediation and Arbitration, 2007, and the Law of the People's Republic of China on Promotion of Employment, 2007).

These labor laws, created in the wake of devastating layoffs from state-owned enterprises (SOEs) and an associated rise in regressive employment practices, have not been universally lauded. They have drawn criticism for incomplete implementation due to loopholes and limited enforcement, and there have been reports of manufacturers moving to countries with lower wages in reaction to the labor laws (Wang et al., 2009). However, the overall effect of the laws has been a positive one, having contributed to wage growth and reduction of income inequality without adversely affecting the balance of trade. Thus, China has been able to see an increase in wages and rights of workers in large part as a result of the laws without losing its export advantage.

This overall positive effect on development that China has been able to realize in part through the 2007–2008 labor laws supports previous arguments and accounts that contradict the prevailing neoliberal standpoint on labor rights in developing countries. For example, Bharadwaj (1990) has argued that India squandered some of its development potentials by focusing too much on commodities and not enough on changes to labor conditions in its development strategy. Martin and Maskus (2001) similarly have linked abuse of workers and violation of labor rights with a reduction in both competitiveness and employment, and Lee and McCann (2011) have argued that enhanced labor regulation presents a significant benefit to employers, providing them with greater certainty regarding market conditions, with the benefits that come from a more prosperous and healthy workforce (i.e., greater productivity) while the coordinated nature of the reforms allows them to gain from such conditions without being undercut by the competition.

The Chinese experience with enhanced labor legislation thus further calls into question the essential refusal of the WTO to allow countries to sanction exporters that violate the International Labor Organization's (ILO) core labor standards (Howse, 1999). This is especially the case due to the fact that WTO justifications for the status quo regarding labor standards have been couched as advocacy for developing-country priorities, with the WTO claiming that undeveloped countries would be against using trade sanctions against countries in violation of standards on the basis that this could manifest itself as trade protectionism (WTO, 1999).

China and SOEs

SOEs are companies created by different levels or branches of government in a country and engage in commercial activities on behalf of the government that created it. The concept, however, can be slightly misleading given that the term "state-owned" can also refer to companies that are only partially owned by a government or a particular level of government. SOEs "account for a significant portion of economic activity worldwide. What is more they often operate in key sectors, such as utilities, infrastructure, and finance, on which large portions of the private sector depend on their operations and downstream competitiveness" (Organization for Economic and Cooperation Development [OECD], 2014).

In many respects, the ideas behind SOEs have evolved alongside the China's economy, particularly because of the backing of a powerful central government. Many, if not the majority, of them have been viewed with a great deal of negative repose by the West, which often characterizes them as "infiltrators to be viewed with suspicion," according to Woetzel (2008: 1). Opinion, however, regarding SOEs is still largely divided, with some casting even positive light on their operations and prospects for what they might bring to a globalized economy. Black and white perspectives of SOEs, as Woetzel (2008: 1) states, "rail to recognize that as the Chinese economy evolves, it is no longer so easy or desirable to pigeonhole state-owned enterprises." As Woetzel (2008: 1) states

> Many observers define a Chinese state-owned company as one of the 150 or so corporations that report directly to the central government. Thousands more fall into a gray area, including subsidiaries of these 150 corporations, companies owned by provincial and municipal governments, and companies that have been partially privatized yet retain the state as a majority or influential shareholder.

An important aspect of SOEs is the relationship that they share with the CCP. Huang and Orr (2007: 109) draw attention to the very tight connection between SOEs and the CCP

> China has 70 million party members, and a typical state-owned enterprise may have hundreds if not thousands of them on staff. Consequently, as long as a company remains a state-owned enterprise, the Communist Party committee plays a pivotal role in key decisions.

Recently, *The Economist* (2014) has identified two main problems with SOEs in China. First

> they have failed to comply with the government's [CCP] order to focus on what are deemed to be "strategic sectors" such as aviation, power, and telecommunications. These are industries that the Communist Party believes it must dominate in order to maintain control of an increasingly complex economy.

This is not entirely surprising given that operators of SOEs are often much more in touch with capitalist market realities and the need to style a corporation based on market demands to ensure its success and longevity. Second

> despite these advantages, SOEs have given progressively less bang for their buck. Faced with mounting losses in the 1990s, China undertook a first round of drastic reforms of its state-owned companies. There were mass closures of the weakest firms, tens of millions of lay-offs and stockmarket listings for many of the biggest, which made them run a little more like private companies.

This second point should also come as no surprise because the CCP has too much control over SOEs, forcing them to operate in artificial and, therefore, restricted ways. Li (2008: 5) points to "ambiguous property rights" and "soft budget constraints" as factors prohibiting SOEs from operating efficiently.

China's Economic Development in Twenty-First Century

The first major economic boom to have taken place in China after the Second World War was directly related to the economic reforms undertaken by the CCP in 1978. The world witnessed China go through such tremendous changes that scholars and researchers from around the world took notice. Many wondered if the reforms were to have an overall positive or negative impact on China and its future. For example, questions rose about the ability of the CCP to feed its growing population (Brown, 1995). Pessimism continued to grow over the years with others considering China to be moving toward the "brink" (Chang, 2001) and on the verge of collapse (Henderson, 1999). Contrasting the overarching view that China was moving down a one-way street to collapse are those who envisioned a (dormant) rising giant (Hu and Khan, 1997), a strong future for a resilient country, and a horizon of immeasurable opportunity.

From these perspectives emerged the idea that China would eventually become the next (if even "fragile") superpower (Shirk, 2008) that would ultimately rival the United States (Murray, 1998) with others claiming that with its surge of unprecedented power (Zhu, 2012) comes a looming "threat" (see Gertz, 2000; Timperlake and Triplett, Jr., 2002; Miller, 2006). Some of the expedients of China's rising economic power have been attributed to its "leading place in heavy industries," explains Miller (2006), "like steel and shipbuilding reflect[ing] the dramatic advances that China's economy has made in the past two decades." He explains further that the

> ubiquity of Chinese products serving lower income consumers at Walmart and of Chinese-made clothing in high-end department stores underscores how much China's low labor costs are making it the manufacturing hub of the world, contributing to the hollowing out of the traditional American manufacturing base.

China's extensive economic restructuring and long-term strategic focus on economic prosperity entirely transformed the economic landscape of China. Hu and Khan (1997) explain that "prior to the 1978 reforms, nearly four in five Chinese worked in agriculture; by 1994, only one in two did. Reforms expanded property rights in the countryside and touched off a race to form small nonagricultural businesses in rural areas." Processes of decollectivization coupled with increased prices in order to obtain agricultural products around the country greatly benefited farms that were privately owned including small family farms, and a rising efficiency in the use of labor that had not yet been witnessed in China. This was a direct product of liberalization feeding a more profit-driven outlook. Even small towns became the new seedbeds of business and industry that eventually flourished as the "resulting rapid growth of village enterprises has drawn tens of millions of people from traditional agriculture into higher-value-added manufacturing" (Hu and Khan, 1997). However, this was an area of constrained growth and prematurely labeled a success story. The following figures depict the steady climb in China's GDP per capita against both Western Europe (since 1500) and the United States (since 1952).

Despite the tremendous success experienced by the CCP in its economic reforms and liberalization schemes, the nonagricultural sector fared rather poorly. By the late 1970s, China's agricultural sector boasted approximately 70% of the entire country's labor force, however, it "was not even able to provide China's population with 2,300 calories per capita per day (near the UN-established minimum). Emergency grain imports were frequently needed to meet food deficits" (Zhu, 2012: 109). One of the major problems with the nonagricultural sector and its weak performance in China was, not just the mere presence of SOEs, rather the domination of the sector by these enterprises. The allocation of resources, as well as production activities, was carried out according

Table 5.1 Employment Share, GDP Share, and Total Factor Productivity Growth by Sector

Average Annual Total Factor Productivity Growth (%)				
Nonagricultural Sector				
Period	Agriculture	Nonstate	State	Aggregate
1978–2007	4.01	3.91	1.68	3.61
1978–88	2.79	5.87	–0.36	3.83
1988–98	5.10	2.17	0.27	2.45
1998–2007	4.13	3.67	5.50	4.68
Year	Employment Share (%)			
1978	69	15	16	100
2007	26	62	12	100
Year	GDP Share (%)			
1978	28	27	45	100
2007	10	70	20	100

Source: Brandt, L. and Zhu, X. 2010. *Accounting for China's Growth, Working Papers Tecipa-394,* University of Toronto, Department of Economics, Canada; Zhu, X. 2012. Understanding China's growth: Past, present, and future, *Journal of Economic Perspectives,* 26(4): 103–24.

to CCP planning and implementation as opposed to natural occurring signals within the market (Zhu, 2012). In fact, the domination of the nonagricultural sector by SOEs presents somewhat of a paradox regarding the economic performance of China from 1952 until 1978, with "an average par capita GDP growth rate of even 3 percent" (Zhu, 2012: 110). This is particularly the case given Zhu's (2012: 110) assessment regarding SOES in that, "[m]ost of the state-owned enterprises at that time were inefficient, overflowing with redundant workers, and often producing output for which there was no market demand." The following figure shows total factor productivity (TFP) growth for the aggregate economy, the agricultural sector, and the nonagricultural sector (Table 5.1).

China's Labor Laws in Historical Context

The People's Republic of China (PRC) has had a storied history of attempting to use state policies to temper the effects of increased market openness on labor. This dates back to its response to accelerated growth from foreign involvement with the enactment of the Labor Law and Trade Union Law in 1979, which required private employers to negotiate with unions (Bieler et al., 2008). However, China has also been characterized as gravitating toward piecemeal labor policies with great regional differences in terms of their application, resulting in a "patchwork of half-implemented policies" (Hurst, 2008: 14).

Because of the high number of workers in China, full employment is considered unachievable in the country, and policymakers are aware that high unemployment would be catastrophic (Bieler et al., 2008). Moreover, China has a high percentage of migrant laborers, due to the oversupply of labor in the agricultural sector—a factor which in turn has stemmed largely from the Household Responsibility System (HRS) introduced in the 1980s and the subsequent relaxation of migration rules between different parts of the country in the 1990s (Fang et al., 2010).

The state has always had a role in determining wage levels in Chinese enterprises, but the Wage Guideline System (WGS) (1999) provided labor administration authorities with a frame of reference to perform their work. For example, it lays out reference standards for determining wage levels and is thought to lead to a greater success rate for workers' job applications. As of 2010, the system had been applied in over 100 Chinese cities. In addition, the Minimum Wage Regulations (MWR) (2004) made the rules for the participating regions and cities much more clear and comprehensive, successfully encouraging the regions and cities to adjust the minimum wage more frequently (Fang et al., 2010).

Contextual accounts of the enactment of the 2007–2008 laws in China suggest that the new legislation was spurred on by the social consequences of massive SOE layoffs from 1993 to 2006. In Chinese SOEs and urban collective sector enterprises, 60 million people were laid off between 1993 and 2006—amounting to the net loss of over 40% of urban area employment in the formal sector. By Hurst's (2008) account, these laid-off workers did not find employment again easily. Two regional dynamics that led to the layoffs were the declining certainty of state subsidies to SOEs because of smaller budgets for SOEs (due to a widening of local ties with central China) and the Central Coast and provincial capitals being hit by state-imposed austerity budgets for SOEs (Hurst, 2008).

After the Chinese Communist Party's (CCP) 15th Party Congress of 1997, there was a new imperative for SOEs to not just be self-sustaining but profitable and globally competitive. One way to cut costs in order to become more profitable was to lay off workers. Loans became more conditional on use for things like adopting new technologies, and, thus were harder for SOEs to obtain. This led to higher rates of SOE "exits" in the form of bankruptcy, the sale of the company, or privatization. Large job losses generally accompanied privatization, with the laid-off workers replaced either by migrant laborers from rural areas or by the same workers employed on a contract basis for less with no benefits and a percentage of their severance pay held by the employer as a deposit (Hurst, 2008).

The backlash against these types of abuses that had become rife within the system began to be seen at the CCP's 16th National Congress. While China has generally been observed as following the preferred prescription for modernization of the neoliberal west—namely, "privatization, market-driven development, liberalization and globalization" (Bieler et al., 2008: 94) there was recognition by state leaders at the time of the 16th National Congress that this was not the best way to move the country forward. Instead, strategies for more inclusive growth and prosperity were sought, among the results of which were important changes to labor legislation.

Reforms and Their Impact

The three labor laws introduced by the PRC in 2007–2008 can be summarized as follows:

Labor Contract Law (2007)

Made the practice of employers holding a "deposit for bondage" to keep workers from leaving.

1. Refined the rules surrounding labor contracts including new types of contracts such as a nonfixed-term contract that protects against the arbitrary dismissal of workers
2. Made social insurance contributions mandatory for employers
3. Gave trade unions a more inclusive role in the management of enterprises, and gave local governments more jurisdictions over monitoring compliance (*Labor Contract Law of the People's Republic of China,* 2007; Hurst, 2008)

Employment Promotion Law (2008)

This included 69 articles on employment security, which stipulate the role of enterprises and local governments in training and vocational education, regulate employment agencies and their activities, provide terms for government assistance to self-employed workers, and forbid discrimination against vulnerable groups of workers (*Law of the People's Republic of China on Promotion of Employment,* 2007; Hurst, 2008)[2].

Labor Disputes Mediation and Arbitration Law (2008)

1. Simplified procedures for arbitration and mediation of labor disputes, introducing the *One Arbitration, Final Ruling* law (as opposed to the previous system of multiple trials).
2. Increased the length of time workers can apply for arbitration to one year from 60 days while at the same time providing time limitations of 45 days to 60 days from the time of acceptance of the case to its conclusion. Also, eliminated fees for arbitration and lowered litigation fees, stipulating that a mediation stage should occur before employers and workers go into arbitration. This stipulation recognized grassroots and community-led mediation bodies as legitimate for the mediation process (though there are questions about the authority of these bodies in practice), and put the burden of proof onto employers in some specific instances (*Law of the People's Republic of China on Labor Dispute Mediation and Arbitration,* 2007; Hurst, 2008).

Hurst (2008) has provided some effective criticisms in the scope of these laws, noting that the Employment Promotion Law (EPL) does not stipulate protocols and procedures for the enforcement of its regulations—particularly with regard to discriminatory employment practices—and pointing out that business owners who did not like the open-ended contract have avoided entering into it by employing workers informally or through agencies. He notes that some local governments have waived the necessity for employers to contribute to social security premiums for workers, but workers also wish to avoid entering into contracts in some cases because they do not want to pay their share of the social security premiums either—particularly migrant workers who cannot benefit from locally managed benefits regimes.

Moreover, despite the introduction of "One Arbitration, Final Ruling," employers can still appeal decisions, resulting in the same two-trial process after arbitration that the reform was designed to avoid. The lowered cost of arbitrations has resulted in an overload of cases and caused Chinese officials to put pressure on the disputing parties to settle the cases in mediation. In addition, there have been cases of corruption, with some firms favored politically, meaning they are essentially exempt from inspections and other employers working through employment agencies that are heavily involved in lobbying local governments (Hurst, 2008).

Recent news reports on labor in China also point to the fact that where one problem has been improving, another has worsened. In 2010, China approved the practice of vocational schools supplying interns to work in factories as part of their graduation requirements in order to fill a supposed shortage of workers. While some interns make the same wages as regular workers, others have revealed that most of what they make has to be given to the educational institution requiring their internships—despite working 12-hour days for global tech companies such as Hewlett-Packard and Apple (*Wall Street Journal*, 2014).

However, other expert observers have seen the legislation as an overall improvement, despite its limitations. For example, Fang, Yang, and Meiyan (2010) note that from 2007 to 2008, there was significant growth in both nominal and real wages for migrant workers (20% as opposed to less than 5% in 2002). This dynamic is reflected in the general trend of wages as well, as yearly wages rose by 1.7% from 2008 to 2014 as compared to 1.5% in the four-year period from 2004 to 2008 (Ministry of Human Resources and Social Security [MOHRSS], 2014). China's growth post-2008 has been slower than in the 2000–2007 periods gain of an average of 27%, but there are other factors that explain this: The percentage of the population of working age (16–65) has declined since 2010 and more factories are moving to the central areas, where minimum wages are lower (Zhang, 2012).

The reforms have also coincided with greater demand for the accountability of the All-China Federation of Trade Unions (ACFTU), as enforcement of regulations has been put into the spotlight due to the fact that stronger laws now exist to level the playing field on the Chinese job market. In recent years, the dissatisfaction of Chinese workers with the ACFTU has become harder to ignore. For example, a series of strikes at Honda's auto parts factories in Guangdong province in June 2010 had the establishment of their own union as one of the workers' principal aims. The Chinese state allowed these workers to form their own union, which the lead trainer in China for a global NGO known as Social Accountability International (SAI) believes was a sign that the Chinese government was trying to put pressure on the ACFTU to do a better job of representing workers (Tepper Marlin, 2012).

Concerns that the labor laws have caused factories to move to other countries, voiced early after their implementation, have not borne out either. Although not a constant upward trend, growth in exports did have a significant impact on promoting employment in both manufacturing and service sectors, with less-educated, rural, youth and women demographics most impacted. This growth also had a positive effect on wages and lessened income inequality (Zhang, 2012). Accordingly, China's Gini coefficient has declined from 0.52 in 2010 to 0.50 in 2012 (World Bank, 2014).

Generalizability of the Case

By some accounts, the ability for China to enhance labor regulation without feeling adverse effects from doing so is relatively unique. For example, Bieler et al. (2008) have argued that more robust labor laws would not discourage foreign companies from setting up in China because there are too many other advantages there. Indeed, they highlight that Wal-Mart has recognized unions there when elsewhere they have refused. However, proponents of a "Labor-Ist" approach to development such as Bharadwaj (1990) have long argued that economic development in emerging economies has focused too much on commodities and not enough on changes to labor conditions. Noting that Keynesian economics has given way to free-market theories of economic development on the grounds that Keynesian economics failed to account for stagflation in the 1970s, Bharadwaj critiques this state of affairs on the grounds that the free-market paradigm is errant in its conception of development dynamics.

Among the examples that Bharadwaj cites is India, which greatly expanded its products and services produced, with extensive application of new technology. However, he notes, that had not resulted in higher employment rates, a lower number of families living in poverty, or higher levels of consumption or land ownership by the time of writing. Moreover, he has remarked that shift toward free-market labor processes has resulted in an increase of precarious labor and growing income inequality along lines similar to China (i.e., the urban–rural divide), and underscored back in 1990 that despite the technological and industrial advancements that occurred in the late twentieth century in India, the bulk of India's population still largely employed in the agricultural sector. As of 2012, the percentage of India's population employed in the agricultural sector is still one of the highest in the world, at 47% (World Bank, 2014). Bharadwaj (1990) has attributed such negative effects to the application of neoliberal, free-market-oriented development theories such as Competitive Capitalist Market theory and has asserted that this is not often recognized because macroeconomic analyses have also fallen out of favor with academic and professional specialists on economics in developing countries.

In the context of this kind of global neoliberal consensus described by Barawa, China's experience with labor law enhancement is iconoclastic; however, other globalization theorists do not view divergence from the deregulatory approach proscribed by global trade institutions as quite so unique. Brenner (2010) has written about how globalization along neoliberal lines has urged states to be more competitive with one another, but this is thought to have produced more regional differentiation than homogenization, and more regulatory reorganization than deregulation. Post-2008 the trend has been moving even further in this direction, with states adopting more cus-tom-fitted policy prescriptions for financial recovery and with some states taking steps toward the decommodification and regulation for the public good. However, this has taken place at the national level by powerful states in order to increase their competitive advantage; meanwhile, a substantive transformation of transnational regulatory regimes has yet to occur despite the apparent demand for it by many smaller states.

Implications for the WTO and Global Development Order

Since its inception, there have always been those within the WTO who have seen a large role for the institution as one that ensured proper labor standards. Already, there is a renewed consensus from the 1996 Singapore ministerial conference on what is unacceptable for labor but no consensus on how to enforce this internationally. The ILO is charged with applying these standards but has no authority to affect substantial trade reprisals for those countries who do not comply (Alston, 2004).

From as early as 1998 when the ILO's Declaration on Fundamental Principles and Rights at Work was made, all WTO member governments committed to a narrower set of internationally recognized "core" standards—freedom of association, no forced labor, no child labor, and no dis-crimination at work (including gender discrimination).[1] However, the WTO as an institution has claimed that it is developed countries who are for this and undeveloped countries who are against using trade sanctions against countries who violate these standards on the basis that these sanc-tions could be applied as protectionism masquerading as altruism (WTO, 1999).

However, the WTO's concern about the misapplication of sanctions for protectionist purposes under the guise of upholding basic labor rights is itself a demonstrable red herring. One need only look to other potentially subjective grounds that are considered admissible for sanctions by the WTO and its General Agreements on Tariffs and Trade (GATT) (Article XX[a]) such as the potential to invoke sanctions "when necessary to protect public morals" (WTO, 2015). Indeed, Howse (1999) provided a comprehensive study on how WTO jurisprudence for reviewing labor-based sanctions might best occur. He writes

> measures linked to compliance with fundamental labor rights might well be presumed to be nondiscriminatory and thus not in violation of Article I and III, provided that they are not operated in a discriminatory manner [...] while the rights in the Convention are universal, defining a consensus on the essential content of some of these rights is an ongoing process, quite properly centered in the ILO. A WTO panel then should take account not only of the universality of the rights that are being invoked by the trade-restricting member, but also of the extent to which ILO practice indicates a clear consensus that the practices being sanctioned represent unambiguous violations of the universal content of the right (Howse, 1999: 26).

In light of the experiences of China, India, and others with both commodity-based and labor-based modes of expansion outlined in this chapter, the WTO's stance on the enforcement of labor standards seems much more in keeping with Weiss's (2005) assertion that developed nations have been the architects of multilateral institutions that limit certain activities by less-developed states but leave room for state interventionism and other strategic action by the richer states to retain competitive advantage. In particular, Weiss states that most developed states have shaped global rules to constrain actions while leaving open channels for strategic state action, that states are still the most important actors when it comes to industrial governance, and that the straitjacket of rules at the WTO and other organizations has not stopped states from engaging in state activism.

Thus, the utility of examples such as the Chinese case in the context of labor standards is likely to be applied at the state level for other developing nations, but it is not expected to significantly impact the orthodoxies on development in prevailing global governance institutions. During the UN (2009) the G-77 developing countries stressed the need for representative global market governance and the introduction of measures to protect the most vulnerable states from financial and social ruin, the proposals that actually came out of the Stiglitz Commission failed to challenge the neoliberal paradigm of finance-led growth or to "question the basic logic of profit-oriented, market-mediated capital accumulation and its implications for the 'triple crisis' of finance, development and the environment" (Jessop, 2010: 37).

There are also other opportunities beyond the state level for developing nations to apply policy learning regarding enhanced labor laws. Moses (2000) notes that while trade openness has resulted in a shift away from the use of traditional or Keynesian macroeconomic instruments, other types of instruments have sprung up in their place; for example, an increased tendency to engage in income policymaking and the state targeting of particular sectors through subsidies and other supports. Moreover, despite the fact that WTO rules have become more complex and in some cases intrusive in recent years, developing nations have been increasingly strategic in terms of forging regional alliances and negotiating for shared priorities at the WTO (Barton et al., 2006). Therefore, there is opportunity to reap the benefits of coordination on enhanced labor protections without necessarily requiring the full cooperation of global development institutions.

There are many more details and contextual factors that can and should be evaluated in future studies of this empirical case in order to pinpoint causal variables for the economic and political dynamics discussed. For example, it would be beyond the scope of the chapter to purport to have isolated in any meaningful sense the labor laws in question in terms of their independent impact on China's employment, exports, economic development, and even wages. However, it is apparent that in the years since the three significant labor laws have been passed in China, wages have grown at a faster rate while levels of inequality have been reduced, and that this has not had a long-term adverse effect on exports or other significant economic indicators.

It can in any case be contended that the 2007–2008 labor laws have been implemented to substantial degree while admittedly not an entirely satisfactory one for all observers and that this has not had a noticeably adverse effect on Chinese economic development. This is significant in and of itself because there is demand for greater respect for human rights—including labor rights—in many developing countries, on principle. As Amartya Sen stated, "[t]o the extent that there has been any testing of the proposition that the poor Asians do not care about civil and political rights, the evidence is entirely against that claim" (Nussbaum, 1997: 139). Therefore, it is important to dispel the notion that for developing states to heed the domestic demand for greater upholding of labor rights will negatively impact development. The case is thus one, which flies in the face of WTO proclamations that the enforcement of higher standards for labor is antithetical to the aims of developing nations, and in conjunction with other considerations may be of interest to nations that are behind China on the road to development.

Notes

1. This refers to the ILO's Declaration on Fundamental Principles and Rights at Work (1998) which covers four fundamental principles and rights at work: (1) the effective abolition of child labor, (2) the elimination of all forms of compulsory labor, (3) the elimination of discrimination in respect of employment and occupation, and (4) freedom of association and the effective recognition of the right to collective bargaining (ILO, 1998).
2. While the law was adopted at the 29th Meeting of the Standing Committee of the Tenth National People's Congress on August 30, 2007, it did not take effect until January 1, 2008 and thus, is considered a 2008 law (Hurst, 2008).

References

Alston, P. 2004. Core labor standards and the transformation of the labor rights regime, *European Journal of International Law*, 15(3): 457–521.

Barton, J. H., Goldstein, J. L., Josling, T. E., and Steinberg, R. H. 2006. *The Evolution of the Trade Regime*. Princeton, NJ: Princeton University Press.

Berger, S. 1996. Introduction, in Berger, S. and Dore, R. (eds.), *National Diversity and Global Capitalism*. Ithaca, NY: Cornell University Press.

Bieler, A., Lindberg, I., and Pillay, D. (eds.) 2008. *Labor and the Challenges of Globalization: What Prospects for Transnational Solidarity?* London, UK: Pluto.

Bharadwaj, K. 1990. Paradigms in Development Theory: Plea for 'Labor-Ist' approach, *Economic and Political Weekly*, 25(4): PE20–8.

Brandt, L. and Zhu, X. 2010. *Accounting for China's Growth, Working Papers Tecipa-394*, University of Toronto, Department of Economics, Canada.

Brenner, N., Peck, J., and Theodore, N. 2010. After Neoliberalization?, *Globalizations*, 7(3): 327–45.

Brown, L. R. 1995. *Who Will Feed China? Wake-Up Call for a Small Planet*. New York, NY: W. W. Norton & Co.

Chang, G. G. 2001. *The Coming Collapse of China*. New York, NY: Random House.

Fang, C., Yang, D., and Meiyan, W. 2010. Fast growth, but widening income distribution in China, In OECD, *Tackling Inequalities in Brazil, China, India and South Africa: The Role of Labour Market and Social Policies*. Paris, France: OECD Publishing.

Gertz, B. 2000. *The China Threat: How the People's Republic Targets America*. Washington, DC: Regnery.

Henderson, C. 1999. *China on the Brink: The Myths and Realities of the World's Largest Market*. New York, NY: McGraw-Hill.

Howse, R. 1999. The world trade organization and the protection of workers' rights. *The Journal of Small and Emerging Business Law*, 131: 1–38. Retrieved February 3, 2014 from: http://graduateinstitute.ch/files/live/sites/iheid/files/shared/executive_education/summer_international-affairs_faculty-IA_professors/howseworkers%255B1%255D.pdf.

Hu, Z. and Khan, M. S. 1997. Why is China growing so fast? *Staff Papers (International Monetary Fund [IMF])*, 44(1): 103–31.

Huang, R. H. and Orr, G. 2007. China's state-owned enterprises: Board governance and the communist party, *The McKinsey Quarterley*, (1): 108.

Hurst, W. 2008. *The Chinese Worker After Socialism*. New York, NY: Cambridge University Press.

ILO. 1998. *Declaration on Fundamental Principles and Rights at Work*. Retrieved January 20, 2015 from: http://www.ilo.org/declaration/lang--en/index.htm.

Jessop, B. 2012. Narratives of crisis and crisis response: Perspectives from North and South, in Utting, P., Varghese Buchholz, R., and Razavi, S. (eds.), *The Global Crisis and Transformative Change* (23–42). Basingstoke, UK: Palgrave Macmillan.

Labor Contract Law of the People's Republic of China 2007. *People's Republic of China: Database of Laws and Regulations*. Beijing: Government of the People's Republic of China.

Law of the People's Republic of China on Promotion of Employment 2007. *People's Republic of China: Database of Laws and Regulations*. Beijing: Government of the People's Republic of China.

Law of the People's Republic of China on Labor-dispute Mediation and Arbitration 2007. *People's Republic of China: Database of Laws and Regulations*. Beijing: Government of the People's Republic of China.

Lee, S. and McCann, D. (eds.) 2011. *Regulating for Decent Work: New Directions in Labor Regulation*. Basingstoke, UK: Palgrave Macmillan and the ILO.

Li, M. 2008. *Three Essays on China's State-Owned Enterprises: Towards an Alternative to Privatization*. Saarbrücken, Germany: VDM Verlag.

MOHRSS 2014. China Average Yearly Wages, 1952–2014. Beijing: Government of the People's Republic of China.

Martin, W. and Maskus, K. E. 2001. Core Labor Standards and Competitiveness: Implications for Global Trade Policy, *Review of International Economics*, 9(2): 317–28.

Miller, L. 2006. China an Emerging Superpower? *Stanford Journal of International Relations*, 6(1).

Moses, J. W. 2000. *OPEN States in the Global Economy: The Political Economy of Small-State Macroeconomic Management*. New York, NY: St. Martin's.

Murray, G. 1998. *China: The Next Superpower: Dilemmas in Change and Continuity*. London, UK: St. Martin's Press.

Nussbaum, M. C. 1997. *Cultivating Humanity: A Classical Defense of Reform in Liberal Education*. Cambridge, MA: Harvard University Press.

OECD 2014. State-Owned Enterprises in the Marketplace. Retrieved October 27, 2014 from http://www.oecd.org/daf/ca/soemarket.htm [It says it is a 2014 revision of the *OECD Guidelines on Corporate Governance of State-Owned Enterprises*].

Shirk, S. L. 2008. *China Fragile Superpower*. Oxford, UK: Oxford University Press.

Tepper Marlin, J. 2012. China's Labor Unions: New Tendrils, *Huffington Post*. Retrieved November 16, 2014 from http://www.huffingtonpost.com/john-tepper-marlin/china-unions_b_1762713.html.

The Economist. August 2014. Fixing China Inc.: Reform of State Companies is Back on the Agenda (print edition).

The Wall Street Journal. 2014. China's factories turn to student labor. Retrieved November 15, 2014 from http://www.wsj.com/articles/chinas-tech-factories-turn-to-student-labor-1411572448.

Timperlake, E. and Triplett, W. C., Jr. 2002. *Red Dragon Rising: Communist China's Military Threat to America*. Washington, DC: Regnery.

UN. 2009. *Report by the Commission of Experts (Stiglitz Commission) of the President of the United Nations General Assembly on Reforms of the International Monetary and Financial System*, New York, NY.

Wang, H., Appelbaum, R. P., Degiuli, F., and Lichtenstein, N. 2009. China's New Labor Contract Law: Is China Moving Towards Increased Power for Workers? *Third World Quarterly*, 30(3): 485–501.

Weiss, L. 2005. Global Governance, National Strategies: How Industrialized States make room to move under the WTO, *Review of International Political Economy*, 12(5): 723–49.

Woetzel, J. R. 2008. Reassessing China's State-owned enterprises, *The McKinsey Quarterly*, 59.

World Bank 2014. Employment in agriculture (% of total employment): *World Development Indicators*. Retrieved December 5, 2014 from: http://data.worldbank.org/indicator/SL.AGR.EMPL.ZS.

WTO. 1999. Understanding the WTO: Cross-Cutting and New Issues. Labour Standards: Consensus, Coherence, and Controversy. Retrieved January 29, 2014 from https://www.wto.org/english/thewto_e/whatis_e/tif_e/bey5_e.htm.

WTO 2015. The General Agreement on Tariffs and Trade (GATT 1947). Retrieved February 20, 2015 from https://www.wto.org/English/res_e/booksp_e/gatt_ai_e/art20_e.pdf.

Zhang, C. 2012. Local Labor Market Effects of Exporting in China, MPRA, Paper No. 38615.

Zhu, X. 2012. Understanding China's growth: Past, present, and future, *Journal of Economic Perspectives*, 26(4): 103–24.

Chapter 6

Persistence of Italian Mafia: Violent Entrepreneurs in Developed States

Marinko Bobić

Contents

Introduction

Italy is one of the founding states of the European Union (EU), a polity priding itself on postmodern principles including the absence of the use of violence. Yet, the Italian state in the south has been infested with violence that some compare to civil wars (Saviano, 2007), most of which have been blamed on the existence of the Italian mafia. Thus, there is great difficulty in attempting to understand why the mafia persists in a state when the principles of that state stand in stark contradiction to such organizations. This puzzle forms the basis of the research presented in this chapter. The dependent variable is defined as mafia persistence. In this case, I propose three independent variables: (1) the availability of violent entrepreneurs, (2) the existence of a market for private protection, and (3) the mafia's transformation to serve, and depend on the state. All three variables feed into the resilience of the Italian mafia. The first two independent variables define structural conditions for the mafia to *emerge* while the third variable defines the mafia's ability to *persist*. Of course, there are conditional variables that make these mechanisms work, with the most pertinent one to identify being the Italian state's self-interest in eschewing extensive monetary funds and other resources in order to effectively combat the mafia.

The justification for choosing the Italian mafia is rooted in Van Evera (1997: 47) reasoning that the case of the Italian mafia is sufficiently data-rich to permit effective and productive process tracing that can yield insight into the case of the Italian mafia and spur further research and analyses. The case also provides an extreme value of the dependent variable, namely, the persistence of mafia. Thus, Italy presents a case of intrinsic importance, the mechanisms of which need to be uncovered. As for the method utilized to uncover these mechanisms, I employ a historical process tracing approach, addressing events in Italy as recently as when Silvio Berlusconi was in power. The historical contrast provides natural within-case variance of background conditions in which the mafia has operated. By identifying factors, which have persisted despite these background changes, we can thus identify a causal variable that has persisted (Van Evera, 1997: 64). In such a way, process tracing elucidates conditions utilized by the mafia and translates them into a case outcome. That outcome, as previously noted, is the continuation of the mafia.

It is also worth mentioning that although this is an explanation of a specific case, but that case forms part of a general phenomenon that can be found elsewhere, namely the persistence of organized crime in developed countries. Of course, many would claim that the mafia is more than just organized crime (Paoli, 2003), and while it is true that we can see many features of mafia resembling, for example, religious sects or political actors, there are many good reasons to group the mafia together with organized crime rather than other institutions. The most prominent reason for doing is that former members of the mafia (those who have defected) have acknowledged their former organization as organized crime (Paoli, 2003).

Alternative Explanations

When evaluating alternative explanations, we should consider the possibility that an observed relationship between two variables is not causal; rather, that it could be the effect of a third variable. Some authors have pointed to the failure of the Italian state to monopolize violence as the cause that enabled the mafia to rise and persist (Gambetta, 1993: 1). Indeed, this is similar to Shelley's (1994) argument that the central government has not been able to fully control the bureaucracy, economy, or justice system of southern Italy. The mafia was able to flourish because citizens did not perceive the legal authority of the state (Shelley, 1994: 668). I do not entirely disagree with this observation. It provides an important condition explaining why the state initially failed to provide services that the mafia did. However, although this is an important condition that facilitated the emergence of the mafia, this relationship can change.

Bull and Rhodes (2007: 12) assign the responsibility of the mafia's persistence to problems of Italian governance. They claim that the Italian system is beleaguered by fragmentation, clannish behavior, the power of minority vetoes, and the lack of collective aspiration. Shelley (1994: 669) confirms this, noting that Italian politics operates without a clear majority, which makes it susceptible to external (i.e., nonofficial political and other forms of influence). However, this account is rather top-down, focusing on descriptive accounts of conflict among the elites. Although not an incorrect observation, conflict among elites is partially a consequence of the state's relationship with the mafia.

Geopolitics has also been used frequently to explain why certain countries are sustained in organized crime. Among these explanations we find that Italy proves to be a crucial link for the smuggling of drugs, people, and weapons from former Soviet states, the former Yugoslavia, and Albania (Busuncian, 2007: 98). One such example is the speedboat routes between Albania and Italy. Even though routes change often in response to law enforcement's antitrafficking efforts, Italy nonetheless proves to be a crucial geographical link to the crime from Eastern Europe (Surtes, 2008: 52). However, this phenomenon also seems to be a consequence rather than the cause of the mafia's persistence. That is, the mafia has been able to utilize Italian geographical proximity to other countries rich in crime, rather than the inverse, that Italy's geographical proximity to other countries has provided a lifeline for the mafia. As the subsequent sections will show, the mafia had sustained itself even before these international linkages of transnational organized crime became available.

History

Process tracing attempts to provide a "beginning" to issues studied. For our purposes, we would ideally like to determine the origins of the mafia with the aim of seeing which conditions actually played a substantial role in its emergence in addition to how those conditions may have changed, if at all. However, there is a lack of historical evidence that inevitably interrupts this historical process. The initial emergence of the mafia is, however, offered by an abstract model provided by Gambetta (1993). He identifies that there was a brutish, Hobbesian world of everyday violence in southern Italy. In the interest of protecting themselves, peoples living within this territory would seek the most violent and most prepared "firms" to protect them. There was no state to soften the rules of the game (Gambetta, 1993: 41). People would seek the protection of the mafia to protect themselves and their property, for example, when buying or selling horses (Gambetta, 1993: 19). Yet, the issue of cheating is fundamentally tied to the information. Both a buyer and a seller would need the mafia to supply truthful information about the other. Indeed, Tilly (1982: 182–3) confirms that it would also be in the interest of a stationary bandit to provide protection to the people and extract taxes in return. These early actions of the mafia, however simplified, also closely resemble theoretical foundations of the state, according to Tilly (1982).

The first actual records of the mafia appeared during Italian unification of 1860, but some claim earlier origins. The crucial factor for Gambetta (1993: 77), which explains why the mafia emerged in southern Italy, the way described above and not anywhere else, is lack of trust, which can be attributed to the Spanish strategies of divide and conquer. This policy has resulted in a distrustful population toward one another and especially toward the government and government officials. This condition created a particularly high demand for protection. In many parts of southern Italy this demand was not met by the mafia, however, parts of southern Italy, where former soldiers and villains were left unemployed due to the transformation of the society from feudalism into democracy, the conditions seemed ideal for these men to seek new jobs (Franchetti, 1985: 90–1). Indeed, it is a lack of trust, presence of mobilized men, and the sale of protection that was unique to towns in which the mafia originated.

We can compare this to towns where the mafia did not emerge. In eastern Sicily, for example, the upper class managed to preserve the monopoly over force and has prevented villains, rising from lower classes, from sharing it (Franchetti, 1985: 55). This has been done in such a way that upper classes created their own private police. Clearly, capitalism has exposed class differences, and while in eastern Sicily upper classes retained their power, in the western Sicily the struggle between classes continued until after the Second World War. Although class differences were crucial as to who retained the monopoly on violence, once new clans emerged, they served interests of both the aristocracy and the poor. This is why the highest concentration of land protection was in the fertile citrus groves surrounding Palermo (Paoli, 2003: 567). From here, groups such as *Sacra Unione* (Holy Union) spread to other towns and villages.

One might wonder about other groups that utilized violence. Indeed, banditry was also widespread in southern Italy at the time. However, what has made the mafia unique is its autonomy in choosing and enforcing contracts. As well, other mafia organizations emerged in parallel to the Sicilian mafia such as the Calabrian mafia. There are no historical studies of the Calabrian mafia, and as Paoli (2003: 624) claims, the best evidence of their earliest existence comes from police reports and novels. There is no reason to believe, however, that these two mafia organizations emerged in different circumstances. Both of them utilized their ability to wage violence, exploit protection markets, and work with the state. As such, these similarities seem to be much more important than some subtle differences between the two organizations. As Strange (1996: 112) claims, Sicilian, Calabrian, Campanian, and Apulian mafias have interwoven a thick (and relatively peaceful) network of illicit business, trading, information, and funds.

Globalization and Transformation

Once the mafia became established as an industry specializing in the supply of protection (where landowners were not united), they spread to protect other commercial routes during the nineteenth century to other parts of southern Italy (Gambetta, 1993: 98). With this expansion, in order to adapt, came the transformation of much of the nature and capacity of the mafia. During this period, the strongest characteristic of the mafia was that it resisted the weak state and its exercise of centralized authority. The second important period came during the fascist period of Benito Mussolini, which attacked mafia and forced it underground and abroad, only for the mafia to return with allied armies (Shelley, 1994: 665). Only in this case has the existence mafia become threatened, confirming the view that if a state decides to commit resources to break the symbiotic relationship, it is possible to undermine the mafia. However, fascism did not last long enough to bring about the mafia's demise.

The current period is marked with pressures of globalization on the state including expectations about law and order as well as a popular denunciation of the mafia due to a rising number of literate and educated peoples. When the Italian state launched an attack to uproot the mafia, efforts cost the lives of many public servants and mafia chiefs. The mafia, on the other hand, leaving traditional economic areas, has been engaging in more lucrative illegal activates by trying to compete in the world market, and not surprisingly, this has caused some loss of legitimacy among the population. Moreover, to survive in its lucrative illegal markets, the mafia has been pressured to relinquish its kinship ties that once formed the basis for a shared sense of community and legitimate authority (Paoli, 2003). Such kinship ties were simply too cumbersome and dangerous to maintain with many mafia members defecting to the state or simply pursuing only economic interests (and thus, were more willing to defect when it was in their interests). In essence, the social cohesion that the mafia has relied upon has fallen apart. Those who try to maintain the traditional cohesion realize that they may be facing major opposition. Paoli (2003) contributes a high number of defections of mafia members directly to the failing system of moral values (Paoli, 2003). Betrayal is more common, as is unnecessary killing and engagement in activities that the mafia has traditionally shunned (prostitution, drugs, and abductions). Not surprisingly, the mafia has been recruiting less and exposing itself less to the external world.

Although, there seems to be no controversy over change, not everyone agrees that the mafia has been struggling. Strange (1996: 110) claims that the mafia has been expanding its numbers and the extent of its operations. As such, Sicilian and American Cosa Nostra now operate with Chinese triads as well as Colombian drug cartels. There is much in illegal markets that is becoming more lucrative, drawing many of these organizations together. Indeed, this is what Saviano (2007: 482) recognized with Chinese triads opening factories in Naples and engaging in competition with traditional Italian fields such as the fashion markets. Strange (1996: 114) calls this "Pax Mafiosa," whereby there is now an international society of mafias that is truly global. Just as a figure, seizures of cannabis have multiplied from three to 10 times in roughly a decade. Shelley (1994: 663) also addresses some of the worrisome consequences of the Italian state's policy of selling valuable properties in the south, which are being purchased by the mafia. However, even at this point, it is difficult to refute that the mafia is rapidly transforming, and in doing so, losing touch with its traditions.

Symbiotic Relationship with the State

Despite pressures of globalization, there still exists a symbiotic relationship between the state, the mafia, the population, and even the church. As Gambetta (1993: 21) states, those who seek mafia protection need it to sort out their disputes, to retrieve their stolen property, or to protect their cartels from free riders and competitors. Probably the most convincing reason for the mafia's survival is that it has surrounded itself with networks of willing agents. However, its symbiotic relationship with the state has also been the key to its persistence. Gambetta (1993: 4) argues that the mafia and the Italian state have converging interests. This occurs particularly in the area of keeping law and order, eliminating public hazards, drug overdose, and dealing with common criminals. These interests further converge with members of the mafia guaranteeing the state the sale of votes and illicit interparty arrangements. Moreover, many state institutions view the mafia as a legal system of its own (Gambetta, 1993: 4).

Indeed, with aforementioned struggles that the mafia is facing, the symbiotic relationship with the state may seem confusing. This is so because the state lacks initiative, policy planning and implementations, and resources necessary to deal with the mafia. Whenever the Italian state launches anti-mafia campaigns, there is a split within the state between those who support the campaign and those who oppose it. This is why many of these campaigns have been so violent and ultimately lead to failure. As Saviano (2007) describes, politician tenures in the local administration are often short, ending in either murder or arrest—the former usually for anti-mafia rhetoric and the latter for collaborating with the mafia. Even Berlusconi has tried to derail investigations into the mafia (Shelley, 1994: 662). Perhaps it is in the interest of the government to maintain ties with the mafia, but it is also the inability of the government to free itself from these ties. It has, thus, become a vicious cycle.

The Mafia has also learned from repressive policies of the national government (Strange, 1996: 114). Profitability increases whenever a government declares certain trades in services or goods illegal (i.e., gambling, prostitution, alcohol, guns, and pornography). The increased risk of dealing with these activities raises their price with the mafia keen to take these activities on. While the mafia has accumulated sufficient wealth to maintain order and deliver votes for the government, benefits of this symbiosis have been anything but equal. Thus, although the mafia state symbiosis exists, it is often based on extreme competition with each side trying to obtain greater benefits.

Conclusion

Theoretically, we can confirm the observation that the structural conditions, noted at the beginning of this chapter, define the mafia's persistence when taken in unison. Globalization has been shaping and influencing this relationship, changing both the mafia and the state. This chapter has sought to establish an explanation of the Italian case, incorporating mostly structural approaches, but with an important cultural element, namely the lack of trust (Chubb, 1996: 274). The theory can be further applied. Indeed, this is what research on the Russian mafia has sought to achieve. Interestingly, the Russian mafia draws its strength, in part, from disbanded army soldiers and unemployed athletes. The breakdown of communism provided the market for protection, with the Russian state preferring to neutralize, pacify, or integrate its mafia (Volkov, 2002: 186). In other words, as in the Italian case, the state and the mafia have had a difficult, but collaborative relationship. Indeed, Strange (1996: 112) also confirms the theory, stating that failure of the state apparatus, security forces (and the subsequent disarray), and weakness/lack of resources of law enforcement has cultivated conditions ideal for the mafia to seize up to 80% of some Russian economic sectors. The crucial factor, which created the need for a private protection market, as in the Italian case, was the lack of trust. Shelley (1994: 667) shows that there was no trust in those who had the power to enforce property rights in Russia. Corruption and collusion of the Russian state with the mafia have made the mafia state relationship sustainable (Chubb, 1996: 17–9). Indeed, Fukuyama (1996) confirms that even Chinese triads developed in the absence of trust in society that saw violent entrepreneurs coming together with markets (need for protection) (both of which are driven by the absence of trust in various societal spheres), leading to the mafia and its relationship with the state—the interaction is intensified by the processes of globalization.

As is typical of case studies, there are inherent weaknesses in this research. First, we cannot generalize these results to other cases since we have no varying antecedent conditions, which we can use comparatively. In other words, we cannot test whether there is something specific in Italy that is not present in other countries. Although other countries such as Russia seem to fit the theory, a more robust investigation is needed. Second, this theory is what Van Evera (1997) categorizes as low-uniqueness and low-certitude—decisive explanation is lacking. Rather, we can only use the results here in the total balance of evidence. The evidence offered here is merely probabilistic. Third, this research lacks prescriptive richness, since the causes identified, cannot easily be controlled by human action (Van Evera, 1997). This is problematic because policymakers would not be able to find effective strategies to combat the mafia phenomenon. However, this research at least offers insight into ineffective solutions or conditional solutions. For example, state repression of the mafia would only succeed with a great deal of bloodshed, perhaps undermining the strategy altogether. This is perhaps why Russia has chosen an integrationist approach to the mafia, the success of which remains to be seen.

Further research should address the weaknesses mentioned here. Namely, a fuller investigation into the Russian, and even the Chinese case could serve to expand the applicability of the theory. If such testing fails to expand the applicability of the theory, then antecedent conditions that would explain why the Italian case is different from the Russian and Chinese one should be sought elsewhere. One could also look at different pressures of globalization on each of these states, perhaps explaining some differences that exist between them. Finally, even though there is an existing literature on much of what has been presented in this chapter, there is always room for improvement by looking at evidence, which was not available before, or evidence, which might have been overlooked. If anything, the internal crisis of the mafia in Italy should make insider information more transparent.

References

Bull, M. and Rhodes, M. 2007. Introduction-Italy: A contested polity, *West European Politics*, 30(4): 657–69.

Busuncian, T. 2007. Terrorist routes in South Eastern Europe, *The Quarterly Journal*, 6(1): 85–102.

Chubb, J. 1996. The mafia, the market, and the state in Italy and Russia, *Journal of Modern Italian Studies*, 1(2): 273–91.

Franchetti, L. 1985. *Condizioni Economiche e Amministrative della Province Napoletane*. Bari, Italy: Laterza.

Fukuyama, F. 1996. *Trust: The Social Virtues and the Creation of Prosperity*. New York, NY: Free Press.

Gambetta, D. 1993. *The Sicilian Mafia: the Business of Private Protection*. Cambridge, MA: Harvard University Press.

Paoli, L. 2003. *Mafia Brotherhoods: Organized Crime, Italian Style*. Oxford, UK: Oxford University Press.

Saviano, R. 2007. *Gomorrah*. New York, NY: Farrar, Straus & Girous.

Shelley, L. I. 1994. Mafia and the Italian State: The historical roots of the current crisis, *Sociological Forum*, 9(4): 661–72.

Strange, S. 1996. *The Retreat of the State: The Diffusion of Power in the World Economy*. Cambridge, UK: Cambridge University Press.

Surtes, R. 2008. Traffickers and trafficking in Southern and Eastern Europe, *European Journal of Criminology*, 5(1): 45–60.

Tilly, C. 1982. *Warmaking and Statemaking as Organized Crime*. Center for Research on Social Organization, University of Michigan: Ann Arbor, US.

Van Evera, S. 1997. *Guide to Methods for Students of Political Science*. New York, NY: Cornell University Press.

Volkov, V. 2002. *Violent Entrepreneurs: The Use of Force in the Making of Russian Capitalism*. New York, NY: Cornell University Press.

Chapter 7

Bridging Worlds: Academe and Cultural Agency in Southern Mexico

Robert W. Blake, Elvira E. Sánchez-Blake, and Debra A. Castillo

Contents

Introduction

As in our "Crossing Borders" learning framework addressing agricultural challenges, in this chapter we continue our story of encounters and needed solutions from another perspective. We explained in Chapter 3 that Cornell University has led a wide range of student and faculty from around the world on a multidisciplinary, intergenerational examination of rural and urban development in tropical Latin America for many years.* In 2008–09, *Experience Latin America,* and *Hispanic Theater Production* courses were linked through the felicitous circumstance of a substantial core of students taking both courses. This resulted in a mutual collaboration fueling an integrative process building awareness, knowledge, and culture transmitted through performance. Best known by the troupe name, *Teatrotaller* exists both as a course and as a student organization with the mission of promoting Hispanic culture through the production of high-quality theater

---

* These field courses have been conducted in Puerto Rico, Dominican Republic, Costa Rica, Honduras, Ecuador, and Mexico.

in Spanish. Student-founded in 1993, and primarily attracting undergraduate students with a steady sprinkling of graduate students, staff, and community members, *Teatrotaller* has directed, staged, and performed over 60 Spanish, Latin American, and U.S. Latino plays, which have been performed in festivals over the years in the United States and elsewhere.

This chapter discusses one example of how multiple encounters during living laboratory explorations helped students and faculty members alike to articulate problems and develop subsequent research investigations based on these contextualized settings and inputs by our hosts. In this particular case, it included an exchange of socially conscious theater productions. Beginning with Teatrotaller's presentation of *La mujer que cayó del* cielo, a play by Víctor Hugo Rascón Banda, inspired by the true story of a Rarámuri woman from northern Mexico incarcerated in an insane asylum in the United States, to a mixed audience of indigenous and ladino Chiapanecan people. It also included interactions with indigenous and ladino theater professionals from that Mexican state, which inspired the students to propose creating their own play to introduce the social problems facing southern Mexico to a northern audience back in the United States.

The Experience

In more general terms, our consolidated pedagogical and problem framing approach contributes to the intellectual growth of students and faculty alike, as well as challenging us to think of ways to share this knowledge with different local and international communities. There are many ways to break with the past. Some may go unrealized until the transformation is complete. One's own nature finds a new genesis, emerging as another from a cocoon after rain, or like a liberating flight from the memory into a new self. This is what Petrona de la Cruz tells us in her story of Maya performance as cultural agency, in an interview with Sánchez-Blake, "el teatro ha sido una forma de sanar mis heridas. Pude gritarle al mundo, al público, el dolor que sentía por dentro" (Sánchez-Blake, 2012: 22). Petrona's colleague, Isabel Juárez, added, "romper el silencio tuvo un efecto multiplicativo en las mujeres y sus comunidades. Las miembras de la organización comenzaron a hablar y a ganar confianza. Muchas mujeres ni siquiera sabían que tenían una voz" (Sánchez-Blake, 2014).

Through the years, graduate and undergraduate student researchers have developed projects and publications with the dual purposes of pursuing real-world issues and giving something back to our hosts and others with similar needs and interests. Other outcomes included policy papers or case study reports shared with communities or the government. Recognizing that valuable intellectual work and analysis take place in all disciplines, we have also incorporated cultural agency and performance studies into our portfolio of pedagogical interactions and articulations of researchable problems.

As we have shown, the living laboratory provides opportunities to gain awareness and knowledge of a distant world that encompasses many issues separately addressed by the academy. Farm visits initiated learning and insight about real-world issues concerning food production, land and water, climate change, biodiversity, family and community welfare, and the economic challenges faced by agrarian society. Conversations with farmers, indigenous people, and other hosts helped articulate needs and contemporary challenges; likewise, the opportunity to see plays like the indigenous language play about ancient Maya culture, *Palenque rojo*, with its international-level production values, and Sna Jzt'ibajom's much more modest staging of their "Cómo nació el maíz" gave our theater students a repertoire of images to draw upon. Especially productive in this respect were conversations with the directors of the plays, and the generosity of the members of Sna Jzt'ibajom in opening their house to us, and sharing their unpublished play scripts (even permitting us to adapt them if we wished).

A better understanding about maize provided by *ejido* farmers proved a significant inspiration for all including those whose motivations and intellectual curiosity pointed in the direction of performance. This quintessential nutriment of the Maya, and the important role of maize in Mexican life, from the ancient cosmovision in the *Popol Vuh* to current diets and heritage foods, attracted learners from all backgrounds to a broadly shared cultural common ground. Students and faculty also learned about sacred Maya beliefs from distinguished anthropologist Jan de Vos (2001), and in particularly impressive visits to the San Juan Bautista church in San Juan Chamula with the Chamula leader Don Manuel Pérez López. In this place, past and present blend with sacred rituals and religious ceremonies, epitomizing the syncretism of Christian and Maya creeds, tradition, and modernity, and only through Don Manuel's whispered guidance were we able to sort out the myriad images and activities. Universidad Autónoma de Yucatán (UADY) archeologists Lilia Fernández and Guillermo Kantún helped us to peer beyond a superficial appreciation for the majesty of Maya civilization and heritage at spectacular ruins in Palenque, Uxmal, Toniná, Bonampak, Yaxchilán, Chincultik, and Izapa. Our explorations also included special meetings with the Zapatista authorities at the Oventik *caracol*, a seat of civil government, where the Zapatista concept of "good" and "bad" government was differentiated alongside their model of indigenous regional autonomy. Conversations with personalities who overcame their own challenges, like Antonia López, Antonio Gómez, and Petrona de la Cruz, stimulated considerations of meaning and values, putting the music of their voices in our ears.

Antonia López is a charming, irrepressible *Zinacanteca* businesswoman. She, with her mother and younger sisters, manufactures and markets beauty in colorful hand-loomed weavings, tapestries, and other artisanry, and the woolen embroidery art that distinguishes Zinacantec couture. Like other artisans, Antonia's creations represent another level of cultural transference, where the sunny day brightness of local flower gardens is projected onto woven canvases. Our students wanted to know more about Antonia, to hear her story. Granting the request, she began as anyone might. For Antonia, everything begins with an idea, with a desire—"I wanted to have my own bed." Antonia shared her story, one sadly similar to that of many women around the world: storms of family violence, a drunken father's hurting hands, her injured mother's bed-ridden recoveries, a wish for men more respectful and caring of their families, a father throwing her into the street, disowning her for buying her own bed, and a house in which to put it—pleading to convince her mother to escape the domestic violence and move in with her. This was not a story of abuse, however, but of survival, resilience, and pride. Antonia proudly showed us the house she designed and had built with her own funds, earned by the work of her hands. She bragged about her sisters finishing high school, and her own newly achieved literacy in Spanish, her desire to learn English so as better to serve international visitors and reach other markets. She handed out her business cards, encouraging students to email her, and asked how to develop better business plans. We sat on her bed, in room, and talked. We believe this victory of family, community, and dreams still plays, lingeringly, for those who were witnesses. *Which marks will become indelible? Who is to say, not for a lifetime?* Antonia's story could join the Fortaleza de la Mujer Maya (FOMMA) repertoire of productions.

One final vignette is a story of access denied. Don Antonio Gómez Entzín and his family raise vegetables for the market in San Cristóbal de Las Casas on a steep hillside high above Huitepec. Everyone's hard work pays off when there is enough water for his or her crops. In addition to rainfall, good yields typically require irrigation from the mountaintop stream running on family land just above their farmstead. Gathering together with Antonio, his wife, and children after a guided walkabout we learned more about their livelihood, chores, markets, family, and schools. Family income from vegetable sales was deteriorating because farmers could no longer irrigate their crops. Huitepec waters had been diverted to feed the Coca-Cola bottling franchise at the base of the mountain. We were told the government was supporting corporate demands amid complaints from Huitepec residents of less access to water resources, which are stewarded by them. Along with Antonia's story, this encounter especially provoked reactions and reflections in our group and with Chiapanecans, and beyond about power, privilege, pride, and subaltern needs for cultural and community agency.

Upon returning from Chiapas, co-enrolled *Teatrotaller* students and faculty decided to continue efforts through the creation of a Spanish play to reenact some of the main challenges facing Chiapanecans, projecting their realities, and past and present, onto a local stage. Combining acting and language instruction is not in itself novel—drama techniques have long been shown beneficial to language learning. Ryan-Scheutz and Colangelo (2004: 375) indicate that drama provides language learners "opportunities to speak in less controlled and more creative ways … bring(ing) learners closer to real-life use of the target language." Our students took these lessons a step further into a complexly staged performance in which both cultural and language learning were encouraged through a fully realized devised drama structure.

This seems a natural next step but is by no means an obvious one either for performance or language pedagogy. Not long ago, The Association for Theater in Higher Education (ATHE) devoted a special issue of its journal, *Theatre Topics*, to the question of devising (2005). Reading through the issue is a peculiar experience because there is not a single example of, or case study from, the Hispanic or U.S. Latino world despite the widespread acknowledgment of the influence exerted by Brazilian Augusto Boal's fundamental work in his Theater of the Oppressed. This blind spot adds a rather ironic perspective to comments like that of Berkeley (2001: 3), who stresses that devised theater highlights, "the uses of theatrical performance for ALL students in the work of forming identities and values." At the same time, we take seriously the repeated message of these articles—devised drama and its radical pedagogies are typically seen to have a transformative mission, and it is a performative mode that speaks, or should speak, to all. As Foreman (2005: 97) of the Dell'Arte School comments, "the goal is to create a courageous theater, based on people in relationship, passing beyond the peripheral situations of our lives and into the circumstances that define the human condition."

Profoundly concerned about the limited political and social power of the groups with whom we interacted, our students committed to finding an appropriate artistic response that would supplement other forms of activism in the area. Accordingly, a devised script, *Kan Balaam* (Jaguar Serpent), was cowritten with students through a collaborative initiative to elicit awareness and understanding about socio-cultural issues. Script development began with eager discussions in Chiapas assimilating information that ranged from background facts about subaltern lives, to observations about styles of social interaction, clothing, how men and women in communities speak, and how they occupy space with their bodies. The process was completed at home through extensive research, writing, editing, rewriting, and composing assisted at a crucial stage by input from the well-known Mexican–American playwright, Carlos Morton. Through this challenging process, *Kan Balaam* emerged as an integration of Maya myth and cosmology from the *Popol Vuh* with contemporary conflicts in indigenous communities. Some of these conflicts are many centuries old but manifested anew as modern invasions into the traditional culture and its territories by globalized economic structures.

The title, "*Kan Balaam*," refers to the Maya belief of opposing forces. "*Kan*," the serpent, represents Kukulkán, the Maya god of creation, and his manifestations—the sun, fertility, and life—in opposition to the jaguar (*balaam*) and its manifestations of night, death, and darkness. The *Popol*

Vuh segment was pivotal in linking the overarching metaphor of the continuity between present communities and past beliefs. The story line of *Kan Balaam* focuses on the fate of an indigenous couple (Carlos and Felicita) unable to have children. The couple's infertility dilemma parallels other aspects of their barren lives and landscapes, worsened by drought, and denied access rights to their communal river, which have been ceded to the Coca-Cola bottler. The maize harvest fails and the community faces starvation. Carlos takes to drink and constantly blames his wife for inability to procreate. Meanwhile, a delegate from the bottling plant visits Carlos, offering him a job in exchange for procuring village support needed for construction of another bottling plant near town. The delegate is an old neighbor from their hometown of Chamula, who has become a city person (*ladino*) changing his name, language, and dress. He urges Carlos to do the same by forsaking old ways and traditions. Felicita, overhearing the conversation and fearful of her inebriated husband's response, scurries to the Chamula church to recruit a *curandero* to perform a ritual to make her fertile. The church ritual transports Felicita (and the audience) to the past, where she is reminded of her Maya roots.

The creation scene based on the *Popol Vuh*, where the world including its animals and plants come into being, is completed by emergence of the Man of Maize, who is powerful enough to resist water and fire, but humble enough to worship his creators. Afterward, Felicita sees herself in a past life as a young maiden, Cuzán (*Golondrina*), who is chosen by the Maya king to be offered to the gods by casting her into a sacred *cenote*. In this scene, she discovers her infertility is due to an act of rebellion toward the rain god (*Chaac*) when Cuzán refuses to deliver the message ordered by the Maya priest. By opposing this mandate, a curse falls upon the Maya bringing horrors of bearded white men and white gods who conquered, enslaved, and destroyed their civilization.

When Felicita returns to the present day, the healer empowers her to break the curse. She must convince her husband to understand the gods' message and return to their people's roots. When Felicita tries to do this Carlos is drunk. She falls into despair. Meanwhile, Carlos dreams that Kukulkán and Cocacoalt (the dark Coca-Cola god) fight to gain control of his soul. While Kukulkán attempts to convince him to return to his people because they need him, Cocacoalt invites him to follow his *compadre* in taking up the Coca-Cola offer to forsake his people. When he awakens, Carlos suddenly understands the message and makes up his mind. He searches for Felicita and finds her just as she is about to pitch herself into a *cenote* in despair. As they embrace in a common bond of responsibility to their people, thunder echoes from contented gods with the promise of rain and fertility. In the final act, Carlos has become a leader in his community. He defeats the Coca-Cola delegate by refusing his proposal and condemning intrusion on their lands. Led by Carlos, the entire community joins forces with the Zapatistas pledging support in opposing the invasion. In the end, Carlos and Felicita are blessed with the long awaited promise of a child.

In sum, *Kan Balaam* integrates Maya myths and cosmology with contemporary issues facing Chiapanecan communities as interpreted by students. Students shared their heightened transcultural awareness and learning with a larger audience, in a gesture of gratitude and intellectual responsibility for the gift of shared narratives and information bestowed by gracious Chiapanecan hosts. A church ritual mimicked observations in the San Juan Chamula church melded with an investigation of ritual traditions, not a facile task. All costumes, props, and sets were original creations. We were also fortunate to be assisted by UADY archeologist Dr. Lilia Fernández, who helped finalize costume and set design, advised on types of feathers, gowns, masks, and makeup used by the ancient Maya. She was a critical consultant also in choreographing the "ball game" in the ancient Maya legend scene. The entire theater company worked in an environment of comradeship, where Spanish was the language of the workplace, inspired and spurred by our Chiapas exploration.

Through this second living laboratory, students enhanced cultural understandings and linguistic skills. The urgent social issues addressed in this play gave a particularly forceful quality to their applied research inquiries, an especially satisfying result both in terms of intellectual and personal growth. As one of the students writes in her final reflection on the yearlong course:

> The entire process for the creation of *Kan Balaam* was really an experience and a collective group effort. From its very beginnings as a raw idea in Chiapas, to the script writing, the set making, the masks, the costume design, the lights, the stage—everything came together because there was a communal group goal. It can be argued that the same group effort that was put into the creation of *Kan Balam* is parallel to the community effort of the people of San Juan Chamula in the play when they are trying to get rid of the Coca Cola company … As I watched the play, I felt like I watched my *Experience Latin America* course condensed into one play with all the issues I learned and with classmates from whom I learned while acting them out on stage.

Conclusion

We have illustrated ways in which academe has employed cultural agency to embrace a more inclusive worldview that helps to effectively frame and pursue problems. By trading places, where our hosts from other walks of life and cultures are the professors and subalterns are at the table, students and faculty become colearners and collaborators charged with social responsibility in delivering voice, knowledge, and understanding to extended audiences. We contend that greater academic agency through alliances like those embodied in *Experience Latin America* is needed to achieve equity goals through effective community engagement and applied problem solving. It also helps ensure that all can participate in public policy decisions, which is part of "reinventing our life in society," Godenzzi's (2006) challenge to education.

We have briefly described a series of encounters between social realities and academe. By remembering, reenacting, and transmitting these stories we hope to contribute to a stronger voice with greater understanding and visibility for the forgotten people of our hemisphere. By revealing instances of silences broken and culture performed we have demonstrated the potential realized by bringing *academe to the field* and the *field to academe*, as part of a reinforcing educational process that promotes understanding and social transformation.

We also analyzed the power of performance as an engine of cultural agency that naturally connects with community and reinforces academe. Thus, cultural attitudes and perceptions are transformed, knowledge is created through research and disseminated, and social awareness and respect are raised in ways like those urged by de Schutter (2011). The performing culture theatrical experience described in this chapter condenses into a clear example of the adoption of cultural agency by academe. Exposed to an enabling cultural landscape, one that carries messages of cultural and other substantive contexts, students winnow and amplify them through their own engagements, lenses and reflections, finally delivering them through an egalitarian process to academe and society writ large.

Acknowledgments

We thank Emily Holley and Charles Nicholson for their helpful feedback on drafts of this chapter.

References

Berkeley, A. 2001. Myths and metaphors from the mall: Critical teaching and everyday life in undergraduate theatre studies, *Theatre Topics*, 11(1): 19–29.

de Schutter, O. 2011. *End of Mission to Mexico: Mexico Requires a New Strategy to Overcome the Twin Challenges of 'Food Poverty' and Obesity, Says UN Food Expert*. Geneva, Switzerland: Office of the High Commissioner for Human Rights (OHCHR).

de Vos, J. 2001. *Nuestra Raíz*. Mexico City, Mexico: Ed. Clío, Libros y Videos.

Foreman, R. 2005. Potholes on the road to devising, *Theatre Topics*, 15(1): 91–102.

Godenzzi, J. C. 2006. The discourses of diversity: Language, ethnicity and interculturality in Latin America, in Sommer, D. (ed.), *Cultural Agency in the Americas*. Durham, NC: Duke University Press, pp. 146–166.

Ryan-Scheutz, C. and Colangelo, L. 2004. Full-scale theater production and foreign language learning, *Foreign Language Annals*, 37(3): 374–400.

Sánchez-Blake, E. 2012. Teatro Maya y resistencia indígena: El caso de Chiapas, *Letras Femeninas*, 38(1): 17–31.

Sánchez-Blake, E. 2014. Mayan cultural agency through performance: Fortaleza de la Mujer Maya—FOMMA, in Castillo, D. A. and Day, S. (eds.), *Mexican Public Intellectuals*. London, UK: Palgrave, pp. 163–181.

Appendix: Images from Southern Mexico

La mujer que cayó del cielo, San Cristóbal de las Casas, January 2009.

The audience, San Cristóbal de las Casas.

Kan Balaam (play), Ithaca, April 2009.

Kan Balaam (play), Ithaca, April 2009.

Chapter 8

A New Index to Measure Group Inequalities in Human Development for Sustainability*

Hasnat Dewan

Contents

Introduction

Disparities and inequalities among groups, regions, and between genders are undesirable, and may have serious consequences for the national integrity and social sustainability. However, the fact is that many such inequalities and disparities cannot be eliminated easily. It may take decades of effort to eliminate or significantly reduce such disparities. Therefore, appropriate management of the factors that reduce income, wealth, capabilities, and opportunities for any group, gender, or region is important for the national integrity and social sustainability. A first step for sustainable management of the factors causing inequality is to measure the relevant inequality. This

---

* This chapter is a revised version of the author's published article: Dewan, H. (June, 2010). A new index to measure group inequalities in human development for sustainability, *Review of Business and Technology Research*, 3(1): 467–474.

chapter employs the Human Development Index (HDI) as a yardstick for inequality because it is a weighted average of income, health, and education indices. The section "Literature Review" provides a brief overview of some popular inequality indices. The section "The Equity Index" proposes a new index to measure inequality and provides an equity condition for sustainable human development. The section "Applications" shows how gender inequality and regional disparity can be measured with the proposed index. It also demonstrates how the proposed index differs from the Gender-Related Development Index (GDI) and how that can serve as an early warning system for regional unrest. The section "Conclusion" presents some final observations.

Literature Review

Acknowledging the rights of future generations on resources, sustainability seeks intergenerational equity. Such an objective is implausible and morally and ethically questionable when the sustainability goals do not also include achievement of intragenerational equity. Therefore, monitoring present inequality is an essential first step for the sake of sustainability. Different measures of dispersion are used to compare inequality between groups and individuals in terms of income and opportunities. Any equity index should meet the Pigou–Dalton condition of transfer, which indicates that *ceteris paribus* any transfer from a relatively poor to a relatively rich person must increase the degree of inequality.

The Gini coefficient, which is represented by twice the area between the cumulative income share curve (Lorenz curve) and the line of equal income share, is the most commonly used indicator of income inequality. Atkinson's (1983) measure of income inequality is another popular index. By definition

$$I_{Atkinson} = 1 - \left[\sum_{i=1}^{n} \left(\frac{Y_i}{\hat{Y}} \right)^{1-\varepsilon} f_i \right]^{1/1-\varepsilon}$$

for $\varepsilon \neq 1$

$$= 1 - \exp\left[\sum_{1=i}^{n} f_i \log_e \left(\frac{Y_i}{\hat{Y}} \right) \right]$$

for $\varepsilon = 1$
Where
 Y_i = income of the people in i-th income range
 $\hat{Y}$ = mean income
 f_i = proportion of the people in i-th income range
 ε = inequality aversion parameter

Rawls' (1971) contractual theory of justice assesses inequality in terms of the condition of the least advantaged members of society. There are hosts of poverty indices that reflect the number of poor people and/or their relative incomes in a society. Two well-known composite poverty measures are the Sen Index (1976) and the P (α) measure of poverty (Foster et al., 1984). A combination of headcount index, poverty gap, and Gini coefficient are used to compute these indices.

Besides these income-based poverty measures, in 1997 with the help of Sen et al. the United Nations Development Program (UNDP) introduced a new poverty measure, called the Human Poverty Index (HPI). It uses human development information from the "deprivational perspective." By definition

$$HPI = \left[\frac{(P_1^3 + P_2^3 + P_3^3)}{3} \right]^{1/3}$$

Where
P_1 = % of people not expected to survive to age 40
P_2 = % of adults who are illiterate

$$P_3 = \left[\frac{(P_{31} + P_{32} + P_{33})}{3} \right]$$

P_{31} = % of people without access to safe water
P_{32} = % of people without access to health services
P_{33} = % of moderately and severely underweight children under 5

GDI and Gender Empowerment Index (GEM) are two gender-related development indices but are often mistaken by many as gender-related inequality indices (UNDP, 2009).

Each of the inequality and poverty indices has its merits in measuring certain types of inequality and poverty. However, none of them is used as a universal sustainability indicator. The following section proposes an equity index that measures inequality in terms of human development. Along with other indicators of sustainable development, a nonpositive change in the equity index can ensure economic and social sustainability (Dewan, 2009).

The Equity Index

Individual inequalities are certainly not something to ignore, but unless people can identify themselves with a group, the failure can be attributed to personal incapability. Inequality among individuals may, or probably shall, never be eliminated. Moreover, for variables such as life expectancy at birth only group inequality matters (Sen, 1993). The existence of group inequality indicates that somehow there exists, or may have existed, some factors generally preventing different groups from being equal in terms of their achievements of certain goals.

"Groups" can be defined in various ways depending on needs and purposes. For example, to analyze material well-being, Slesnick (1993) divided households across the United States into 23 demographic groups based on family size, age of household head, region of residence, race, type of residence, and sex of household head. In a plural society, inequality can arise from racial, ethnic, or religious differences. For instance, the UNDP (1993) report showed that, considered alone, Caucasian Americans outranked any other nations in the world while African Americans ranked 31st, and Latino Americans ranked 35th in HDI ranking of all countries. Women's human development is lower than that of men's in all nations. The latest UNDP (2009) report shows that in Australia GDI = 0.966 (rank first) and in Niger GDI = 0.308 (rank 155th), when GDI = 1 is representative of perfect gender equality.

Inequality due to racial, ethnic, or religious reasons may cause serious social tension and unrest. Another form of inequality, which can be a potential source of unrest in a country and has been studied extensively in regional economics, is regional disparities. Social programs in any country are, in general, tailored to groups, rather than individuals. Group inequalities need to be reduced for the sake of a congruent society. If national integrity is somehow threatened due to inequality, that must have a significant impact on sustainable development. A properly defined equity index that measures group inequality can help guide the social planners to devise appropriate policies to address equity issues. Such an index can also be used to evaluate the effectiveness of any policy.

The Equity Index (E), defined below, is a measure of the deprivation of different groups in relation to the highest achiever group of human development. Groups are to be defined based on national characteristics. For country comparisons, groups can be defined based on some common criteria, for example, gender, race and ethnicity, religion, and geographical region. Therefore, a group can be "Caucasian Christian Female from California," or "African-American Muslim Male from New York," and so on.

In light of the above discussions, an Equity Index (E) to measure group inequality is defined as

$$E = \left[\sum_{i=1}^{n} (H_{\max} - H_i)^\gamma \left(\frac{P_i}{P} \right) \right]^{1/\gamma}$$

Where
$H_{\max}$ = Group with the highest achievement in human development
H_i = HDI of the i-th group
(P_i/P) = Relative population in the i-th group and
γ = Inequality aversion parameter ($\gamma \geq 1$)

Since life expectancy for women is greater than that for men, necessary adjustments have to be made while computing gender inequality with this index. Although regional disparities in terms of longevity and educational attainment are not desirable, uneven growth in income in different regions is not inconsistent with the "Growth Pole Theory" of economic development. Therefore, some may suggest that rather than regional GDP, regional GNP or personal income can be a more appropriate indicator to compute E. Alternatively, E can be computed from regional longevity and educational attainment data only. This methodology, however, implicitly assumes that income disparity has the same distribution as that of longevity and educational attainment. The third option is to use regional GDP when E reflects geographical income disparity.

Comparative Statics of E

By definition, the equity index is a weighted average of order γ of group inequality in human development. If a society is more concerned about group inequality or disparity, it can assume that $\gamma > 1$. That will put more weight on larger disparities. When $\gamma = \infty$, a society is unwilling to accept any group inequality in human development. More affirmative action programs from the social planners can be expected when $\gamma > 1$. For country comparisons, $\gamma = 1$ can be assumed.

The following partial derivatives provide good insights about the comparative statics of E:

i. $\delta E/\delta P_i|_{P \ fixed} = (H_{\max} - H_i) > 0$. That means if the relative population in a deprived group i increases, E will increase.

ii. $\delta E/\delta H_i|_{H_{max}\,fixed} = (P_i/P)(-1) < 0$. That means everything else equal if the human development of group i increases, E will decline at a rate (P_i/P).

iii. $\delta E/\delta H_{max}|_{H_i\,fixed} = (\sum P_i/P) > 0$. That means if H_{max} increases relative to all H_i, E will increase.

(i) and (ii) above indicate that E fulfills the Monotonicity Axiom, which implies that E will not decrease unless relative human development of group i improves, or the population in group i decreases. The policy implication of (iii) above is that increasing the welfare of the highest achiever group relative to other groups is not consistent with equity objectives.

The proposed index has the following properties. Proofs of the properties are beyond the scope of this short chapter.

Property 8.1

E is homogeneous of degree one in H_{max} and H_i, and in P_i and P.

Property 8.2

E meets the Pigou–Dalton condition of transfer for all $\gamma > 1$.

The Pigou–Dalton condition indicates that everything else remaining the same, any transfer from a relatively poor to a relatively rich person must increase the degree of inequality. This is similar to Sen's (1976) weak transfer axiom, which indicates that, "a transfer of income from one poor household to another poor household where the latter is relatively "richer" than the former" causes an "increase in the poverty measure" (Blackwood and Lynch, 1994). Since E measures group inequity, the Pigou–Dalton condition is defined here in terms of groups rather than individuals.

Property 8.3

E is consistent with Rawlsian justice.

Rawlsian justice implies that the fastest way to decrease E is to increase human development of the most deprived group, when H_{max} does not decline.

Property 8.4

The elasticity of substitution between L_i and Q_j, $\sigma_{Li,Qj} \neq 0$.

Q_j = Quality of life = $1/3(ED_j + Y_j)$, where ED_j = educational attainment of the j-th group and Y_j = income of the j-th group. If there is a tradeoff between the improvements in the quality of life for group j and the increase in life expectancy (L) for group i, it is expected that one would prefer the increase in L_i, when i is the deprived group. Since there is perfect substitutability between the components of HDI, the rate of substitution between L_i and Q_j in the equity index is not infinite. In other words, $\sigma_{Li,Qj} \neq 0$.

Equity Condition for Sustainability

Meeting the basic needs of the present generation without compromising the ability of future generations to meet their needs is considered sustainable development (Brundtland, 1987).

A nonpositive change in the equity index is a necessary, but not a sufficient condition for sustainability. It is a necessary condition, particularly when the basic needs are defined in terms of end goals of life or the HDI (Dewan, 2009). Even if only per capita income or consumption is used to measure sustainability (sustainable economic growth), as preferred by most mainstream economists, this equity index remains relevant. There is a high correlation between income or consumption and the HDI. Following is the desirable equity condition for a society:

$$\frac{dE_t}{dt} = \frac{d}{dt}\left[\sum_{i=1}^{n}(H_{max,t} - H_{it})^{\gamma}\left(\frac{P_{it}}{P_t}\right)\right]^{1/\gamma} \leq 0$$

where t = time.

Applications

The equity index can be used to measure any type of group inequality in human development. The following two subsections show the relevance of the proposed index as one of the sustainability conditions by measuring gender inequality and regional disparity.

Gender Inequality

Women constitute on average about half of the population in a country, but in terms of human development, rights, or participation in national decision-making they lag behind men in almost every country on the planet. The UNDP has been computing GDI and GEM for different countries every year since 1995. Not in a single country, have women been able to surpass the achievement of human development by men. Women's role in national decision-making and their participation in professional and technical jobs widely vary from country to country. GDI and GEM together capture such gender differences. However, they are not inequality indices. Based on the definition of equity index in Section "The Equity Index," gender inequality can be computed as

$$E = \left[(H_{male} - H_{female})^{\gamma}\left(\frac{P_{female}}{P}\right)\right]^{1/\gamma}$$

where $\gamma \geq 1$.

A comparative study between GDI and E ranking for 33 countries from a randomly selected 1992 Human Development Report shows that the correlation coefficient, r (Rank$_{GDI}$, Rank$_E$), is 0.424. Table 8.1 shows GDI and E ranking of 10 selected countries.

It is, therefore, evident that the ranking is sensitive to the indicator used. It is shown in Section "The Equity Index" that the proposed index has all the required properties of a good inequality index. A negative change in the equity index is indicative of lower gender gap, which is desirable for sustainability.

Regional Disparity

Based on the definition of equity index in Section "The Equity Index," an index for regional disparity can be calculated as

Table 8.1 GDI and E Ranks of 10 Countries

Country	E Rank	GDI Rank	GDI Rank – E Rank
Sweden	1	1	0
Finland	2	3	1
Norway	3	2	– 1
Paraguay	4	28	24
France	5	4	– 1
Denmark	6	5	– 1
Myanmar	7	32	25
Czechoslovakia	8	14	6
Australia	9	6	– 3
New Zealand	10	7	– 3

$$E = \left[\sum_{i=1}^{n} (H_{\max} - H_i)^{\gamma} \left(\frac{P_i}{P} \right) \right]^{1/\gamma}$$

where i represents a region.

Inequality in terms of regional human development may have significant implications for sustainability. Regional inequality in human development in a country can often be interpreted by the concerned groups as "injustice" and be a source of unrest. That may even lead to the disintegration of a nation. As "country" is usually used as a unit of analysis, all sustainability conditions will likely change if a country disintegrates. Since HDI uses income, health, and educational information, regional inequality in human development must be monitored for the sake of economic and social sustainability in a nation. Changes in the decomposed regional inequality index can serve as an early warning system for potential sources of unrest.

While other forms of inequality are unjustifiable, regional disparities are sometimes justified by the primate city model or the growth pole theory. According to Higgins (1978), the growth pole concept has meaning in a stage of development where industrialization takes place based on the exploitation of natural resources. Zero regional disparity in a pure geographic sense is not feasible. In fact, in many developing countries, poverty areas exist within each region in a very asymmetrical manner (for examples from India, see Mathur, 1978). Most developing nations have the "syndrome of collective poverty" (Friedmann, 1978). It can be argued that these nations cannot afford to slow down growth rates in relatively high-income regions for accelerating growths in relatively low-income regions. "Growth rates, of income or of jobs, are customary indicators of regional economic differences" (Malecki, 1991). However, the choice of different income measures may substantially change the ranking of different regions in a nation (Hansen, 1995). Therefore, it is important to use the appropriate income measure in the equity index, which depends on the purpose of computing the index.

For intragenerational equity, it must be ensured that the region of origin of a person in a country does not become a deciding factor in attaining human development. People from all regions should have access to the same "opportunity set" in realizing their potentials and attaining equal quality of life. In a country, a person can find the best opportunities in life in a place other than his or her birthplace. Therefore, regional GNP rather than regional GDP is a more appropriate income measure to use for computing the equity index. Educational attainment and life expectancy, then, must be computed for each group of people born in a particular region, rather than for those living temporarily in a region. If the equity index is defined in such a way, it will not reflect the regional disparity in human development in a pure geographic sense. Rather, it will measure if the geographical origin is a source of difference in attaining human development.

From Western European survey data, Hansen (1992) concludes that, "even though the strongest geographic attachment of most people is to their own locality or region, there is nonetheless a pronounced willingness to be taxed to support regional development policies for economically lagging regions." Therefore, the people in resource-rich regions may approve resource-transfer, at least to some extent, from their regions to resource-poor regions in a nation, when the people in resource-rich regions are economically advanced. However, if the people in a resource-rich region lag behind in attaining end goals of life, that can be a problem for national integrity. The breakup of Bangladesh from Pakistan in 1971 could be a good example.

Proposition

A significant disparity in human development and other developmental and socio-cultural indicators may lead a deprived region to threaten to break away. The threat is "credible" if the region's resource-base is strong.

Assuming a constant-sum bargaining game between a country and a resource-rich region in the country, it can be shown that breaking away from the country is a dominant strategy for the region. This is particularly true if the quality of life in the region is not according to local expectations relative to that in the rest of the country. On the other hand, for a relatively resource-poor region staying together is the optimum strategy. Even if the region is a low achiever in human development or a large receptor of pollutants, its threat to break away may not be "credible" from economic considerations. Therefore, a national policy of lesser access to opportunities in a resource-poor region may be consistent with Summers' (1992) infamous policy prescription of exporting pollution to underdeveloped regions. However, the equity index would suggest that such a policy is not coherent with sustainability objectives.

The above proposition implies that sustained low human development regions are probably relatively resource-poor. Any effort to improve human development in those regions will likely require resource transfer from high human development regions, which is consistent with social justice. E can be defined both for understanding disparity among geographic regions and for measuring inequity among people due to the regional origin. Change in E over time is a good indicator to assess if the country is moving toward convergence or divergence in terms of regional opportunities.

Conclusion

For sustainability and national integrity, equal opportunity and an environment for flourishing human potential have to be assured for everyone in every nation. Any form of discrimination based on skin color, race, ethnicity, religion, gender, or region that decreases human potential is inconsistent with sustainability objectives. The proposed equity index can be used as an evaluation tool for equity programs. It can help identify appropriate indicators of inequality, and thus, help manage group inequalities. The proposed index is sensitive to the number of groups used to compute the index. Therefore, one has to be cautious about interpreting the value of the index. It should also be noted that in a pluralistic society, sources of unrest and threat to central governance could originate from other issues not directly related to economic growth or achievement in human development. The equity index, as defined, will not capture such sociocultural disparities. Therefore, a complete set of sustainability indicators must include sociocultural and other indicators along with the equity index. The equity index measures only one dimension of sustainability. Its universality to measure any form of group inequality is its strength.

References

Atkinson, A. B. 1983. *The Economics of Inequality*. Oxford, UK: Clarendon.

Blackwood, D. L. and Lynch, R. G. 1994. The measurement of inequality and poverty: A policy maker's guide to the literature, *World Development*, 22(4): 567–78.

Brundtland Commission 1987. *Our Common Future*. Oxford, UK: Oxford University Press.

Dewan, H. 2009. Re-defining sustainable human development to integrate sustainability and human development goals, *The International Journal of Environmental, Cultural, Economic, and Social Sustainability*, 5(4): 147–62.

Foster, J., Greer, J., and Thorbecke, E. 1984. Notes and comments: A class of decomposable poverty measures, *Econometrica*, 52(3): 761–66.

Friedmann, H. 1978. World market state, and family farm: Social bases of household production in the era of wage labour, Comparative Studies in Society and History, 20: 545–86.

Hansen, N. 1992. Regional policies for equity: Can they be justified?, in Savoie, D. and Brecher, I. (eds.), *Equity and Efficiency in Economic Development*. Montréal, Canada: McGill-Queen's University Press.

Hansen, N. 1995. Addressing regional disparity and equity objectives through regional policies: A skeptical perspective, *Papers in Regional Science*, 74(2): 89–104.

Higgins, B. 1978. Development poles: Do they exist?, in Lo, F. and Salih, K. (eds.), *Growth Pole Strategy and Regional Development Policy*. Oxford, UK: Pergamon.

Malecki, E. J. 1991. *Technology and Economic Development: The Dynamics of Local, Regional and National Change*. London, UK: Longman.

Mathur, O. P. 1978. The problem of regional disparities: An analysis of Indian Policies and Programs, in Lo, F. and Salih, K. (eds.), *Growth Pole Strategy and Regional Development Policy*. Oxford, UK: Pergamon.

Rawls, J. B. 1971. *A Theory of Justice*. Cambridge, MA: Belknap Press of Harvard University Press.

Sen, A. K. 1976. Poverty: An ordinal approach to measurement, *Econometrica*, 44(2): 219–31.

Sen, A. K. 1993. Life expectancy and inequality: Some conceptual issues, in Bardhan, P., Datta-Chaudhuri, M., and Krishnan, T. N. (eds.), *Development and Change: Essays in Honour of K.N. Raj*. Oxford, UK: Oxford University Press.

Slesnick, D. T. 1993. Gaining ground: Poverty in the Postwar United States, *Journal of Political Economy*, 101(1): 1–38.

Summers, L. 1992. *Internal Memo*, World Bank, Breton Woods, NH.

UNDP. 1992, 1993, and 2009. Human Development Report. New York, NY.

Chapter 9

Coordination Failure in Global Common Pool Governance?*

Jan-Erik Lane

Contents

Introduction

Economists and environmentalists alike underline that there is, in principle, no contradiction between economic growth on the one hand, and preservation of the environment on the other. They go on to offer many examples of innovations that foster both growth and ecology concerns. Thus, Singapore, for instance, has spearheaded several forms of economic development and economic growth that are also environmentally sustainable. An entire city in China has been built upon the use of renewable sun energy. Moreover, almost all carmakers have planned for the construction of electricity or hydrogen cars. Many urban sites employ so-called green buses. This feasible coherence between economic growth and environmental sustainability holds at the microlevel in the economy, encompassing a host of interesting and promising projects, especially in rich countries. However, at the macrolevel, especially at the global level, matters are entirely different,

---

* This chapter is a revised version of the author's published article: Lane, J-E. 2015. Planet Earth in the 21st century: Coordination failure in common pools governance, *International Journal of Sociology and Anthropology*, 7(4): 107–11.

as economic activity, in general, consumes lots of energy, which results in a constantly increasing emission of greenhouse gases (GHGs). This global contradiction between economic growth and ecological sustainability, both valued by many people, most probably is a major challenge of the twenty-first century, because there is a limit to the increase in CO_2 equivalent emissions, as far as climate change is concerned. Too much global warming may change basic living conditions around the entire world. The aim of this chapter is merely to pin down exactly these macrorelationships between economic activity, energy consumption, and GHGs, as they hold for the planet today when measured at the total or aggregated levels (Enerdata, 2015; Energy Information Agency, 2015; World Bank, 2015; World Resources Institute, 2015).

The Relevance of Economic Growth

Economists and politicians emphasize the need for balanced growth on many occasions. Zero economic growth has been pledged by a small group of people, talking about the global limits to growth. They are often rebutted by the argument that growth and environment do not necessarily collide. This is true—at the microlevel. One understands the quest of, for instance, France for economic growth, having experienced the misfortunes that a long period of almost zero growth leads to budget cuts, loss of public service employees, too little investments, reductions in welfare spending, cutting back on culture projects, and so forth. Development theory provides a key role for economic growth for the ambition of peripheral nations to *catch-up* with core nations. The European Union and even the United States (Table 9.1) look upon the recent surge in economic growth in the new economic giants with envy.

The GDP measures on income or production do not take environmental costs into account. Instead, polluting industries such as the airline business, shipping, and the car sector contribute considerably to the GDP. It has been argued that the GDP standard indicator should be revised to include the subtraction of ecology costs. Now, the generation of total income or production for a year comes with the emission of GHGs. Figure 9.1 portrays the close connection between GDP and total emission, using LN numbers for most recently available data.

Figure 9.1 shows that on the global macrolevel, the variation in economic development has strong implications for the emission of all four kinds of GHGs: the richer and larger a country

Table 9.1 Economic Affluence in the Twenty-First Century (LN Gross Domestic Product [GDP] Per Capita in Constant Value USD for 2005)

Year	2000	2003	2006	2009	2013
Euro Area	10.3	10.3	10.4	10.3	10.4
EU	10.2	10.2	10.2	10.2	10.3
Brazil	8.39	8.40	8.49	8.57	8.67
India	6.36	6.47	6.68	6.85	7.06
China	7.02	7.26	7.57	7.87	8.18
US	10.6	10.6	10.7	10.7	10.7

Source: World Bank 2015. *GDP Per Capita*, Washington, DC.

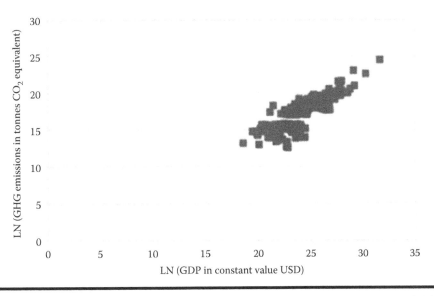

Figure 9.1 Total Emissions and GDP: Equation: LN GDP—LN Green House Gases [GHG] Total: $y = 0.81 \times$, R2 = 0.708. (Adapted from World Bank 2015. *GDP Per Capita*, Washington, DC; World Resources Institute 2015. *GRG Emissions Totals*, Washington, DC.) GDP versus GHG for 158 countries in 2011.

economy, the more emissions it releases. This finding is, of course, the rationale for the basic argument that we need another kind of economic growth that builds upon carbon neutral technology. This is no doubt feasible in theory, but in practice, we are stuck with the fossil fuel economy, especially after the turn to shale oil and gas. Moreover, the destruction of forests and depletion of fresh water sources continue.

At global reunions among the politicians and experts, there is much talk about the emissions per capita. Developing countries underline that they tend to display lower emissions per capita than advanced economies. Is this true? Figure 9.2 suggests an answer to the question of the distribution of the total GHGs, which is a most policy-relevant issue.

The findings, however, strongly suggest that emissions per capita are only weakly associated with GDP per capita. Thus, a few rich countries have rather low emissions, whereas some developing countries have substantial emissions per person. Thus, a global policy for ecological sustainability with regard to emissions control must be the responsibility of all countries on the globe, all people being concerned. It is true that a few rich countries have very high emission per capita (the United States, Australia, and the Gulf States), but most of the emissions originate in the very populous countries in the world, especially in Asia, besides the United States.

Economic development can be environmental friendly. Many micro-projects have reduced carbon emissions and, yet delivered goods and services more efficiently. However, what counts at the macrolevel is the overall additions and subtractions. Take the example of Singapore, whose government is very much aware of the energy environmental conundrum. Although it must be admitted that Singapore is conducting many advanced projects to promote ecological sustainability, it should be pointed out that it is a huge hub for air traffic and see shipping, which both result in GHGs. In addition, Singapore has coal-fired power stations and consume huge amounts of electricity (water cleaning, waste treatment, and air conditioning in almost all private housing

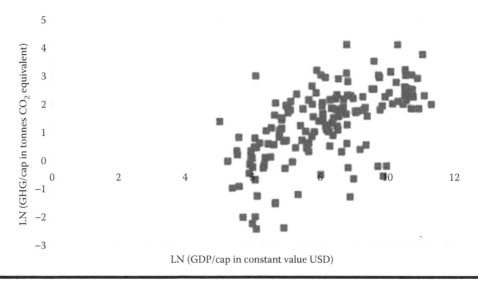

Figure 9.2 Emissions per capita and GDP per capita: Equation: LN GDP/CAP—LN GHG/CAP: $y = 0.52 \times$, R2 = 0.370. **(Adapted from World Bank 2015.** *GDP Per Capita*, **Washington, DC; World Resources Institute 2015.** *GRG Emissions Totals*, **Washington, DC.) GDP/Capita versus GHG/capita for 158 countries in 2011.**

and public buildings). The same contradictory finding applies to the United Arab Emirates where extensive investment procedures take place within ecologically friendly projects. However, the fact remains that the CO_2 emission per capita here is the largest in the world, as in Qatar. To understand the close link between total GDP and total emissions, one needs to look at global energy consumption.

Energy Consumption

Economic activity in all forms consumes directly or indirectly huge amounts of energy. This leads to the emission of GHGs, directly or indirectly. To take a somewhat drastic example: the rapid increase in consumption of meat energy has resulted in an enormous growth in the number of cows in the world, which produce methane that is very conducive to climate change and global warming. Figure 9.3 illustrates the close connection between total GDP and total emissions today.

It is also the case that rich countries consume more energy per person than poor countries as higher levels of affluence require more energy. The situation is paradoxical, as rich countries can invest in environment-friendly technology, but they also consume more energy for upholding their lifestyle, as depicted in Figure 9.4.

More affluent or luxurious lifestyles are exhibited not only through bigger cars but also in more heating and air conditioning. Electricity is needed in affluent countries. If it is not to be produced by nuclear energy, as in Germany, a country may actually rely more upon coal-fired power stations. As with Germany, massive amounts of imports of coal from developing countries, like Colombia, with dismal ecological effects both abroad and at home.

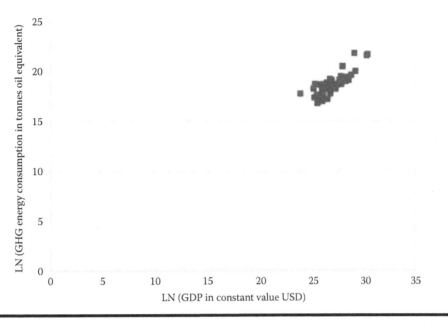

Figure 9.3   GDP and Energy Consumption: LN GDP—LN Energy Consumption: $y = 0.71 \times$, $R2 = 0.695$.

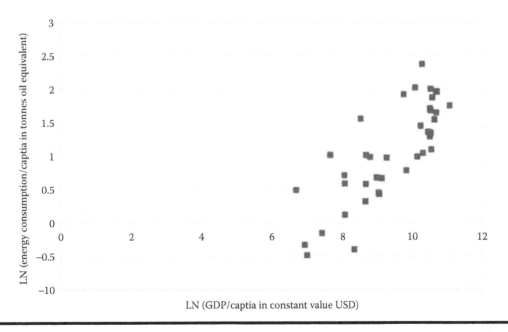

Figure 9.4   GDP Per Capita—Emissions Per Capita: LN GDP/CAP—LN Energy Consumption/ CAP: $y = 0.47 \times$, $R2 = 0.641$.

Three Global Models

Global ecological sustainability is not enhanced as long as total carbon equivalent emission increase, that is, augments sharply year in and year out in reality. Two factors increasing GHGs on the macro or global level are world population and economic activity:

$$\text{Total GHGs} = \text{LN GHG} = 0.520 * \text{LN GDP} + 0.477 * \text{LN Pop}, R2 = 0.76 \tag{9.1}$$

This equation models the global situation today. One can imagine what happens to total GHGs emissions and ecological sustainability when the world population reaches nine billion people and GDP doubles.

The major factor behind yearly increases in GHGs by some 3%, besides many promising innovations, is the constantly augmenting need for energy. Other factors matter, like the cutting or burning down of forests, and the acidification of the seas and oceans. Finally, we can look at the following equations:

$$\text{LN Energy} = 0.477 * \text{LN Pop} + 0.43 * \text{LN GDP}, R2 = 0.88 \tag{9.2}$$

Again, the increase in energy consumption predictions for the next two decades from the Energy Information Administration's (EIA) Annual Energy Outlook (AEO) for 2014, mirrors the projected growth in world population and the optimistic scenario for economic production or the stylized economic growth rates of 3%–5% per year. I would suggest that the energy factor is the central one behind the global warming process, which is supported by the following equation:

$$\text{LN GHG} = 1.0109 * \text{LN Energy} - 0.133 * \text{LN Pop} + 0.1052 * \text{LN GDP}, R2 = 0.95 \tag{9.3}$$

Energy consumption with rising levels of affluence has a stronger impact on the emission of GHGs rather than population growth alone. However, when population increases combined with increases in energy usage due to a rise in affluence, then emissions augment.

Emissions

Levels and Rates of Increase

EIA (2015) recently stated that, "economic growth takes off but pollution stalls." This information refers to a slight increase in GDP but CO_2 emissions either increasingly or decreasing. However, this confounds levels and rates of change. Today, the yearly output of CO_2 emissions stands at approximately 30 gigatons. If this *level* of output continues for a decade or more, global warming will not halt at two degrees. Whether it increases slightly from one year to another will not change the major challenges of rising temperatures, desertification, acidification, and fresh water shortages. Should the present level of CO_2 emissions continue yearly for more than a decade, then the danger of a 6% increase in global temperatures *is not* improbable.

Conclusion

The G20 group of states and governments needs to do something to promote the use of energy from renewable resources. As this group represents almost 80% of global populations, the G20 could embark upon an ecologically sustainable energy policy without either free riding or the kind of massive transaction costs that have plagued the United Nations efforts thus far. Changing the energy patterns is the only realistic option, as the quest for economic growth emerges from an unstoppable human drive. One can look upon the planet as a giant common-pool. Managing the resources in this common-pool presents such severe collective action problems that humankind has yet to find a policy mix that can "fix" the problems. Otherwise, we face the most dismal "tragedy of the commons" ever. It is up to the governments of the large, populous, and economically strong to find and implement coordination mechanisms that reduce the economic dependency upon fossil fuels. There is no guarantee against a major coordination failure. Approaching the planet as a giant common-pool with an atmosphere necessary for life, one must not assume that teleology will somehow stop freeriding and reneging, preventing coordination failure (Ostrom, 1990). The simple need for action, policies, and coordination will not call forth institutions and enforcement or policing. The city of Shanghai boasts that it has succeeded in building a large coal-fired power plant that emits no GHGs. To create a global *common-pool resource regime* (CPR) of all cities burning coal for electricity to rebuild them without CO_2 emissions would require much more than "voluntary cooperation."

References

Enerdata 2015. *Global Energy Statistical Yearbook, 2014—Total Energy Consumption*, Grenoble, France.
Energy Information Agency 2015. *Annual Energy Outlook 2015—With Projections to 2040*, Washington, DC.
Ostrom, E. 1990. *Governing the Commons*, Cambridge, UK: Cambridge University Press.
World Bank 2015. *GDP Per Capita*, Washington, DC.
World Resources Institute 2015. *GRG Emissions Totals*, Washington, DC.

Chapter 10

Bernard Stiegler on Agricultural Innovation*

Pieter Lemmens

Contents

Introduction

This chapter discusses the relevance of the work of the French philosopher of technology Bernard Stiegler (1952) in addressing technoethical and technopolitical issues in agricultural innovation, in particular, the use of genetic engineering technologies. Before specifically dealing with his work on agriculture and agricultural innovation, I briefly introduce the broader scope of his work and the most important aspects of his views on technology and technological change. I then focus on his theory of agriculture as a technical system as seen from his more encompassing view on the coevolution of humanity and technology. Emphasis is placed on his notion of proletarianization and its effects on farmers and people around the world due to the corporate-controlled deployment

---

* This chapter is a revised version of the author's published article: Lemmens, P. 2014. Bernard Steigler on agri-culture as a technical system, *Sustainable Agriculture Research*, 3(4): 76–81.

of genetic engineering technologies in industrialized agriculture. I further discuss Stiegler's main theoretical insight that technologies must be considered as *pharmaka*, meaning they can both *obstruct* and *advance* the psychic and social individuation processes involved in the sociotechnical practices they support and, can do so, simultaneously. Given their pharmacological nature, like any other technology, genetic engineering technologies *can* and *should* be redeployed as tools to reverse the process of proletarianization and institute a new system of agriculture where farmers regain their lost ability to participate in the innovation processes and, therefore, the evolution of the technical *milieu* that constitutes their existence.

Main Philosophical Ideas

Human Individuation and the Technical Milieu

Stiegler's philosophy of technology and technological change is rooted in a philosophical-anthropological conception of man. The premise of his thinking is that man is fundamentally characterized by what he calls an "original lack of origin" or *défaut d'origine*. In contrast to animals, man is a being who is "substantially without essence" (i.e., a creature with no intrinsic or natural qualities). The proprium of man consists in his thoroughly accidental character and precisely for that reason; the human condition is essentially the condition of technicity. In contrast to the metaphysical tradition unto Heidegger, Stiegler claims that man is a prosthetic being by essence (Stiegler, 2009b). Man's temporal and historical mode of being (i.e., his involvement in a process of permanent becoming) is grounded in the original default.

Stiegler understands the structurally incomplete, technically constituted, and conditioned process of becoming characteristic of man based on the theory of *individuation* developed by French philosopher of technology Gilbert Simondon. Salient to this theory is the idea that individuals do not precede the process of their individuation, which means there is no fixed principle of individuality. According to Simondon, psychic individuals can individuate only within and relative to a collective, as a process of psycho-collective co-individuation. Stiegler adds a third term to this model: technology or the process of technical individuation (Stiegler, 2007). The human individuation process, therefore, involves not two but three terms, and it is the third term, that of the individuation of the technical system or technical *milieu*, that possesses a certain primacy, since technical innovation is the initiating factor in the typically human process of individuation (Stiegler, 2013). This does not mean, to be sure, that technology would be "asocial" in the sense that it would externally determine processes of psycho-collective individuation, yet it "over-determines" them in the sense of conditioning them.

The technical system is the pre-individual *milieu* (also a term of Simondon), which allows the articulation of the individual psyches and the collective in the first place, but is also formed through the process of psycho-collective co-individuation. The relation between psyches, collectives, and the technical *milieu* is *transductive*—a relationship in which the constituting terms coconstitute each other and only take shape in their relationship to one another. Stiegler speaks here of "organs" and calls the study of the ever-changing relations throughout history between psychic organs, social organizations and the artificial organs of the technical *milieu* "general organology"—extension of Simondon's notion of mechanology (Stiegler, 2013).

The articulation of the processes of psychic individuation with the processes of collective individuation through the technical *milieu* constitutes a process of "transindividuation" that results in the formation of the "transindividual" (once again a term by Simondon). This comprises everything that is shared by all individuals and metastabilizes itself in a certain way in the form of culture, language, customs, modes of production, social rules, moral principles, and so on. The pre-individual *milieu* is both the product and the process of transindividuation and the condition of the processes of psychic and collective individuation (Stiegler, 2007). It includes techniques that act as external memory supports, initially only implicitly, but with the emergence of so-called "mnemotechnics" like writing explicitly. It is constantly evolving, from clay tablets, papyrus, parchment, and from the printing press to radio, television, cinema, and the Internet. Thus, the human is principally characterized by the adoption of always new technologies (Stiegler, 2009a).

Techno-Evolution and Epiphylogenesis

Stiegler also theorizes technology and technological change from an evolutionary perspective on the human as a technical lifeform. He shows that human evolution is essentially a techno-evolution—the process of anthropogenesis is fundamentally technogenic. Techniques act as external memories that are unique to the human species. What constitutes the humanity of the human and differentiates humans from other animals is a process of technical exteriorization, as Stiegler claims with French archeologist and paleoanthropologist André Leroi-Gourhan. Human evolution is based on the transmission and accumulation of external, artificial memory supports that have initiated an entirely new process of evolutionary differentiation operating outside of the biological organism (i.e., not of genetic differentiation but differentiation of technical prostheses) that nevertheless permanently interact with human biology (Stiegler, 1998).

Human culture, tradition, spirit, and so on, are ultimately based on the very possibility of inheritance of technical artifacts that act as memory traces—as material carriers of exteriorized experience (Stiegler, 2004a). The process of hominization, then, *is* the process of technical exteriorization (and its subsequent interiorization). Stiegler calls the third, technical type of memory unique to humans epiphylogenetic memory and the process of evolution based on it epiphylogenesis, since it involves the transmission of individual (epi-) experience to the species (phyllo-) (Stiegler, 1998). Anthropogenesis and human history can be described as a process of epiphylogenesis. Within this process, different stages or epochs can be distinguished. Each epiphylogenetic epoch makes certain forms of knowledge and experience possible. It provides the technological conditions of possibility for thinking and being in a certain period and structures as such what Heidegger thought of as the epochality of history. It includes both artifacts and symbols. Language and technology are two equiprimordial dimensions of the same process of exteriorization on which the evolution of man essentially rests (Stiegler, 2004a).

Stiegler's Pharmacological Conception of Technology

What sets Stiegler apart from most other philosophers is his emphasis on the fact that human existence is essentially technically constituted and conditioned, which implies, among other things, that human autonomy cannot exist without heteronomy (Stiegler, 2013). In his most recent work he lays increasing emphasis on the fact that any technology, but in particular mnemotechnology, has the character of what he calls (after his teacher Jacques Derrida, who borrowed this term from Plato) a *pharmakon* (Stiegler, 2013). This Greek word means both medicine and poison, in the sense of that which can both heal and make us sick. That is to say, technology functions for humans—as the animal that is fundamentally open and indeterminate and therefore in essential need of prostheses—simultaneously as that which "comes to the rescue" of his indeterminacy in the sense of compensating for it, "curing" it as it were, and as that which can "poison" this indeterminacy, acting as a barrier to his freedom and thereby undermining his existence and world-disclosive capacity rather than supporting it.

In the case of mnemotechniques, this means that they can both elevate and frustrate the mind, lead to both subjectivation and desubjectification, and can be employed for emancipation and individuation as well as disciplining and disindividuation of the mind. In Foucauldian terms: they can act both as technologies of power and as technologies of the self. They can enhance autonomy and sociality but also heteronomize subjects and atomize societies. As a crucial aspect, technologies and the technical systems they constitute are in need of practices of care. As supported by a system of *pharmaka*, each culture is, therefore, necessarily a system of care: care *for* and *through* the *pharmaka* (Stiegler, 2013).

Processes of individuation and subjectivation are crucially, and from the very outset, pharmacological in nature and the human being—as a being without origin—is a substantially pharmacological being. Fighting against the toxifying tendencies within the technical *milieu* of the mind presupposes that philosophy develops a critical pharmacology of technology. One of the technical *milieus* that are suffering from toxification due principally to the capitalist employment of the new and emerging *pharmaka* that enable its revolutionization is the global agricultural system.

Stiegler's View on Agricultural Innovation

Agriculture as Technical System and System of Care

Throughout its evolution and history, humans have always had to adopt new technologies—new technical systems. The arrival of a new technical system however, as Stiegler shows following the French historian of technology Bertrand Gille, always causes a disruption in the social system, suspending and actually destroying the system of care based on the preceding set of technologies and the skills evolved around them (Stiegler, 2009b). Initially, then, technological revolutions are destructive of ways of life and modes of existence. They bring about maladjustment between the technical system and the social system, giving rise to a fundamental disorientation. Only by adjusting itself to the new technical system can the social system invent a new system of care based on the possibilities offered by the new technical system. Presently, agriculture is confronted with a new technological base (i.e., biotechnology, in particular, the technologies that can manipulate life on the molecular level) that may destroy traditional lives of farmers all over the world. They also embody the possibility though of a *new agriculture*.

Like all culture, agriculture is a system of care (Stiegler, 2007). This is to say that it is a kind of therapeutic (from the Greek word *therapeuein*: to care, to take care of) in the sense that the practice of agriculture as the cultivation of (vegetable) life and with it, the creation of artificial ecosystems, always entails a violation of the natural world—a disequilibration and disruption of ecological balance. Traditional farmers are those who take care for the living, and this always means selecting the living through technics. As a technically equipped and educated selector-cultivator, the traditional farmer is not simply a reproducer but also a producer of life. He breeds new life and new varieties, and in doing so, he also transforms his own way of life or his world. In domesticating plants (and animals), the traditional farmer also domesticates (in the sense of elevating) himself. Moreover, in transforming the world, in forming a new world, he must take care of this world and this taking care, as the very essence of agriculture, is a therapeutics that involves techniques, which have essentially the character of *pharmaka* and necessarily involve knowledge (i.e., the know-how [*savoir-faire*]), skills, and expertise based on these technologies.

It is, in particular, this know-how that "makes the farmer," that constitutes his way of life, that is to say, his existence.

The appearance of a new technical system always involves the appearance of a new kind of society and new social roles—a new modality of the process of psychic and collective individuation based engendered by a novel process of technical individuation (Stiegler, 2013). Agricultural systems must also be understood as processes, involving a common technological base and a variety of sociotechnical roles. Agriculture actually entails a fourth process of individuation as well, which is the process of vital individuation of the plants and it can be argued that agriculture is centered upon the care for, and the technical improvement of, processes of vital individuation of crops. What distinguishes contemporary agriculture from traditional agriculture is that today it is possible to directly intervene in these processes of vital individuation. This enables both a proletarianization of agricultural innovation, as currently happens predominantly, but it can also become the basis of a new mode of agriculture, which supposes a process of deproletarianization.

The Biotechnology Revolution and the Corporate Control of Agriculture

At the moment, we are in the midst of a huge rupture in the technological base of agriculture, particularly due to the new genetic engineering technologies that enable intervention in the very processes underlying the development and evolution of life. With these technologies becoming prevalent, the care and responsibility for the living are more and more transferred from farmers to biotechnologists. This could in principle lead to fruitful cooperations and to a sharing of responsibilities, but problematically, today these technologies are everywhere turned into private property by major agrotech multinationals with the principal aim of acquiring monopolies and ensuring profits, not of providing farmers with new innovative breeding tools.

Corporate control of these technologies represents the biggest threat to the know-how of farmers and to the care and responsibility for the living accompanying it. As Kloppenburg has shown, genetic engineering technologies ideally enable capitalist penetration of agriculture and the conversion of farming into wage labor activity thereby transforming the farmer into a proletarian (Kloppenburg, 2004). This process of proletarianization of the farmer allows for the exploitation of his labor force but what is even more troubling for Stiegler, is the fact that this proletarianization involves a reduction of the existence of the farmer to the level of subsistence, substituting a mode of living with a mode of employment. Reduced to a subsistence mode of living, farmers lose the knowledge and know-how through which they have always exercised their care and responsibility for the living. While discharging the farmer of the care and responsibility for biological innovation, corporate-led, privatized agriculture is not replacing it with an alternative practice of care and responsibility. It replaces it instead with a systemic carelessness and a complete absence of responsibility.

The Proletarianization of the Farmer and the Ruining of Agriculture as a System of Care

From the perspective of Simondon, taken over by Stiegler, the proletarian is the one who, dispossessed of the means of production and turned into a unit of labor power, has lost his know-how and it is in this that the real, and most problematic essence of proletarianization consists (Stiegler, 2010a). Most problematic because it implies a dispossession of (the means of) taking care and responsibility for the living, which is exercised by farmers through their know-how and more broadly through their way of life or their *savoir-vivre*. It is this care and responsibility, which elevates them above subsistence level and makes them into existent human beings that farmers all over the world do not want to lose.

The new genetic engineering technologies enable an expropriation of the most important and most central means of production in agriculture (the seed) through the appropriation of the germ-plasm. This implies an expropriation of the know-how and knowledge of farmers and turns them into proletarians, disengaged from the responsibility for the living. This responsibility for breeding and selection will no longer be in the hands of the farmers but is delegated to scientists, who are themselves, just like farmers, increasingly functioning as employees for big corporations. Farmers' modes of existence are in fact short-circuited and thereby made obsolete through these new tech-nologies (Stiegler, 2007). In the context of contemporary finance capitalism, which has become a purely speculative endeavor increasingly, carelessness and irresponsibility have become systemic features (Stiegler, 2010a).

Rejection of the privatization and corporatization of agriculture often goes hand in hand with an outright rejection of genetic engineering technology as such. However, the introduction of these technologies in agriculture does not necessarily imply their proletarianizing—and, there-fore, careless and irresponsible—deployment by capitalism. They can be (re)possessed and (re) appropriated by farmers and turned into new tools for taking care and responsibility, tools for a new, thoroughly technologized, and industrialized yet not proletarianized agriculture. The refusal of corporate agriculture should not lead to a refusal of the (bio) tech neologization of agriculture as such. What should be rejected is the proletarianizing ways in which they are put to use.

Stiegler's thesis is that grammaticization, the discretization and formalization of the continu-ous flows of natural processes that enable their exteriorization (Stiegler, 2004b), is the principal factor behind proletarianization, that is to say: its condition of possibility (Stiegler, 2004b). This dramatization of life in fact enables the short-circuiting of the process of reproduction of living organisms and, with it, the short-circuiting of the knowledge and know-how of those who have traditionally been endowed with the care and responsibility for the reproduction of these organ-isms and as selectors also with their production (i.e., with the creation of new life): the farmers. This actually makes the traditional lives of farmers obsolete, proletarianizing their mode of exis-tence. The upshot of this is a loss of participation of the farmers in the development of their "own" technical milieu, which is to say: in the very conditions determining agricultural production. This results in the formation of dissociated milieus, in which there is no association anymore between farmers and the technical system, neither between farmers among each other. This finally means ruining of their existence (and consistency) and its reduction to subsistence. Ultimately, agricul-ture becomes a system of care-collapses. What is needed is a reversal of this process (i.e., a process of proletarianization) and this can only come about as a therapeutic based on the very same tech-nologies that are at the basis of proletarianization (Stiegler, 2013).

Deproletarianization and the Pharmacological Turn

As Stiegler contends, technologies, as the material effects of grammaticization processes, are intrinsically ambiguous, in the sense that they can both foster and intensify and ruin and erode processes of psychic and social individuation, they can both support and undermine psychosocial individuation processes. In other words, technologies can be conducive of both disindividuation and individuation (the former being synonymous with proletarianization). It is for this reason that Stiegler theorizes technologies fundamentally as *pharmaka* (Stiegler, 2010b). As previously men-tioned, technologies as *pharmaka* can simultaneously poison processes of psych collective indi-viduation and be employed to cure these processes. As a matter of fact, the *only* way to cure the poisoning effects of technological *pharmaka* is via these very same *pharmaka*, and that is by developing new practices around and on the basis of these *pharmaka*—practices of care (Stiegler, 2007).

This pharmacological view of technology is anything but a refashioning of the traditional idea of the neutrality of technology. On the contrary, the fact that technology *conditions* any process of individuation in a pharmacological way implies that psyches and collectives cannot "use" or "apply" technologies as they see fit from an autonomous and sovereign subjective standpoint. Instead, they have to *negotiate* with this condition as that which is foundational to their practices and can, as such, both support and undermine these practices. On the other hand, the fact that technologies condition processes of individuation does not rule out the fact that they can be redesigned by "users" to support new and alternative "applications." That which ultimately decides whether *pharmaka* act as a poison or function as a medicine—as a therapeutic—is the presence or absence of a practice of care, economic practice to be sure, but one in which care is the ultimate value of the valorization process. This restores, according to Stiegler, the original sense of the word economy, as "to economize" originally means to take care (Stiegler, 2013). Without a practice of care, *pharmaka* "support" proletarianization, which means the absence of any practice and the exclusion of the user from participation in the evolution of the technical system, which he depends on nevertheless.

Now, what the privatization and, thus, desocialization of the new biotechnologies by the big agrotech companies precisely prevents, is the formation of such practices of care around these technologies. The processes of innovation in agriculture are everywhere privatized and put under control—ultimately—of finance capitalism, short-circuiting the farmers as selectors (i.e., destroying the processes of psycho-collective individuation and inducing dissociative), careless *milieus* deprived of the possibility of responsible action. The new biotechnologies offer the possibility of a new, globalized, and industrialized agriculture, but only on the condition that they can be appropriated by the actors within the technical milieu in which they are introduced, so that they can develop new practices and new modes of existence on the basis of these technologies. This possibility is currently frustrated because of the excessive privatization—dispossession and enclosure of these technologies. The corporations who have massively taken hold of all these new, powerful, and promising tools for innovation are emphatically unable—by virtue of their very nature *as* corporations—to rebuild a system of care, and to restore a long-term perspective, which is absolutely necessary for the creation of a new global agriculture, especially in the light of the global environmental and food crises.

The impending proletarianization of agriculture, made possible by and implemented through biotechnology, needs to be countered with a resolute project of deproletarianization, that is, not by rejecting the new biotechnologies but by re-appropriating them, socializing them, and turning them into elements of a new technical milieu that can function as the basis of a new, global agriculture. The future of biotechnologies agriculture cannot be entrusted to private companies who are totally devoid of care and incapable of taking responsibility for life on earth, both the life of crops and the life of the people who live from these crops. To prevent a rampant decline of agriculture into agribusiness and to allow for the possibility of reconstituting agriculture as a system of care, one needs to socialize the new technologies and make the future of agriculture subject to our collective responsibility. The deproletarianization of agriculture, an absolute necessity for the future of humankind, therefore needs to go hand in hand, as Kloppenburg (2010) emphasizes, with a battle for the repossession of the means of taking care of agricultural production, which has always been a social activity—a process of psycho-collective individuation based on the sharing of knowledge and know-how.

The first steps toward repossession and deproletarianization, as Lemmens (2014) argues, may already be on the horizon with the introduction of the principles of open source innovation in the agricultural context. Open source innovation, which originated the world of software development, not only involves a "repossession" of the means of production through the creation of a "protected commons" (Kloppenburg, 2010), but also an effort to re-autonomy the knowledge production and creation of know-how that is continuously expropriated from farmers with a view to restore this knowledge and know-how at the psycho-collective level and, so, to regain the ability to participate in the transformation of their own technical *milieu* and its modes of production, and as such to become the creators and authors again of their own life-worlds and their own existence—and to be able to take care and responsibility for it. Open source may be the vital first step in the transformation of the new biotechnical *pharmaka* from corporate biotechnologies of control-from-the-outside into commonly owned biotechnologies enabling a caring and more intelligent agriculture, endogenously "controlled-from-within," that is, agriculture as a genuine system of care (Kloppenburg, 2010). This may eventually lead to a trajectory of agricultural innovation that deviates from the dominant tendency of increasing biotechnologization. However, from Stiegler's perspective—and considered as a phase within the history of grammatization—biotechnology appears as something that is here to stay. Its ultimate destination, however, is anything but decided and will depend on the ways in which social actors adopt it.

References

Kloppenburg, J. 2004. *First the Seed: The Political Economy of Plant Biotechnology.* Madison, WI: The University of Wisconsin Press.

Kloppenburg, J. 2010. Impeding dispossession, enabling repossession: Biological open source and the recovery of seed sovereignty, *Journal of Agrarian Change*, 10: 367–88.

Lemmens, P. 2014. Re-taking care: Open source biotech in light of the need to deproletarianize agricultural innovation, *Journal of Agricultural and Environmental Ethics*, 27(1): 127–52.

Stiegler, B. 1998. *Technics and Time 1: The Fault of Epimetheus.* Stanford, CA: Stanford University Press.

Stiegler, B. 2004a. *Philosopher par accident: Entretiens avec élie during.* Paris, France: Éditions Galilée.

Stiegler, B. 2004b. *De la misère symbolique: L'époque hyperindustrielle.* Paris, France: Éditions Galilée.

Stiegler, B. 2007. Zorg dragen: Landbouw en industrie, *Ethische Perspectieven*, 17(3): 213–27.

Stiegler, B. 2009a. *Acting Out.* Stanford, CA: Stanford University Press.

Stiegler, B. 2009b. *Technics and Time, 2: Disorientation.* Stanford: Stanford University Press.

Stiegler, B. 2010a. *For a New Critique of Political Economy.* London, UK: Polity.

Stiegler, B. 2010b. *Taking Care of Youth and the Generations.* Stanford, CA: Stanford University Press.

Stiegler, B. 2013. *What Makes Life Worth Living: On Pharmacology.* London: Polity.

HUMAN RIGHTS

Chapter 11

Foreign Aid and Human Rights: Putting Investment into Perspective

Sebastian D. T. Jedicke and Scott Nicholas Romaniuk

Contents

Introduction

The issues of poverty and inequality can be ascribed to the colonial period, in which the major European powers divided the world into spheres of influence and areas of control. Although nearly all former colonies gained their independence by the end of the twentieth century, the problems of these countries have not disappeared. Dependency on foreign aid is a serious issue throughout the African continent and other parts of the periphery and semiperiphery, and due to the diversity of challenges, it is difficult to determine how to cultivate development. As a direct result of poverty, disease is a major obstacle to development, and foreign aid helps in ensuring humanitarian assistance in the form of medicine and education (Sachs, 2012a, b). Other scholars, namely Moyo (2010) and Easterly (2003), present the opinion that the deeply rooted problems of Africa, for example, cannot be solved with foreign aid alone, as the problem lies with issues such as corruption; and if not solved, countries will never be able to sustain themselves due to their reliance on aid. In this chapter, I examine whether foreign aid helps or hinders "development" by evaluating and contrasting the views of three prominent development scholars. We present the argument that the only way to break the cycle of dependency on foreign aid is to develop economically; fighting disease with foreign aid is a great humanitarian deed yet, aid promotes the problems of corruption and a weak economy, more than it solves it, thereby, preventing countries from developing and becoming self-sufficient. While the humanitarians amongst us wish to see aid as the product of selflessness, a belief in equality, and to protect human rights, the reality is different. The second aspect of this article discusses the value of human rights and how they are linked to foreign aid. In the third section, three case studies are presented: Democratic Republic of Congo (DRC), Iraq, and Turkey. With these, I attempt to demonstrate why donor countries continue to provide bilateral aid despite signs of either poor development or blatant violations of fundamental rights that foreign aid ultimately seeks to "correct."

Foreign Aid: Shortcomings of Temporary Solutions

"Foreign Aid Works—It Saves Lives," argues that foreign aid is successful; he refers to a study by Gabriel Demombynes and Sofia Trommlerova, which looks at how anti malaria nets have contributed to a significant decrease in the mortality rate of infants in Kenya (Demombynes and Trommlerova, 2012). This example is representative of Sachs overall argument that foreign aid saves lives and, therefore, aids development. However, the question remains: *How we can measure the success of foreign aid?* A great deal of financial resources have gone into helping developing countries, yet, despite billions of U.S. dollars of aid given the situation does not appear to improve substantially, as the news reports of human rights violations and suffering, on a daily basis. From a humanitarian and statistical standpoint, foreign aid contributes to development, leads to decreased mortality rates, and increased birth rates, bringing these statistical values closer to those of developed countries. Sachs, Easterly, and Moyo agree that aid helps combat disease. Furthermore, it cannot be argued that building schools, wells, and hospitals is not beneficial for the development of a country from an infrastructure point of view. However, an increased population means that wealth needs to be evenly distributed among people and communities, and for economically weak countries struggling with poverty, failure to do so causes them to be even more reliant on foreign aid in order to combat poverty. Although improved infrastructure and education through foreign aid might be in place now, this does not mean it is, or can be used efficiently. As Moyo suggests, political instability and unrest disrupts development, and even educated elites of countries such as Zambia cannot help their country because the flaws inherent within the political system and the rampant corruption that habitually prevents significant progress (2010). *Does foreign aid reach the ones in need?* Easterly (2007) contends as follows:

> Africa continues to be the poorest region in the world, even though it is the most aid intensive in the world, it had the worst economic growth, and it basically had zero rise in living standards since independence despite 568 billion dollars going to Africa over that time period.

While foreign aid has the potential to positively impact development because of its influence on poverty and disease, the results might be short-lived because all it does is *relieve* poverty (Easterly, 2003, 2007). However, one should not be so quick to dismiss foreign aid as either shallow in effect or producing only short-term results. In fact, the problem might be associated with financial commitments rather than the formulation of development policy and subsequent implementation of development projects. Sachs (2012b) reasons that there is simply not enough being *done* for aid and that a figure of USD $40 billion aid per year has to be reached in order to achieve even greater progress and results. He identifies a critical point in terms of financial commitment that, once reached, can begin to yield positive results. Therefore, aid dependency is intricately connected to a threshold of support not being made, which in-turn results in developing countries becoming stuck at certain levels of development.

Over the past two decades, the World Bank has increased its efforts for decentralization in developing countries with the view of bringing governments closer to various peoples and communities (Lessman and Markwardt, 2012: 1723). This would make aid more efficient, in principle, as local authorities could then identify specific needs and assign priorities to development projects to combat disease and poverty. Easterly (2007) states that this as a potential solution as the money does not reach areas in greatest need given that it gets lost through corruption in the process. In countries where a stable political framework is in place, such as South Africa, aid is more effective and can be of assistance to development (Moyo, 2009). However, this does not apply to countries in which corruption is a problem. Giving money to autocratic rulers only facilitates their rule, enhances existing levels of corruption, and tightens the government's grip on the country's wealth. Both Moyo (2009) and Easterly (2007) argue that not only are many African countries polluted with corrupt officials, but the aid-giving process *itself* is corrupt. *What accounts for this?* Transparency issues and lack of accountability to ensure that the money is being used for its intended purpose become the primary suspects. When countries, corrupt or not, become aid-dependant, they undergo an interesting yet simple process whereby they become more accountable to the country providing aid rather than to their own people (Easterly, 2007). In other words, a foreign government sets the agenda on how to *fix* a developing country rather than allowing recipient countries' extensive levels of autonomy. As Easterly (2007: PAGE) explains in an interview, aid comes with "lots of conditions attached, which often destroys the effectiveness of the aid." Sachs (2012b) dismisses the focus on corruption in turn, claiming that "hunger translates to instability." In a sense, aid does help development, as it is required for stability, which in turn is needed for progress. Such progress in medical aid has been made and is extremely successful as evidenced by how effective the fight against malaria has been. That same model can be applied to other points.

When evaluating the research conducted by these three scholars, it becomes clear that the difference of opinion stems from a fundamental discrepancy. Sachs (2012a, b) argues in favor of the positives that are being done and looks to the future with optimism. Although Africa, for example, has been slow in developing, he points to the rather controversial Millennium Development Goals (MDGs). In this vein, he argues that there is progress being made and that, "a lot of countries will not meet the goals by 2015, but the way to achieve the goals has become more and more clear" (Sachs, 2012b). Moyo (2010) argues that countries have started to perceive "governments start to view aid income as permanent income" and goes on to explain that there needs to be more focus on Foreign Direct Investment (FDI) and trade in order to substitute the aid model. She further evaluates the differences in aid, suggesting, what Sachs calls "progress," is "a good idea in the short term, but it is not going to help in the long term not work in the long term [...] view those types of intervention as a band aid solution" (Moyo, 2010). This corroborates with the arguments made by scholars such as Easterly (2003:2) where "[w]e find that aid has a positive impact on growth in developing countries with good fiscal, monetary, and trade policies but has little effect in the presence of poor policies." Unfortunately, we might thus see aid as neither a short-term nor a long-term solution. To support the latter, aid does not work to promote development, as the fundamental framework required to achieve this is not in place because of issues such as corruption.

Easterly (2003) and Moyo (2010) argue against aid as a suitable or effective way to help countries and promote development because it only masks the real problems of corruption and an overall ill-managed bureaucracy (i.e., political system). Accordingly, they identify problems such as a lack of accountability and transparency in the aid-giving process resulting in development being hindered finding its ways to areas of countries for which it was never intended. While they do not dismiss the arguments of Sachs, who accredits the development and progress as part of the MDGs and reducing the devastating impact that malaria has had in Africa and other parts of the world to the work of aid, notes that still more has to be done. In spite of this, Moyo (2010) puts this kind of aid into perspective as short-term solutions that do not address economic underdevelopment and inequality. Aid does not solve political instability, end or prevent human right violations, nor necessarily find its way to those areas that need it most. Both Easterly (2003, 2007) and Moyo (2010) concur with the argument that aid leads to aid dependency, which will always encumber the intentions of aid donors through even major development plans because it worsens existing political and, thus, social problems. This leads to a critical question: *Why is foreign aid such a widely used concept by Western governments when they do more bad than good and appear to have little to no gain from doing so?*

Human Rights: Rights with No Value?

Human rights violations have become part of the day-to-day life of many parts of the world. They are represented in various extremes such as the repression of freedom of speech (a verity that is even found breeding ground in even the most advanced liberal democratic societies), the prevention of people from realizing political, social, and economic statuses on the basis of self-determination, the prevention of the freedom of movement, tyranny over religious expression, and even outright political violence (sometimes systematic campaign of violence against one's own population in the form of physical and mental torture, and abuse as well as unfair prosecution, and even genocide). The list of human right violations is endless, and they even occur in countries that are receiving a wealth of foreign aid by Western governments and organizations such as the World Bank. Over the past several decades, the international community has often responded to human rights violations and punished human rights violators when they have reached extreme levels. Examples include the ending of Apartheid in South Africa; the North Atlantic Treaty Organization's (NATO) invention in South East Europe (SEE), which resulted in the prosecution of human rights violator and war criminal Slobodan Milošević; and the U.S. led invasion in Iraq in 2003 which rid the country of Saddam Hussein, whose authoritarian leadership violated human rights and discriminated the Sunni minority for years. *What happens when human rights violations are being punished? How do they get resolved and is there a framework in place that protects the individuals?*

Generally, it is assumed that human rights violations widely go unpunished and are simply ignored because there is no effective governing body, which has the legislative rights as well as the executive power to do so. Individuals also find it incredibly difficult to bring about major changes to the foreign policy aims of a state. This is logical given that a country like the United States would not adjust its foreign policy so as to focus considerably on human rights violations in Nigeria by a violent regional terrorist group like Boko Haram and governmental forces if neither actor poses a threat to the U.S. national security agenda. The attacks of 9/11 on the Twin Towers and the Pentagon resulted in the Bush-Cheney-Rumsfeld administration declaring the "War on Terror" (WoT) and in official documentation of the Office of the United Nations High Commissioner for Human Rights (OHCHR) (2008:4), a simplistic notion was put forward under which conditions of human rights can be made flexible for counterterrorism (CT) purposes. That provision states

> for each measure, one must determine whether, given the importance of the right or freedom, the impact of the measure on the enjoyment of that right or freedom is

proportional to the importance of the objective being pursued by the measure and its potential effectiveness in achieving that objective.

If CT policies can be altered in the name of protection of human rights while, and through, violating the rights of the citizens whom they are meant to protect, it is of little surprise that foreign aid is given to governments that actively, and knowingly to the donors, violate human rights themselves. Thus, *human rights* is merely a loose term while in regards to CT, the WoT is only a "war" of extraordinary measures constructed in the midst of an act of macro-securitization, as the term justifies the tools "we" in order to fight an elusive enemy—if we are to assume that that WoT was/is, in fact, a "war" directed at terrorists/insurgents and not merely a tactic. The WoT is fought within the legal limits and the process of litigation of human rights shapes and dictates policy choice to a large extent as it determines the extremes to which it is both conducted—constantly pushing the boundaries of what is legally justifiable (Duffy, 2008:582). Therefore, we can conclude that the protection of human rights does, to a large extent, fail to influence decision-making by individual states if it fits the foreign policy aims. This raises the question: *What framework is in place to ensure the protection of human rights?*

There are a wide variety of pressure groups, nongovernmental organizations (NGOs), social movements, and other institutions of various kinds that, through different funding sources, pursue the protection of human rights. *How do human rights violations impact foreign aid payments?* With regards to bilateral aid, we find that there is, in fact, little impact. According to Lebovic and Voeten (2009:82), studies on the matter suggest that, "despite their self-proclaimed commitment to human rights, aid allocations are largely based on the political objectives of donors and, less so, on the economic needs of recipients and/or their rights practices." Moreover, the allocation of aid should be regarded as rewarded according to "economic (trade), historical (colonial ties), political (United Nations [UN] voting), and military relevance (security ties) to the donor," as opposed to being based on their adherence to human rights and *rewarding* or *punishing* them. In *The Cost of Shame: International Organizations and Foreign Aid in the Punishing of Human Rights Violators*, Lebovic and Voeten (2009:93) employ a healthy body of empirical findings to investigate the relationship between human rights violations and foreign aid in the form of multilateral aid. Their research demonstrates that a "UNCHR resolution is estimated, in most model specifications, to coincide with a drop in a country's multilateral aid share of around 40 per cent," meaning that, "poor human rights performance are correlated with large reductions in World Bank and multilateral loan commitments, but have no impact on bilateral aid allocations."

The protection of human rights is a difficult affair as the institutions that are meant to protect them have little leverage to enforce them. If bilateral aid is not significantly affected by human rights violations, then a decrease of roughly 40% in multilateral aid will do more harm than good in humanitarian terms as it is fair to assume that countries that violate human rights would be prone to neglecting allocation of sufficient amounts to human development projects—even, more so, if a shortage of funds occurs. Thus, cutting a state's funds based on human rights violations can be a double-edged sword as it is very difficult to reduce foreign aid for specific projects and still ensure aid allocation, for instance, for education, reduction of poverty, and improvements in gender equality, does not suffer due to lack of transparency. If the UN and the World Bank are serious about creating an effective framework for protecting human rights, they need to do more than hoping and providing money for problematic and corrupt states. This requires cooperation with individual donor countries and the establishment of an aid package plan similar to the Marshall Plan, which effectively reconstructed (at least Western) Europe following the Second World War.

Importance of Foreign Aid

We have so far discussed the ineffectiveness of foreign aid in attaining an independent country with a self-sufficient economy, and consistent economic growth. We have also established that a lack of respect toward upholding human rights on a global scale is represented in both, not only in policy action by governments but also in their foreign aid allocation. We now discuss reasons why foreign aid is an important foreign policy tool by displaying three different examples of how foreign aid is employed with the aim of obtaining positive results; by engaging with the Democratic Republic of Congo (DRC), Iraq, and Turkey.

While the majority of aid can be viewed as an altruistic practice to stabilize countries scarred by civil war and poverty, there are always underlying political benefits. This decade's failed states consist of Afghanistan, Angola, Burundi, the DRC, Liberia, Sierra Leone, and Sudan (Rotberg, 2003: 10). The situation in DRC is representative of how aid is intended to prevent state failure. The DRC is resource-rich, however, UN sanctions monitors reported in 2014 that, as a result of corruption and lack of transparency, "98% of the gold produced in [the] DRC 'is smuggled out of the country' and that as a result, [the] DRC and Uganda—the main transit country for Congolese gold—'are losing millions of dollars annually in tax revenue and tolerating a system that is financing armed groups'" (Arieff, 2014: 12). This is an example of how the path that the DRC is currently pursuing toward state failure is already negatively affecting surrounding countries. Furthermore, for the international system, a failed state is problematic as events such as violent civil war and unrest can spread across borders, and can develop a local conflict into a regional conflict or war. Additionally, we should underscore the notion that failed states are prone to hosting terrorist and other criminal organizations that can have a detrimental impact on local and regional economies as well as the international economy overall. In the case of the DRC, aid alone achieves very little. Instead, the country needs to create its infrastructure and economy to eventually become self-sufficient and decrease its reliance on foreign aid. Until then, however, the United Nations Organization Stabilization Mission in the Democratic Republic of the Congo (MONUSCO) and other projects work together in an attempt to reestablish human rights through humanitarian work, aimed at health and education, to protect the vulnerable population from the human rights violators who rule the country. The United States is currently the largest contributor of MUNESCO peacekeeping operations. However, the allocation is an issue heavily discussed in the United States, as an investment of this nature requires justification. Therefore, the Arieff (2014: 18) identifies the following aspects instrumental for Congress' decisions about the future of U.S. aid:

1. The impact and strategic design of U.S. aid to DRC such as whether aid flows to the areas of greatest need and/or the highest U.S. national interests
2. The degree to which U.S. aid to DRC and neighboring states can or should be conditioned or restricted as a tool of policy leverage
3. The relative effectiveness of various tools for exerting U.S. influence such as diplomacy, foreign assistance, and U.S. actions in multilateral fora
4. The degree to which the Kabila government has shown progress in confronting deeply ingrained problems related to the security sector, economic governance, accountability for human rights abuses, and state capacity

This illustrates that foreign aid is seen as a business decision, human right violations do not impact the decision making for bilateral aid because human rights usually fall beneath such issues as national security. While neglecting human rights violations appears an amoral policy, the national interests, or the promotion of national interests through moral concerns, are at the heart of the nation state.

The United States has frequently employed the WoT as very convenient justification for fighting the war against organizations such as the Islamic State of Iraq and Syria (ISIS) and al-Qaeda in the problematic and strategically important region of the Middle East. Iraq, a country with a wealth of natural resources and some of the world's largest natural oil and gas reserves, had large parts of its country destroyed due to the Iraq War, which commenced in 2003. The official justification for the war was the need to defeat "a regime that developed and used weapons of mass destruction [WMDs], that harbored and supported terrorists, committed outrageous human rights abuses, and defied the just demands of the United Nations and the world" (US Department of State [DoS], 2003). However, it was revealed that Iraq never possessed WMDs, and it is widely speculated that the war was about ensuring Iraq would remain a reliable source of oil for the United States. As early as 2001, the UN noted, "Iraq continues to face significant technical and infrastructural problems, which unless addressed will inevitably result in the reduction of crude oil production" (Council on Foreign Relations [CFR], 2003: 20). The problem, if solved, benefitted not only countries such as the United States, but also there was hope that, "Iraqi gas might feed into a pipeline system carrying gas from several potential suppliers across Turkey to Europe, if such a system is built" (CFR, 2003: 25). Iraq received USD $174 million of foreign aid prior to the conflict in 2000, a figure that would increase enormously by 2008 (United Nations Development Program [UNDP], 2011: 157). This makes Iraq the highest recipient of official development aid, the reason behind this is that a democratic and stable Iraq will have a significant impact on peace in the Middle East and also strong economic benefits. Moreover, it could provide Europe (specifically members states of the European Union [EU]) with a way of diversifying its energy portfolio, thereby reducing its energy dependency on Russia.

One of the highest recipients of foreign aid in 2014 was Turkey. There is a long-standing donor–recipient relationship between Turkey and the United States as well as the EU. Geopolitically, Turkey is of significant value because it connects the "West" with the "East" and, therefore,, poses a great security risk if it were to become and remain politically unstable. During the Cold War, Turkey was home to U.S. nuclear weapons due to its proximity to the Soviet Union and, as compensation received large amounts of bilateral foreign aid. It has since been one of the main recipients of U.S. foreign aid despite habitual human rights violations (Lee, 2011: 8–9). However, the benefits of maintaining close relations with Turkey far outweigh(ed) concerns about human rights violations. In a 1992 report, Human Rights Watch (HRW) stated that, "the Bush [a] dministration, like the Reagan [a]dministration, has never linked human rights to foreign aid for Turkey" (Callaway and Matthews, 2008: 154). While the United States used the "carrot and stick" approach to promoting human rights in Turkey, the emphasis was placed on "carrot" rather than "stick." Irrespective of promises made to the Turkish government by the United States, the human rights situation in Turkey has generally remained the same. This was certainly the case until Turkey's ambitions to join the EU were made abundantly clear during the late 1990s. Due to the political instability that can be caused through human rights violations, the situation had to significantly improve in order to fulfill the conditions set by the EU otherwise accession for Turkey would have remained an impossibility—and could not be justified purely by means of geopolitical/geostrategic importance. Overall, the EU-U.S.-Turkey foreign aid donor–recipient relationship can be summed up as one in which the United States "did not, and does not, in practice, link US foreign aid to human rights in Turkey, whereas the European Union clearly and unambiguously links accession to membership to human rights" (Callaway and Matthews, 2008: 157).

Conclusion

Conceptually, foreign aid is heavily linked to human rights. However, the reality is that Western governments, the majority of which are donors, are willing to accept what can only be described as a "necessary evil" in the achievement of national security and foreign policy matrices. We might actually refer to the practice as a utopian notion where states perceive foreign aid as being provided based on merit and with the intention of moving toward the protection and strengthening of human rights. Unilateral aid, as the discussion presented in this chapter has shown, retains an element of humanity when it comes to the protection of human rights; however, the underlying policy function of foreign aid is to ensure the stability of the international economic system by ensuring that state failure does not occur. The World Bank and the UN simply cannot seize aid packages completely on the basis that human rights violations are occurring. *Why?* Such measures will simply contribute to continued violations. Thus, institutions require a framework in which they reward governments for improving human rights situations—seeking not only to protect but also to strengthen them—however, we should acknowledge that they lack the physical tools to do so as diplomacy has proven its many limitations. Bilateral aid limits the effectiveness by neglecting human rights violations through the pursuit of rationalist foreign policy goals. The example of the DRC shows that economic benefits and regional geopolitical effectiveness of bilateral aid determines investment. The WoT embodies the achievement of foreign policy aims through extraordinary measures, the implementations of which are justifiable through the flexibility of international human rights law. Moreover, the case of Iraq exemplifies that underlying economic and security benefits are an integral part of the reason the U.S.-led invasion in 2003 actually came to fruition while security concerns resulting from terrorist and insurgent groups/organizations played a secondary role. Finally, the example of Turkey displays that governments are not motivated to improve their human rights situations unless there is considerable material benefit for that country, making both human rights violations and foreign aid an effective foreign policy tool.

References

Arieff, A. 2014. Democratic Republic of Congo: Background and US Policy. Congressional Research Service Report No. R43166, Washington, DC.

Callaway, R. L. and Matthews, E. G. 2008. *Strategic US Foreign Assistance the Battle between Human Rights and National Security*. Farnham, UK: Ashgate.

Council on Foreign Relations. 2003. *Guiding Principles for US Post-Conflict Policy in Iraq*. New York, NY.

Demombynes, G. and Trommlerova, S. K. 2012. What Has Driven the Decline of Infant Mortality in Kenya? World Bank Policy Research Working Paper No. 6057, Washington, DC.

DoS. 2003. *Winning the War on Terror*. Washington, DC.

Duffy, H. 2008. Human rights litigation and the 'war on terror', *International Review of The Red Cross*, 90(871): 573–97.

Easterly, W. 2003. Can Foreign Aid Buy Growth?, *The Journal of Economic Perspectives*, 17(3): 23–48.

Easterly, W. 2007. *Riz Khan*. Interviewed by Riz Khan [video], Al Jazeera.

Lebovic, J. H. and Voeten, E. 2009. The cost of shame: International organizations and foreign aid in the punishing of human rights violators, *Journal of Peace Research*, 46(1): 79–97.

Lee, H. J. 2011. *The Impact of US Foreign Aid on Human Rights Conditions in the Post-Cold War Era*. PhD thesis No. 12068, Iowa State University.

Lessmann, C. and Markwardt, G. 2012. Aid, growth, and devolution, *World Development*, 40(9): 1723–49.

Moyo, D. 2009. *Dead Aid: Why Aid Is Not Working and How There Is a Better Way for Africa*. New York: Farrar, Straus, and Grioux.

Moyo, D. 2010. Why Aid to Africa Has Been a Disaster. Interviewed by Allan Gregg [video], TV Ontario (TVO), November 24, 2012.

OHCHR. 2008. Human Rights, Terrorism and Counter-Terrorism. Fact Sheet No. 32.

Rotberg, R. I. (ed.) 2003. *When States Fail: Causes and Consequences*. Princeton, NJ: Princeton University Press.

Sachs, J. 2012a. Foreign Aid Works—It Saves Lives. *The Guardian*.

Sachs, J. 2012b. Jeffrey Sachs on Development Aid. Interviewed by Larry Elliot [video], *The Guardian*, April 12, 2012.

UNDP. 2011. *Towards Human Resilience: Sustaining MDG Progress in an Age of Economic Uncertainty*. New York: UNDP.

Chapter 12

Discrimination and Hate: Overcriminalization or New Normativity?[*]

Charis Papacharalambous

Contents

Introduction

Hate crime laws present a new paradigm in criminal law: they require incrimination of civil and human rights violations. Their *militant* nature undermines the traditional inflexibility of *pro reo* and *pro libertate* axioms in criminal law. They also represent a *holistic* incrimination approach as they should cover (according to the definition of "hate" one chooses) every form of relevant behavior—conceived of as a part of an organic whole.[†] Indeed, hate crimes are in this regard a candidate for a methodology, which has been (as allegedly representing epistemologically a version

---

[*] This chapter is a revised version of the author's published article: Papacharalambous, C. 2013. Discrimination and hate: Over-criminalization or new normativity? *International Law Research*, 2(1): 195–205.
[†] This characteristic may lead to a variety of scopes of law application and is also prone to promote a fear of crime panic (see Jacobs/Potter, 2001: 11–28, 45–64).

of "organicism" and politically a version of "totalitarianism") the target of critique in Popper's *"Poverty of Historicism"* (Popper 2005:63–5 [=Chapter I.7, 132–53] [=Chapter III.23–4]). Finally, hate crime laws found liability in a primarily *subjective* mode (i.e., on the fact that the perpetrator is motivated by prejudice). A good example is s. 28(1) of the 1998 UK Crime and Disorder Act, whereby it is crucial either that racial hostility was demonstrated during the commission of an offense or that the offense was motivated by such hostility.

All this has been exposed to a steady critique. It is argued that criminal legislation against hate crimes can tentatively become purely *symbolic*, satisfying ideological and media needs through law rhetoric, which can obliquely enhance or spread societal divisions and prejudices, while in parallel—the argument continues—*empirical verification* of the necessity for hate crime laws is to a significant degree lacking (Jacobs and Potter, 2001:65–91, 130–44). Further, hate crime laws seem to infringe on constitutional rights (especially free speech) by punishing more severely not the conduct based on the bigot's view, but merely and preemptively the bigot's view itself—producing the so-called "chilling effect" of the respective law restrictions onto the right (Jacobs and Potter, 2001:111–29). It is also said that such legislation prepares difficulties to judges and prosecutors, makes police work more perplexing and turns (by using the prison system) counterproductive—because it is this system itself that generates bias-based attitudes (Jacobs and Potter, 2001:92–110).

Dilemmatic Stand of the Reaction of the Democratic Legal Systems in the West

Through all this, the courts are very often confronted with a real mess. The United States (U.S.) Supreme Court decisions *R.A.V. v. City of St. Paul* (1992) and *Virginia v. Black* (2003) are outstanding in this respect: on the one hand they try to conserve the free speech field as wide as possible, extending it also to speech forms, which remain constitutionally unprotected in principle (the respective "categorization method" is being made thematic below); on the other, they try to deal with the incrimination requirement by recurring to labels such as "virulence," criminally relevant "secondary effects of the speech," or "compelling state interest" in disavowing certain opinions or teachings as false or merely offending (Christou, 2007:94–8, 204; see on this case law also Weinstein 2010b: 84–8; Jacobs and Potter, 2001:121–9). One has to bear in mind that both decisions have been issued on cases of Klan or Klan-like burnings of wooden crosses in the garden of Afro-American family houses (see on this case law Heyman, 2010: 164 footnote 27).

In this framework it is hardly possible to maintain a sound distinction between (marginally still allowed) *content-based* and *viewpoint-based* laws against hate conduct. The first incriminate the message conveyed as *per se* violating legal interests; insofar as these laws constitute principally already illegitimate speech regulations—in that they surpass either the indirect act prohibitions or the "pure speech" restrictions concerning circumstances of the pronouncement ("content neutral speech regulations"). However, they are still held independent of the viewpoint underlying the message. The laws of this second category are namely laws directly incriminating such underlying views and are therefore considered as pure censorship (see on all these distinctions in the U.S. doctrine, Christou, 2007: 89–93). Worse than this blurring of boundaries is the fact that hate crime has totally fallen out of sight here, because there is no way to combat it without exactly involving viewpoints in the criminal law (see especially on this critical point, Christou, 2007: 98–9). This is another mode of saying that *the word is the harm*, that these notions are in hate speech inseparable from one another—whereas in hate *crimes* in the strict sense, the severity of hate conduct is extremely legible in an autonomously occurring result (Levin, 1999: 11–9).

As it is well argued, hate speech causes harm not only by directly traumatizing target group victims in a way analogous to causing short-term effects on vulnerable victims through abusive conduct, but also by indirectly promoting a social environment of inequality and (looming or exercised) violence (Sumner, 2010: 207–11). The more remote the incriminated conduct is from the real perpetration of a hate crime, the more illegitimate it becomes as an inchoate crime; if instigation presupposes a primary act and incitement is a legitimate inchoate form of crime, provisions generally incriminating promotion or dissemination of hatred lose any linkage to a criminal conduct—as long as "hatred" is a feeling that is not criminal in itself (Sumner, 2010:212–20; Weinstein, 2010a: 53–55). However, given the abstractly endangering nature of hate speech, it should be possible for a democratic (although not absolutely and exclusively liberal) state to recur to such "doubly inchoate" conduct not only for symbolic reasons, but by taking very seriously the need for a preemptive reaction to hate speech due to the latter's characteristics.

Main Forms of Dealing with Hate through Criminal Law

The embarrassment hate crime laws present to the criminal law system is apparent in that all modes of traditional doctrinal attempts to deal with it must fail. We can discern three of them.

Violation of a Person's Reputation?

The connection of hate with *honor or reputation violation* is the first one. The *first* problem here is that one is forced to affirm the construct of "group libel" and insofar to accordingly transform the individual-based conception of harm—that in general is traditionally ascribed to libel. A *second* problem arises from the fact that one thus seems to promote identity politics in favor of collective entities, which is strongly debated in the fields of constitutional law and liberal political theory. For the majority of the academics in the United States, the only decision favoring group libel laws—the *Beauharnais v. Illinois* from 1952, a case of white supremacist propaganda—has been revised (Christou, 2007:161–215; Weinstein, 2010a: 58–60; Weinstein, 2010b: 87–8). On the above as well as to the entanglement of identity politics with symbolic criminal legislation, see Jacobs and Potter (2001:65–78, 114–7, 130–44; cf.). For the well-known differentiated approach of conceding the existence of rights related to collective identities *within* a liberal political frame, see Kymlicka (1996: passim, and especially Chapters 2 through 4 and 6 through 9).

Further—and especially concerning the common law tradition, more specifically the U.S. law—there is no such thing as "honor," which can be identified in the continental criminal law; to be protected is rather the reputation understood as "market value" the damage of which can be recovered through tort law compensation. This can be achieved only under the terms of the critical statement being false and done with actual malice (Christou 2007:125–30, 141–6, 154, 160–1).

After *N. Y. Times v. Sullivan*, the U.S. Supreme Court made even libel laws dependent upon more demanding scrutiny requirements, thus "constitutionalizing" them too (Christou, 2007:155–60). *Finally*, defamation is criminalized only as long as it constitutes a public order offense; as to the rest, hate speech is considered as extreme political expression and thus in the United States principally protected through the First Amendment: according to the "strict scrutiny" procedure, the possibility of granting constitutionality to criminal law restrictions of free speech is almost equal to null.* At the European level, however, the recognition of the group libel through hate speech is obvious throughout the recent case law of the European Court of Human Rights (hereafter ECtHR). Thus, at a more universal level we have a clear case of *ambiguous treatment* in identifying hate with libel. Clear of course is that the ECtHR treats extreme speech in a more austere manner when associations or parties are active; this is so because of the danger for others' rights or the public order their organizational structure represents, see Christou (2007:372, 375–6; see Hare 2010a: 72–4).

Profound Assault on Dignity? A Crux for Liberalism

A second alternative is the connection of hate crime with *violation of human dignity*. In the *civil law tradition* (i.e., in the German criminal law) one could uncover a stream of legal thought strongly affirming an axiological concept of dignity upon which a distinction between, say, "deep personhood" and "mere" personality in the sense of exerting social roles is based; according to this distinction, hate crime can be more clearly shown to be a violation of this deep substrate of the person over which one cannot dispose (ethnicity, biologically determined capabilities, sexual orientation, and the like). Such offenses—especially when committed in public—deserve punishment in the spirit of this tradition. As to the rest, one can recur to the general civil and criminal laws or to the eventual specific antidiscrimination laws (see respectively: Christou, 2007:216–34, 244–7).

In contradistinction to this, *the U.S. law* promotes criminalization of discrimination in the commercial private sector (except contracts or agreements affecting highly personal relations like hiring a governess or getting married); this is the case with prohibitions of entry to people of color. On the other hand, this tradition dismisses restrictions of hate speech even when the latter is publicly expressed. No metaphysical dignity is recognized and any approach of the person going beyond the notion of a procedurally intact claimant connotes for many liberal ideals of solidarity suspect of crypto-communitarian preoccupations (Christou, 2007: 211–5, 234–8, 241, 244–7).

The only way to bring someone to justice is then to have a case where an "act" instead of mere "speech" is at stake. This is the famous *act–speech dichotomy* established with the Supreme Court decision in *Chaplinsky v. N. Hampshire* from 1942 and its "categorization approach"—according to which obscene, profane, or extremely aggressive speech has been subtracted from First Amendment protection (in the Court case a Jehovah witness has called a policeman "god damned fascist" and "racketeer"). This can be of no concern as long as a result or at least a conduct hate crime has been committed; in the case of hate speech, the victims remain without protection in the framework of a (considered as "free") "marketplace of ideas"—the "firstness" of which is inflexibly presupposed on the grounds of an abstract deontology based on an unreflectively assumed methodological individualism: whenever individuals are not endangered the speech runs free—principally without context-dependent balancing—as long as only a "definitional" balancing is held as proper (Christou, 2007: 51–74, 133–9; for a recent exhaustive review of the characteristics of the "marketplace of ideas" topic, see Salton 2012: 1–6). Israel (1999:108) very correctly notes that this "marketplace"

---

* As to the differentiations among "strict scrutiny," "intermediate scrutiny," (reserved for deteriorations of speech acts and aiming at protection of important public goals), and "rational basis test" (on issues of freedom of action in general or of contractual freedom, whereby restrictions are normally held as in conformity with the First Amendment), see Christou, 2007: passim (material taken from here and there) and at 31 and footnote 18, 58–9, 351 and footnote 47, 386.

has become a poor regulator. When a speech issue becomes politicized there is no intellectual free trade, but an intense competition of sound bites and phrases calculated to catch the attention of a bored public emerges. The press has an appetite for the "other side."

One tries to heal this in attempting to trace some harm behind the speech; if the latter can be conceived of as intralinguistic effect (namely as inherent in the speech and occurring through it) his is embracing *John Austin's "speech–act" theory*. According to this, the victim of hate speech is, in a sense, forcibly "silenced" in his/her very right to behave freely and spontaneously. If criminal law, the argument continues, punishes "perlocutionary" effects, namely extralinguistic effects of the speech—as is the case with instigation or incitement—there is reason to punish also the illocutions as something less than incitement but sufficiently more than mere words (Christou, 2007: 238–43). One could add to this also, that in any case what is at stake in terms of hate speech is not the epistemic aspect, the truthfulness or not of "facts" raised by a pronouncement, but the very moral/ethical aspect of its normative unacceptability, an aspect more suitably envisaged by a rather "positive" (normatively disciplined) as opposed to a "negative" (morally neutral) account of freedom rights (Christou, 2007: 38–9, 103–5).

The *problem* with this is that for the enactment of criminal law sanctions, the judgment should be secure; that is, based on a clear-cut distinction between free and harmful conduct. Wherever the judgment is controversial as to whether what has been done is harm, then the *in dubio principle* prevails. We could resist this by widening the protection scope up to the "offense principle."* We could abandon the requirement of having a "palpable" violation for punishing hate. That hate speech violates fundamental rights is in any case well established theoretically (see a well-founded approach on this focusing on recognition denial through hate in Heyman, 2010: 165–9; see Christou, 2007: 186–7 and at footnote 453). In most cases of hate speech, the very meaning of it offends, it redeems no social value and counterarguing against legitimizes it (Israel 1999: 106–9). This discussion is, of course, still open: Owen Fiss assumes a harm caused by hate speech, and Joseph Raz also argues that toleration of hate speech means primarily its acceptance—that is unbearable for a democratic state. Others argue differently; for instance, R. Dworkin senses concessions to "paternalism" behind these arguments (see on these standpoints, Christou, 2007: 105–7, 243, 246–7, 381–2).

It seems all the more that liberalism must deny normatively well-established rights if it insists in being strictly coherent. Thus, it cannot guarantee gender equality and protection from domestic violence if religious freedom is granted a space within which women are clearly disempowered (Evans, 2010: 364, 368–74). More fundamentally, the very implication of modern liberalism that legitimacy can only be the outcome of a deliberative procedure (whereby the best argument shall prevail) is completely idealistic; its Habermasian/Rulsian impetus sidesteps the very meaning of value-laden controversies, devalues their passionate nature through overrationalizing the conflict of beliefs and imposes the U.S. particularity of autonomy's and individual freedom's glorification upon cultures structured otherwise (on this and especially the Israeli–U.S. cultural/legal differentiation, see Reichman, 2010: 336–7, 342–5, 350–2; analogously, see Christou, 2007: 41–3

---

* Joel Feinberg's well-known distinction can be followed here, especially the qualifications he makes thematic through dealing with "profound offenses" whereby also expressions of hate are primary candidates. Cf. Feinberg, 1987: 50–96; see respectively also Herring, 2008:24. See Christou, 2007: 328–30, as to the utilization of the offense principle in the jurisdiction of the German Constitutional Court concerning hate speech and public security.

on the U.S. "individualism" vs. German "Republican communitarianism" differentiation). Even sociologically, one can discern in the United States a deeply rooted idiosyncratic culture of aggressively displaying disrespect to Eurocentric hegemonic elite norms, which produces a populist "leveling down" effect, so contrary to the European "elitist" normativism (see on this view of J. Q. Whitman, i.e., Post 2010: 137–8; Christou, 2007: 114–6).

This is the case unless we conceive of liberalism not in the sense of mere agnostic toleration (whereby free speech serves the wider social benefits) but in a principled sense whereby free speech is a non-instrumental value in itself, capable of combating adverse values such as religious oversensitivity. In conformity with an according cosmopolitan interpretation of Article 10 European Court of Human Rights (ECtHR), freedom of (even emotively charged) speech outbalances a supposed "right not to be religiously offended" (Cram, 2010: 316–27; analogously favoring a non-instrumental value of free speech also Weinstein 2010a: 60–1). On the other hand, the value is nonetheless inherently "thin" as long as normative expectancies are concerned, whereas the "communitarian" alternative looks rather overly-"thick" as long as liberties and rights are concerned: even if value-laden, liberalism is still *too morally oriented* to form something more effective than the complementary flip side of an equally *too much concrete ethics-oriented* communitarian stance. What lacks both is democratic militancy. With regard to such an argument, one cannot save liberalism by trying to reintegrate extremist speech into an overinclusive liberal polity based on "agonistic respect" backed by a discourse ethics—lying principally outside the legal-repressive paradigm and deliberatively proceeding so that extremism may function as collaterally benefiting liberalism in making the latter's legitimacy deficits publicly thematic (cf. this sympathetic attempt by Malik, 2010: 107–20).

In addition, the attempt to save liberalism through Robert Post's theory on "democratic legitimacy" is failing: where racist speech offends a group, not all citizens are "silenced" or "alienated" as this theory would require to allow hate speech to be censored. Protection succumbs thus, practically, again to toleration—since it tacitly presupposes that only peculiar individuals may be candidate offenders, the public conflict turns surreptitiously "reprivatized" (cf. differently Cram, 2010: 327–30; similarly in favor of boundless freedom of expression on liberalistic–pragmatic grounds is Baker, 2010: passim and at 146, 150–7). At least, such theoretical patterns—allegedly displaying the "perennial essence" of a "polity"—turn easily abstract-essentialist or ahistoric (Heinze, 2010b: 190–203). In case one fills liberalism with more thick values, one comes up with nonliberal consequences: if (which is correct) the First Amendment philosophy is to be interpreted as primarily "other-rights-based," that is, not as an absolute value, then the path opens even for the incrimination of private hate speech because it simply negates the rights of others as it is not a right itself any more (Heyman, 2010: 163–4). As Heyman writes

> the balancing of rights is subject to a crucial constraint; an asserted right can derive no value from its negation of another right. If rights like personal security, personality, and equality have positive value, the negation of those rights cannot also have such value (Heyman, 2010: at 164, footnote 25).

This is fine, but then the liberalist edge is cut—and this is the crucial point that Heyman's view uncovers. The exclusion of the hate speech perpetrators is suggested exactly in the manner that common crime is usually excluded; that is, without legitimacy concerns. It is the peculiarity of hate speech that liberalist accounts risk missing. They fail to account for the fact that hate speech is not speech in the meaning of a contribution to a noncoerced dialog—since it, by its very essence, blocks the very possibility of beginning any kind of deliberation. Insofar it is not exertion of a right but a systematic and purposeful display of the intent to imminently damage deliberation through rights negation. Far from searching in "unconventional" ways for truth, hate speech destroys the elementary conditions for pursuing truth. If then political discourse is meant as promotion of emancipation and formation of social and interpersonal relations in a democratic manner, hate speech *is not a political attitude* (see, respectively, on all these aspects the lucid text of Heyman, 2010: 169–77).

No other meaning can be given to provisions explicitly excluding racism and anti-Semitism from political discourse, like those of Articles 19 para 3 and 20 para 2 of the 1966 International Covenant on Civil and Political Rights (admitted by Hare, 2010a: 70–1, 76). It is only consistent with supporting the U.S. one-sidedness in protecting free speech when it is argued that the European standards do not serve the freedom of extremists, anti-Semitists, and racists enough (cf. this anti-European, hard core "common law" approach in Hare, 2010a: 78–80). Of course, no argument in favor of liberalism can be made out of abusively referring to clear cases of *politically motivated selectivity*. There, certain contributions to the political arena are excluded and remain unprotected merely due to their "unconventional" nature—disliked by the establishment, as the notorious *Dennis v. US (1951)* has disappointingly shown (see the respective admission of Weinstein, 2010a: 42–3; Weinstein 2010b: 91).

On the other hand, it must be said in favor of another position that Post has maintained that hate speech is this time more accurately discerned. He correctly argues that treating hate speech as endangerment is incorrect. Hate speech is not dangerous like incitement is, it cannot be dealt with as more or less imminent ("clear and present") danger, it is not principally punished for what it may engender (even if empirically this may be the case); opposite to this, hate speech is principally punished, Post continues, because it violates essential social norms of civility and respect, because it is already a *harm* insofar and *not merely a risk* for letting something else occur (Post, 2010: 129–30, 134–6; cf. to this Weinstein, 2010a: 55–8). The experience of causal connection between speech and violence, as Post (2010: at 136) puts it:

> underscores the subjective sense of disorder that arises whenever social norms of propriety or civility are *violated* [emphasis added] [...] But hate speech regulation is distinctive in that it seeks to repress speech merely because it has 'the tendency' to produce violence or disorder. Law that seeks to suppress speech with this "tendency" is in reality law that seeks to suppress *violations* of essential social norms.

This approach is followed here as long as it both stresses the *specific harmfulness* of hate speech and the *inadequacy* of treating it as a security or public order issue.* But let us see this last option in more detail immediately below.

Shortcomings of the "Public Order" Viewpoint

There is finally a third option: the connection of hate crime with *security interests*. One recurs here to Justice Holmes' formula of a "clear and present danger" emanating from the Supreme Courts'

---

* A contradistinction to both militant-democratic and liberal account for hate crimes constitutes the peculiar "pacifistic" approach of Jacobs/Potter, 2001: 144–53, inclined to promote as criminal policy the total extinction of antihate laws for the sake of "integrity" and "non-division" of society. It goes without saying that this *a-political* stance (insofar as political cannot but mean schism and conflict) is totally incompatible with the position supported here.

case law during the intrawar period. Modified (through the interpretations of Justices Learned Hand and Brandeis) from context-dependent judging toward "classic" incitement incrimination, the test found its best application in *Brandenburg v. Ohio (1969)*. However, this option of solving the problem is futile because such rubrics are destined to deal with crimes against the *state* (such as treason or espionage), which are totally alien to hate crimes (see Christou, 2007: 295–303).

Public order has surfaced also as legal interest violated by hate conduct. This is largely the case in Germany. Notwithstanding the risk that public order may be, through the respective legislation and case law there, so overpowered that it may paternalistically promote pure loyalty instead of autonomously engendered respect for the Constitution, the German solution is basically rightly oriented: undifferentiated formal-negative protection of free speech is subjected to a more ethics-based conception safeguarding the material conditions of moral autonomy and thus propelling the latter (cf., with critical overtones, Christou, 2007: 248–87, especially at 257, 262–3, 276–82. In favor of the German model specifically as to delegitimizing and combating exclusively neo-Nazism, see Papacharalambous, 1991: 287–9, 350–1, with further references). Analogous is the Greek antihate legislation (Christou, 2007: 352). In addition, the British legislative development from 2006 to 2008 concerning the abolition of blasphemy and the introduction of "incitement to religious hatred" aims, in a more functionalistic manner, at security purposes—replacing an outmoded and content-based criminal law prohibition deemed oppressive.

That the public order protection tends through this development to produce a kind of "normative inflation" by multiplying punishable incitement beyond the well-established core of racial hatred is a problem already noticed: for example, religious groups are deemed necessary to protect— groups that are competitive among themselves, well equipped as to budget and logistics and publicly influential (see i.e. Hare 2010b: 296–310). The French paternalist model of guiding society through the state is another variation of promoting security interests. Apart from the involvement of the executive for dissolving dangerous associations (which is similar to the German model of organization dissolution) at an administrative law level (see i.e., Mbongo, 2010: 222, 226–7), the criminal law system establishes a very widened net of provisions—which to a significant degree goes very far beyond security interests in that it protects also human dignity and (group) reputation against hate speech, even when a speech has not been publicly pronounced (Mbongo, 2010: 227–8).

Similar is the construct of the so-called "fighting words" in the United States, which nonetheless has been practically dismissed by the Supreme Court jurisprudence because of "vagueness" or "over-breadth." As to hate speech, the construct seems in its insistence on close interpersonal communication rather outmoded and (due to the weak position of hate speech vulnerable victims) rather misplaced—thus merely symbolically declaring the legal disapproval of provocative conduct in general (Christou, 2007: 288–95). Besides, even this construct has not healed the paradox of hate speech laws conceived of in a static and abstract manner: nonextension of hate laws to ever-new categories of protected persons or groups means discrimination, whereas such extension censors massively (Heinze, 2010a: passim, who pleads for the abolition of hate laws within "longstanding, stable, and prosperous democracies" totally thus soothing and neutering hate laws as politically keen laws: at 285; cf., opposite to this approach, the political nature of *not* adequately applying hate laws within a racism-friendly societal environment is observed by Molnar, 2010).

Progress in the field brought the so-called "true threats" doctrine. Even if a true threat requires a speaker-based approach, it can guarantee punishment to a significant degree by using criteria of "reasonableness." Helpful is also the fact that differently from incitement, true threat lets a communication through the net and the ascription of a purely "normative" causation suffice. *Virginia v. Black* (2003) has mainly given the doctrine its contours without closing all possible loopholes, as a holistic incrimination of hate speech would have it. However, true threats can principally let normative criteria suffice and not require naturalistic causation in the strict sense, capturing also illocutions beyond the perlocutionary pronouncements—an issue already earlier hinted at as crucial (see above under subchapter 3.2; Christou, 2007: 303–21, 325–6, 369). Along these lines, the incrimination of a "threat" as such in the Cypriot Penal Code (art. 91A introduced through L. 56(I)/2001)—namely of terrorizing or intimidating the victim by menacing with the commission of a violent act—was a development in the right direction.

Concluding on the Quintessence of Hate Speech

The whole premise of punishing hate crime by omitting to accurately and comprehensively target it is *misplaced*. The possibilities for misusing hate laws based on security interests for reactionary purposes aside (see on such misuses i.e., Malik, 2010: 99–105), such laws entirely disregard the *new normative underpinnings* of the hate crime prohibitions. We should recall Nazi laws against Jews and opponents; the international crimes as they have been formed from Nuremberg to the International Criminal Court (ICC); cases such as the disputable old decision of Illinois Supreme Court in re: *Village of Skokie v. NSP of America* (1978); further, harassment and domestic violence or the social toleration of widespread commission of heinous organized crimes such as trafficking in humans—escorted by the perpetuation of an incrimination model as totally outmoded as the one based on "individual responsibility."

What is common in these types of conduct and in the respective legal and judicial reaction against them?

First, we have basically to do with *group-based* crimes. Not the individual but a common characteristic of it—shared with others in a way the individual cannot dispose of—is the target of the attack, hence the imminence and the tendency of spreading inherent in the conduct.

Second, the criminal law reaction against discrimination should be *per se* preventive and proactive by principally allowing liability to be established without requiring strict application of causation terms or of the correspondence principle between *actus reus* and *mens rea*; that thus some concessions to a *de facto* reversal of the burden of proof are made is to be admitted, but this cannot put in doubt the legitimacy of abstract endangerment as a generally well-established doctrinal feature, able to apply also here.[*] Prevention will do especially where hate crime and racism turn all the more "terroristic" as in the United States (see, respectively, the historical account attempted in this regard by Petrosino, 1999: passim; as to Afro-Americans see also Torres. 1999: passim). In Cyprus, the antidiscrimination laws enacted in 2002 and 2004—aimed at the necessary harmonization with the respective European Union (EU) directives—follow this pattern in establishing reversal of burden of proof (outside criminal proceedings), affirmative action, and administrative monitoring authorities; especially to be mentioned is L. 42(I)/2004 granting enhanced competences to the Ombudsman Against Racial Discrimination.

Third, the *perpetrator's error* as to the qualifications of the victim has to be dealt with as "error in persona" and not as genuine error of fact, which could negate criminal intent.

Fourth, the *motives* become crucial instead of "intention" (being technically understood as voluntariness plus knowledge plus willfulness), because fighting against discrimination and hate means rather reaffirmation of law aims through an entire punishment of "mere guilty mind"

---

[*] Hate crimes are thus to be considered as "implicit endangerment offenses" as Antony Duff puts it, meaning that no concretely proven danger is required in the conduct in order for it to be punished—even if the lack of harm indicates a lesser wrong (see indicatively Ashworth, 2011: 165–6).

externalizations without further act than traditional fragmentary sanctioning of acts (deemed to be legally, if not already morally, principally "neutral"). Hate speech is not to restrict through qualifications of *mens rea* requirements an allegedly wide ("complete crime type") conduct (as to this traditional restrictive legislative mode see Christou, 2007: 359) but instead to expand comprehensively incrimination of hate conceived of principally and basically as an inchoate offense. The identification of *actus reus* and not *mens rea* issues is at stake. Therefore, "mere advocacy" may be freed from punishment when one, in exerting scientific research, attacks certain groups without obviously lashing out at individuals (see Christou, 2007: 356). However, the key word there is *may*.

A context-dependent interpretation can possibly uncover that the advocacy is actually not that much "mere." This is of course different from saying that individuation of penal treatment should die out; personality-based psycho-legal arguments (presented during the process as defenses by lawyers) may have their *particular and nongeneralizable* merit (see Dunbar, 1999: 72–5). Importantly, this cannot outweigh the holism of an animus-based incrimination as a *principle*. Therefore, any argument going beyond psychopathy and aiming at (*generalizable*) justification or excuse should be interpreted with regard to criminal responsibility as mere "technique of neutralization" (see on such defendants' attempts Byers et al., 1999: passim). Prior to these techniques, "an actus reus exists in words" (succinctly so Israel, 1999: at 107 in fine).

Fifth, (and this is narrowly connected with the previous topic) hate crime laws are militant political weapons of a democratic state and cannot be conceived of properly by reducing them to traditional crime laws. That means of course that antihate criminal law must be *holistically* constructed and construed (and consequently it must not leave loopholes of protection) but by the same token and in contradistinction to the usual criminal law paradigm it should not become "universalistic" in the pejorative sense. The strong moral–political commitment antihate laws express, that is, the democratically required protection of decency of the socially vulnerable, prevent such sublimations so common in the ideology of legalism. You cannot, for instance, label every discrimination a "hate act;" you can only by ridiculing antihate laws apply them against those counteroffending the genuine perpetrators (for instance, by labeling as hate speech the stigmatization of a racist as "racist" or "outcast"). Analogously, applying hate crime laws may be *in concreto* redundant (see, for instance, *DPP v Pal* [2000], where an Asian has uttered racial insults against another Asian out of anger). On the other hand, it was an initial mischief that in the United States a 2007 Draft for a Local Law Enforcement Hate Crimes Prevention Act (LLEHCPA)—which would have enormously facilitated prosecutorial work—has been withdrawn due to a promised presidential veto (Human Rights *first* 2008: 137, 175). Finally, the Law (being conceived as a legislative response to the brutal hate-motivated murders of M. Shepard and J. Byrd, Jr. back in 1998) passed Congress on the October 22, 2009, having extended bias categories under federal protection to include gender identity, sexual orientation, and disability; it has been signed into law by President Obama on the 28th of October of the same year (see on this history, LLEHCPA, 2009).

This leads us also to another crucial conclusion: you cannot sever the acts and purposes from the underlying system of ideas of the perpetrators. This is somehow commonplace in the human rights law doctrine. As Finnis puts it concerning religious fundamentalism, "sharia" or "jihad" are inseparable from a certain religion, inherent and not extraneous to it and incompatible to the secularized democracy ideal guiding the ECtHR in *Refah Partisi et al. v. Turkey (2003)* (Finnis, 2010: 436–41; equally as to the gender equality perspective McGoldrick, 2010: 426). As also *Şahin v. Turkey (2007)* (a headscarf "hijab" prohibition case) amply shows the ECtHR jurisdiction has often recurred to public order considerations as to conduct and expressions held illegitimate; in such contexts the behavior need not harm, offend, or exert pressure on somebody and from a strongly supported feminist point of view the antiwoman symbolism of the dress may suffice for its prohibition. Besides, the respective French 2004 Law prohibiting the wearing of conspicuous religious insignia inside educational institutions seems to have worked effectively—even concerning the Muslim parents who preferred that their girls unveil if this was the condition that they continued going to school (McGoldrick, 2010: 410–1, 422–4).

Also noteworthy is that restrictions of overly broad antidiscrimination laws seem more persuasive if proposed in a political climate already sufficiently ensuring minorities' rights. Thus, if the British *Hammond v. DPP (2004)* case seems to blatantly contradict the older ECtHR standpoint expressed, that is, in *Handyside v. UK (1976)* and protecting "offending, shocking, and disturbing" expressions (whereas the Swedish Supreme Court's decision in re *Åke Green (2005)* in favor of the *Handyside* spirit seems to be a finer balancing judgment) this is not unrelated to the fact that homophobic speech has become so discredited that antihomosexual speech without a harm link may hardly be any more felt as "insulting." The crucial point is not the inflexibility of "definitional balancing" toward the virtues of proportionality thinking (cf. adversely Leigh, 2010: 388–99). The directness of violation of democratic values is very crucial in any event. If *Hammond* may exhale a spirit hostile to core free speech right, *Norwood v. DPP (2003)*, a case, which resulted in conviction for placing in an apartment window a poster with anti-Islam pronouncements and pictures, may not (Weinstein, 2010a: 30–50). It may, on the contrary, display—even if one abides by the requirements of restrictive interpretation—that

> express advocacy of policies antithetical to democracy is not a legitimate part of the public discourse by which people govern themselves and thus may be suppressed without violating the core democratic free speech principle (Weinstein, 2010a: at 48).

It must be admitted that this militant and comprehensive approach is exposed to some serious critique and that further work has to be done on the dogmatic features of "assault" or of "unprovoked random attacks" aiming at eventually achieving a coherent restraint of general and widely used incriminations of "hate," which can overburden the freedom of political communication. Conversely, no hurdles are visible in punishing certain views or specific utterances in which historically hate conduct has been crystallized—which are clearly normatively unbearable and which offend without ever being able to further scientific discussion (an example is the Holocaust denial in the first place). Further, why should we perfectly individualize the symbolic harm at each possible victim's psyche, when normatively a hate crime is not otherwise intelligible but as a group-based one? Finally, what does impede us to criminalize hate conduct whereas we are (normally) not willing to allow a conduct promoting—for example—rape or pedophilic tendencies?

We have then to accept that the criminal law against hate and discrimination should by definition be *maximal, not minimal*. There is a good reason for all this: criminal protection of the citizens' equality status is hypocritical if the law will not contribute to the eradication of the evil's roots. To be clear: Criminal law has to take sides against the misery engendered by a market democracy becoming all the more crime generating and immoral. Insisting on an outmoded and undifferentiated "liberalism of safeguards and balances in favor of the defendant" overlooks that in the modern criminal law doctrine individual guilt is being bypassed by an increasing focusing on "collective" forms of guilt (such as organized crime; national, trans-border and international macro-criminality; corporate crimes, and so on). It also overlooks that the old-fashioned ethically colorless criminal law positivism should be progressively replaced by politically and ethically engaged criminal legislation in the framework of a "thick" democracy concept borrowing from strong republican principles, understood as full of concrete political content and not merely as tools for achieving formal "politeness" (my point of departure is a strongly anti-Habermasian one;

on the three democracy models, liberal, republican, and procedural-deliberative, see Christou, 2007:331–6).

In this framework there are good reasons why also nonindividualized hate speech ("abstract hate speech") is also to be incriminated. This is namely so not only because deontology is not to be interpreted necessarily from the viewpoint of the individual or because teleology indicates social or communitarian values, but also because democracy as a normatively "thick" notion is an "ought to" and a "*telos*" simultaneously in- and for-itself (cf. the theorizing on these aspects followed by Christou, 2007: 378–87). Accordingly, merely bypassing the problem of hate speech through technically inspired regulations will not do (cf. Dworkin's "partnership democracy" in Christou, 2007: 336–8). Contrary thus to the US conception concerning dealing with hate (cf. Christou, 2007: 324), *democracy precedes freedom*. The probable objection warning with an eventual "Guantánamo syndrome" fails: the latter is not the culmination of political correctness but rather the official legitimization of prejudice and hate—which is exactly what has to be fought against.

References

Ashworth, A. 2011. The criminal law's ambivalence about outcomes, in Craft, R., Kramer, M. H., and Reiff, M. R. (eds.), *Crime, Punishment, and Responsibility*. Oxford, UK: Oxford University Press.

Baker, C. E. 2010. Autonomy and hate speech, in Hare, I. and Weinstein, J. (eds.), *Extreme Speech and Democracy*. Oxford, UK: Oxford University Press.

Byers, B., Crider, B., and Biggers, G. 1999. Bias crime motivation. A study of hate crime and offender neutralization techniques used against the Amish. *Journal of Contemporary Criminal Justice*, 15(1): 78–96.

Christou, V. 2007. *Die Hassrede in der verfassungsrechtlichen Diskussion* (Hate speech in the constitutional law discussion). Baden-Baden: Nomos.

Cram, I. 2010. The Danish Cartoons, offensive expression, and democratic legitimacy, in Hare, I. and Weinstein, J. (eds.), *Extreme Speech and Democracy*, Oxford, UK: Oxford University Press.

Dunbar, E. 1999. Defending the indefensible. A critique and analysis of psycholegal defense arguments of hate crime perpetrators. *Journal of Contemporary Criminal Justice*, 15(1): 64–77.

Evans, C. 2010. Religious speech that undermines gender equality. in Hare, I. and Weinstein, J. (eds.), *Extreme Speech and Democracy*. Oxford, UK: Oxford University Press.

Feinberg, J. 1987. *Offense to Others: The Moral Limits of the Criminal Law*. Oxford, UK: Oxford University Press.

Finnis, J. 2010. Endorsing discrimination between faiths: A case of extreme speech?, in Hare, I. and Weinstein, J. (eds.), *Extreme Speech and Democracy*. Oxford, UK: Oxford University Press.

Hare, I. 2010a. Extreme speech under international and regional human rights standards, in Hare, I. and Weinstein, J. (eds.), *Extreme Speech and Democracy*. Oxford, UK: Oxford University Press.

Hare, I 2010b. Blasphemy and incitement to religious hatred: Free speech dogma and doctrine, in Hare, I. and Weinstein, J. (eds.), *Extreme Speech and Democracy*. Oxford, UK: Oxford University Press.

Heinze, E. 2010a. Cumulative jurisprudence and hate speech: Sexual orientation and analogies to disability, age, and obesity, in Hare, I. and Weinstein, J. (eds.), *Extreme Speech and Democracy*. Oxford, UK: Oxford University Press.

Heinze, E. 2010b. Wild-West cowboys versus cheese-eating surrender monkeys: Some problems in comparative approaches to hate speech, in Hare, I. and Weinstein, J. (eds.), *Extreme Speech and Democracy*. Oxford, UK: Oxford University Press.

Herring, J. 2008. *Criminal Law: Text, Cases, and Materials*. Oxford, UK: Oxford University Press.

Heyman, S. J. 2010. Hate speech, public discourse, and the first amendment, in Hare, I. and Weinstein, J. (eds.), *Extreme Speech and Democracy*. Oxford, UK: Oxford University Press.

Human Rights First 2008. *2008 Hate Crime Survey*.

Israel, M. 1999. Hate speech and the first amendment. *Journal of Contemporary Criminal Justice,* 15(1): 97–110.

Jacobs, J. B. and Potter, K. 2001. *Hate Crimes: Criminal Law and Identity Politics.* Oxford, UK: Oxford University Press.

Kymlicka, W. 1996. *Multicultural Citizenship: A Liberal Theory of Minority Rights.* Oxford, UK: Clarendon.

Leigh, I. 2010. Homophobic speech, equality denial, and religious expression, in Hare, I. and Weinstein, J. (eds.), *Extreme Speech and Democracy.* Oxford, UK: Oxford University Press.

Levin, B. 1999. Hate crimes. Worse by definition. *Journal of Contemporary Criminal Justice,* 15(1): 6–21.

LLEHCPA 2009.

McGoldrick, D. 2010. Extreme religious dress: Perspectives on veiling controversies, in Hare, I. and Weinstein, J. (eds.), *Extreme Speech and Democracy.* Oxford, UK: Oxford University Press.

Malik, M. 2010. Extreme speech and liberalism, in Hare, I. and Weinstein, J. (eds.), *Extreme Speech and Democracy.* Oxford, UK: Oxford University Press.

Mbongo, P. 2010. Hate speech, extreme speech, and collective defamation in French Law, in Hare, I. and Weinstein, J. (eds.), *Extreme Speech and Democracy.* Oxford, UK: Oxford University Press.

Molnar, P. 2010. Towards improved law and policy on 'hate speech' – The 'clear and present danger' test in Hungary, in Hare, I. and Weinstein, J. (eds.), *Extreme Speech and Democracy.* Oxford, UK: Oxford University Press.

Papacharalambous, C. 1991. *Das politische Delikt im legalistischen Rechtsstaat: Beitrag zu einer Theorie der illegalen politischen Kommunikation* (The political offence under the legalistic State of Law. Contribution to the theory of the illegal political communication). Frankfurt, Germany: Peter Lang.

Petrosino, C. 1999. Connecting the past to the future. Hate crime in America. *Journal of Contemporary Criminal Justice,* 15(1): 22–47.

Popper, K. 2005. *The Poverty of Historicism* (translated into Greek by Ath. Samartzis). Athens, Greece: Eurasia.

Post, R. 2010. Hate speech, in Hare, I. and Weinstein, J. (eds.), *Extreme Speech and Democracy.* Oxford, UK: Oxford University Press.

Reichman, A. 2010. Criminalizing religiously offensive satire: Free speech, human dignity, and comparative law, in Hare, I. and Weinstein, J. (eds.), *Extreme Speech and Democracy.* Oxford, UK: Oxford University Press.

Salton, H. T. 2012. A godless constitution?: Faith, politics, and speech in the bill of rights of the United States," *International Law Research,* 1(1): 1–12.

Sumner, L. W. 2010. Incitement and the regulation of hate speech in Canada: A philosophical analysis, in Hare, I. and Weinstein, J. (eds.), *Extreme Speech and Democracy.* Oxford, UK: Oxford University Press.

Torres, S. 1999. Hate crimes against African Americans: The extent of the problem. *Journal of Contemporary Criminal Justice,* 15(1): 48–63.

Weinstein, J. 2010a. Extreme speech, public order, and democracy: Lessons from *The Masses,* in Hare, I. and Weinstein, J. (eds.), *Extreme Speech and Democracy.* Oxford, UK: Oxford University Press.

Weinstein, J. 2010b. An overview of American free speech doctrine and its application to extreme speech, in Hare, I. and Weinstein, J. (eds.), *Extreme Speech and Democracy.* Oxford, UK: Oxford University Press.

Case Law

Beauharnais v. Illinois 343 US 250, 1952.

Brandenburg v. Ohio 395 US 444, 1969.

Chaplinsky v. N. Hampshire 315 US 568, 1942.

Dennis v. US 341 US 494, 1951.

DPP v. Pal, CrimLR 756 (Divisional Court), 2000.

Hammond v. DPP, EWHC 69 (Admin.), 2004.

Handyside v. UK, ECtHR, 1 EHRR 737, 1976.
Norwood v. DPP, EWHC 1564 (Admin.), 2003.
N. Y. Times v. Sullivan 376 US 254, 1964.
Prosecutor General v. Åke Green [=Supreme Court of Sweden, Case B 1050–05, November 29th of 2005], 2005.
R.A.V. v. City of St. Paul, Minnesota 505 US 377, 1992.
Refah Partisi et al. v. Turkey, ECtHR, 37 EHRR 1 (Grand Chamber), 2003.
Şahin v. Turkey, ECtHR, 44 EHRR 5 (2007).
Village of Skokie v. NSP of America 373 NE 2d 21 (Ill. Supreme Court), 1978.
Virginia v. Black 538 US 343, 2003.

Chapter 13

Work Discrimination against Women Employees in Malaysia[*]

Zaiton Othman and Nooraini Othman

Contents

Introduction

The Malaysian economy has been growing quickly over recent years, and partially due to women workers. Women account for approximately half of the population of Malaysia, and in addition to their traditional role in the unpaid domestic sector of the economy, women have participated in various sectors of employment such as manufacturing, business, agriculture, and general services. The percentage of women in the labor force increased from 44.7% in 2000 to 45.7% in 2005. Their share of total employment increased from 35.6% to 36.7% over the same time. During this period, women were mainly involved in the manufacturing, wholesale and retail trade, agricultural, and general services sectors. In terms of occupational structure, a higher percentage of women were employed in high-paying jobs mainly due to improvements in their educational achievements. The proportion of women in the category of senior officials and managers increased from 4.8% in 2000 to 5.4% in 2005. In the professional category, women were mainly employed

---

[*] This chapter is a revised version of the authors' published article: Othman, Z. and Othman, N. 2015. A literature review of work discrimination among women employees, *Asian Social Science*, 11(4): 26–32.

as doctors, dentists, lawyers, architects, and engineers. The percentage of women in this category was 7.2 in 2000 and increased to 7.5 in 2005 (Ninth Malaysia Plan, 2006–2010).

Many studies have indicated that the possibility for Malaysian women to participate and succeed in careers inherently depends on their ability to manage their roles as wife, mother, and worker at the same time. In more general terms, career success depends on the interplay among work, family factors, organizational demands, women's sociodemographic characteristics, and the development climate within the country (Maimunah and Ahmad, 1999; Maimunah and Roziah, 2006). The Malaysian Gender Gap Index recorded a reduction in gender inequality from 0.34 in 1980 to 0.25 in 2009. However, the reduction was not equally found in all four dimensions of the index. The education and health indices registered very low inequality values of 0.041 and 0.121, respectively, the economic participation index registered a moderate inequality value of 0.246, and the empowerment of women index registered a high inequality value of 0.578 (Economic Planning Unit, 2011). The report (Economic Planning Unit, 2011) further stated that despite increased participation at all levels of education, women's participation in the labor force has not substantially changed since the 1980s. Women workers have participated in almost all types of occupations. They are part of the fundamental human resources that provide the best skill and talent, ideas, and innovation. The Convention on the Elimination of All Forms of Discrimination against Women (Ministry of Women and Family Development, 2004) stated that because women compose half of the population, their engagement, empowerment, and contribution helps the country to achieve economic performance effectively. According to the Global Gender Gap Report (2009), the most important determinant of a country's competitiveness is its human talent, which includes the skills, education, and productivity of its workforce—women account for one-half of the world's potential talent base.

Empowering women and providing them with equal rights and opportunities to fulfill their potential is necessary to achieve business and economic progress. Therefore, it is important for Malaysia to provide gender parity of participation and opportunities for women workers to fully utilize their skills and talents. To achieve such parity, gender gaps must be closed or at least we must strive to reduce them significantly. Given the current gender parity in education, the goal of gender equality is nearly achievable, and with government commitment, equal employment opportunities for all residents can become a reality. In addition to the Malaysian government's efforts in promoting gender parity by providing equal education opportunities for all residents, the government incorporated the principle of nondiscrimination in the CEDAW into the Federal Constitution with the amendment of Article 8(2) to state that no discrimination can be made on the basis of gender (Ministry of Women and Family Development, 2004). The government also established an independent Commission on Human Rights in 1999, which promotes and protects human rights (Ministry of Women and Family Development, 2004), and adopted the Malaysian Gender Budget, which underlines the government's commitment to gender equality (Ministry of Women and Family Development, 2005). In addition, in 2006, the Malaysian government established the Non-Aligned Movement (NAM) Institute of Women's Empowerment (NIEW), which provides training for women's empowerment and gender equality to participants from NAM nations (Abdul Aziz, 2008).

Female workers from many parts of the world face different types of discrimination at their workplaces. It is reported that employment discrimination will not disappear even if men and women possess the same qualifications such as education level and experiences (Haspels and Majurin, 2008). The discriminatory practices faced by some women workers in Malaysia are reflected in hiring, promotion, job assignment, termination, compensation, and various forms of harassment (Bhatt, 2005). Sipe et al. (2009) stated that gender discrimination occurs when employers' selection, evaluation, promotion, and reward allocation decision are made based on an individual's gender. In the ILO Action Guide (Haspels and Majurin, 2008), discrimination at work is defined as a difference in work-related opportunity or treatment for which there is no objective or legitimate justification. Gender discrimination negatively affects women's incomes and opportunities for career development. This chapter discusses the nature and forms of discrimination faced by women employees with some reference to Malaysia. Discussions about how the government, employers, and educational institutions can better enhance their roles in handling and, possibly, curbing work discrimination and positively enhancing the level of women's mental health will also be highlighted in this chapter.

Nature and Forms of Discrimination

Promotion

Koshal et al. (1998) stated that women in Malaysia are underrepresented at all management levels because women are discriminated against in terms of promotion to higher ranks despite their continued high performance. Women perceive unequal opportunities for advancement after recruitment. This is perhaps one of the reasons for the lack of women at senior level. Norms of executive performance in Malaysia continue to exist on a "masculine managerial model."

Koshal et al. (1998) stated that women workers must work harder to obtain the same reward that men receive for the same work. Ismail and Ibrahim (2008) found that 49.9% of women employees in Sagamax agreed that women, in general, must work *harder* and *longer* to prove their credibility to achieve the same progress as men. Studies by Ismail and Ibrahim (2008) also revealed that women have been discriminated against in terms of promotion opportunities. Women workers face more promotion resistance than men due to the perception that male workers are more suitable for managerial positions. Negative attitudes toward women who seek higher managerial positions in organizations are influenced by the existence of a male managerial model. This type of prejudice restricts women's recruitment and promotion to higher positions in organizations. In the study by Koshal et al. (1998), only 66% of men compared to 88% of women felt comfortable having a woman as their boss. This implies that a "male managerial model" remains widely accepted in Malaysia and that norms of executive performance are unconsciously based and influenced by this model. Their studies found that more women managers perceived resistance to their career advancement from both male and female subordinates. It is also stated that male managers do not perceive women as exhibiting interactive leadership style. Women face a great deal of resistance to promotion to positions of higher rank even though they are qualified to meet the challenge of the position (Koshal et al., 1998).

Discrimination against women in the workplace also exists in other parts of the world. Women are viewed by a high proportion of male managers as unfit to fill the senior management position (Wood, 2008). Antecol et al. (2009) discovered that sex discrimination is one of the main factors that influence workers' job satisfactions and intentions to quit their jobs. A study by Wood (2008) revealed that in Australia, gender stereotyping influenced women's attitudes toward promotion to higher management ranks. Both men and women employees believed that women are likely to progress to senior positions of management slower due to gender stereotyping attitudes. Huang (1998) found that males are significantly overrepresented in management positions (33.3% of the sample) compared to females (15.94%). Gender stereotyping continuously influences the career advancement of female managers in middle management positions in Australia. Although studies showed that some extraordinary women rise to the top, only a few remain in top positions. According to Noble and Moore (2006), many women who aspire to leadership positions find it impossible to obtain them, whereas others who do obtain such positions eventually leave. Hutchings (2000) indicates that the results of her study in Thailand suggest that women are not represented at the managerial level in numbers that are comparable to their workforce membership. According to Cai and Kleiner (1999), given that management was traditionally viewed as a male occupation, women had great(er) difficulty in moving up the career ladder. This is due to the perception that most women managers are less likely to possess the attributes of successful managers than male managers. A study by Orser and Leck (2009) also shows significant discrepancies in the percentage of women in higher-level management.

A study by Mun (2010) concluded that women in Japan face discrimination in obtaining male-type jobs. Male-type jobs provide higher wages and require longer training and even "masculine" characteristics. Wage gaps, in this scenario, will likely increase due to large training differentials, and because women face job discrimination. Women's lower earning in the labor market is one of the results of gender discrimination (Besen and Kimmel, 2006). The same scenario is evident in Pakistan as Sadaquat and Sheikh (2010) found that the employment of women in higher-paying jobs is very limited and their advancement is slow compared to men. Most women occupy lower positions and suffer from gender discrimination. In a study of the hospitality industry, Burgess (2003) found that women continue to be pushed into lower-status jobs. This is either caused by the lack of opportunities for promotion or attitudes toward their employment. There are fewer females at the senior management levels.

According to the abovementioned studies, women are underrepresented in organizations' higher-ranks. One perception is that a worker needs certain masculine traits to be in the managerial ranks. Moreover, due to the perception that women are ineffective as managers because they do not possess the requisite "masculine" characteristics or traits, there are few women at the higher managerial levels. Mihail (2006) found that gender stereotyping persists within the Greek culture and, therefore, also exists in workplaces in Greece. In the study, gender was found to be the most influential factor in forming attitudes toward women as managers. Organizational cultures often reflect continuing gender stereotypes, and studies show that the perception that "women take care and men take charge" is a prevailing stereotype of the difference between men and women, and that women are not as skilled as men when it comes to problem-solving (Bible and Hill, 2007). As stated by Wood (2008), senior management and leadership positions continue to be perceived as a male domain and will continue to exert a negative influence on the career advancement of women. This notion is in line with Brink and Stobbe (2009), who found that women students are viewed as lacking the competence needed to pursue a career in earth sciences due to the perception that they are not physically strong enough to perform the hard work that is typically required of an earth scientist.

Pay Equality

The fewer number of women in higher positions contribute to the gender earnings gap. Women tend to be concentrated in lower-ranking positions that are lower paid (Fernandez, 2009). The study by Fernandez also suggested that although wage discrimination exists in all occupations, it is most prevalent in male-dominated occupations. Equality in men and women's education does not appear to be a sufficient condition for pay equality. This is evident in Kuwait, where Hosni and al-Qudsi (1988) found that even with higher educational attainment, women continue to earn lower wages than men. This pay differential is due to wage discriminatory practices.

In Turkey, gender discrimination exists in the form of gender wage gaps. Kara (2006) stated that women receive a 30% lower wage and that women are paid less than men in all occupations.

In Turkey, discrimination occurs more often in private sectors than in public sectors. A study by Ismail and Ibrahim (2008) revealed that 78.7% of women workers perceived that they were not being paid as well as their counterparts for the same job and that they were being subjected to gender-related discrimination. Orser and Leck (2009) also provide evidence of earnings disparities between genders, as their findings show a gender compensation gap at the senior management level. Burgess (2003) explained that data collected in her survey show evidence of differences between male and female earnings. In the United Sates, the gender pay gap decelerated in the 1990s and was expected to continue declining over time. However, this gap is unlikely to disappear completely. The gender pay gap is clearly tied to the effect of discrimination against women (Blau and Kahn, 2000). A study by Broyles (2009) discovered that nearly 20% of the earnings gaps for female chemists are due to employer discrimination and these women were earning over USD $3000 less income per year.

According to the Haspels and Majurin (2008), gender discrimination will continue to exist despite the increase in education level and experience of women in the workforce. This notion is supported by Tam (1996), who revealed that employers' gender discrimination contributed to the gender income gap. Gender discrimination might affect the behavior of woman workers, which, in turn, negatively affects their productivity level, thus reducing their earnings. In terms of education level, even though relatively more women are educated, they continue to face gender inequality such as earnings gaps. The increasing number of women who are enrolling in education is not sufficient to eradicate gender inequality (Durbin and Fleetwood, 2010).

Training Opportunities

A study by Hutchings (2000) indicates that discrimination against women workers exists in Thailand, where the majority of organizations are resistant to incurring the time and costs associated with introducing policies that can help to reduce gender inequality. The absence of specific training programs, organizations' policies, and women's underrepresentation at managerial levels indicate the existence of discrimination against women in Thailand. In their study of a large sample of medical professionals, Carr et al. (2000) found that 75% female respondents chose gender discrimination as one of the most important factors that hindered their careers. The study revealed that these respondents' formal and informal training did not adequately prepare them to address gender discrimination in the workplace.

Ways to Address Work Discrimination

Othman's (2011) research revealed a need for women workers to understand the existence of discrimination against them in the workplace. They need to understand their equal rights as employees and that there are ways to avoid discrimination. It would be beneficial to educate and prepare women for the discrimination issues before they enter the workforce. An introduction to the issues can begin as early as the primary and secondary school levels. It could be done by eliminating all types of sexism and stereotyping of women's roles from textbooks, references, and other materials used in teaching and learning processes.

Then, the effort can be continued at the college and university level. Education concerning gender discrimination and other discriminatory employment practices should be provided in relevant courses such as human resource management (HRM) and business law. Students should be exposed to the forms and nature of discrimination, ways to avoid discrimination, and how to handle discrimination and to increase their knowledge and understanding of the issue. The effects of gender discrimination such as the limited opportunity for promotion and pay inequality, may be minimized if these future workers are better prepared for discrimination. The negative impacts of discrimination on self-confidence, job satisfaction, and career commitment may also be reduced if women are better prepared with greater knowledge.

In addition, employers should continuously attempt to address and reduce gender discrimination through policies, training, and enforcement (Cai and Kleiner, 1999; Sipe et al., 2009). Employers may encourage employees, especially women employees, to file complaints or reports of any discriminatory practices against them. The employees should be ensured that if they compile and submit a report, they will not be perceived as "troublemakers" or "agitators," which could result in undeserved performance ratings, increased workloads, or other negative retaliatory moves (Leslie and Gelfand, 2008). Employers should be aware that internal discrimination claims are much less costly than external claims such as legal claims. External claims are costly in terms of both time and money. By encouraging internal discrimination claims, organizations are able to retain talented employees and reduce the possibility that workers who perceive themselves as victims of discrimination will file external claims against the organization (Cai and Kleiner, 1999).

In addition, organizations may provide their managers, decision-makers, and policy-makers with training programs, seminars, or workshops on discrimination in the workplace. Providing these actors with knowledge and trainings will allow them to increase their understanding, awareness, and ability to avoid discriminatory practices and, thus, will increase the organization's ability to prevent valuable employees from leaving the organization or filing legal claims of discrimination.

Finally, the government, specifically the Ministry of Human Resources (Malaysia), could increase and continue to implement antidiscriminatory tools and regulations to reduce the gender gap. The courts and the government of Malaysia must be committed to implementing comprehensive laws with effective remedies if violated. The government must promulgate legislation with a clear gender equality objective that is applicable in all circumstances. Some of the main concerns are the definition and understanding of "gender equality," "direct discrimination," and "indirect discrimination." The legislation must also be construed in accordance with the provisions of CEDAW (Abdul Aziz, 2008).

Othman (2011) further states that women workers' experience of discrimination in the workplace, as measured by the high percentage of negative responses, is surprising and differs from expectations, even though the majority of previous research indicates that discrimination against women in the workplace exists. According to previous studies, discrimination against women occurs more often at the higher position or decision-making levels, and fewer discrimination practices occur at lower levels of management.

This result may be due to the higher level of education that Malaysian women receive(d). As Huang (1998) explains, the gap between male and female workers can be narrowed effectively by women's pursuit of higher levels of education. Women in Malaysia surpassed men in enrollment and academic achievements in many situations, and they seem to be closing the gender gap in the socioeconomic arena (Nadchatram, 2005). Women in Malaysia have made encouraging progress in many key areas, such as education and employment and, thus, have experienced increased participation in power sharing and the decision-making process. Although inequality persists in Malaysia, due to women's increased education levels, the gap can be narrowed further still (Ministry of Women and Family Development, 2003).

The other factor that may lead to lower levels of discrimination is the Malaysian government's efforts in curbing the discriminatory practices in the workplace. The government, especially the Ministry of Human Resources and the Ministry of Women, Family, and Community

Development, has developed and implemented many antidiscrimination tools and programs that help to control and reduce the discrimination practices against women workers. Antidiscriminatory laws, procedures, and policies were also developed to provide guidelines and help in handling claims of discrimination against women.

Conclusion

Despite the Malaysian government's efforts to increase gender equality in Malaysia, gender discrimination against women persists in the workplace. Discrimination against women in the workplace exists in nearly every country in the world. Studies have shown that discrimination practices such as gender pay gaps, sexual harassment, occupational gender segregation, discrimination in hiring and promoting, and stereotyping, occur worldwide. The government of Malaysia has made several commitments to promoting gender equality and women's empowerment. A National Policy on Women was adopted in 1989. In 2001, the government amended Article 8(2) of the Constitution to prohibit any form of gender discrimination, and in August 2009, it launched the second National Policy on Women and the Women's Development Action Plan (Economic Planning Unit, 2011). The Tenth Malaysia Plan (2011–2015) stated a policy objective of increasing the number of women in key decision-making positions. This objective is in line with the CEDAW Committee's recommendation to establish concrete goals and timetables to accelerate the representation of women in elected and appointed bodies in all areas of public life. Today, women hold nearly two-thirds of public service positions, and many women occupy middle-management positions.

Although there is evidence that discrimination exists more in upper-level management positions and less in lower-level jobs, the relevant parties must monitor discrimination practices consistently and continuously at all levels. Alternatives to address discrimination discussed above may help to further reduce and minimize discrimination practices against women workers. Efforts taken to improve the situation and to reduce discrimination practices must be intensified and performed continuously. This will ensure that women workers will continue to enjoy their equal rights and employment benefits, which will in turn reduce their stress levels, enhance their levels of mental health, and increase their job satisfaction in addition to their contribution to social and economic welfare.

Acknowledgment

This work is supported by Universiti Teknologi Malaysia under the Research University Grant (RUG-Flagship), vote no: 01G96.

References

Abdul Aziz, Z. 2008. *Mechanisms to Promote Gender Equality in Malaysia: The Need for Legislation.* London, UK: Women Living Under Muslim Laws, Dossier 29.

Antecol, B., Barcus, V. E., and Cobb-Clark, D. 2009. Gender bias behavior at work: Exploring the relationship between sexual harassment and sex discrimination, *Journal of Economics Psychology*, 30(5): 782–792.

Besen, Y. and Kimmel, M. K. 2006. At Sam's Club, no girls allowed: The lived experience of sex discrimination, *Equal Opportunities International*, 25(3): 172–187.

Bhatt, J. K. 2005. *Gender Discrimination in Employment-How Far Does Article 8 of the Federal Constitution Guarantee Gender Equality?* Shah Alam, Malaysia: Universiti Teknologi MARA.

Bible, D. and Hill, K. L. 2007. Discrimination: Women in business, *Journal of Organizational Culture, Communications and Conflict*, 11(1): 65–76.

Blau, F. D. and Kahn, L. M. 2000. Gender differences in pay, *Journal of Economics Perspectives*, 14(4): 75–99.

Brink, M. V. D. and Stobbe, L. 2009. Doing gender in academic education: The paradox of visibility. *Gender, Work and Organization*, 16(4): 451–470.

Broyles, P. 2009. The gender pay gap of STEM professions in the United States, *International Journal of Sociology and Social Policy*, 29(5/6): 214–226.

Burgess, C. 2003. Gender and salaries in hotel financial management: It's still a man's world, *Women in Management Review*, 18(1/2): 50–59.

Cai, Y. and Kleiner, B. H. 1999. Sex discrimination in hiring: The glass ceiling, *Equal Opportunities International*, 18(2/3/4): 51–55.

Carr, P. L., Ash, A. S., Friedman, R. H., Szalacha, L., Barnett, R. C., Palepu, A., and Moskowitz, M. M. 2000. Faculty perceptions of gender discrimination and sexual harassment in academic medicine, *Annals of Internal Medicine*, 132: 889–896.

Dessler, G. 2008. *Human Resource Management* (11th ed.). Upper Saddle River, NJ: Pearson Education.

Durbin, S. and Fleetwood, S. 2010. Gender inequality in employment: Editor's introduction, *Diversity and Inclusion: An International Journal*, 29(3): 221–238.

Economic Planning Unit. 2011. *The Millennium Development Goals at 2010*, Kuala Lumpur.

Fernandez, J. L. 2009. Intra-occupational gender earnings gaps in Malaysia, *Journal Kemanusiaan*, (14): 20–36.

Global Gender Gap Report. 2009. Harvard University and University of California, Berkeley.

Haspels, N. and Majurin, E. 2008. *Work, Income and Gender Equality in East Asia (Action Guide)*. International Labour Organization. Bangkok: ILO Subregional Office for East Asia.

Hosni, D. A. and al-Qudsi, S. S. 1988. *Sex Discrimination in the Labor Market of Kuwait*. University of Central Florida, FL and Kuwait City, Kurait: Kuwait Institute for Scientific Research.

Huang, T. 1998. The impact of education and seniority on the male-female wage gap: Is more education the answer? *International Journal of Manpower*, 20(6): 361–374.

Hutchings, K. 2000. Class and gender influences on employment practices in Thailand: An examination of equity policy and practice, *Women in Management Review*, 15(8): 385–403.

Ismail, M. and Ibrahim, M. 2008. Barriers to career progression faced by women: Evidence from a Malaysian multinational oil company, *Gender in Management: An International Journal*, 23(1): 51–66.

Kara, O. 2006. Occupational gender wage discrimination in Turkey, *Journal of Economic Studies*, 33(2): 130–143.

Koshal, M., Gupta, K. A., and Koshal, R. 1998. Women in management: A Malaysian perspective, *Women in Management Review*, 13(1): 11–18.

Leslie, L. M. and Gelfand, J. M. 2008. The who and when of internal discrimination claims: An interactional model, *Organizational Behavior and Human Decision Processes*, 107: 123–140.

Maimunah, I. and Ahmad, A. 1999. *Women and Work: Challenges in Industrializing Nations*. London, UK: Asean Academic Press.

Maimunah, I. and Roziah, M. R. 2006. *High-Flying Women Academics: A Question of Career Mobility*. Subang Jaya, Malaysia: Pelanduk.

Mihail, D. 2006. Gender-based stereotypes in the workplace: The case of Greece, *Equal Opportunities International*, 25(5): 373–388.

Ministry of Women and Family Development. 2003. *The Progress of Malaysian Women since Independence 1957–2000*. Kuala Lumpur, Malaysia: Government of Malaysia.

Ministry of Women and Family Development. 2004. *Report to the UN Committee for the Convention on the Elimination of All Forms of Discrimination against Women (CEDAW), (First and Second Report)*. Kuala Lumpur, Malaysia: Government of Malaysia.

Ministry of Women, Family, and Community Development 2005. *Gender Budgeting in Malaysia*. Kuala Lumpur.

Mun, E. 2010. Sex typing of jobs in hiring: Evidence from Japan, *Social Forces*, 8(5): 1999–2026.

Nachadtram. 2005. *Women in Malaysia*. Kuala Lumpur: UNICEF Malaysia. Retrieved February 15, 2011, from http://www.incef.org/malaysia/support6066.html.

Ninth Malaysia Plan, 2006–2010. 2006. Government of Malaysia, Kuala Lumpur.

Noble, C. and Moore, S. 2006. Advancing women and leadership in this post-feminist, post-EEO era, *Women in Management Review*, 21(7): 598–603.

Orser, B. and Leck, J. 2009. Gender influences on career success outcomes, *Gender in Management: An International Journal*, 25(5): 386–407.

Othman, Z. 2011. Discrimination against Women in Workplace, unpublished Masters thesis. Serdang, Malaysia: Universiti Putra Malaysia.

Sadaquat, M. H. and Sheikh, Q. A. 2010. Employment situation of women in Pakistan, *International Journal of Social Academics*, 38(2): 98–113.

Sipe, S., Fisher, D. K., and Johnson, C. D. 2009. University students' perception of gender discrimination in the workplace: Reality versus fiction, *Journal of Education for Business*, 84(6): 339–349.

Tam, T. 1996. Reducing the gender gap in an Asian Economy: How important is women's increasing work experience?, *World Development*, 24(5): 831–844.

Wood, G. 2008. Gender stereotypical attitudes. Past, present, and future influences on women's career advancement, *Equal Opportunities International*, 27(7): 613–628.

Chapter 14

Employee Rights: The Equity–Equality Conflict as a Dilemma in the Management of Reward Systems[*]

Steen Scheuer

Contents

Introduction

The general aim of this chapter is to investigate the causal relationship between a willingness to contribute in the workplace and the effect of employees' social norms. The employment relationship is an exchange relationship, but "once the wage has been determined, this sets the stage for conflicts over work effort" (Hechter, 1987: 127). Not only effort but also contribution, more generally, is in focus here; this encompasses commitment, persistence, willingness to change, to submit novel ideas, and so on. These aspects are highly sensitive to fairness issues—issues that impinge on the question of variance of social norms in employment situations and among different kinds of

---

[*] This chapter is a revised version of the author's published article: Scheuer, S. 2011. The equity-equality conflict: Dilemmas in the management of reward systems, *Journal of Management and Sustainability*, 3(3): 158–165.

employees including institutional factors that support or minimize the effectiveness of particular normative statement in the workplace condition.

The factors that determine workplace actors' appeal to social norms of fairness in some situations and what "fairness" is perceived as consisting of is of interest here. Questions such as *When is a pay level considered relativity fair, and when is it not? When are contingent pay systems (i.e., pay-for-performance systems) perceived as fair and when are they not? When can differences in contribution (equity) overrule the social norm of equality? Which contingent reward structure should be applied for teamwork members, if any? Which reward structure should be utilized to motivate employees to a continuous search for smarter working procedures and solutions?* These are central concerns of motivation theory in which rational choice decisions are counterbalanced by endowment effects or other fairness concerns.

Management is placed in a dilemma between what is—an economically rational structure of incentives, on one hand, and that, which is considered equitable (in accordance with employment rights) by employees, on the other. Since equality in reward counts for more among a considerable fraction of employees, while equity in contribution counts more for most employers, this is an inherent dilemma—constantly having to be negotiated and solved, but never reaching any "final solution" in any company. Based on this dilemma, implications for management are described, and recommendations for the utilization of and limitations for pay variance among peers are given.

Motivation and Fairness

Social norms of fairness and normality are important forces that influence our conduct in the employment relationship. Besides incentives, the conception of what is normal and what is fair strongly impinge on our conceptions and, thus, on our agency. The issue of social norms of fairness has been widely discussed in sociology, economics, and psychology, and the impact of social norms on economic microdecisions have by now been established (Kahneman et al., 1986a,b, 1990; Elster, 1989a, 2007, 2009; Joas, 2000; Boudon, 2001; Kahneman, 2011) including the importance of institutional and legal factors in forming employees' conceptions of fairness (Fehr et al., 2009). However, "fairness concerns" is a quite general term since fairness may relate to equity as well as equality norms and values; thus, the point of reference for evaluating "fairness" may differ quite profoundly. Equity fairness refers to a balance between contribution and reward (Elster, 1989a) and, thus, the employment relationship between company and employee while equality fairness brings the reward of the individual employee in relation to that of his/her colleagues. Since both the effort and the value of the contribution are usually less visible than reward differentials, it turns out to be difficult to bring equity into play among colleagues. *Who should do it?*

Within the employment context, one basic problem related to social norms is the fact that while the contractual salary payment is binding, the desired level of contribution is not, and it is only enforceable in the general sense that an employee may be warned, demoted, or fired as a result of poor performance (in the employer's eyes). This is the nature of the open-ended psychological contract (Marsden, 2004a; Rousseau, 1995). This contract puts social norms of the fairness at the center stage. The impact of fairness on daily workplace interactions may appear slight, but the impact of unfairness is substantial. The perceived level of pay fairness (including perceptions of pay relativities) can certainly have a negative effect on the contribution levels of employees (Abell, 1995; Fehr et al., 2009:366, 369). Fairness is enforced, but sometimes this is to the detriment of all participants' outcomes (Axelrod, 1984). This is important because effort, commitment, persistence, change willingness—in other words, motivation—are important indicators of individual and organizational performance. In fact, the proponents of what is sometimes labeled "New Pay" (i.e., more flexible pay systems such as contingent pay, performance-based pay, etc.) to a quite substantial effect seem to neglect fairness effects when they argue an ever-increasing utilization of individualized performance-related payment systems (PRP) (Lawler, 1990, 2000; Schuster and Zingheim, 1992).

Therefore, since the employment relationship may be seen as an iterated Prisoner's Dilemma (PD) between the employer and the employee (Axelrod, 1984) or as a continuous renegotiation of the effort bargain (Marsden, 2004b), for management it is important to understand the nature and substance of the particular social norms present and to understand which factors may facilitate or hinder changing these norms. This is particularly pertinent for companies and organizations undergoing constant change impetuses, that is, with the increasing use of high-involvement management—where increases in delegation, empowerment, and involvement may sometimes be seen to have ambiguous consequences. These ambiguous consequences result when more demanding jobs are not followed by social supportive supervision, by rewards or by a lack of delegation of the actual powers needed—thus transgressing employees' norms of equitable fairness (Bryson et al., 2012; Böckerman et al., 2011; Wood and Bryson, 2009).

When judging an exchange or the change of the conditions of an exchange, our choice of reference point may be either some ethical standard or the "normal" procedure and conditions in a situation: the cardinal rule of fair behavior is that one person should not achieve a gain by simply imposing an equivalent loss on another (Kahneman et al., 1986a: 731). If there is a lack of emphasis on this, if there is a deficiency in the ability of management to convince employees on this point, or indeed if employee representatives consciously frame a conflict in precisely such terms, then this may generate a sense of lack of fairness among employees and, thus, provoke workplace conflicts (Scheuer, 2006a).

Endowment Effects and Employment Rights: Equity versus Equality

In much of the literature, the consideration of norms is related to issues of the pay/work–effort relationship, while less has been done in terms of considering other important motivational aspects of the employment relationship—especially various issues of intrinsic motivation. While an employee may feel intrinsically motivated to undertake a specific task in the desired direction (with the desired intensity and persistence effort), social norms in the work group may contribute to or detract from this motivation in the same manner that extrinsic motivation may be perceived as crowding out or crowding in the motivation of the employee (according to Motivation Crowding Theory) (Lawler, 1990; Frey, 1998, 2002; Ryan and Deci, 2000; Frey and Osterloh, 2010; Latham, 2012).

Some social norms relate to ownership in the broad sense, implying "ownership" of a job, of a particular level of salary, and of particular rights and small privileges in the workplace. This has been labeled the endowment effect (Kahneman et al., 1990; Thaler, 1980). It is, thus, against the sense of equity that one should lose an endowment (such as tolerate a salary reduction or an unwanted lengthening of working hours) much more than the loss of prospective gain (i.e., loss of an expected pay bonus) although even a pay reduction appears to be acceptable in certain circumstances (Kahneman et al., 1986a). This may explain why pay increases for the lower-paid may be seen by others (the higher paid) as a loss of an endowment (a privilege, a right, or a sense of ownership) and be reframed as a smaller percentage increase, and thus, an incurred loss (Elster, 1989a, 2009).

Examples of this type of reasoning often occur publicly in collective bargaining occurring in coordinated market economies (Hall and Soskice, 2001). In liberal market economies—and indeed in local company bargaining—this type of argumentation may be less prevalent (at least in the quasipublic discourse) but the deliberations behind them may nevertheless loom large in the minds of groups of employees and in the group-oriented subculture, that is, in the informal organization.

The problem, then, is this: norms of equity may thus run flat in the face of norms of equality. The status quo is not the same as equity since equity expresses a norm of "to each according to his X" where X may be education, experience, position in the status hierarchy, etc., and this may not be met by status quo—although strongly entrenched nonequitable practices may prevail due to the institutionalizing effects of more or less subconscious taken-for-granted modes of evaluation, that is, through isomorphic processes (Scott, 1995). Equality is also different from these two, since equality may not only express the requirement of equal treatment in the face of differences in race, religion, gender, age, sexual orientation, etc. but also represents a social norm of more equal distribution of income and wealth in society—regardless of education, seniority, position, etc. Equality may be local (company- or profession-based) or societal (Elster, 1989a: 224–231, 1989b; Scheuer, 2000). The adherence to social norms does not reduce conflict in society, and it does not solve all distributional problems. Since social norms among employees will be heterogeneously distributed, a "normative confrontation" will often occur in the workplace context, and it requires both procedures for conflict resolution and a reciprocal insight in and understanding of the social norms underlying the bargaining positions of the other part. Endowment effects—when conceived as employment rights—and social norms are relatively resilient, but they have dynamic properties, depending inter alia on framing (Boudon, 2001; Joas, 2000).

Employees in work situations exert individual agency. The decisions that agents continuously make form the core of the issue of work motivation. Work motivation may generally be defined as the process that determines how energy is used to satisfy needs and, thus, motivation is a cognitive resource allocation process in which the agent chooses the time and energy to be spent on an array of more or less work-related tasks. Motivation includes direction, intensity and persistence of the expended effort, and this process is future-oriented in that agents anticipate the amount of satisfaction that they suppose will occur when outcomes are received (Latham, 2012: 193; Pritchard et al., 2002; Vroom, 1964).

Motivation and Incentives

Much progress has been made in the understanding of human work motivation even though the influence on motivation from social norms is still not well understood. Some of the concepts from classic motivation are still heavily utilized, especially Herzberg's distinction (1966) between intrinsic and extrinsic motivational factors. Moreover, the debate between (psychological) intrinsic motivation theories and (economic) extrinsic or incentive theories is still very much alive (Deci, 1975; Deci and Ryan, 1985; Frey, 1998, 2002; Lawler, 2000; Ryan and Deci, 2000) while some have attempted to integrate the two perspectives (see Steel and König, 2006). Both Deci's and Frey's contributions make much of the possible out-crowding effects of extrinsic incentives, especially when they are experienced as "controlling" (Frey, 1998; Andersen and Serritzlew, 2012). This may be an expression of an individual wish not to be controlled (or to be controlled less) but it may also have spilled over from fairness norms based on the status quo, which might imply that pay bonuses generally are controlling. However, some evidence points in the opposite direction, since those who report having pay-for-performance systems generally consider their company more equitable than those who do not have such an arrangement (Scheuer, 2006b). This is the case even for those not obtaining a bonus; therefore, it does not express any simple economic satisfaction with a higher salary (a simple rational choice valuation); rather, it expresses satisfaction with the implicit deal underlying such an arrangement (i.e., an acceptance of the deal as normatively fair).

More recent theories have appeared under the label of "Public Service Motivation" (Perry and Hondgehem, 2008). This theory connects the traditional motivational aspects of work with the impact of the employee's interest in serving the public good, and the effect of variations in motivational systems has been shown in various particular work contexts (Andersen and Serritzlew, 2012; Andersen et al., 2011). More generally, others have pointed out how the introduction of choice and competition among public sector institutions may enhance performance (Grand, 2003, 2007, 2010; Marsden, 2004b; Thaler and Sunstein, 2008).

An important contribution to motivation theory is Latham and Locke's goal-setting theory, which furthered equity theory and expectancy theory in establishing that companies must supply employees with relatively specific and obtainable goals in their work defined (i) from the work's basic characteristics and (ii) from an understanding of the goals and preferences of employees (Latham and Locke, 1979, 1991; Locke, 2000; Locke and Latham, 1990, 2004; Tversky and Kahneman, 1986; Wicker et al., 1993). This theory explicitly states that feedback and recognition are not enough, but they are mediated by the setting of specific goals. Further, the ability to perform faced with difficult goals is mediated by the level of goals set by individual employees themselves: people with high goals and high self-efficacy have higher performance yet lower expectancies of success than those with low goals and a low-performance level. Furthermore, goal setting is a discrepancy-creating process, for example, motivation requires "feed-forward" control in addition to feedback since employees with high self-efficacy often set themselves even higher goals, creating a novel discrepancy. Many of these processes will become influenced by employees' social norms, which may add to or detract from perceived self-efficacy and individual goal setting.

Companies require substantial pay variance (often also a degree of variance between peers) but they also need to be seen as fair in their pay policies by every group of employees. This is the basic dilemma of companies, and, thus of its reward system and for its whole system of Human Resource Management. One way of managing is to keep actual pay levels and individual pay secret, perhaps even forbidding employees to exchange this information; however, this approach is hardly ever completely successful and it also diminishes confidence levels between management and employees.

What is considered normal or ideal varies with attributes of the employment situation or the employee such as employment status, employment sector, employment tenure or age, level of formal education, and (perhaps) gender. Added to this may be attitudinal factors such as institutional membership and political orientation. While theories of social norms and fairness constraints, in general, have received quite some attention, relatively, little has been written concerning how social norms vary according to these variables in the employment setting. However, one should not only look at the prevalent social norms in the working populace. One must also specify how these very norms are contingent upon (a) aspects of social status, personal attributes and attitudes and (b) institutional characteristics (i.e., trade unionism, collective bargaining) of the work situation. At the same time, there is the issue of establishing exactly when an action by management turns unfair and when change programs, therefore, may run into trouble. From this, we can pose the following question: *Can choosing a reward structure that is economically and rationally fair potentially impede upon teamwork (and other dynamic forms of cooperation)?*

Propositions for Human Resource Management

Following is a discussion of a number of consequences of the above considerations for HR management. These consequences concern the most specific aspects of payment and reward structures, and their theoretical and analytical underpinnings.

1. Under contingent pay, systems that entail a degree of choice are perceived as fair. This ensures perceived fairness of outcomes (even when the individual misses the incentive) while systems that entail increased perceived control are less so. This impinges strongly on employee motivation and effort (Allgulin and Ellingsen, 2002; Andersen and Pallesen, 2008; Frey, 1998, 2002; Frey and Osterloh, 2010; Sewell and Barker, 2006).

2. Contingent pay systems (ever so economically marginal) enhance management's insights into the individual employee's contribution. However, insights should be perceived as non-controlling, that is, enabling some choice.

3. Under contingent pay-systems, social norms based on equity will vary positively with employment status, the level of formal education, and membership of trade unions or associations—with high-status unions having the strongest support.

4. Under contingent pay-systems, framing may impinge on actors' activation of their respective social norms of equity and equality—respectively, enabling greater or lesser envy towards the differentiation of rewards.

5. Under teamwork, pay differences among participants matter little, but contingent team rewards may hinder cooperation (contribution) by some participants, depending on the size of the relative differentials, depending on (1) framing and (2) size of relative differences. Specifically, very small or very large variations in contingent team reward are particularly impeding (U-shaped) (Auriol et al., 2002; Arrowsmith and Marginson, 2010; Barker, 1993, 1999).

6. *In temporary teamwork (e.g., Task Forces), how can contingent teamwork reward be implemented and framed to avoid envy?* Either one may mete it out percentage-wise or may have to move parts of the rewards for higher earners to other fora.

7. *In permanent teamwork (e.g., standing committees or quality circles), how can envy be minimized?* This can be done by changing the framing, that is, by making contingent rewards less relative to basic pay (i.e., more egalitarian), or by moving rewards for the higher earners out of the teamwork.

8. Local (i.e., collegial) perceived fairness of relative pay distribution increases with principal's insight in individual performance and with members' perception of principal's fairness in t-1 (Prendergast, 2002; Rotemberg, 2002). This also increases the perceived fairness of own pay. Perceived fairness also increases when a collective bargaining procedure is in place while the perceived fairness of own pay does not (Sisson and Marginson, 2002).

9. Collective bargaining agreements enhance fairness perceptions both in times of slack and when times are good, and, thus, enable rationalization processes and contingent pay increases or reductions. It does, however, probably require more "linearity," that is, stricter egalitarianism in increases and reductions than management might otherwise prefer.

10. It is considered as unfair to reduce nominal pay due to excess labor supply or even under low company profits, and it can only be perceived as fair under impending company losses (Elster, 1989, 2009; Kahneman et al., 1986a, 1990).

11. Firms that operate with bonus systems or profit sharing encounter less resistance in reducing overall pay during slack (Kahneman et al., 1986a: 740). Firms that have collective bargaining

procedures in place can also more easily reduce nominal pay without becoming perceived as unfair (Ingram, 1991; Traxler et al., 2007).

Conclusion

In the debate for and against the utilization of incentives in the employment relationship, there is often very strong polarization. You are either for or against it. However, theories turning their back entirely on economic incentives when it comes to motivation seem to ignore that any wage structure (even complete egalitarianism) contains a kind of incentive. Maybe not a kind, however, which one will think further the productive and concerted efforts of employees. Therefore, one may underscore that there are many options in the introduction or the rearrangement of a performance and reward management system, especially concerning: (1) the formalization of the criteria for bonuses and rewards, (2) the share of the reward package allocated to variable pay, and (3) the degree of "publicity" connected to the contingent rewards.

In other words, contingent economic rewards may be "high-powered" or "low-powered" (Langbein, 2010: 15–16). In situations where there are reasons to believe that the divisive nature of contingent individual rewards is detrimental to collective performance—or where high-powered incentives may be perceived as controlling and thus crowd out intrinsic motivation or task motivation—it may be wiser to go for the low-powered contingent reward system in order to avoid employees' perception of the system as a transgression of their rights in the employment relationship. This will enable management to reward good individual performance while simultaneously keeping intrinsic (task) motivation, a good sense of equity while (not in the least) avoiding the divisive effects on collaborative efforts due to a sensed transgression of rights. Most companies are, after all, supposed to be collaborative efforts.

References

Abell, P. 1995. The new institutionalism and rational choice theory, in Scott, W. R. and Christensen, S. M. (eds.), *The Institutional Construction of Organizations*. London, UK: Sage.

Allgulin, M. and Ellingsen, T. 2002. Monitoring and pay, *Journal of Labor Economics*, 20(2/1): 201–216.

Andersen, L. B. and Pallesen, T. 2008. 'Not Just for the Money?:' How financial incentives affect the number of publications at danish research institutions, *International Public Management Journal*, 11(1): 28–47.

Andersen, L. B. and Serritzlew, S. 2012. Does public service motivation affect the behavior of professionals?, *International Journal of Public Administration*, 35(1): 19–29.

Andersen, L. B., Pallesen, T., and Pedersen, L. H. 2011. Does ownership matter?: Public service motivation among physiotherapists in the private and public sectors in Denmark, *Review of Public Personnel Administration*, 31(1): 10–27.

Arrowsmith, J. and Marginson, P. 2010. The decline of incentive pay in British manufacturing, *Industrial Relations Journal*, 41(4): 289–311.

Auriol, E., Friebel, G., and Pechlivanos, L. 2002. Career concerns in teams, *Journal of Labor Economics*, 20(1): 289–307.

Axelrod, R. 1984. *The Evolution of Cooperation*. New York, NY: Basic.

Barker, J. R. 1993. Tightening the iron cage: Concertive control in self-managing teams, *Administrative Science Quarterly*, 38(3): 408–437.

Barker, J. R. 1999. *The Discipline of Teamwork: Participation and Concertive Control*. Thousand Oaks, CA: Sage.

Böckerman, P., Bryson, A., and Ilmakunnas, P. 2011. *Does High Involvement Management Improve Worker Wellbeing?*, Center for Economic Performance (CEP) Discussion Paper, The Center for Economic Performance, London, UK.

Boudon, R. 2001. *The Origin of Values: Essays in the Sociology and Philosophy of Beliefs*. New Brunswick, NJ: Transaction.

Bryson, A., Dale-Olsen, H., and Barth, E. 2012. Do higher wages come at a price?, *Journal of Economic Psychology*, 33(1): 251–263.

Deci, E. L. 1975. *Intrinsic Motivation*. New York, NY: Plenum.

Deci, E. L. and Ryan, R. M. 1985. *Intrinsic Motivation and Self-Determination in Human Behavior*. New York, NY: Plenum.

Elster, J. 1989a. *The Cement of Society: A Study of Social Order*. Cambridge, UK: Cambridge University Press.

Elster, J. 1989b. Social norms and economic theory, *Journal of Economic Perspectives*, 3(4): 99–117.

Elster, J. 2007. *Explaining Social Behavior*. Cambridge, UK: Cambridge University Press.

Elster, J. 2009. Norms, in Hedström, P. and Bearman, P. (eds.), *The Oxford Handbook of Analytical Sociology*. Oxford, UK: Oxford University Press.

Fehr, E., Goette, L., and Zehnder, C. 2009. A behavioral account of the labor market: The role of fairness concerns, *Annual Review of Economics*, 1: 355–384.

Frey, B. S. 1998. *Not Just for the Money: Economic Theory of Personal Motivation*. Cheltenham, UK: Edward Elgar.

Frey, B. S. 2002. *Inspiring Economics: Human Motivation in the Political Economy*. Cheltenham, UK: Edward Elgar.

Frey, B. S. and Osterloh, M. 2010. *Successful Management by Motivation: Balancing Intrinsic and Extrinsic Incentives*. Berlin, Germany: Springer.

Grand, J. L. 2003. *Motivation, Agency, and Public Policy: Of Knights and Knaves, Pawns and Queens*. Oxford, UK: Oxford University Press.

Grand, J. L. 2007. *The Other Invisible Hand: Delivering Public Services through Choice and Competition*. Princeton, NJ: Princeton University Press.

Grand, J. L. 2010. Knights and knaves return: Public service motivation and the delivery of public services, *International Public Management Journal*, 13(1): 56–71.

Hall, P. A. and Soskice, D. 2001. *Varieties of Capitalism: The Institutional Advantage of Competitive Advantage*. Oxford, UK: Oxford University Press.

Hechter, M. 1987. *Principles of Group Solidarity,* Berkeley, CA: University of California Press.

Herzberg, F. 1966. *Work and the Nature of Man*. New York, NY: World Publishing.

Ingram, P. 1991. Changes in working practices in British manufacturing industry in the 1980s: A study of employee concessions made during wage negotiations, *British Journal of Industrial Relations*, 29(1): 1–13.

Joas, H. 2000. *The Genesis of Values*. Cambridge, UK: Polity.

Kahneman, D. 2011. *Thinking, Fast and Slow*. London, UK: Allen Lane/Penguin.

Kahneman, D., Knetsch, J. L., and Thaler, R. 1986a. Fairness as a constraint on profit seeking: Entitlements in the market, *American Economic Review*, 76(4): 728–741.

Kahneman et al. 1986b. Fairness and the assumptions of economics, *Journal of Business*, 59(4): 285–300.

Kahneman et al. 1990. Experimental tests of the endowment effect and the Coase theorem, *Journal of Political Economy*, 98(6): 1325–1348.

Langbein, L. 2010. Economics, public service motivation, and pay for performance: Complements or substitutes?, *International Public Management Journal*, 13(1): 9–23.

Latham, G. P. 2012. *Work Motivation: History, Theory, Research, and Practice*. London, UK: Sage.

Latham, G. P. and Locke, E. A. 1979. Goal setting: A motivational technique that works, *Organizational Dynamics*, 8(2): 68–80.

Latham, G. P. and Locke, E. A. 1991. Self-Regulation through goal setting, *Organizational Behavior and Human Decision Processes*, 50(2): 212–247.

Lawler, E. E. 1990. *Strategic Pay: Aligning Organizational Strategies and Pay Systems*. San Francisco, CA: Jossey-Bass.

Lawler, E. E. 2000. *Rewarding Excellence. Pay Strategies for the New Economy*. San Francisco, CA: Jossey-Bass.

Locke, E. A. 2000. Motivation, cognition, and action: An analysis of studies of task goals and knowledge, *Applied Psychology. An International Review*, 49(3): 408–429.

Locke, E. A. and Latham, G. P. 1990. *A Theory of Goal Setting and Task Performance*. Englewood Cliffs, NJ: Prentice-Hall.

Locke, E. A. and Latham, G. P. 2004. What should we do about motivation theory? six recommendations for the 21st century, *Academy of Management Review*, 29(3): 379–387.

Marsden, D. 2004a. The 'Network Economy' and models of the employment contract, *British Journal of Industrial Relations*, 42(4): 659–684.

Marsden, D. 2004b. The role of performance-related pay in renegotiating the 'Effort Bargain:' The case of the british public service, *Industrial and Labor Relations Review*, 57(3): 350–370.

Perry, J. L. and Hondgehem, A. 2008. *Motivation in Public Management: The Call of Public Service*. Oxford, UK: Oxford University Press.

Prendergast, C. 2002. Uncertainty and incentives, *Journal of Labor Economics*, 20(2): 115–137.

Pritchard, R. D., Paquin, A. R., DeCuir, A. D., McGormick, M. J., and Bly, P. R. 2002. The measurement and improvement of organizational productivity, in Pritchard, R. D., Holling, H., Lammers, F., and Clark, B. D. (eds.), *Improving Organizational Performance with the Productivity Measurement and Enhancement System*. Huntington, NY: Nova Science.

Rotemberg, J. J. 2002. Perceptions of equity and the distribution of income, *Journal of Labor Economics*, 20(2/1): 249–288.

Rousseau, D. M. 1995. *Psychological Contracts in Organizations: Understanding Written and Unwritten Agreements*. London, UK: Sage.

Ryan, R. M. and Deci, E. L. 2000. Intrinsic and extrinsic motivations: Classic definitions and new directions, *Contemporary Educational Psychology*, 25(1): 54–67.

Scheuer, S. 2000. *Social and Economic Motivation at Work: Theories of Work Motivation Reassessed*. Copenhagen, Denmark: CBS Press.

Scheuer, S. 2006a. A novel calculus? institutional change, globalization and industrial Conflict in Europe. *European Journal of Industrial Relations*, 12(2): 143–65. http://dx.doi.org/10.1177/0959680106065032.

Scheuer, S. 2006b. Årsbonus som incitamentløn: Større indsats eller mere splittelse?, *Ledelse og erhvervsøkonomi*, 70(2), 100–111.

Schuster, J. R. and Zingheim, P. K. 1992. *The New Pay: Linking Employee and Organizational Performance*. New York, NY: Lexington.

Scott, W. R. 1995. *Institutions and Organizations*. London, UK: Sage.

Sewell, G. and Barker, J. R. 2006. Coercion versus care: Using irony to make sense of organizational surveillance. *Academy of Management Review*, 31(4): 934–61. http://dx.doi.org/10.5465/AMR.2006.22527466.

Sisson, K. and Marginson, P. 2002. Coordinated bargaining: A process for our times?, *British Journal of Industrial Relations*, 40(2): 197–220.

Steel, P. and König, C. J. 2006. Integrating theories of motivation, *Academy of Management Review*, 31(4): 889–913.

Thaler, R. 1980. Towards a positive theory of consumer choice, *Journal of Economic Behavior and Organization*, 1(1): 39–60.

Thaler, R. H. and Sunstein, C. R. 2008. *Nudge: Improving Decisions About Health, Wealth, and Happiness*. New York, NY: Penguin.

Traxler, F., Brandl, B., and Glassner, V. 2007. Pattern bargaining: An investigation into its agency, context, and evidence, *British Journal of Industrial Relations*, 46(1): 33–58.

Tversky, A. and Kahneman, D. 1986. Rational choice and the framing of decisions, *Journal of Business*, 59(4): 251–278.

Vroom, V. H. 1964. *Work and Motivation*. New York, NY: John Wiley and Sons.

Wicker, F. W., Brown, G., Wiehe, J., Hagen, A. S., and Reed, J. L. 1993. On reconsidering maslow: An examination of the deprivation/domination proposition, *Journal of Research in Personality*, 27(2): 118–199.

Wood, S. and Bryson, A. 2009. High involvement management, in Brown, W., Bryson, A., Forth, J., and Whitfield, K. (eds.), *The Evolution of the Modern Workplace*. Cambridge, UK: Cambridge University Press.

Chapter 15

Securing the Future of the Community: Child Protection in ASEAN*

Palapan Kampan and Adam R. Tanielian

Contents

---

* This chapter is a revised version of the authors' published article: Kampan, P. and Tanielian, A. R. 2014. Securing the future of the community: Child protection in ASEAN, *Asian Social Science*, 10(11): 172–84.

Introduction

The Universal Declaration of Human Rights (UDHR), while not a treaty per se, is considered the foundation of international human rights law (United Nations [UN], 2013). Broader historical human rights emerge from the international customary law, some intersecting with *jus cogens*, or peremptory norms—which prohibit genocide, slavery, human trafficking, and racial discrimination (Cornell University, 2013). Treaties addressing other aspects of human rights (such as expression, religion, employment, education, and health care) exist because states agree that such principles should be written into law and that people should be the subjects of such rights. The argument is made that children cannot be holders of rights due to legal and intellectual capacity, and because of problems relating to the exercise of rights while a minor (Archard, 2010). Such arguments are easily held irrelevant because in fact children do have rights and adults have duties to protect those rights. The 1989 Convention on the Rights of the Child (CRC) is a milestone treaty, which outlined the fundamental rights of children to life, nationality, religion, expression, health care, education, and freedoms from exploitation or abuse. The CRC is the most widely ratified international human rights treaty, with only the United States and Somalia withholding ratification. Optional Protocols accompany the CRC and address in further details the involvement of children in armed conflict, the sale of children, child prostitution, and child pornography.

This chapter reflects upon effects of the CRC and related treaties since their inception with a focus on the Association of South East Asian Nations (ASEAN). Successes and failures are considered on several points: nutrition, child soldiers, child sexual exploitation, human immunodeficiency virus infection and acquired immune deficiency syndrome (HIV/AIDS), substance abuse, child labor, violence, and education. As part of preparation for the 2015 launch of the ASEAN Economic Community (AEC), issues relating to children's rights in ASEAN are analyzed with the aim of providing information and conclusions that can help improve conditions in the region. Creative, aggressive policy changes are promoted. Ultimately, the future of the AEC is in the hands of families and individuals in the region, without whose cooperation, children cannot enjoy rights they are guaranteed under international and domestic laws.

Methodology

This research focuses on secondary data including literature, legal materials, and statistics relevant to child protection and children's rights. Aims of the study were to assess both successes and failures in the area of child protection and to offer suggestions for continued improvement in view of apparent systemic or paradigmatic shortcomings. The inclusion of numerical data implies some element of quantitative methods in the research; however, the enormous scope of societies under study in combination with the extreme secrecy, accompanying criminal practices created epistemological conflicts. While the statistical data retrieved from secondary sources were not disputed, we approached such numbers as estimates and reference cases, which supported opinions on issues or demonstrated the need for further action.

Qualitative methods supported broader legal analysis and literature review. Subjectivity associated with morality and deontological ethics was preempted by legal positivism. Conflicts of legideals were mitigated by ranking paradigms from international to local jurisdictions. *De lege ferenda* recommendations for executive and legislative branches are proffered in support of existing principles at multiple levels. Pragmatism was also a concern during formation of conclusions. We undertook the research with the outlook that our systems are fundamentally imperfect and subject to multiple constraints, thus making no singular plan or criticism universally valid. Considering that consequential harm persists short of massive improvements in child protection systems (and given the limited economic resources available) our interpretations of the data are made with a sense of eclectic utilitarianism, whereby our ultimate goal is mere universal children's rights in practice.

Research Procedure

All data and materials were collected from secondary sources. Most of the searches were conducted via electronic databases using keyword strings such as "child protection," "human rights," "child abuse," and associated terms that were mentioned in multiple texts relevant to the research. Documents were initially sorted into "legal" and "article" categories. The "legal" category included treaties, statutes, constitutions, and cases. The "article" category contained academic, governmental, intergovernmental, and nongovernmental organization (NGO) research findings. Upon review of the documents, we found eight main themes: nutrition, child soldiers, child sexual exploitation, HIV/AIDS, substance abuse, child labor, violence, and education. Literature, statistics, and legal documents were again separated by theme for analysis and interpretation.

Convention on the Rights of the Child: 25 Years of Mixed Results

State parties to treaties like the CRC are bound to enact laws implementing certain provisions, but sovereign states also exercise discretion when interpreting obligations and developing domestic enforcement systems. The result is an uneven application of treaty provisions between and among nations. Due to differences in the legal system or tradition or relating to public budgets, treaties often serve as guiding principles or ideals, which are not always considered pragmatic. Ultimate power in any municipal jurisdiction is vested in local, state, federal, or other domestic government. Thus, while states have formally agreed that children are rights holders, abuse of those rights is still prevalent (Voice of America [VoA], 2009; the United Nations Children's Fund is a United Nations Program [UNICEF], 2013). Notwithstanding, the need for further protection and enforcement of children's rights, the CRC, and its Optional Protocols, led to constrained successes.

Nutrition

Consistent progress has been made worldwide through the application of CRC Articles 24 and 27 and implementing policies at the domestic level. Cambodia, Indonesia, Laos, Philippines, Thailand, and Vietnam saw the prevalence of undernourishment decrease from an average 36% of the population in 1990 to 14.5% in 2011 (World Bank, 2013). Prevalence of stunting in Southeast Asia saw an estimated decline from about 43% of children in 1990 to around 28% in 2005 (Gillespie et al., 2001). However, while conditions have improved in recent decades, the prevalence of malnutrition in Southeast Asia is greater than the average among developing nations (World Health Organization [WHO], 2013).

Proper diet and growth is not a superficial concern, nor is being underweight or malnourished merely a matter of cultural perception. Potterton (2009) found malnutrition related to 60% of deaths in children under five. Another study found malnourished children are 20% less literate (Save the Children, 2013). The Food and Agriculture Organization of the United Nation (FAO)

(2012) stated, "adequate nutrition is essential for economic growth, good health and physical and cognitive development." In 2007, East and South Asia were tied for the highest degree of malnutrition in the world, with no improvement over the previous decade unlike in Sub-Saharan Africa (ibid). While some quarter of the world's children have been considered "seriously underweight" (UNICEF, 2006a), those numbers have been higher in developing ASEAN states. UNICEF (2006b) estimated that six million children under the age of five were underweight in Indonesia, three million in the Philippines, and two million in Vietnam. A two-way relationship is noticed, where poor economic and social conditions lead to and emerge from poor nutrition.

Child Soldiers

CRC Article 38, referring to customary International Humanitarian Law Rules 136–7, proscribes recruitment and involvement of children in armed conflict. Numerous other multilateral agreements likewise ban the use of child soldiers, which is listed as a war crime under Article 8 of the Rome Statute. In the 10 years following the Optional Protocol, the use of child soldiers decreased significantly among state militaries (Lederer, 2008; Child Soldiers International [formerly the Coalition to Stop the Use of Child Soldiers or CSUCS], 2012). However, there are still believed to be some 800,000 active child soldiers worldwide, comprising about 40% of all armed forces (Kaplan, 2005; Chatterjee, 2012). Nonstate militias, terrorist organizations, and rebel forces and gangs now pose the greatest threat globally.

Longstanding conflicts in Southeast Asia draw attention to the consistent use of child soldiers in the region. Myanmar has oft been cited as having the highest number of child soldiers in the world (Bachhuber, 2003; Tran, 2009; Healey, 2011). The Secretary General of the UN (2011) recently reported the involvement of children in armed conflict in Myanmar, Philippines, and Thailand. These egregious violations of children's rights shed light on the deficiencies of our international legal system, which operates on good faith standards whereby independent nations are solely responsible for honoring their agreements (with little to no feasible means of remedy for individuals).

Despite overwhelming political support for the CRC and Optional Protocols, the treaty itself has no direct authority within domestic systems, where laws are implemented and enforced. Two areas where there have been consistent improvements—child soldiers and nutrition—provide examples of the scope and severity of the larger issues, where each percent improvement represents only a drop in the bucket. Facts and figures suggest that protection of children's rights resembles that of adults' rights. There is some minimum level of enforcement, but no utopian paradise is emerging regardless of political and social interest.

ASEAN 2015: The Need for a New Approach

Scheduled to launch in 2015, the AEC could be a breakthrough in regional political, social, cultural, environmental, and economic relations. Considering the population diversity and social dynamics of the region, increased flow of goods, services, capital, labor, and people also pose unique threats to public safety, health, security, and wellbeing. For the AEC to be as successful as its proponents wish, both public and private sectors in ASEAN will need to undertake some fairly radical changes. Handshakes and document signings among politicians alone will not be enough to ensure a smooth transition into a harmonized union. Massive grassroots and informal local efforts will be crucial in building any sustainable development, peace, and stability in South East Asia (SEA). Enforcement is vital in the short term, and a cultural transition needs to occur in the medium to long term.

Child Sexual Exploitation

Southeast Asia has long held the dubious distinction of having one of the world's largest populations of child prostitutes. Estimates of the exact number of children involved in illicit sex trades vary, but presence of minors in tourist brothel establishments is well known in places such as Thailand, Cambodia, and the Philippines, among which there could be roughly one million child prostitutes (Tumlin, 2000; Jacquemin, 2011). Numerous studies have exposed the scourge of child sex exploitation in ASEAN, linking the trade to organized crime, disease, psychiatric illness, poverty, statelessness, and corruption (Tanielian, 2013).

The region's tropical climate, pristine beaches, and open-door visa policies make it a popular international travel destination, but what is good for the tourism industry is also bad for society as sex tourists troll the bars and towns for exotic thrills. An American ambassador to the Philippines estimated that "40% of foreign tourists come to the Philippines for sex" (Rosales, 2011). That figure is suspected to be closer to 60% in Thailand, where sex is "an essential economic pillar" (Rusing and Urbina, 2005; Shahabudin, 2012). These statistics are in spite of statutory prohibition of all prostitution in those nations.* Evidence of a failure to protect is found in the fact that prostitution, including child prostitution, proliferates openly and freely throughout the region, without significant prevention or enforcement by public or private sectors. All 10 ASEAN members have laws prohibiting sex trafficking and exploitation of minors (International Criminal Police Organization [INTERPOL/ICPO], 2010), yet the region has become a prime destination for child sex tourists (Bergman, 2013).

Cases like *United States versus Kent Frank*[†] and *Regina versus Klassen*[‡] caught media attention and showed extraterritorial law enforcement is possible in response to grave human rights abuses like child sex tourism; however, such actions cannot abrogate domestic authority. The territoriality principle of international law generally supplants the nationality principle. Hence, cooperation between states can aid in prosecution for criminal offenses—whether in the nation where the offense occurred or in the nation to which the accused belongs—but a foreign nation may not conduct investigations or make arrests abroad without explicit permission from the state in which such actions are undertaken. Consequently, responsibilities for enforcement and adjudication are best left to the sovereign nation in which offenses occur.

Eradication of any criminal trade is usually an unrealistic target, but a reduction by more than half within 10 years would be feasible with the right type and amount of attention. Reactive policing is perpetually required, but to tackle thorny turpitude such as child sex trades, proactive policing and heavy community involvement are essential. Government officers and civilians alike should take the independent initiative to gather and disseminate information, analyze issues, and develop strategies that go beyond mere education on the topic.

Neighborhood watches, community hotlines, peer counseling, and early detection initiatives must provide a support system, which not only rescues those caught in illicit trades although prevents new entrants. Comprehensive, effective protection systems will undoubtedly challenge

---

* Thailand Prostitution Prevention and Suppression Act (1996). Philippines Revised Penal Code (1930). Art. 202.
† United States v. Frank, 599 F.3d 1221 (2010).
‡ Regina v. Klassen, 24292 BCSC 1762 (2008).

cultural norms related to privacy, the status quo regarding expressing dissent, and traditional Confucian opposition to legalism and coercive state power (Bloom, 2009; Deng, n.d.). Without changes in attitudes toward communicating openly and honestly about social ills, progress will be minimal.

HIV/AIDS

Like most macropublic health and crime statistics, numbers of HIV/AIDS infections are inexact. Statistical uncertainty and social taboos increase the complexity of these problems. What is sometimes overlooked is how the disease spreads across geographical regions. Rapid economic growth and mobility within and across national borders also affect how the disease impacts a society or region (the United Nations Educational, Scientific, and Cultural Organization [UNESCO], 2004). With more than two million cases of HIV/AIDS in the Greater Mekong Sub-Region (GMS), relaxed international visa and travel restrictions within the AEC could lead to the growth of HIV/AIDS infections.

A UNICEF (n.d.) study from Southeast Asia showed 30% of sex workers aged 13–19 are infected with HIV. Thailand—the wealthiest nation in the GMS—has the highest rate of HIV infection in Southeast Asia (Bergman, 2013) showing the disease is not exclusive to the most impoverished. Ruangkanchanasetr et al. (2005) found high-risk behavior associated with HIV/AIDS—such as drug use—was prevalent among adolescents in Bangkok. Studies have concluded that campaigns for condom use in commercial sex establishments have helped slow the spread of HIV/AIDS (UNICEF, n.d.), but limited or logistical growth models are not necessarily the most attractive trends. Rather, we should aim for a more parabolic curve to see a reduction in the total number of cases in the near future.

Reducing the prevalence of HIV/AIDS requires dramatic changes in behavior and cognition among major sectors in society. Education and awareness campaigns are imperative. However, education is perhaps the simplest component of a functional plan. Attitudes regarding the value of life will need to shift so that people who are aware of the disease can justify taking action to prevent its spread. This entails higher-order changes in socioeconomic paradigms.

Substance Abuse

In 2003, the United Nations reported that

> [t]the Asian and Pacific region has some of the toughest laws against drug abuse and drug trafficking. Yet, the region is losing the war on drug abuse. Increasing numbers of young people are joining the ranks of drug users. At the same time, the age of initiation into drug use is declining throughout Asia and the Pacific to as low as 12 years.

Studies of over the past decade have shown that 5%–7% of Thai adolescents engage in drug use, with rates among boys reaching nearly 14% (Pengpid and Peltzer, 2013). Whereas Western teenagers use cannabis more often than other drugs, methamphetamine is the most commonly used drug among Thais. In 2010–2011, Thailand ranked fourth in the world for reported methamphetamine seizures (United Nations Office on Drugs and Crime [UNODC], 2013a). Year-on-year growth was 60% between 2011 and 2012, when 227 million pills were seized (UNODC, 2013b). Prevalence of people who inject drugs has decreased in Thailand, but the country remains a hub for heroin trafficking. Domestic Thai market preferences may have shifted away from the opiates the Golden Triangle nation was famous for in the 1960s–1980s, but opium cultivation has stubbornly remained an issue. The Narcotics Control Board Deputy Secretary-General Pitaya Jinawat reported that local politicians or ex-state officials finance most opium growers in the Kingdom (Kheunkaew and Khamthita, 2008). While estimated production for 2013 was low, Thailand's role in the Golden Triangle opiate trade is still active (Australia Network News [ANN], 2013).

Myanmar remains the primary suspected source of methamphetamine pills in East and Southeast Asia, and the world's number two producer of illicit opiate drugs (UNODC, 2013a,b). Opium cultivation has remained a persistent and increasing problem in Myanmar despite government campaigns to eradicate the drug (Stout, 2013). Among the three Golden Triangle nations—Myanmar, Laos, and Thailand—opium poppy production has risen for seven consecutive years (UNODC, 2013c). The region accounted for 18% of global illicit opium production in 2013. Children and young people in Southeast Asia are exposed not only to cultures and societies heavily affected by illicit drug cartel activity but also to abuse of legal substances like alcohol and tobacco. While some people view illegal and legal drugs as separate issues, other studies confirm positive relationships among all risky behavior (United Nations Economic and Social Commission for Asia and the Pacific [UNESCAP], 2003; Kulsudjarit, 2004; Pengpid and Peltzer, 2013; UNODC, 2013a). Psychoactive drugs are normal goods by economic terms, and studies show these positive correlations between income and legal and illegal drug use (Petry, 2000; Institute of Alcohol Studies [IAS], 2011; Hu and Stowe, 2013). As income rises within the AEC, so too do threats to public health and safety in the way of increased use of and exposure to a variety of legal and illegal drugs.

The problem of drug use among people under age 18 cannot be effectively addressed without taking a more comprehensive approach. Rather than merely stigmatizing illegal drugs and their users, experts in multiple disciplines related to public health, law, psychiatry, education, and social sciences have overwhelmingly endorsed major overhauls to antidrug strategies with the aim of creating "evidence-based policy" or moving away from rhetoric and ideology toward more scientific handling of the issues (International Center for Science in Drug Policy [ICSDP], 2010; Obama, 2013).

Doctors and scientists involved in the Vienna Declaration believe that "we cannot end AIDS until we end the war on drugs" reflecting the complex matrix of associated ills. However, ending the war on drugs in Southeast Asia would challenge a prime component of the political status quo. It is easily arguable that such a paradigm change would not be popular or appropriate in the region. Still, each year more experts admit that the war on drugs has failed (Annan and Cardoso, 2013; Law Enforcement Against Prohibition [LEAP], 2013; McDonald, 2013).

A twenty-first-century strategy for ASEAN could rely upon facts and statistics related to health and safety in general. Worldwide, alcohol use is the world's third largest risk factor for disease burden, whereas illicit drug use ranks 18th (WHO, 2009). Drunkenness—rather than illegal drug intoxication—is associated with most murders and violent crimes (Bureau of Justice Statistics [BJS], 2007; DrugScope, 2013). Public and private initiatives should focus on creating and sustaining a more functional community where risks are better managed, and reckless behavior is not supported or ignored. Both alcohol and drug laws need to be enforced. Offenders and abusers need treatment and guidance options through local departments of health and groups like Alcoholics Anonymous and Narcotics Anonymous, whether inside or outside of correctional facilities (Smart Justice, 2013).

Real and sustained change throughout the AEC will require changes of mind, which are the most difficult changes to put into action. Children and young people will need to feel comfortable talking about their thoughts, feelings, and behavior related to illicit drugs and related issues. Creating a supportive atmosphere will not be simple, considering that popular government initiatives from the previous decade included extrajudicial killings of drug suspects (Economist, 2008). Until opinions, irrational fears, and superstitions are replaced by solid facts and trust in science, progress will be minimal.

Child Labor

Every country in ASEAN except Myanmar ratified both the 1973 International Labor Organization (ILO) Convention No. 138 regarding minimum working age and 1999 Convention No. 182 concerning the worst forms of child labor. Article 32 of the CRC similarly requires a minimum age of employment while Articles 33–36 pertain to the worst forms of child labor (i.e., slavery, sexual exploitation, child pornography, and trafficking in children). Despite the popularity of these treaties among national legislatures, widespread violations are found in practice. Perhaps child labor is the most noticeable area where rhetoric and formal policy are starkly contradicted by daily practice. There certainly exist arguments on behalf of parents and community members that suggest child labor is necessary for basic economic survival, but those points do not change the gravity of the situation where children's rights are being openly and wantonly abused.

Minimum working age for children is 15 under Article 2(2) of Convention No. 138, yet UNICEF (2011) reported on five ASEAN member states wherein greater than 7% of children age 5–14 were involved in labor. Although national laws state a minimum working age of 15,[*] the World Bank (2013) estimated 35% of children age 7–14 in Cambodia work, 13% in the Philippines, and 15% in Thailand. Numbers were negligible in the wealthiest three countries in ASEAN—Singapore, Brunei, and Malaysia. Regional rates of child labor exceed worldwide averages for respective national income groups (ILO, 2013). Indonesia,[†] Laos,[‡] and Vietnam[§] labor laws allow some employment of persons under age 15, despite ratification of Convention 138.

Not a single member of ASEAN received a positive review from the U.S. Department of State in the 2013 Trafficking in Persons Report. Cambodia, Malaysia, Myanmar, and Thailand were placed on the Tier 2 Watch List (2WL). It should be considered no coincidence that Thailand is a neighbor to each of the other three AEC members on the 2WL, given that Thailand is frequently cited as the number one destination country for trafficking in the GMS (Punkrasin, 2008; International Organization for Migration [IOM], 2012). Regardless of law, policy, ideology, religion, or formal doctrine prohibiting these abuses, Southeast Asia is known for all of the worst forms of child labor (*see* ECPAT, 2013).

Changing the labor market will be a challenge for most nations in ASEAN, where large portions of the workforce are in agriculture. Reports showed children most frequently work in agriculture. Gross Domestic Product (GDP) per capita (purchasing power parity [PPP]) is less than USD $10,000 in seven of ten ASEAN member states (Central Intelligence Agency [CIA], 2013). ASEAN has three of the world's least developed countries—Cambodia, Laos, and Myanmar. Absent miraculous economic growth, community-led changes should be directed at the long term with more planned parenthood, birth control, and education on family economics. Children should not be viewed as another farm hand. In the short and medium terms, only government enforcement can make a dent. Schools will need to report absences against registries of local

---

[*] Cambodia Labor Code (1997). Art. 177; Thailand Labor Protection Act, §44 (1998); Philippines Labor Code (1974). Art. 139.

[†] Indonesia Act Concerning Manpower (2003). Art. 68–70.

[‡] Laos Labour Law (2006). Art. 41.

[§] Vietnam Labour Code (2012). Art. 164.

residents to make sure children are enrolled and attending. However, in the world of small, family owned businesses, enforcement will interfere with perceived parental rights, and social harmony could be disrupted until people come to terms with living within the letter of their laws.

Violence

CRC Article 19 theoretically protects children from all forms of violence while Article 28 protects them from violence in schools. Most violence against children relates to harmful traditional practices that have been normalized for millennia. 94% of children age 2–14 in Vietnam and 74% of children in the same age group in Laos reported experiencing violent disciplinary methods (UNICEF, 2011). UNICEF (2012) reported multiple studies from ASEAN showing trends of abuse: 30% of Thai sixth grade students reported physical abuse, 50% or more of children in Cambodia experienced physical abuse, and about 50% of children in the Philippines experienced corporal punishment in schools. High and higher numbers are found all around the region, and qualitative reports support an assertion that violence against children is prevalent in ASEAN (Ratarsarn, 2005; UNICEF, 2005; UN, 2006).

Overt, multifaceted public and private action, and support for changes of habit and culture, which have for ages endangered the safety and wellbeing of children, are needed to stop the violence, but no change can happen without mothers and fathers simply protecting their children.

Education

In 2010, mean years of schooling among adults aged 25 and older in ASEAN was 6.65 years. Adults age 25 and older in Cambodia, Indonesia, Laos, Myanmar, and Vietnam had less than six years of schooling on average (United Nations Development Program [UNDP], 2010). While six out of ten ASEAN members are on track to meet MDG two on primary school enrollment (UNICEF, 2007), primary education alone will not lead to significant improvements in income and quality of life in a competitive AEC. Thailand, with its higher GDP per capita compared to other nations in the region, serves as a standard of comparison for the medium human development group— Thailand, Philippines, Indonesia, Vietnam, Cambodia, Laos—yet only 29% of females and 36% of males age 25 and older in Thailand have at least a secondary education (UNDP, 2013).

Discussion

While the birth of a child is often anecdotally related to the happiest moments in a person's life, we find a breadth of evidence that as the child matures, individuals and societies exhibit less joy about the life. It is unarguably a parent's responsibility to feed, clothe, shelter, protect, and begin to teach a child, but for a variety of reasons many parents are unable or unwilling to carry out their basic duties. Ideally, the State should step in and replace the parent in some way such that the child's development, health, and wellbeing are not severely impeded. Such an ideal system breaks down, however when the State does not have sufficient funds or political infrastructure to give benefits or place children in protective custody.

Within ASEAN, the average income lies below USD $4,000 per year[*] and inflation outpaces wage gains (Australia DFAT, 2013). Education and good food are normal goods, so we can

---

[*] 2013 GDP per capita USD $3,852.

conclude that lack of education and food implies a lack of economic means. Ideally, when a family is unable to provide necessity goods for a child, the government should supplement income or provide benefits. However, tax revenues in ASEAN fall far below the Organization for Economic Cooperation and Development (OECD) average levels, and individuals are unable to contribute further to tax bases, leaving seven of ten ASEAN governments without means to provide for and protect their people (OECD, 2013; World Bank, 2013).

The data and literature showed a trend across all themes: there simply is not enough money to fix the problems. Despite some variance between nations' domestic statutes, their apparent missions are generally in sync with prominent international values. The ASEAN Human Rights Declaration (2012) reaffirms commitments toward human rights. What is being said and written is sufficient, but the disparity between stated commitments and actual results draws concern.

Annual Human Development Reports (UNDP, 2013) show correlations between income, institutional, and social quality. In essence, microindividual cases are representative of macrocollective conditions. People from poorer nations are more likely to experience extremely troublesome life phenomena such as human rights abuses. In turn, persons subjected to human rights abuses are more likely stuck in deep poverty (Amnesty International, 2013). Economic essentials such as secondary education, student busing, free school lunches, social housing, food stamps, and child protective services cannot be established and maintained without dramatic changes in public budgets.

Real, sustained, quantifiable improvements of living conditions and quality of life require both macroeconomic growth, which supports per capita income growth, and more active local enforcement against human rights violators. Paradoxical conditions clearly exist whereby law enforcement cannot be funded without increased government revenue, which in turn cannot rise without the economic benefits of more civil societies. Lacking reform in tax collection, public budgets will not likely support doubling or tripling of enforcement and corrections budgets, especially since prisons are already overcrowded in the region (Walmsley, 2011; International Center for Prison Studies [ICPS], 2012). There are, fortunately, some important factors that have not yet been seriously considered.

Disruptive Policy Innovation for Social Change

If police were to act in more *ex officio* capacity and undertake more proactive efforts on the issues of child sex tourism, it is likely that large seizures of cash and property could be witnessed, which could fund further efforts in the fight against children's rights abuses. Legalization of adult prostitution, such as in Singapore, could also help government officials regulate the age of sex workers while increasing tax bases and exponentially reducing money laundering. In the meantime, drinking establishments should be searched or raided for minors, and alcohol distribution outlets should be the subjects of investigations for furnishing to minors. Fines should be assessed for violations of laws, which would then increase police budgets. Furthermore, a comprehensive system of liquor, dancing, hotel, travel, tourism, and other entertainment licenses would increase public budgets, thereby giving governments more power to enforce laws.

WHO (2009) considers opium and related drugs "essential medications." Few people are aware of licit opium cultivation worldwide, such as in Australia (Tasmanian Government Department of Justice [TASDOJ], 2013), India (Bureau of Narcotics, 2013), Turkey (UNODC, n.d.), and Great Britain (Allen-Stevens, 2001). Considering that the problem of opium cultivation in the Golden Triangle region is persistent and supported by "local politicians and ex-state officials" (Kheunkaew and Khamthita, 2008), a licensing scheme could be developed to handle political concerns and improve tax revenues. Should opium crops be licensed and distributed through proper hospital channels, *ex officio* action against illicit producers in Thailand, Laos, and Myanmar would likely be easier to rationalize.

If public budgets can be increased significantly through some aggressive new policy, and/or by more active enforcement of older policies, then expenditures in education and social infrastructure may support broader improvements. Education and counseling services give people valuable skills and know-how that can generate long-term returns, making individuals more self-sufficient, more productive, and more socially responsible. Children can be fed balanced meals at schools that have the budgetary power to offer free or subsidized nutrition based upon reported family reported income. Instead of turning a blind eye to vises of the region, authorities can look for opportunity in even the foulest segments of consumer markets. However, only with a more mature, humble approach can one man's trash become another man's treasure.

Conclusion

None of the literature or legal documents reviewed suggested that child protection today is at an entirely acceptable level. While most children today enjoy more rights than those in generations past, abuse is still at intolerable levels. Poverty and human rights abuse are clearly related, placing a greater burden to protect upon governments whose people are impoverished such as those in the Mekong Sub-Region. Governments, unfortunately, cannot print their way out of economic turmoil, and lacking public revenues displace burdens of protection back onto private communities.

Potential revenues are available in the short- and medium-term through creative initiatives and much-needed political changes. There are enormous opportunities for macroeconomic growth in the medium- to long-term for the AEC, but there are no guarantees that such growth will occur or that its impacts will be distributed evenly. Alternative means of providing security and stability need to be explored and debated in the short term, perhaps offered to the public by way of a democratic vote. By engaging in academic research and discussion of issues—with the aim of suppressing invalid arguments while supporting fact-based reasoning—real change can occur in ASEAN.

Still, increased government action is no panacea for human rights abuses. Governments are neither omnipotent nor infallible. Human rights abuses exist in every country, caused and perpetuated by a complex range of factors from inequity and mental illness to prejudice and passive aggression. While few people are directly involved in human rights abuses, it requires a great deal of ignorance and indirect support from bystanders who may consider altruism irrational. Police and courts need to react swiftly when violations occur, but proactive measures are probably the best route toward more civility.

The most difficult part of any process of change will likely be to gain genuine support in communities. Modern political conditions in the ASEAN region are such that people may think and feel as though they love and support their governments or nations, but in practice they fail to uphold the fundamental principles upon which the states were formed. Human rights abuses not only violate *sui generis* statutes but also trample Constitutional ideals. Unfortunately, courts are often ineffective and inefficient forums for handling cases involving constitutional or human rights abuses, save the most appalling of incidents.

Human rights, whether for children or adults, emerge from the heart of communities based upon liberties that people agree are universally valid. Practice and protection of such rights must be a personal endeavor occurring in the home, at work, at school, and everywhere life takes place. Massive failures to protect children's rights as identified in this article are evidence that insufficient numbers of adults recognize and respect rights of children. Continuance of such atrocities is not legally defensible, but where the law itself is viewed with a suspicious eye and spoken of with a disdainful tone, little progress can be made.

References

Allen-Stevens, T. 2001. First license is granted for British drug poppies, *Farmers Weekly*.

Amnesty International 2013. *Poverty and Human Rights*, London, UK.

Annan, K. and Cardoso, F. 2013. Kofi Annan: Stop the "War on Drugs," *Cable News Network (CNN)*.

Archard, D. 2010. Children's rights, *Stanford Encyclopedia of Philosophy*. Center for the Study of Language and Information, Stanford University, Stanford, CA.

ASEAN Human Rights Declaration (November 19, 2012). Phom Penh, Cambodia.

Australian Government, Department of Foreign Affairs and Trade (DFAT) 2013. *ASEAN 10*, Canberra, Australia.

Bachhuber, E. 2003. *Reluctant Warriors?: A Comparative Analysis of Children in Armed Conflict in Colombia an Myanmar*, Monterey Institute of International Studies, Monterey, CA.

Bergman, J. 2013. Can Burma avoid the curse of sex tourism? *Time*.

BJS 2007. *Drug Use and Crime*, Washington, DC.

Bloom, I. 2009. *Introduction to Confucian Thought*, Asia for Educators, Columbia University, New York, NY.

Chatterjee, S. 2012. We needn't wait for conflicts to end for children to be removed from armed organizations, *Forbes*.

Child Soldiers International 2012. *Louder than Words*, London, UK.

CIA 2013. *GDP per capita (PPP)*, Washington, DC.

Cornell University 2013. *Jus Cogens*, Ithaca, NY.

Deng, F. n.d. *Corrective Justice in the Confucian Legal Tradition: A Nonexistent Concept*, Peking University Law School, Peking, China.

DrugScope. 2013. *How Much Crime is Drug Related?* London, UK.

Economist 2008. *Thailand's Drug Wars: Back on the Offensive*, London, UK.

ECPAT 2013. *End Child Prostitution, Child Pornography & Trafficking of Children for Sexual Purposes*, Bangkok, Thailand.

FAO 2012. *FAO Statistical Yearbook: World Food and Agriculture*, Rome, Italy.

Gillespie, S., Haddad, L., and Allen, L. 2001. *Attacking the Double Burden of Malnutrition in Asia and the Pacific*, Asian Development Bank, Manila, Philippines.

Healey, J. 2011. *Former Burmese Child Soldier to Speak in Congress*, Huffington Post.

Hu, X. and Stowe, J. 2013. *The Effect of Income on Health Choices: Alcohol Use*, Southern Agricultural Economics Association Annual Meeting, Orlando, FL.

IAS 2011. *Consumption levels by income earned*. Retrieved December 26, 2013, from http://www.ias.org. uk/Alcohol-knowledge-centre/Socioeconomic-groups/Factsheets/Consumption-levels-by-income-earned.aspx.

ICPS 2012. *World Prison Brief: Asia*, London, UK.

ILO 2013. *Marking Progress against Child Labor*, Manila, Philippines.

ILO Convention (No. 138) 1973. Minimum Age Convention.

ILO Convention (No. 182) 1999. Worst Forms of Child Labor Convention.

India Central Bureau of Narcotics (CBN) 2013. *Licit Cultivation*, New Delhi, India.

International Centre for Science in Drug Policy (ICSDP) 2010. *The Vienna Declaration*, Vancouver, Canada.

INTERPOL/ICPO 2010. *Legislation of INTERPOL Member States on Sexual Offences against Children*, Lyons, France.

IOM 2012. *Child Trafficking and Labor Trafficking Cases Rising*, Geneva, Switzerland.

Jacquemin, C. 2011. Mekong Responsible Tourism, UNWTO. http://ethics.unwto.org/sites/all/files/docpdf/jacqueminpresentation-baliseminar2011.pdf.

Kaplan, E. 2005. *Child Soldiers Around the World*, Council on Foreign Relations (CFR), New York, NY.

Kheunkaew, S. and Khamthita, T. 2008. *Golden Triangle Opium Production on the Rise*, Bangkok Post, Bangkok, Thailand.

Kulsudjarit, K. 2004. Drug Problem in Southeast and Southwest Asia, *Annals New York Academy of Sciences*, 1025: 446–57.

LEAP 2013. *Law Enforcement against Prohibition*, Medford, MA.

Lederer, E. 2008. Conflicts using child soldiers declines, *The Seattle Times*.

McDonald, H. 2013. *"It is Time to End the War on Drugs:" Says Top UK Police Chief*, The Guardian, London, UK.

Obama, B. 2013. *A 21st Century Drug Policy*, Office of National Drug Control Policy, Washington, DC.

OECD 2013. *Revenue Statistics and Policy Challenges in Asia,* Development Center and Center for Tax Policy and Administration, Paris, France.

Pengpid, S. and Peltzer, K. 2013. Prevalence and psychosocial correlates of illicit drug use among school-going adolescents in Thailand, *Journal of Social Science*, 34(3): 269–75.

Petry, N. 2000. Effects of increasing income on Polydrug use: A comparison of heroin, cocaine, and alcohol abusers, *Addiction*, 95(5): 705–17.

Potterton, L. 2009. Fighting malnutrition, *International Atomic Energy Agency (IAEA) Bulletin*, 50–2: 43–4.

Punkrasin, C. 2008. *Letter from the Permanent Mission of Thailand to the United Nations*, UN, New York, NY.

Ratarsarn, Y. 2005. *Recommendations from Children on Violence against Children*, UNICEF, New York, NY.

Rosales, A. 2011. *US Ambassador's Statements on RP's Sex Tourism Have Basis—DFA*, Philippines Department of Foreign Affairs (DFA), Manila, Philippines.

Ruangkanchanasetr, S., Plitponkarnpim, A., Hetrakul, P., and Kongsakon, R. 2005. Youth risk behavior survey: Bangkok, Thailand, *Journal of Adolescent Health*, 36(6): 227–35.

Rushing, R. and Urbina, J. 2005. Fatal Attraction: A Qualitative Study of Western Clients of Sex Workers in Thailand, paper presented at Conference *Violence: A Game for Men*? Guadalajara, Mexico, June 21–23, 2006.

Save the Children 2013. *Food for Thought Report*, London, UK.

Shahabudin, S. 2012. *Strategies of Civil Society to Address AIDS in Asia: Emphasis on the Sex Sector,* UN, New York, NY.

Smart Justice Alliance. 2013. http://smartjusticealliance.org/documents/

Stout, D. 2013. Burma's opium production has hit record levels because farmers have no choice, *Time*.

Tanielian, A. 2013. Illicit supply and demand: Child sex exploitation in ASEAN, *National Taiwan University Law Review*, 8(1): 97–140.

TASDOJ 2013. *Poppy Production in Tasmania*, Hobart, Australia.

Tran, M. 2009. Burma rebels vow to stop using child soldiers, *The Guardian*.

Tumlin, K. 2000. Trafficking in children and women: A regional overview, paper presented at *Asian Regional High-level Meeting on Child Labor*, Bangkok, Thailand.

UN 2006. Rights of the Child, General Assembly Report A/61/299.

UN 2011. Children and Armed Conflict, A/65/820–S/2011/250.

UN 2013. The Foundation of International Human Rights Law.

UNDP 2010. *HDI Trends 1980–2010*, New York, NY.

UNDP 2013. Human Development Report.

UNESCAP 2003. *Adolescent Substance Use: Risk and Protection*, New York, NY.

UNESCO 2004. *HIV/AIDS in the GMS*, New York, NY.

UNICEF 2005. Regional Assessment on Violence against Children in East Asia and the Pacific Region.

UNICEF 2006a. A Quarter of the World's Children Seriously Underweight.

UNICEF 2006b. Progress for Children.

UNICEF 2007. MDG2: Achieve Universal Primary Education.

UNICEF 2012. Child Maltreatment: Prevalence, Incidence, and Consequences in the East Asia and Pacific Region.

UNICEF 2013. Child Protection: Statistical Indicators.

UNICEF n.d. HIV/AIDS in the Region: Impacts and Risk Factors.

UNODC 2013a. World Drug Report, New York, NY.

UNODC 2013b. Record-High Methamphetamine Seizures in Southeast Asia.

UNODC 2013c. Golden Triangle Opium Production Rises 22% in 2013, Says UNODC.
UNODC n.d. Turkey Program.
US Department of State (DoS) 2013. *Trafficking in Persons Report*, Washington, DC.
VoA 2009. *Children's Rights Still Violated 20 Years after Convention*, Washington, DC.
Walmsley, R. 2011. *World Prison Population List*, International Center for Prison Studies, London, UK.
WHO 2009. *Access to Controlled Medications Program*, Geneva, Switzerland.
WHO 2013. Millennium Development Goals.
World Bank 2013. *World Development Indicators*, Washington, DC.

Chapter 16

Researching International Humanitarian Law: A Decision-Making Process Model for Operationalizing State Practice[*]

Matthew T. Zommer

Contents

---

[*] This chapter is a revised version of the author's published article: Zommer, M. T. 2014. Operationalizing international humanitarian law: A decision-making process model for assessing state practice, *International Law Research*, 3(1): 150–8.

Introduction

The subject of international humanitarian law (IHL) contains multiple opportunities for accessing and gathering historical and contemporary examples of the primary source material. However, a review of the literature reveals the absence of a consistent and coherent model for examining this material. Specifically, the subject of state practice is underoperationalized for research purposes. The aim of this chapter is to provide a common methodological framework for researching and disseminating IHL source material. Two salient shortcomings in the literature reviewed influenced this chapter's development. First, the literature contains an overemphasis on treaty rule analysis, often failing to include examples of state practice. Second, a portion of the literature is advocacy-driven, often ignoring examples of negative state practice. The decision-making process model advanced in this chapter addresses these limitations and provides an inclusive framework for assessing IHL.

This chapter emerged from the author's experience researching historical and contemporary U.S. practice with IHL; specifically, issues surrounding enforcement, reciprocity, and reprisals. It has also been informed by conflicting theories and disciplinary debates between scholars of International Law (IL) and International Relations (IR). In particular, the author has considered the interdisciplinary imbalance that places an emphasis on IR theory, often leaving IL methodology perspectives and theories underutilized. Jeffrey Dunoff and Mark Pollack's recent collection, *Interdisciplinary Perspectives on International Law and International Relations* (2013), is the most extensive work to date addressing the empirical and theoretical interaction between IL and IR. The authors conclude that a majority of the interdisciplinary work has involved the application of IR as a "discipline to IL as a subject" (Dunoff and Pollack, 2013: 649). In turn, the authors recommend that IR scholars make greater use of lawmaking process approaches that take into consideration the dynamics of customary IL. Applying this recommendation to IHL (a subject of shared interest between both disciplines) this chapter seeks to foster discussion and to maximize the collection and organization of the large volume of primary source material that often goes underutilized.

Three terms are often used to describe the constraints and acceptable practices exhibited during times of war: law(s) of war, law(s) of armed conflict, and IHL. For consistency, IHL is used throughout this chapter to describe the body of rules and customs that regulate behavior during times of armed conflict. IHL is comprised of three broad categories: rules concerning weapons, rules concerning warfare (including rules pertaining to permissible tactics and targeting), and humanitarian rules governing the treatment of victims of conflict (Delupis, 2000). Furthermore, IHL is divided into two types: convention law (often referred to as positive law) and customary law.

Convention law consists of codified rules found in multinational treaties. A significant portion of the academic literature on IHL examines the subject from this treaty rule-based perspective.

This emphasis is not surprising considering that treaties are the end product of an often extensive and well-publicized multinational diplomatic negotiation process. However, problems arise when IHL analysis is limited solely to treaty rules and fails to consider examples of state practice. When the analysis is restricted to treaty rules, it results in an incomplete and potentially misleading view. The danger associated with such limited analysis is well articulated by Roberts and Guelff (2000) who conclude that "any work concerning the laws of war which is limited to international agreements risks distorting not only the form but also the substance of the law" (Roberts and Guelff, 2000: 7).

Customary international law (CIL), on the other hand, is non-codified and often consists of emerging trends based on state behavior. As defined by the U.S. government, CIL is the "general and consistent practice of states which is followed by them from a sense of legal obligation [*opinio juris*]" (Restatement (Third) of Foreign Relations Law of the United States (1987) § 102 (2)). From a conceptual and research perspective, there is considerable nebulousness and overlap in the source material comprising state practice and *opinio juris*. Furthermore, there exists ongoing debate among scholars and jurists on how to weigh the importance of state practice and *opinio juris* (Price, 2004). Conceptual and evidentiary difficulty particularly lies in attempts to determine *opinion juris*, the "psychological" element of CIL (Goldsmith and Posner, 1999). Arguably, when considering state practice (as opposed to *opinion juris*), there is greater evidentiary clarity due to the availability of documented primary source material. In turn, there is less need to make interpretive decisions concerning intent. Finally, the largest study to date on customary IHL (discussed next in greater detail) found that separating state practice from *opinion juris* to be difficult and largely theoretical.

It is outside the scope of the present work to evaluate the conceptual differences between the two elements that comprise CIL. Furthermore, this chapter does not advance arguments concerning the customary status of specific IHL rules. Instead, the present focus is on creating a methodological model that can aid in researching and organizing primary source material that potentially relates to both state practice and *opinion juris*. From a research perspective, CIL is conceptually vague, complex, and because of its dynamic nature, it is also in need of constant updating of the source material. Thus, the challenge facing the scholar researching IHL is to operationalize the subject into a clearer, delineable, and observable phenomenon. To address this challenge, an expansive view—or what Michael Byers refers to as the "inclusive approach"—to state practice is adopted (Byers, 1999).

Sources of Customary IHL: The ICRC Study

In 2005, the ICRC published the report *Customary International Humanitarian Law* (henceforth the ICRC study) (Henckaerts and Doswalk-Beck, 2005). At over 5000 pages, the ICRC study is unprecedented in both size and scope. The central part of the work, Volume 1, contains 161 proposed rules that cover the full range of IHL. Volume II provides the background material for each rule contained in Volume 1. Though an important addition to the literature, the ICRC study has been criticized on a number of grounds including failure to consider negative state practice (Bellinger and Haynes, 2006), lack of historical context and advocacy bias that ignores contradictory examples (Parks, 2005), and nontransparency in selection of state practice and the failure to acknowledge the United States as a persistent objector to Additional Protocol I to the 1949 Geneva Convention (Scoobie, 2007). However, many of the authors who offer these critiques accept that the methodology employed by the ICRC to assess state practice is, in fact, sound. According to

Table 16.1 Sources of Customary IHL

Policy statements	Opinions of official legal advisers
Executive decisions	Official protests
Treaty reservations	Threatened use of weapons
Statements of treaty interpretation	Military communiqués during conflict
Travaux Préparatoires	Rules of engagement
Legislative hearings	Memoirs
Military manuals	Diplomatic correspondence
Instructions to armed forces Confirmed battlefield violations	National case law and legislation

the ICRC study, state practice consists of both physical and verbal acts. Physical acts include battlefield behavior, use of certain weapons, and treatment of individuals. Verbal acts, on the other hand, are more extensive and include military manuals, national legislation, diplomatic protests, and opinions of official legal advisors.

For the purpose of this chapter, the most important critique of the ICRC study is that it failed to employ—in an objective and systematic manner—the methodology that it endorsed. The influence of the ICRC study on the present work is fittingly summarized by George H. Aldrich, "I believe it is a very important study, but I think its importance rests on it's being used as a basis for further work and as a spur to such works, rather than on its conclusions" (2005: p. 504). With this in mind, the sources of state practice utilized in the following research model is borrowed heavily from the ICRC study with additions from Ian Brownlie's *Principles of Public International Law* (1990) and the author's research on IHL. Together, these sources comprise the raw material of state practice and are listed in Table 16.1.

As can be surmised, such an extensive amount of source material is challenging to collect and organize. Furthermore, the way in which primary source material is organized implies and gives meaning to how IHL develops and is interpreted. By solely examining the end product (codified treaty rules) one fails to address the underlying dynamics that shape and influence the practice of IHL. Whereas the ICRC study simply lists material considered to reflect state practice, this chapter advances a more nuanced model that permits source material delineation and organization. The model developed below considers IHL as a dynamic decision-making process that includes the creation, dissemination, and application of source material.

IHL as a Decision-Making Process

The decision-making process model of state practice is conceptually influenced by the International Law as Process (ILP) approach to IL —which was, in turn, influenced by the policy-oriented approach developed by Lasswell and McDougal (1992). Commonly referred to as the New Haven School of International Law, the ILP perspective rejects the view that international law consists solely of neutral "rules" that exist to be "impartially applied" (Higgins, 1994: 2).

In contrast, according to ILP, the international law operates in a dynamic manner that permits development and change. Furthermore, the process approach assumes that multiple actors and stakeholders (including both state and nonstate actors) influence decision making. For example, state-affiliated decision-makers can fall within a conceptual hierarchy that includes political and military leaders, legislators, diplomats, legal experts, military practitioners, and soldiers. Nonstate decision-making influence, on the other hand, is predominately found in the special status and role of the ICRC, a unique hybrid NGO that significantly influences IHL by arranging conferences, drafting treaty provisions, and applying pressure on governments to apply and adhere to IHL (Finnemore and Sikkink, 1998).

The model below focuses primarily on U.S. state practice post-World War II. The United States is an excellent case study for several reasons. First, primary source material is readily available through considerable holdings at national and presidential archives and is often updated through declassification policy. Second, it has actively participated in IHL treaty-making resulting in detailed records. Third, the United States has established an extensive military training regime that is regularly updated. Finally, the United States has had to address questions regarding the application of, and adherence to IHL, as it has regularly engaged in numerous armed conflicts. The decision-making process model that follows allows for the organization and dissemination of source material and permits multiple interpretations. While divided into four categories, the source material may overlap into more than one category depending on interpretive choices.

Law Creation Records of the Treaty Conference (Travaux Préparatoires)

The official records (*travaux préparatoires*) of a treaty conference serve as an important resource regarding individual nations' positions as they developed throughout the negotiation process. Often referred to as the "Final Report," the conference negotiation history is often extensive. For example, the *travaux préparatoires* for the 1949 Geneva Conventions are over 2000 pages in length—while the negotiation history for the 1977 Additional Protocols (I and II) to the 1949 Geneva Conventions extend over 8000 pages in 17 Volumes. In addition to official *travaux préparatoires*, reports, and minutes of meetings between government experts and diplomats negotiating IHL questions are useful tools for capturing state practice. Primary source material at the treaty stage is readily accessible and features prominently in the IHL literature.*

Diplomatic Correspondence

During treaty conferences where IHL is established, extensive official communications take place between diplomats and their respective nations, between state coalitions, and between states and the ICRC. Often, these take the form of classified cables and communiqués. These documents help reveal how an individual state negotiates, makes concessions, and establishes unified positions on and interpretations of IHL. Locating these official papers involves the use of archives and/or document declassification. For example, in the United States, the National Archive and

---

* The US Library of Congress facilitates an online web page dedicated to military legal resources that include (among other items) negotiating history, drafts, and the Conference of Government Experts relating to the Geneva Conventions.

Records Administration (NARA) holds in its collection hundreds of State Department diplomatic cables containing proposed rule revisions, individual state positions, and voting records from the diplomatic conferences (1974–1977) that culminated in the 1977 Additional Protocol to the 1949 Geneva Convention.* In England, the National Archives contain similar communiques from the Foreign and Commonwealth Office (FCO) and the Ministry of Defence (MOD) which highlight negotiation positions and draft provisions—including NATO consultation on specific IHL rules.†

Domestic Executive-Level Agency Decision-Making

In the United States, inter/intra domestic federal agencies actively engage in IHL decision-making. This decision-making process can be seen in memoranda, reports, and position papers that argue and interpret the legal, policy, and military implications of treaty rules under negotiation. These documents provide a wealth of information and reveal how individual agencies (i.e., Department of State, Department of Defense, and National Security Council) interpret draft rules provided by the ICRC. Locating source material at this stage involves consulting archival finding aids. In the United States, NARA utilizes numbered record groups based on document provenance. For example, State Department documents relating to ICRC draft rules can be found in NARA Record Group (RG) 43: International Conferences, Commissions, and Expositions, RG 59: General Records of the Department of State, RG 353: Interdepartmental and Intradepartmental Committees and RG 383: U.S. Arms Control and Disarmament Agency. Department of Defense and military RG location is even more complex and requires an examination of at least 15 different document locators at NARA. Furthermore, this does not include national security-related documents that are located at individual presidential archives.

Postconference Publications

Although this research model emphasizes primary source material created at the time of the event, incorporating postconference publications written by participants helps to fill lacunae in the historical record. Scholarly articles, reports, and memoirs provide useful information, especially in cases where individual committee minutes are unavailable. The ICRC's strict confidentiality policy (only ICRC general archives prior to 1965 are open to researchers) often necessitates the use of secondary source material to clarify individual state positions. For example, Frits Kalshoven—who acted as Rapporteur for a number of committees that addressed the controversial issue of reprisals during the 1974–1977 Diplomatic Conferences—published a series of articles that provide a rare picture of the behind-the-scenes workings of the ICRC conferences (Kalshoven, 2007). Furthermore, U.S. Delegates George Aldrich and Richard R. Baxter subsequently published articles relating their experiences at the diplomatic conference that provide valuable insight into the position of the United States and other delegations (Baxter, 1977; Aldrich, 1991).

---

* Many of these documents are available online and can be located through the NARA Access to Archival Databases (AAD).

† Although these documents are not available online they can be located through the National Archive catalog and are available for viewing at the National Archives, Kew.

Ratification

Domestic Executive-Level Decision-Making

A corollary to treaty creation, postsigning treaty ratification decisions involve interagency and executive-level decision-making. In the United States, this often includes legal opinions submitted by the Department of State, Department of Defense, and the Joint Chiefs of Staff (among other executive-level agencies and groups). Analysis of these records often reveals interagency tensions over IHL treaties and specific treaty rule interpretation. In addition to the aforementioned NARA document locators, the archives at presidential libraries contain documents that reveal national security and executive-level decision-making. For example, the decision by the Reagan Administration to not submit Additional Protocol I for ratification was preceded by numerous interagency and White House staff reports and memoranda.* In England, similar interagency decision-making and debate between FCO and MOD accompanied the decision to add a treaty reservation to the 1977 Additional Protocols on the subject of reprisals.

Legislative Decision-Making

In the United States, legislative decision-making relating to IHL treaties often includes special sessions, hearings, and reports from Congressional working groups—including the House Committee on Foreign Affairs/Armed Services, the Senate Committee on Foreign Relations, and other legislative groups and hearings. Reports from these meetings can help clarify official government position and may reveal (among other things) differences between political party affiliates. At the ratification stage, treaty reservations or interpretative statements may also be discussed and approved. Many of these documents are available online and through the Library of Congress Online Catalog.

Dissemination

Dissemination involves incorporating IHL rules into military doctrine and includes the related concepts of implementation, promulgation, and training. State practice is reflected in the numerous field manuals, pamphlets, regulations, training circulars, and training films that are produced by governments to train their military. Reisman and Leitzau (1992) refer to the dissemination of IHL as "an essential component in the international lawmaking process" and "a necessary step if law is to be transformed from an exercise in theory to a matter of practice" (Reisman and Leitzau, 1992: 1 and 3). Furthermore, dissemination of IHL is clearly required by the 1949 Geneva Conventions. According to Article 126 of Geneva Convention III (1949)

> The High Contracting Parties undertake, in time of peace as in time of war, to disseminate the text of the present Convention as widely as possible in their respective countries, and, in particular to include the study thereof in their programs of military and, if possible, civil instruction, so that the principles thereof may become known to all their armed forces and to the entire population.

---

* The author has located and secured the release of multiple documents relating to this decision through the Ronald Reagan Presidential Library (FOIA Case# F10-046).

Additional examples of wording that indicate the mandatory nature of dissemination can be found in Convention I (Art. 47), Convention II (Art. 48), and Convention IV (Art. 144). To date, the most extensive comparative analysis of military training is the ICRC study.* As primary source material indicating state practice, training materials are important because they can capture and illustrate changes in training emphasis over time.

Application

The application of IHL to an armed conflict can be viewed from different perspectives. The initial application often involves executive-level decisions and the formal announcement that a specific treaty or treaty rule is applicable. This can be triggered by the acknowledgment that the conflict has become international in scope or through the official recognition of a belligerent (Bill, 2000). Source material can take the form of official policy pronouncements (and protests) or documentation of behind-the-scenes decision-making—including legal memoranda and reports addressing the overall legal status of the conflict, the status of combatants and prisoners, or the use (or threatened use) of specific weapons.

A second type of conflict application arises during armed conflict and may occur in response to violations (suspected, accused, or actual) or in response to pressure from allies or the ICRC. These may include the threatened use of weapons or other forms of retaliation in response to enemy violations. Though recent attention has focused on the controversial U.S. post-September 11 "Global War on Terror" detainee policy, similar IHL decision-making debates occurred in other post-World War II U.S. conflicts and include the controversy over forced versus nonforced prisoner preparation during the Korean War (Hermes, 1966), the decision to apply to the 1949 Geneva Conventions early in U.S. involvement in Vietnam (Prugh, 1974), and the threatened use of weapons and treatment of prisoners during the 1990–1991 Gulf War (Roberts, 1993).

In addition to internal memoranda and policy statements, another important primary source is the official military directives authorizing—and setting parameters for—the use of force. These directives (often referred to as Rules of Engagement) contain elements of IHL and provide essential source material. Official military histories are also helpful in locating specific documents. For U.S. foreign policy decisions and diplomatic history, the Department of State historical series Foreign Relations of the United States (FRUS) is useful as a primary source location tool. Another example of source material at the application stage can be found in firsthand accounts of decision-makers (memoirs and diaries). For example, the publication of Scharf and Williams' *Shaping Foreign Policy in Times of Crisis* (2010) provides unprecedented insight into the workings of the Department of State Office of the Legal Adviser. Although, U.S. courts have historically veered away from interpreting IHL, contemporary decisions such as Hamdan versus Rumsfeld (2006) provide judicial insight into the application stage of the decision-making process.

Adherence

Establishing state practice of nonadherence to IHL is a highly controversial, inherently politicized, and widely contested subject. A contemporary IHL scholar or historian would, in fact, be

---

* Ongoing updates to the ICRC Study being conducted between the British Red Cross and the ICRC at the Lauterpacht Center for International Law, University of Cambridge, has led to extensive additions to source material indicating state practice.

hard pressed to provide an example of an armed conflict where IHL violations have *not* occurred. One research challenge, in this case, is determining whether violations are isolated occurrences at the battlefield level or whether they are part of a broader policy or systemic practice. Another challenge involves the over-reliance on secondary accounts that assume independent verification. In general, there are inherent problems when attempting to conduct empirical and objective research on the subject of nonadherence to IHL. The "fog of war" needs to be considered where basic facts are difficult to ascertain. Perpetrators often conceal violations and adversaries may promote embellished or exaggerated rumors of violations or, conversely, may downplay or deny violations (see Morrow, 2014 for discussion). Furthermore, transparent democracies, by their nature, will arguably be exposed to incidences of nonadherence before nondemocracies will. As it stands, much of the state practice source material reflecting IHL nonadherence relies on the work of investigative journalists, personal memoirs and diaries, and NGOs working to ensure respect for IHL.

Discussion

International Relations

International humanitarian law is more than the application of treaty rules. Rather, it is a dynamic decision-making process involving multiple actors, with different degrees of authority. Within the scholarly field of IRs, the theory most compatible with this view is constructivism. Brunnée and Toopego (2013) go so far as to state that constructivism can "help provide a more coherent account of customary international law [...] than other IR theories and even than international law itself" (Brunnée and Toopego, 2013: 139). With its focus on ideas, interests, institutions, and norms—coupled with the acknowledged role that nonstate actors have on influencing state behavior—constructivism is well-placed to appreciate a research model that considers IHL as a decision-making process with varied examples of primary source material.

The decision-making process model can also be used to address important compliance questions including *Why do states comply with international law? How can nonstate actors influence state compliance?* Furthermore, the source material outlined in this model would be helpful in refining or supporting existing research. For example, the process model provides additional material for constructivist research on the role of NGOs in facilitating the internationalization of norms (see Finnemore and Sikkink, 1998). Furthermore, the process model can provide an important research tool when assessing how IHL norms advance, remain stable, or regress. The same source material could potentially address core realist concepts—including the primacy of state power, the emphasis on security interests over norms, the focus on state sovereignty, and the concept of compliance through coercion (threatened or actual).

Historical Perspective

A portion of the IHL literature is either implicitly or explicitly geared toward humanitarian advocacy. This is not surprising when one considers the subject matter and the populations that have been and continue to be directly impacted by compliance or noncompliance with IHL. The emphasis on advocacy, however, conflicts with the historical perspective. In Peter Novick's seminal work on objectivity in historical research, *That Noble Dream*, the objective and detached position of the researcher is described as follows: "The objective historian's role is that of a neutral, or disinterested, judge; it must never degenerate into that of advocate or, even worse, propagandist" (1998: p. 2).

A related tendency is to view IHL primarily through the lens of its codified success. The second half of the twentieth century witnessed the proliferation of IHL treaties in addition to the creation of human rights instruments. If conclusions are based solely (or largely) on the success of codification, then there is cause for optimism for efforts to alleviate human suffering through international treaty law. In the context of IHL, the result can be a narrative that presents IHL in an overly optimistic light and either ignores negative examples of state practice or, worse yet, chooses to emphasize only positive examples of state practice. This is reminiscent of Herbert Butterfield's book "The Whig Interpretation of History," where history is presented as the inevitable march towards advancement and improvement (1931).

A narrative of IHL progress does not necessarily stand up to examples of state practice. For example, focusing solely on contemporary twenty-first century U.S. state practice we witness long established IHL rules being questioned as policy or veering toward nonadherence. The most well-known and discussed example is U.S. policy relating to detainee treatment and the indefinite detention of prisoners at Guantanamo Bay, Cuba. Other recent examples have opened legal gray areas arguably long considered resolved including assassination (targeted killing) and mercenaries (private military contractors). On the other hand, the policy change by the United States to no longer produce or acquire antipersonnel land mines, and to take steps to sign the Ottawa Convention (Gladstone, 2014) illustrates positive practice. The onus of responsibility is on the scholar to include a balanced consideration that includes examples of both negative and positive state practice.

Limitations

The decision-making process model was developed and applied specifically to the United States. Thus, generalizability proves a serious limitation. Arguably, replication to other states will be limited to transparent nations with open source archives. In addition, liberal states participate more actively in negotiating international agreements than totalitarian and undemocratic states (Slaughter, 1995). For example, liberal states possess disaggregated political and decision-making institutions (executive, administrative, legislative, and judicial) thus producing a greater "paper trail" of primary source material. A potential research bias, therefore, exists to focus solely on the practice of liberal and transparent nations while ignoring the very states that are arguably most prone to violating IHL.

Although domestic courts are considered as a source, the role of international courts and tribunals in shaping and interpreting IHL at the domestic level—and the role that these courts can potentially play in IHL enforcement and compliance—is not included. While a promising avenue for future source material, there currently exist conceptual and methodological difficulties in pursuing this potential contribution to state practice (see Conant, 2013). Finally, a research avenue not explored in this article is the role that interviewing decision-makers and stakeholders may have in ascertaining IHL state practice. For example, Ratner's (2011) important work on the ICRC, facilitated through his insider status to this usually secretive organization included access to committee meetings and interviews with numerous ICRC officials. While an insightful and significant addition to the IHL literature, this work stands as an exception. However, future research should consider the possibility of exploring past and present decision-makers and practitioners of IHL for primary source interviews.

Conclusion

From the perspective of a scholar conducting research on the subject of state practice of IHL, applying the proposed model involves both opportunities and challenges. In addition to the standard literature review, the decision-making process model involves the collection of extensive original source material through archival research and government declassification programs. The model proposed in this chapter turns for inspiration to historians in archives and investigative journalists who are working on government declassification, a largely foreign research milieu to both IL and IR scholars. However, this "outsider" perspective works as an advantage because the research model proposed exists apart from the interdisciplinary divide and debate between (and within) international law and IRs. In turn, this research model can potentially act as a methodology bridge between the two disciplines, thus providing the raw material for interdisciplinary dialog and theory development.

International customary law and normative arguments are, by their nature, premised on both historical and contemporary practice because both make statements about change over time. The IR/IL literature, however, is largely void of a discussion concerning what role (if any) the historical perspective and objectivity should play when writing about IHL. This gap has become more glaring as contemporary state practice calls into question long-established assumptions. The decision-making model proposed in this chapter helps to address these discrepancies while opening an avenue for the interdisciplinary dialog on this important subject.

This chapter set out to provide a common methodological framework for gathering and organizing primary source material reflecting state practice of IHL. In creating a decision-making process model containing diverse source material, I have sought to convey and advance what Finnemore and Toope (2001) refer to as a "richer view of international law." The model developed is both inclusive and dynamic. Furthermore, although influenced by the process approach to international law, it is not tied to theoretical assumptions that could limit its applicability. Therefore, both IL and IR scholars can utilize the decision-making process model, thereby creating a common research design bridging both disciplines.

Acknowledgments

An earlier version of this chapter was presented at the World International Studies Committee Fourth Global Conference, Frankfurt 2014. I wish to thank the Citadel Foundation for research support.

References

Aldrich, G. 1991. Prospects for United States ratification of additional protocol I to the 1949 Geneva conventions, *The American Journal of International Law*, 85: 1–20.

Aldrich, G. H. 2005. Customary international humanitarian law, *The British Yearbook of International Law*, 76: 503–24.

Baxter, R. R. 1977. Humanitarian law or humanitarian politics? The 1974 diplomatic conference on humanitarian law, *Harvard International Law Journal*, 78: 1–26.

Bellinger, J. and Haynes, W. J. 2006. U.S. Joint Letter from John Bellinger III, Legal Adviser, U.S. Department of State, and William J. Haynes, General Counsel, U.S. Department of Defense to Dr. Jakob Kellenberger, President, International Committee of the Red Cross, Regarding Customary International Law Study. https://www.icrc.org/eng/assets/files/other/irrc_866_bellinger.pdf.

Bill, B. 2000. *Law of War Workshop Deskbook*. Charlottesville, VA: The Judge Advocate's School, US Army.

Brownlie, I. 1990. *Principles of Public International Law*. New York, NY: Oxford University Press.

Brunnée, J. and Toopego, S. 2013. Constructivism and international law, in Dunoff, J. and Pollack, M. (eds.), *Interdisciplinary Perspectives on International Law and International Relations: The State of the Art*. New York, NY: Cambridge University Press.

Butterfield, H. 1931. *The Whig Interpretation of History*. UK: W.W. Norton.

Byers, M. 1999. *Custom, Power and the Power of Rules: International Relations and Customary International Law*. New York, NY: Cambridge University Press.

Conant, L. 2013. Whose agents? The interpretation of international law in national courts, in Dunoff, J. and Pollack, M. (eds.), *Interdisciplinary Perspectives on International Law and International Relations: The State of the Art*. New York NY: Cambridge University Press.

Delupis, I. D. 2000. *The Law of War*. New York, NY: Cambridge University Press.

Dunoff, J. and Pollack, M. (eds.) 2013. *Interdisciplinary Perspectives on International Law*. New York, NY: Cambridge University Press.

Finnemore, M. and Sikkink, K. 1998. International norm dynamics and political change, *International Organization*, 52: 887–91.

Finnemore, M. and Toope, S. 2001. Alternatives to 'Legalization:' Richer views of law and politics, *International Organization*, 55(5): 743–58.

Gladstone, R. 2014. US Lays Groundwork to Reduce Land Mines and Join Global Treaty, *New York Times*, Article A4.

Goldsmith, J. L. and Posner, E. A. 1999. A theory of customary international law, *The University of Chicago Law Review*, 66: 1113–77.

Hamdan v. Rumsfeld Secretary of Defense, et al. 2006. 548 US 557 (2006).

Henckaerts, J. M. and Doswalk-Beck, L. 2005. *Customary International Humanitarian Law*. New York, NY: Cambridge University Press.

Hermes, W. G. 1966. *Truce Tent and Fighting Front*. Washington DC: Office of the Chief of Military History of the United States Army.

Higgins, R. 1994. *Problems and Process: International Law and How We Use It*. New York, NY: Oxford University Press.

Kalshoven, F. 2007. *Reflections on the Laws of War: Collected Essays*. Leiden, Netherlands: Nijhoff.

Lasswell, H. and McDougal, M. 1992. *Jurisprudence for a Free Society: Studies in Law, Science, and Policy*. New Haven, CT: New Haven Press.

Morrow, J. D. 2014. *Order within Anarchy: The Laws of War as an International Institution*. New York, NY: Cambridge University Press.

Novick, P. 1998. *That Noble Dream*. New York, NY: Cambridge University Press.

Parks, W. H. 2005. The ICRC Customary Law Study: A Preliminary Assessment, Proceedings of the American Society of International Law (ASIL), Washington, DC, USA.

Price, R. 2004. Emerging customary norm and anti-personnel landmines, in Reus-Smit, C. (ed.), *The Politics of International Law*. New York, NY: Cambridge University Press.

Prugh, G. S. 1974. *Law at War: Vietnam 1964–1973*. Washington DC: Department of the Army.

Ratner, S. 2011. Law promotion beyond law talk: The Red Cross, persuasion, and the laws of war, *The European Journal of International Law*, 22(2): 459–506.

Reisman, W. M. and Leitzau, W. K. 1992. Moving international law from theory to practice: The role of military training manuals in effectuating the law of armed conflict, in Robertson, H. B. (ed.), *The Law of Naval Operations*. Newport, RI: Naval War College Press.

Roberts, A. 1993. Law of War in the 1990–91 Gulf Conflict, *International Security*, 18(3): 134–81.

Roberts, A. and Guelff, R. 2000. *Documents on the Laws of War*. New York, NY: Oxford University Press.

Scharf, M. and Williams, P. 2010. *Shaping Foreign Policy in Times of Crisis*. New York, NY: Cambridge University Press.

Scoobie, I. 2007. The approach to customary international law in the study, in Wilmshurst, E. and Breau, S. (eds.), *Perspectives on the ICRC Study on Customary International Humanitarian Law*. New York, NY: Cambridge University Press.

Slaughter, A. M. 1995. International law in a world of liberal states, *European Journal of International Law*, 6(4): 503–38.

Chapter 17

Gender Conjectures and Politics of Land Right Deprivation in South-Eastern Nigeria

Amaka Theresa Oriaku Emordi and Emeka Thaddues Njoku

Contents

Introduction

Gender conjectures thrive in a society's culture to form beliefs and perceptions, which have become the lens through which the sexes are perceived (Grigsby, 2009). This is the case among the Igbo tribe of south-eastern Nigeria, where land and property rights are hinged on conjectures against the female sex. Even though these conjectures have been created on the basis of false information, they are deeply ingrained in the culture of the Igbos and are commonly reflected in various narratives used to depict the female gender. Conjectures such as *ndi si na zu anyu mairi,*[*] *ama onye ozo,*[†] *nwanyi*

---

[*] *Ndi si na zu anyu mairi*: An Igbo narrative that refers to women as people that urinate from the back.
[†] *Ama onye ozo*: This is another Igbo narrative that infers a woman belongs to another man's compound.

adighi enwe ala[*] are common inferences that facilitated the continuous subjugation and relegation of women in Igbo land,[†] not only in the family and the larger society but also within the state.

These conjectures may appear normal; yet, have great consequences on the social status of women and their relevance in the society. More relevant to this chapter is the conjecture "*Nwanyi adighi enwe ala*" (see above for notation). The invocation and propagation of these conjectures through systematic processes of socialization aid in the complete deprivation of women in Igbo land as regards the capacity to own landed properties. It has become almost a taboo to conceive any right for women to own landed property; hence, this practice has hampered the ability of women to contribute to the socioeconomic development of the state, as most rural women have been impoverished due to these cultural practices.

This chapter is divided into three parts: the first part examines the legal displacement of Igbo women on their rights to own landed properties in Nigeria; the second part gives empirical evidence of how these conjectures (which reflect in various narratives) have played out in ensuring that women are perpetually denied their rights to own lands in south-eastern Nigeria; and the third part examines the responses of women to these conjectures and their implications in the socioeconomic development of the state. The concluding part discusses useful suggestions.

Land Laws and Gender in Nigeria

Prior to the introduction of a uniformed right of occupancy system, Nigeria operated a plural system of land tenure, which comprises four systems of tenure under the state land laws. Two of these operated nationwide while the other two followed the northern and southern dichotomy of Nigerian land tenure in southern Nigeria—regulated by customary law, with roots in the traditional perception of the land. Traditionally, the Igbos held the view that land had socioeconomic and spiritual significance. It was perceived as sacred, given by a superior being for the benefits of all members of the community and belonging to everyone—the living, the dead, and the unborn. Furthermore, the living are perceived as trustees of ancestral lands for the sustenance of themselves and the generations unborn (Oshio, 1990). Moreover, as part of the traditional norms—which now are reflected in the customary laws in south-eastern Nigeria—male children have a kind of perpetuity of land in various communities, to the exclusion of women. The reason for this practice is the conjecture that women in Igbo custom are *ama onye ozo*, which means that as soon as they are married they belong to their husband's people other than that of their immediate family. Thus, they cannot hold land in perpetuity like their brothers.

However, a major land reform in Nigeria—the 1978 Land Use Act—nationalized all land in the country and by implication transferred the responsibility of the land administration to committees constituted at the state and local government levels. One justification given for the Act was the rationalization that the customary land tenure system was a constraint on agricultural development. However, the enactment of the 1978 Land Use Act further deprived the women (particularly on Igbo land) the rights to own or exhibit any form of control over landed properties in two ways: First, the act did not completely abolish the extant customary land law and tenure in Nigeria. Most sections of the preexisting customary law were preserved. For instance, Sections 34, 35, 36, and 51 subsection 1 paragraphs 3 and 15 (which stated that an individual or a community

---

[*] *Nwanyi adighi enwe ala*: This means women do not own land. It is a common belief in the Igbo tradition that women lack the basic rights to own or acquire, inherit, or sell landed properties.

[†] Igbo Land: Used to refer to the Igbo ethnic group of the part of Nigeria in the south east.

utilizing or residing on a land in conformity with the customary laws of the land) were maintained. Thus, the various discriminatory customary practices on land and property rights against women in Igbo land were upheld, as the 1978 Land Use Act did nothing to address these prejudiced cultural practices. Second, under the 1978 Land Use Act the ownership or administration of land—specifically in urban areas—was transferred to various committees within the state and local governments. However, men in the south east largely constitute these committees or governments, at both state and local levels.

Women do not have a place, or a say in decision making in these forums and, are thus, marginalized. In the same vein, government at both regional and local levels in charge of the administrations of lands for agricultural development under the Land Use Act in the south-east did not consider the roles or place of rural women in the development of agriculture in these communities, even though they are the major stakeholders. This was well captured by Ekenta et al. (2010) who carried out a gender analysis of land ownership structures and agricultural production in south-eastern Nigeria. His findings reveal that women, even though without the right to land, were more involved in agriculture than their male counterparts. According to him, an agricultural productivity analysis between 2008 and 2011 revealed that females had a higher level of production output than males. Moreover, while land inheritance and ownership of hectares of land favored males over females, females had overall higher productivity in crops production. This, reiterates the positions of Englert and Daley (2008: 180) who argue that, "land is the main resource from which millions of people in rural Africa derive their livelihoods [and women] do the majority of work, producing between 60% and 80% of all food grown [But] most women [...] do not hold secure rights to the land [and] a woman's right to access and control is still tied to her status as a daughter, sister, mother or wife."

According to Section 26 of the Marriage Act (1990),* a woman can inherit part of her deceased husband's property and estate, including land. The property of the deceased is administered in accordance with the wishes of the deceased if he had a will. However, these policy instruments have not yielded much fruit in Igbo land. Even with the strengthening of the women's movement and emphasis on empowerment, the deprivation of women to landed properties remains unabated in south-eastern Nigeria, as these are only practiced in theory. In reality, the multiplicity of the laws on inheritance leave a gap that permits the courts and self-styled traditionalists (including unscrupulous relatives of the deceased) to choose the laws that are beneficial to their self-interest and to the disadvantage of the woman. Specifically, in Igbo land the customary law provides that a woman cannot inherit the land from her husband's estate. The relatives of the deceased usually regard such property as family property or collectively owned. Acquisitions of property with a spouse are not recognized, even when it is proven that the woman worked alongside her husband to acquire the properties for him. A woman in this cultural practice only has the right to an estate or land through her male child. This means that a childless woman under this practice cannot inherit anything.

Gender Conjectures and Land Rights Denial in South-Eastern Nigeria

In many African societies, there exist various forms and levels of the infringement of human rights—distinctively property rights of women by their male counterparts through diverse

---

* See the Nigerian Marriage Act of 1990.

cultural systems—and these violations have become well established over the years (Bankole, 2001; Okello, 2003). Perhaps, nowhere in Nigeria is this property rights violation more pronounced than in Igbo land—in the south-east part of the country. In Igbo land, these violations were facilitated through various conjectures that were detrimental to the socioeconomic development of the Igbo women. These conjectures were constructed by the menfolk in Igbo land for the continued placement of women in a subservient position in the society. An infamous conjecture in Igbo societies that *nwanyi adighi enwe ala* clearly shows the classification of women within the societal structure. This conjecture is traced to the place of the woman within the family in Igbo traditional societies. A girl child born in any family is not considered a member of that family as she would eventually leave; hence, she lacks the qualification to be bequeathed any property from her father.[*] Therefore, due to the inheritance of properties, the male child is given preference.

The inheritance of the female child is premised on the magnanimity of her in-laws, but this is largely dependent on her ability to give birth to a male child, as she cannot inherit anything on her own but through her male children. Thus, women strive to have male children to secure their rights in the family because a woman who has no son loses the right to own properties completely.[†] Nevertheless, in some cases a woman with male children who are not fully grown may still be denied the rights to her husband's properties.[‡] Moreover, a woman who gives birth to female children only—in the event of the death of her husband—will have to surrender her husband's properties to her husband's family. This is mainly applicable to landed properties, as land is regarded as the most significant property anyone can inherit in Igbo societies. Although, in most Igbo societies, a father may decide to bequeath other properties to her female children when he is alive, such a gesture cannot include any portion of land within his ancestral home.[§]

Even in a situation where a woman and her husband acquired both landed properties and other properties collectively, the woman is denied from participating in any issue that may arise as regards the property. Specifically, in cases of boundary disputes, settlement of disagreements and other decisions that may arise on the property, the woman is completely excluded from such discussions or allowed to contribute.[¶] In addition, a part of the belief among the Igbos is that a woman on her own cannot purchase land; she has to go through a man. For this to be done, a man must give their consent and also do the negotiations on her behalf. Should a woman because of her financial status make an attempt to buy a land directly within any Igbo community, the owners will not give her audience or discuss land matters with her.

The Igbos believe that it is condescending to discuss land matters with a woman. In most cases, the woman ends up being duped by the sellers.[**] Consequently, women occupy a very disadvantaged position in terms of property rights within the traditional social structures, and in the context of scarcity, their rights are likely to be the first to be challenged. All these are

---

[*] Author's interview with a woman cultural group leader in Eziada in Urualla, south east Nigeria on February 10, 2015.

[†] Author's interview with a leader of Igbo Women Cultural Organization (*Obi buru notu*) at Obinze Owerri Imo state on February 2, 2015.

[‡] Author's interview with a Pan Igbo women cultural organization leader, (Obinwanne) in Obiohia Imo state in the south east of Nigeria on February 20, 2015.

[§] Authors' interview with an Igbo man in Umuahia Abia State, south east Nigeria on January 17, 2015.

[¶] Author's interview with key stakeholder of the Elders' Council of the Apex-Igbo Socio-cultural Organisation, Ohaneze Ndigbo (Ibadan, January 2015).

[**] Author's interview with an Igbo cultural traditional holder in Umuahia, Abia State, south east Nigeria on February 18, 2015.

largely traced to culturally embedded discriminatory conjectures and practices against women within the societies both in the customary and formal land tenure systems (Emeasoba, 2012). The continued survival of these traditional practices in Igbo land contravenes various international human rights resolutions of the United Nations in which Nigeria is a signatory. The international human rights law stipulates that women and men have equal rights as regards ownership of properties. Conversely, in Nigeria, customary law largely defines property rights; this is acutely the case in the Igbo land, where these laws are significantly biased against women (Okello, 2003). The continued existence of these discriminatory norms entrenched in the customary laws of south-eastern Nigeria has huge political implications for the state; specifically, the perception of Nigeria as a major violator of International human rights by the comity of nations.

Responses of Women and the Socioeconomic Implications of Gender Conjectures and Land Rights Denials in Nigeria

The espousal and entrenchment of the "*nwanyi adighi enwe ala*" conjecture has significant psychological and socioeconomic effects on women in Igbo land, specifically rural women in this area. According to Mill (cited in Mukherjee and Ramaswamy, 2007) in situations where women are helpless about their particular social conditions, they tend to acquiesce themselves to the situation and even became consenting parties to their marginalization; ultimately policing their fellow women into complying with the culture. The response of rural women to these inherent discriminatory practices in Igbo societies gives credulity to the postulations of these scholars. The lack of rights to ownership of landed properties in Igbo land affects the psyche of women to the point that they have come to accept the conjectures and, hence, see themselves as properties of men. Moreover, this has been attributed to the fact that the women believe that they have to be of good conduct to their husbands so that their husbands can take care of them since they largely depend on their men or husbands for survival.

The cultural practices also render women very poor.* Therefore, by their responses they acquiesce themselves to poverty, hunger, illiteracy, and subjugation by their male counterparts. These subjugated conditions which the women face in Igbo land are further facilitated by the fact that women cannot farm on their father's or husband's land without permission, and cannot also acquire land for themselves for the purpose of agricultural development to improve their lives. Women cannot own, harvest, or plant cash crops such as kola nut and palm fruits to make money but are made to depend on whatever their husbands give them. A woman (in the absence of her husband, the elders, and her husband's siblings) has no right to plant or harvest a cash crop. However, to obtain the consent of a male relative is usually a herculean task.† On a yearly basis, a woman's husband gives her permission to farm the land, but only her husband has the right to harvest and sell the produce from the farm.‡ This deprivation of access to land and cash crops is the main reason Igbo women in the rural settings are so impoverished.§

---

* Author's interview with an Igbo traditional custodian in Orlu Imo, south east Nigeria on February 19, 2015.
† Author's interview with an Igbo traditional custodian in Orlu Imo, south east Nigeria on February 19, 2015.
‡ Author's interview with an Igbo cultural traditional holder in Umuahia, south east Nigeria on February 18, 2015.
§ Author's interview with an Igbo traditional custodian in Orlu Imo, south east Nigeria on February 19, 2015.

Conclusion

In this chapter, we stressed the role of cultural conjectures as one of the factors that aided the continued deprivation of property rights to women in south-eastern Nigeria. These conjectures have survived over time through the systemic processes of cultural socialization, which depict the male child as traditionally superior to the female child in diverse ways—particularly in terms of properties. These conjectures are reinforced by narratives such as *ndi si na zu anyu mmiri*, *ama onye ozo, nwanyi adighi enwe ala*. These facilitate the subjugation of women in the social structure of the Igbo societies. Regrettably, in response to these systemic deprivations of the property rights of women in Igbo land, these conjectures have not been questioned enough by women's groups. Rather, Igbo women—specifically rural women—have accepted these cultural conjectures as their way of life. Moreover, the concurrence of norms has had huge consequences on the rural women, as they have become economically dependent on the men for survival.

We equally argue that the denial of the rights of women to inherit, own, acquire, and sell landed properties in Igbo communities of south-eastern Nigeria is a complete departure and violation of international conventions on the rights of women and girls—to which Nigeria is a signatory. Hence, the denial of women's right could continue to portray Nigeria as a major violator of international human rights laws. In the long run, this denial could incrementally affect the country politically and economically, as developed nations will be forced to tie the issuance of foreign aid to the levels at which Nigeria upholds international human rights resolutions. Thus, there is a need for women's groups, government, and other stakeholders to fight collectively in ensuring that these cultural conjectures and practices in Nigeria—distinctively in the Igbo land—are eradicated.

References

Bankole, D. B. 2001. Inhuman and dehumanizing treatment of widows in our society: A rape on women empowerment, *Journal of Gender and Development*, 2(1): 160–164.

Ekenta, C. M., Mohammed, A. B., and Afola, K. O. 2010. Gender analysis of land ownership structures and agricultural production in Imo State, Nigeria, *Journal of Economics and Sustainable Development*, 3(9): 67–73.

Emeasoba, U. R. B. 2012. Land ownership among the Igbos of South East Nigeria: A case for women land inheritance, *Journal of Environmental Management and Safety*, 3(1): 97–117.

Englert, B. and Daley, D. (eds.) 2008. *Women's Land Rights and Privatization in Eastern Africa*. Martlesham, UK: Eastern Africa Series, James Currey Fountain.

Grigsby, E. 2009. *Analyzing Politics An Introduction to Political Science*. Independence, KY: Wadsworth.

Mukherjee, S. and Ramaswamy, S. 2007. *A History of Political Thought: Plato To Marx*. New Delhi, India: Prentice Hall.

Okello, R. 2003. Men's property: Why East African women have no land rights, *The East African*.

Oshio, E. P. 1990. The indigenous land tenure and nationalization of land in Nigeria, *Boston College Third World Law Journal*, 10(1): 43–62.

Chapter 18

Monitoring the Right to Health: The Political, Social, and Ethical Impact of Patient Satisfaction*

Emmanuel Kabengele Mpinga and Philippe Chastonay

Contents

Introduction

The concept of patient satisfaction has a long history of controversy and debate, and patient satisfaction remains an important topic of scientific investigation. However, little is known about its relations and importance regarding the monitoring of the right to health. From the 1950s, patient satisfaction became an important topic in health care settings (Abdellah and Levine, 1957), and

* This chapter is a revised version of the authors' published article: Mpinga, E. K. and Chastonay, P. 2011. Patient satisfaction and the monitoring of the right to health: Some thoughts based on a review of the literature, *Global Journal of Health Science*, 3(1): 64–69.

there has been a growing scientific interest in this field ever since. Medline reports from 1968 to 1977 show that fewer than 100 publications on patient satisfaction exist, whereas there are nearly 4000 publications between 1998 and 2007 (Medline). Early on, many articles centered on the development and utilization of specific tools (Risser, 1975; Ware et al., 1977a,b; MacKeigan and Larson, 1989; Wilson et al., 2006). However, over time more focus was placed on the clarification of the concept of patient satisfaction (Williams, 1994; Wagner and Bear, 2009), particularly on the identification of essential components of patient satisfaction (Hall and Dornan, 1988; Perreault et al., 2001) as well as its specific explanatory factors (Huang et al., 2004; Bautista et al., 2007). Furthermore, studies explored the relationship between patient satisfaction and the quality of care (van Campen & Sixma, 1995; Hutchison et al., 2003) as well as its evolution over time, in different groups of patients, in various healthcare settings, and in different cultural or geographical contexts (Lochoro, 2004; McCabe et al., 2008; Piron et al., 2008; Allan et al., 2009; Kikwilu et al., 2009).

From Risser (1975) to Mrayyan (2006), and with the input of Lochoro (2004) and Wolosin (2005), the concept of patient satisfaction has moved from a more theoretical to a more technical and operational approach. Risser (1975) considers patient satisfaction as the degree of convergence between the expectations that patients have of ideal care and their perception of the care they actually receive. Lochoro supports this point of view, noting that patient satisfaction corresponds to the gap between the expected and perceived characteristics of a service (Lochoro, 2004). These considerations are based on the work of Donabedian, who defines patient satisfaction as the expression of patients' judgment on the quality of care received in all aspects but particularly as it relates to the interpersonal process (Donabedian, 1988). Wolosin (2005) considers patient satisfaction as an indicator of the quality of care and integrates into its definition patients' experiences as a key element of (un)satisfaction. He argues that when experience exceeds expectations, this leads to satisfied patients, while experiences, which fail to meet expectations cause dissatisfaction. Patient satisfaction ultimately reflects their response to experience and interactions with caregivers. Mrayyan (2006) enriches the concept with new dimensions, arguing that patient satisfaction becomes the degree to which nursing care—as well as public health activities—meets patients' expectations in terms of the art of care, technical quality, physical environment, availability and continuity of care, and the efficacy/outcomes of care.

Components of Patient Satisfaction

The components of patient satisfaction can be summarized as "the quality and accessibility of medical care, availability of health services and structures, affordability of costs, information, and participation of the patient." More specifically, the key constituents of patient satisfaction are the quality of medical care (including competent health professionals, adequate infrastructure, and health services), appropriate diagnostic and therapeutic procedures, adequate information on disease and therapy, equity in the accessibility to diagnostic, therapeutic and preventive measures, reasonable costs and affordable health insurance system for the individual and the community, acceptable "waiting times" and appropriate "hostelry," and the participatory approach of care and prevention (i.e., the integration of the patient and his family in the decision procedures) (Risser, 1975; Ware et al., 1977a,b; Hall & Dornan, 1988; Baker, 1991; Mahon, 1996; Lochoro, 2004).

Patient Satisfaction: How to Measure It

Patient Satisfaction Studies

Measuring patient satisfaction is not an easy task. It requires (a) a clear definition of the objectives, (b) the identification of the target populations, (c) well-defined tools and ways of collecting the data, and (d) a strategy for analyzing the data and its utilization. It can focus on the process and/or the results of care. It also allows patients to evaluate services and treatments they have received. Finally, measuring patient satisfaction allows the identification of possible problems and suggests ways of improving the quality of care or public health interventions (Druss, 1999; Harris et al., 1999). Patient satisfaction measuring tools are numerous and vary accordingly to the field investigated. For example, in oncology, a review of the literature on 1803 studies reported 36 different tools available to measure patient satisfaction. In the field of diabetes research and treatment between 1987 and 1997, eight different tools have been developed and used: these include the Diabetes Attitude Scale, Diabetes Treatment Satisfaction Questionnaire, Treatment Satisfaction and Psychological Wellbeing, the Ipswich Diabetes Self-management questionnaire, Diabetes Care Profile, Diabetes Quality of Life (DQOL), and Picker Patient Satisfaction Survey. Such a proliferation of tools implies that for any given research question, the appropriate tool must be chosen, one that has proven its validity, viability, acceptability, and feasibility (Paddock et al., 2000; Richardson et al., 2007; Panvelkar et al., 2009).

In various regions around the world, patient satisfaction studies are widely used to evaluate the quality of care as well as the acceptability and impact of public health programs. They have been implemented in various cultural contexts and in different health systems as well as among patients suffering from specific pathologies (Perreault et al., 2001; Hutchison et al., 2003; Huang et al., 2004; Wolosin, 2005; Mrayyan, 2006; Wilson et al., 2006; Bautista et al., 2007; Piron et al., 2008; Allan et al., 2009). Over the past 30 years, patient satisfaction might well be one of the most studied topics in health sciences, if one considers the number of published articles, the diversity of analytic approaches, and the extent of the debate. It is also necessary to mention the variety of tools developed in order to measure patient satisfaction, many of which have been validated, thereby allowing international comparison and long-term follow-up (Mahon, 1996; Hendriks et al., 2002; Defossez et al., 2007). The measurement of patient satisfaction is of great value to the health system because it allows practitioners to (a) describe and characterize levels of function; (b) identify existing problems in a given sector; and (c) evaluate the quality of care (Sitzia & Wood, 1997).

Reports have been made stating that patient satisfaction studies have a real impact on the attitudes and behavior of health professionals, and that they are likely to bring about improvements in the health service industry (Greco et al., 2001). A French study, for example, reports that among healthcare professionals of a university hospital, 94% have a positive opinion of patient satisfaction studies, 60% are aware of the results of such studies undertaken in their department, and 40% report that those studies have brought about improvements in the services and have caused them to modify their own behavior (Boyer et al., 2006).

Limits of the Patient Satisfaction Concept

Two recent reviews have analyzed the major critiques of the patient satisfaction concept and its related studies. The first one is a review of the literature by Hekkert et al. (2009). The authors report the critiques and observations undertaken by Fizpatrick and Hopkins (1983); Pascoe (1983); Williams (1994); Avis et al. (1997); Sitzia and Wood (1997); Sixma et al. (1998); Jenkinson et al. (2002); Merkouris et al. (2004); the second is a review by Gill and White (2009) based mainly on the studies of Sofaer and Firminger (2005); Gonzales et al. (2005); Gilbert and Veloutsou (2006); Hawthorne (2006) and Heidegger et al. (2006). The major criticisms mentioned in these reviews are the lack of consensus on the concept of patient satisfaction, its subjectivity, the weak discriminative power of the measuring tools, the lack of validity *per se* of those tools as well as the strong focus on clinical settings of the studies.

The lack of consensus around the concept of patient satisfaction has "historical reasons" due to the fact that a large number of studies on patient satisfaction were performed prior to the clarification of the concept, and were determined by the monodisciplinary nature of the approach of many researchers, be they nurses, physicians, psychologists, or managers. At present, a consensus seems at last to have emerged (Leplege & Coste, 2002). The subjectivity of patient satisfaction studies is primarily a result of the fact that they measure personal perception as well as the values and attitudes of patients. However, although this can be considered as a weak point by many researchers, others consider such subjectivity to be a strong point. This is so because it integrates the psychological dimension of the evaluation of care by the patients (Ware et al., 1977a,b; Hekkert et al., 2009).

The weak discriminative power of patient satisfaction studies relates to the high satisfaction scores commonly reported (75%–90%). However, this might well be related to the patient *per se* rather than to methods of collecting the information—tools of collecting data, scale of measuring, and ways of submitting the questionnaires to patients—as has been suggested by some (Ross et al., 1995; Ware et al., 1977a,b). This underlines the importance of validating data collecting tools. The strong focus on clinical settings of patient satisfaction studies is quite real, yet this has been diminishing over the years (Wolosin, 2005). Two strong points of patient satisfaction studies are of a technical nature: their high participation rate and their statistical power. High participation rates have been reported in several reviews. Sitzia and Wood (1997: 39), having reviewed 219 articles from 141 different scientific journals, report a mean participation rate of 72.1%; Asch et al. (1997: 40), having reviewed 178 studies published in medical journals, report a participation rate of 60%. High statistical power relates to the thousands of patients employed in those studies.

Patient Satisfaction and the Right to Health

When considering the respect and protection of the health of populations, the obligation of states is determined by national and international laws as well as by human rights conventions and treaties. General Observation 14 of the Committee for Economic, Social, and Cultural Rights (CESCR) of the United Nations Economic and Social Council (ECOSOC), commenting on the right to health, reaffirms the essential components of the right to health as state obligations. These components are the availability of health services, health infrastructure and public health programs, the nondiscriminatory (physical, economic, and informational) access for all to health care and prevention programs, the acceptability (ethical, gender-related, and cultural) of health services and programs, and the quality of care—health procedures and programs must be scientifically and medically sound, which in turn implies competent health professionals, adequate medication, and appropriate infrastructure (ECOSOC, 2000; E/C.12/2000/4). These rights to health constituents correspond perfectly with patient satisfaction components, as described in the literature and presented previously. This suggests that patient satisfaction could serve as a potential indicator of the right to health, allowing researchers to monitor to what extent the right to health has been integrated into a given health structure, specifically, or in the health sector more broadly. Beyond these technical aspects, patient satisfaction studies present some other strong points regarding the monitoring of the right to health.

First, it is fitting that a democratic society should take into account the opinion of patients in any health policy decision; promoting a participative process in the evaluation of health care activities seems to be a central value of modern societies. This is reported to restore confidence in public services, improve the quality of care, and strengthen social links in the community. It also seems to promote a pluralistic model of decision-making (Taylor, 2009). Second, in parallel to the socioeconomic and technological evolution in recent decades, there has been an evolution of the patient-health professional relationship. This has led to new expectations and demands regarding health care practice, toward a health care practice centered on the patient, which in turn envisages a patient-health professional relationship based on partnership rather than paternalism (Mead and Bower, 2000; Taylor, 2009). Third, in many countries, patient satisfaction studies have become an important indicator of the quality of care, and in some regions, they are even a legal obligation. In France, patient satisfaction studies have been labeled as a "priority" since 1996 (Revilla et al., 2008) while in the United Kingdom, they have been identified as a reform priority since the 1980s (Sitzia & Wood, 1997). Fourth, the health system of the future should be patient-centered, with the patient acting as a key evaluator (IOM, 2001). Finally, in promoting partnership among the various actors of the health system including patients, health professionals, managers, and politicians, patient satisfaction contributes to the protection and the promotion of the right to health care. As an example one might mention the "[c]ore questionnaire for patient satisfaction project" undertaken in the Netherlands in close collaboration with the Dutch Inspectorate for Health and the national Hospital Association; these patient satisfaction surveys, undertaken throughout the country's hospitals, are published annually on the Internet (Hekkert et al., 2009).

Conclusion

The literature suggests that patient satisfaction studies, whether in their founding concepts or in their more technical aspects, have a potential political, social, and ethical impact, which strengthens their usefulness as a monitoring tool of the right to health. Patient satisfaction builds on ethical, deontological, and moral foundations. The principles of autonomy—free choice and participation, beneficence and nonmaleficence, scientific soundness, technical competency, and capacity for empathy—should be respected by health professionals and be an integral part of the mechanisms of implementation and surveillance quality of care and basic rights of patients. Perhaps patient satisfaction could be considered in the future as a right to health indicator making its contribution in monitoring the progress states have achieved in regard to implementing the right to health for the populations they are in charge of. Indeed, patient satisfaction studies yield valuable information on issues such as accessibility/inaccessibility to quality health care, true/false patient participation, the adequate/inadequate circulation of information, and the appropriate/inappropriate allocation of resources, and may ultimately be of interest to health policy decision-makers.

References

Abdellah, F. G. and Levine, E. 1957. Developing a measure of patient and personnel satisfaction with nursing care, *Nursing Research*, 5: 100–108.

Allan, J., Schatter, P., Stocks, N., and Ramsay, E. 2009. Does patient satisfaction of general practice change over a decade?, *BMC Family Practice*, 10(13): 1–10.

Asch, D. A., Jedrziewski, M. K., and Christakis, N. A. 1997. Response rates to mail surveys published in medical journals, *Journal of Clinical Epidemiology*, 50(10): 1129–1136.

Baker, R. 1991. The reliability and criterion validity of a measure of patients' satisfaction with their general practice, *Family Practice*, 8: 171–177.

Bautista, R. E., Glen, E. T., and Shetty, N. K. 2007. Factors associated with satisfaction with care among patients with epilepsy, *Epilepsy and Behavior*, 11(4): 518–524.

Boyer, L., Francois, P., Doutre, E., Weil, G., and Labarere, J. 2006. Perception and use of the results of patient satisfaction surveys by Care Providers in a French Teaching Hospital, *International Journal of Quality in Health Care*, 18(5): 359–364.

Defossez, G., Mathoulin-Pelissier, S., Ingrand, I., Gasquet, I., Sifer-Riviere, L., Ingrande, P., Salamon, R. et al. and REPERES Research Network 2007. Satisfaction with care among patients with No-Metastatic cancer: Development and first step of validation of the REPERES-60 questionnaire, *BMC Cancer*, 7: 19.

Donabedian, A. 1988. The quality of care: How can it be assessed?, *Journal of American Medical Association*, 260(12): 1743–1748.

Druss, G. B. 1999. Patient satisfaction and administrative measures as indicators of the quality of mental health care, *Psychiatric Services*, 50(80): 1053–1058.

E/C.12/2000/4 du 11 août 2000.

ECOSOC 2000. *Le droit au meilleur état de santé susceptible d'être atteint*. Observation générale 14 du comité des droits économiques sociaux et culturels.

Fitzpatrick, R. and Hopkins, A. 1983. Problems in the conceptual framework of patient satisfaction research: An empirical exploration. *Sociology of Health and Disease*, 5(3): 297–311.

Gill, L. and White, L. 2009. A critical review of patient satisfaction, *Leadership in Health Services*, 22(1): 8–19.

Gilbert, G. R. and Veloutsou, C. 2006. A cross-industry comparison of customer satisfaction, *Journal of Services Marketing*, 20(5): 298–308.

Gonzales-Valentin, A., Padin-Lopez, S., and de Ramon-Garrido, E. 2005. Patient satisfaction with nursing care in a regional university hospital in southern Spain, *Journal of Nursing Care Quality*, 20(1): 63–72.

Greco, M., Brownlea, A., and McGovern, J. 2001. Impact of patient feedback on the interpersonal skills of general practice Registrars, results of a longitudinal study, *Medical Education*, 35: 748–756.

Hall, J. A. and Dornan, M. C. 1988. What patients like about their medical care and how often they asked: A metaanalysis of the satisfaction literature, *Social Science Medicine*, 27: 935–939.

Harris, E. L., Swindle, W. R., Mungai, S. M., Weinberger, M., and Tierney, W. M. 1999. Measuring patient satisfaction for quality improvement, *Medical Care*, 37(12): 1207–1213.

Hawthorne, G. 2006. *Review of Patient Satisfaction Measures, Australian Government*, Department of Health and Ageing, Canberra, Australia.

Heidegger, T., Saal, D., and Nuebling, M. 2006. Patient satisfaction with anaestesia care: What is patient satisfaction, how should it be measured, and what is the evidence for assuring high patient satisfaction? *Best Practice Reseasrch and Clinical Anaesthesioogyl*, 20(2): 331–346.

Hekkert, K. D., Cihangri, S., Kleefstra, S. M., van den Berg, B., and Kool, B. R. 2009. Patient satisfaction revisited: A multilevel approach, *Social Science Medicine*, 68–75.

Hendriks, A. A. J., Oort, F. J., Vrielink, M. R., and Smets, E. M. 2002. Reliability and validity of the satisfaction with hospital care questionnaire, *International Journal of Quality in Health Care*, 14: 471–482.

Huang, J. A., Lai, C. S., Tsai, W. C., Weng, R. H., Hu, W. H., and Yang, D. Y. 2004. Determining factors of patient satisfaction for frequent users emergency services in a medical center, *Journal of the Chinese Medical Association*, 67(8): 403–410.

Hutchison, B., Østbye, T., Barnsley, J., Stewart, M., Mathews, M., Campbell, M. K., Vayda, E. et al. and Ontario Walk-In Clinic Society 2003. Patient satisfaction and quality of care in walk-in clinics, family practices and emergency departments: The Ontario walk-in clinic study, *Canadian Medical Association Journal*, 169(1): 977–983.

IOM Committee on Quality of Care in America 2001. *Crossing the Quality Chasm: A New Health System for the 21st Century*. National Academic, Washington, DC.

Jenkinson, C., Coulter, A., Bruster, S., Richards, N., and Chandola, T. 2002. Patients' experiences and satisfaction with health care: Results of a questionnaire study of specific aspects of care, *Quality Safety Health Care*, 11: 335–339.

Kikwilu, E. N., Kahabuka, F. K., Masalu, J. R., and Senkoro, A. 2009. Satisfaction with urgent oral care among adult tanzanians, *Journal of Oral Science*, 51(1): 47–54.

Leplege, A. and Coste, J. 2002. *Mesure de la santé perceptuelle et de la qualité de vie: méthodes et application*. Paris, France: Estem Editions.

Lochoro, P. 2004. Measuring patient satisfaction in UCMB health institutions, *Health and Policy Development*, 2(3): 243–248.

MacKeigan, L. D. and Larson, L. N. 1989. Development and validation of an instrument to measure patient satisfaction with pharmacy services, *Medical Care*, 27(5): 522–536.

Mahon, Y. P. 1996. An analysis of the concept patient satisfaction as it relates to contemporary nursing care, *Journal of Advanced Nursing*, 24: 1241–1248.

McCabe, M. P., Roberts, C., and Firth, L. 2008. Satisfaction with services among people with progressive neurological illnesses and their careers in Australia, *Nursing Health Science*, 10(3): 209–215.

Mead, N. and Bower, P. 2000. Patient centeredness: A conceptual framework and review of the empirical literature, *Social Science Medicine*, 51: 1087–1111.

Merkouris, A., Papathanassoglou E. D., and Lemonidou, C. 2004. Evaluation of patient satisfaction with nursing care: Quantitative or qualitative approach? *International Journal of Nursing Studies*, 41(4): 355–367.

Mrayyan, M. T. 2006. Jordanian nurses' job satisfaction, patients' satisfaction and quality of nursing care, *International Nursing Review*, 53: 224–230.

Paddock, E. L., Veloski, J., Geviritz, O. F., and Nash, D. B. 2000. Development and validation of a questionnaire to evaluate patient satisfaction with diabetes disease management, *Diabetes Care*, 23: 951–956.

Panvelkar, N. P., Saini, B., and Armour, C. 2009. Measurement of patient satisfaction with community pharmacy services: A review, *Pharmacy World and Science*, 31: 525–537.

Pascoe, G. C. 1983. Patient satisfaction in primary health care: A literature review and analysis, *Evaluation and Program Planning*, 6(3–4): 185–210.

Perreault, M., Katerelos, T. E., Sabourin, S., Leichner, P., and Desmerais, J. 2001. Information as a distinct dimension for satisfaction assessment of outpatient psychiatric services, *International Journal of Health Care Quality Assurance*, 14(2/3): 111–120.

Piron, L., Turolla, A., Tonin, P., Piccione, F., Lain, L., and Dam, M. 2008. Satisfaction with care in post-stroke patients undergoing a telerehabilitation program at home, *Journal of Telemedicine and Telecare*, 14(5): 257–260.

Revilla, A., Taboulet, P., Plaisance, P., and Taboulet, P. 2008. La satisfaction des patients aux urgences est-elle comparable à celle des soignants?, *Urgence Pratique*, 90: 5–8.

Richardson, A., Medina, J., Brown, V., and Sitzia, J. 2007. Patients' needs assessment in cancer care: A review of assessment tools, *Support Care Cancer*, 15(10): 1125–1144.

Risser, N. L. 1975. Development of an instrument to measure patient satisfaction with nurses and nursing care in primary care settings, *Nursing Research*, 24(1): 45–52.

Ross, C. K., Steward, C. A., and Sinacore, J. M. 1995. A comparative study of seven measure of patient satisfaction, *Medical Care*, 33(4): 392–406.

Sitzia, J. and Wood, N. 1997. Patient satisfaction: A review of issues and concepts, *Social Science and Medicine*, 45(12): 1829–1843.

Sixma, H., Kerssens, J., van Campen, C., and Peters, L. 1998. Quality of care from the patients' persepctive: From theoretical concept to an new measuring instrument, *Health Expectations*, 1(2): 82–95.

Sofaer, S. and Firminger, K. 2005. Patient perceptions of the quality of health services, *Annual Review of Public Health*, 26: 513–559.

Taylor, K. 2009. Paternalism, participation, and partnership-the evolution of patient centeredness in the consultation, *Patient Education and Counseling*, 74: 150–155.

van Campen, C. and Sixma, H. 1995. Quality of care and patient satisfaction: A review of measuring instruments, *Medical Care Research and Review*, 52(1): 109–133.

Wagner, D. and Bear, M. 2009. Patient satisfaction with nursing care: A concept analysis within a nursing framework, *Journal of Advanced Nursing*, 65(3): 692–701.

Ware, J. E., Jr., Davies A. R., and Stewart, A. 1977a. The measurement and meaning of patient satisfaction: A review of the literature, RAND, Santa Monica, CA.

Ware, J. E., Jr., Snyder, M. K., and Wright, R. 1977b. Some issues in the measurement of patient satisfaction with health care, Santa Monica, RAND, Santa Monica, CA.

Williams, B. 1994. Patient satisfaction: A valid concept, *Social Science and Medicine*, 38(4): 509–516.

Wilson, A., Hewitt, G., Matthews, R., Richards, S. H., and Sheppard, S. 2006. Development and testing of a questionnaire to measure patient satisfaction with intermediate care, *Quality Safety and Health Care*, 15(5): 314–319.

Wolosin, R. J. 2005. The voice of the patient: A national representative study of satisfaction with family physicians, *Quality Management in Healthcare*, 14(3): 155–164.

Chapter 19

European Models of Citizenship and the Fight against Female Genital Mutilation*

Renée Kool and Sohail Wahedi

Contents

---

* This chapter is a revised version of the authors' published article: Kool, R. S. B. and Wahedi, S. 2014. Criminal enforcement in the area of female genital mutilation in France, England, and the Netherlands: A comparative law perspective, *International Law Research*, 3(1): 1–15.

Introduction

Recent research by the United Nations illustrates clearly that the global (criminal law) attention for the practice of female genital mutilation (FGM) is a matter of the last few years (United Nations Population Fund [UNFPA], 2014). However, at the European level, the question of how to deal with FGM has confronted societies for some decades. After the initial struggle with the question of whether the perpetrator's cultural background should result in impunity or absence of guilt, it has become clear that by standards derived from the notion of respect for human rights and human dignity, FGM is an unacceptable cultural practice. Human rights standards—interpreted in conformity with the classical liberal standards and values predominant in Western thinking with its focus on the harm principle—support this view. In this context, the keywords are "harmful traditional practices" and "gender-based violence" (European Institute for Gender Equality [EIGE], 2013) often supplemented by the statement that crimes contradictory to the "views of civilized nations" are involved (Dustin, 2010; van den Brink and Tigchelaar, 2012). This view is laid down in (among others) the recently adopted Istanbul Convention on preventing and combating violence against women and domestic violence (Council of Europe, 2011) and the European Parliament resolution 2012/2684 (RSP) on ending FGM (European Parliament, 2012).

Critical of qualifying FGM a harmful cultural practice is Dustin who argues that such a qualification could be seen to be a result of the "external messiah syndrome" which has dominated the Western thinking with regard to cultural practices of minorities considered harmful and inadmissible by liberal societal standards (Dustin, 2010: 19). In this context, she has raised the question of why the practice of female circumcision is challenged while "cosmetic interventions" on female genitalia have been widely accepted across the Western world. Next, it is argued that by qualifying FGM as a "bad tradition" the right to culture is absorbed, as it were, by the—from a Western perspective—"superior" right to physical and psychological integrity (van den Brink and Tigchelaar, 2012).

The calls for a ban on FGM—based on the notion that it is a harmful and painful gendered practice to females—do not answer the more underlying question of why female circumcision cannot be considered a cultural exception in law, as is the case for some other (controversial) cultural (surgical) interventions such as male circumcision and cosmetic surgery (Kool and Wahedi, 2014; Wahedi, 2012). The question arises furthermore, whether Western legal systems are legitimized to qualify a non-Western cultural practice in terms of right or wrong and, if they are allowed to do so, is the only use of legal measures sufficient in this context to eliminate this practice (Gunning, 1992; Dustin, 2010). In line with this, the question arises furthermore, why despite the consensus on the punishability of FGM its criminal enforcement diverges in Western Europe (Leye et al., 2007). To address the differences in outcome, we studied the criminal law approach to FGM in three countries: France, England, and the Netherlands. The term England is used to refer to the policy pursued in England and Wales, countries of the United Kingdom. Although to outsiders this distinction might seem a bit contrived, it is commonplace in British/English literature, especially in relation to societal views on the unlawfulness of harmful cultural practices. In this chapter, we compare not only the legal framework and the underlying policy but also the underlying national views on citizenship. Our basic assumption is that national views on citizenship influence the way in which Western European societies deal with multiculturalism and harmful cultural practices. We believe strongly that this approach offers an explanation for the divergent enforcement practices in the area of FGM.

Methodology

This qualitative study focuses on the question as to whether a particular notion of citizenship in the studied countries influences the criminal prosecution of FGM. Our choice for these countries is based on our perception that outcomes in enforcement actions banning FGM diverge strongly in these countries. We assume a relationship between the different outcomes in legal enforcement and the different notions of citizenship in the studied countries. Based on this intellectual goal and theoretical assumption, the conceptual framework of this study consists of works concerning notions of citizenship, different researches on the admissibility of "harmful" cultural practices, cultural exceptions in law, and the way substantive criminal law, so far, has reacted to such practices. This qualitative legal research is based on comparative (legal) literature, case law, and legislation concerning the theme that is studied. It should be noted that the use of various notions of citizenship is meant as heuristic to explain the differences in criminal law approach to FGM and its criminal prosecution within the studied states (van der Burg, 2011).

This chapter begins with a short description of the phenomenon of FGM. This description is viewed from the human rights perspective that qualifies this practice as "harmful cultural practice" with the ensuing obligation of penalization. This is followed by a European consensus on the punishability of FGM and a more specific description of the French, English, and Dutch legal approaches to FGM in the context of prevailing views on citizenship. This chapter concludes by asserting that the outcome of the criminal approach to harmful cultural practices is to a certain extent declared by a particular notion of citizenship.

Human Rights as a Basis for Criminalizing the Practice of FGM

The World Health Organization (WHO) describes FGM as follows: "the partial or total removal of the external female genitalia, or any other injury to the female genitalia for non-medical reasons" (WHO, 2011). Worldwide, an estimated 130–150 million girls and women are genitally mutilated in one way or another; approximately another three million girls are estimated to run the risk of being circumcised. FGM is practiced mainly in parts of Northern Africa and Asia and also in the Middle East. Recent empirical studies have shown that this practice has been exercised in Iraqi Kurdistan (Wadi, 2010) and even in the Islamic Republic of Iran (Ahmady, 2015). Next, it is reported that FGM occurs in Western Europe. This ranges from small operations (removal of the foreskin of the clitoris) to larger ones (the removal and sewing up of the labia majora or minora, sometimes in combination with the removal of the clitoris). Removal of the foreskin, which is generally considered a relatively mild form of FGM, is compared to male circumcision (Siesling, 2006; Limborgh, 2011; van den Brink and Tigchelaar, 2012). As FGM, as a rule, is practiced outside a medical context, more substantial health risks are usually involved.

There is no clear explanation for this age-old tradition. There are various reasons for practicing FGM: sometimes it is based on religious beliefs, although it is argued that religious texts do not explicitly support this (Kalev, 2004; Leye et al., 2007; Otto, 2014). Other times, FGM involves an initiation ritual within a group from which the woman derives status (Berkovitch and Bradley, 1999). A critical interpretation hereof is reflected in human rights texts, assuming a gendered practice. This view, however, is not undisputed. Various scholars have referred to the existence of a "double standard" in the fight against FGM (Shweder, 2002; Dustin, 2010). The aforementioned interpretation clarifies matters, as it reveals the "political" nature of international legislation (including human rights) and the underlying conceptualization of cultural practices. Such rules are the result of political negotiations; where the Western liberal discourse is predominant when human rights are involved. In female-related matters such as FGM, gender has been the dominant frame for some decades. Although this frame contains inconsistencies, that is, cosmetic surgery increasing in popularity in the West (breast enlargement, corrections of the labia, etc.) is hardly ever problematized; it strongly affects the evaluation of cultural practices that are qualified as gendered (Lewis, 1995; Dustin, 2010; Smith, 2011; van den Brink and Tigchelaar, 2012). In this context, it is argued by Brems that the increased thinking in terms of women's rights and the related interest in gender has led to a fundamental subordination of the right to culture (Brems, 1997). However, from a more pragmatic point of view the subsumption of FGM under human rights violations also fits in with the prevailing Western opinion that human rights are universal by nature (van den Brink and Tigchelaar, 2012).

The most far-reaching effect hereof may be found in the judgment that this is a cultural practice "in contradiction with the views of civilized nations." Within the sphere of influence of the European Convention on Human Rights (ECHR), which is decisive for Europe, the applicability of this qualification has direct consequences for the requirements of criminal legality. On the basis of Article 7 ECHR, the applicability of this qualification requires no previous, knowable penalization any more: punishability is so obvious that no misunderstanding is possible on the basis of a moral intuition shared by all. In addition, one often resorts to the argument of the universality of human rights. However, an easy appeal to this exceptional category impairs the interest of both foreseeability and recognizability of punishability (requirement of legality) that is also protected as a human right. At the national level, one more or less automatically appeals to the applicability of this category, in the event that the punishability of cultural offenses or related jurisdiction issues is concerned.

In the case of FGM, there may be good reasons for this. As a rule, major (possibly irreversible) violations of a person's physical and mental integrity are involved, which are carried out without permission of the person concerned. This is not applicable, however, to genital mutilations that are performed on adult women at their own request. Even those were sometimes made punishable explicitly, that is, Article 5 (1) (3) and (5a) of the Belgian Criminal Code and Article 5 of the English Female Genital Mutilation Act 2003. However, what if we are dealing with lighter variants of FGM? As a result of the "indivisibility" of the gender frame and of the "generous" use of the label "contradiction with the views of civilized liberal nations," these are also qualified as (at least potentially) punishable behavior—with the ensuing claim for both national and international jurisdiction.

Leaving aside the correctness of such a categorical criminalization, one cannot avoid the conclusion that the predominant human rights frame—which views FGM as a violent and, therefore, criminal practice—contains inconsistencies that raise questions as to the legitimacy of penalization and criminal enforcement. Although one might presume otherwise, FGM was not initially recognized as a human rights violation (Berkovitch and Bradley, 1999; Kalev, 2004; WHO, 2011; van den Brink and Tigchelaar, 2012; UNFPA, 2014). After a slow start in the fifties, it even took until the mid-1990 for FGM to be put on the human rights agenda. Since then, states have been under an obligation to develop legislation providing effective protection against FGM at the state level (Wheeler, 2004).

This has been realized at the European level, as is shown by the Istanbul Convention, the resolution of the European Parliament of June 2012 on ending FGM and the case law of the European Court of Human Rights (ECtHR) among others. A restriction applies with regard to this last source: no case has yet been brought before the ECtHR claiming the infringement of a Convention right on account of the lack of criminal law protection offered against FGM.

Nevertheless, in its decisions on the application of migration law, the ECtHR has clearly indicated that member states are under an obligation to provide adequate and effective protection against FGM (*Omeredo versus Austria*; *Izevbekhai* et al. *versus Ireland*; *Collins and Akaziebie versus Sweden*). Although in these cases FGM was deemed to violate Article 3 ECHR, prohibition of torture and inhumane treatment (Van Boven and Puig, 2005), one may presume that FGM will also violate criminal law protection to be offered under other provisions of the Convention such as the right to life (Article 2 ECHR).

With regard to the aforementioned serious violations, the ECtHR, as a rule, deems it appropriate to resort to criminal law—resulting in the need for an adequate criminalization and effective enforcement hereof (Kool, 2010). Both the association of female circumcision with mutilation and the starting point of criminalization and effective enforcement suggest that the ECtHR will not be inclined to accept a cultural defense easily. This is in line with other human rights conventions that explicitly exclude an appeal to tradition to justify violent practices against girls and women. Consider in this regard among others Article 12 (5) of the Convention on preventing and combating violence against women and domestic violence (Council of Europe, 2011).

European Consensus on the Punishability of FGM: Some Specific Criminal Law Provisions on the FGM Practice

As indicated previously, FGM is a crime in all the member states of the EU (EIGE, 2013a). Additionally, there are periodic calls across the European states to adopt specific criminal law provisions on FGM (Kool, 2005; Kool et al., 2005; Siesling, 2006; Voorde, 2007). Reference is often made to countries that consider FGM a specific offense. Such specific prohibitions are often a *lex specialis* of assault and injury offenses. As such, Sweden was among the first countries prohibiting FGM specifically. In 1982, the Swedish "Act Prohibiting the Genital Mutilation of Women" took effect—according to which is illegal to cut any female genitalia. The consent of the victim is in this context irrelevant. Any attempt to practice this offense is considered punishable in Sweden by imprisonment of not less than two years and not more than ten years. In 2006, two court cases of FGM were registered in Sweden. It should be noted that the principle of extraterritoriality applies to the FGM crime (EIGE, 2013b).

Belgium is another European country in which FGM has been a specific offense since 2001. Article 409 of the Belgian Penal Code criminalizes all variants of FGM with a minimum prison sentence of three years and a maximum of five years. Even the attempt to FGM is prohibited by the Belgian Penal Code. If a minor is circumcised, the defendant will face a minimum prison sentence of five years and a maximum of seven years; if death occurs as a result of FGM, the defendant could face an imprisonment of at least ten years with a maximum of 15 years. The principle of extraterritoriality is applicable, meaning that FGM practiced outside Belgium constitutes a crime.

Cyprus also has a specific criminal law provision on FGM. Since 2003, Article 233A of the Cypriot Penal Code prohibits all forms of FGM. The consent of the victim does not justify this practice, and the defendant could face a maximum imprisonment of five years. However, to date, there have not been any cases of FGM registered in Cyprus. In contrast to many other European states, the principle of extraterritoriality is only applicable to FGM cases after a court decision (see EIGE).

Since 2003, the Spanish Penal Code has specifically prohibited the practice of FGM with a minimum prison sentence of six years and a maximum of 12 years. It should be noted that circumcision of fragile groups of women could affect the length of the imprisonment there. On the other hand, the consent of the victim might reduce the duration of the imprisonment (EIGE, 2013c).

Italy has criminalized FGM specifically as a crime against fundamental human rights. Since 2006, the Articles 583bis and 583ter of the Italian Penal Code have declared all variants of FGM illegal and punishable by imprisonment from four to 12 years (Doe, 2011). Next, punishment can be decreased from three to seven years imprisonment for lighter versions of FGM, or increased if a minor is circumcised. To date, very few cases have reached the courtrooms in Italy (see EIGE).

In Ireland, the Criminal Justice (FGM) Act 2012 clearly excludes "cultural defenses" for FGM and penalizes the practice of it with imprisonment up to 14 years, potentially in combination with a fine of up to €10,000.

Since 2013, Article 226a of the German Penal Code has made FGM illegal. The practice hereof is threatened with an imprisonment of *at least* one year.

The specific criminal law provisions on the practice of FGM across Europe illustrate the great disapproval of this practice. However, specific criminal provisions on FGM apparently have not affected the criminal prosecution of this practice. Hereafter, we elaborate on France, England, and the Netherlands (as particular case studies) to see whether the notion of citizenship might be of influence on the criminal law approach (and the results hereof) to FGM.

Intermezzo: Notions of Citizenship

Although magnification should be avoided and as factual (im)possibilities set the political agenda, a comparative analysis of the criminal law approach to FGM calls for a closer look at society's views on multiculturalism, which in their turn are to be related to views on citizenship. FGM is a cultural offence and this colors the issue of the prosecutorial discretion. Moreover, in case of prosecution, a cultural defense may be advanced. The answers of the criminal justice system to both the question of prosecutorial discretion and the question of assessment of the cultural defense are (also) determined by views in society on the need for immigrants to assimilate, and the extent to which they are allowed to hold and to practice cultural minority views. Although the (mostly) major and irreversible character of FGM limits the "workspace" of criminal law, society's views on multiculturalism also are relevant here.

We use three models of citizenship derived from literature: the republican, the ethnocultural, and the multicultural model (McCormick, 2005; Netherland Scientific Council for Government Policy/Wetenschappelijke Raad voor het Regeringsbeleid [WRR], 2006). The model a country belongs to depends on factors such as the degree to which newcomers are eligible to obtain citizenship of the host country, and the way in which a country recognizes diversity.

Anticipating the "country's analyses," it can be said that France fits in with the republican model. It is more complicated to decide, which models apply to England and to the Netherlands. In the past, and to a certain degree this still is true for England, both countries applied a multicultural model (Koopmans et al., 2005). This model embraces diversity and accepts differences. However, under the influence of a growing globalisation and a global fear of Muslim terrorism and even Muslim takeover of civil achievements, in recent years, views on citizenship have emerged that fit in better with an ethnocultural model. Like the republican model, this model focuses on a culturally homogeneous society, resulting in less scope for diversity.

Bearing in mind the relativity of these models, we have made "country analyses." As France is the only European country that, by far (and without any specific legal prohibition of FGM), actively enforces in the area of FGM—or so it appears—we have taken the liberty of elaborating on this case.

France: From Laissez-Faire to Assimilation

In the past decades, France (like other Western European countries) has had a pressing need for labor immigrants (WRR, 2001). Until the early 1970s it conducted a "laissez-faire" immigration policy—which as a result of the subsequent economic crisis made way for an "ethnocentric assimilation policy" (Guiné and Moreno Fuentes, 2007: 490). The French preference for a centralist approach and universalism resulted in a more restrictive assimilation policy aimed at maintaining French unity, minimizing the cultural differences, and mandating cultural assimilation of newcomers (WRR, 2001). The emphasis shifted to restricting immigration and to "*integration à la française*" (Winter, 1994; Wihtol de Wenden, 2003; Jugé and Perez, 2006). This assimilation policy had its impact in various areas including the approach of FGM; while no accurate numbers are available in France for FGM, it has been estimated that at least 61,000 women and girls or more have been subjected to FGM in the country, with four thousand more at risk (Leye et al., 2007; EIGE, 2013d).

This new assimilation policy did not focus on FGM from the onset. On the contrary, due to the belief that the newcomers were prepared to live according to the French values and to distance themselves from their original cultural background, a blind spot for cultural inequalities existed for quite some time—especially with regard to the position of women and children. Those data were ignored and, therefore, not registered, as a result of which they remained invisible (at least officially). The idea that an official care policy had to be developed in order to prevent "social, ethnic or religious particularism" (i.e., FGM) within the minority group was insufficiently recognized for a long time (Guiné and Moreno Fuentes, 2007: 491).

The death of a baby—baby Bobo—in 1982 as a result of wounds inflicted upon her during her circumcision opened up a debate about FGM practices in France (Winter, 1994; Kool et al., 2005). The tone of the resulting major media coverage indicated that the prevention policy pursued so far would no longer suffice. It became obvious that baby Bobo was not the only victim, care providers working in infant and youth health care (*Protection Maternelle et Infantile* [PMI]) reported having been confronted before with (the consequences of) FGM. In the *arrondissements* in which many immigrants had settled (especially around Paris), these circles insisted that enforcement be tightened up.

The fact that PMI played a prominent role in opening up the FGM debate has to do with the fact that the parents of children born in France are obliged to have their children undergo medical examinations until the age of six, irrespective of their residency status. An examination of the genitals is a part hereof. In conformity with the French views on obedience owed to the authorities, this obligation, as a rule, is not questioned (Nijboer et al., 2010). In addition, a PMI doctor, discovering a genital mutilation during a medical check, is under an obligation to report this to the *procureur de la République,* despite his/her duty of confidentiality. Consider in this regard the Articles 4 and 44 of the *Code de Déontologie Médicale.* Breaching the duty of confidentiality— apart from the exceptions following from Article 226-14 French Code Penal—constitutes a crime, but here an exception applies. Many care workers are not acquainted with the duty to report. As a consequence, hereof, directives were drafted for the PMI doctors. It appears from the case law that immediate action is only required if the danger to the patient's health is of an imminent and constant nature (Henrion, 2003).

Despite the fact that not all PMI doctors are willing to report, a larger degree of cooperation between doctors and criminal authorities exists in France than it does elsewhere (Nijboer et al., 2010). An important fact at the time was that most reports coming in after baby Bobo's death led to two identifiable cutters. As a result, more cases were discovered, and criminal prosecutions were initiated—such as the Keita (1991) and Greou (1994) cases (for a description of these and other French legal cases, see Appendix 5 in Nijboer et al., 2010). In this context, one could assert that a complex variety of factors has contributed to the success France has had in prosecuting cases.

There are more factors, however, the organization of French criminal investigation (and more specifically the prominent presence of the investigating judge) also plays a role. When the police are on the track of a cutter, they call in an investigating judge with wide, independent investigative powers. In combination with PMI's readiness to provide information in connection with the report, building a criminal case is relatively easy. According to Nijboer et al. (2010) in each of the cases tried, indications against the cutter as well as (one of) the parent(s) were present. The victim is examined by a forensic gynecologist at the request of the *procureur de la République* and with the permission of the possibly appointed temporary guardian. This is done to prevent the advance in court—on the basis of a countercheck report—of the defense that the girl has not been genitally mutilated (Nijboer et al., 2010). Here again, parents responding to an invitation for a conversation and doctors collecting such information is more "self-evident" in the French setting than elsewhere.

It should also be noted that French reports mainly originate from PMI doctors in the Paris region. This region has a high concentration of immigrant groups practicing FGM, and one is often confronted with the medical consequences of genital mutilation. This does not alter the fact that there are concentrations of these groups in other parts of France as well; however, activities by the judicial authorities are at a lower level there (Nijboer et al., 2010). What is more, Nijboer et al. conclude that, as a rule, the French police are not actively involved in investigating FGM, with the exception of the cutter cases. In this respect, they point out that, "the reactive character of the French criminal approach to FGM is not only of a formal-legal nature. A fact of a more cultural nature is that in the event of a report of a FGM already committed, relatively few man-hours are invested in investigating possible other cases and more evidence" (Nijboer et al., 2010: 167).

The last (cultural) factor that is important for a correct understanding of the French "success" is the fact that interest groups are entitled to join as a party during a preliminary judicial investigation. Unlike the Dutch regime, for instance, these interest groups have far-reaching procedural authorities. They may inspect documents or make requests, that is, have someone summoned as an expert (Nijboer et al., 2010). The NGOs involved in the criminal proceedings—including the leading women's rights organizations *Ligue pour le Droit des Femmes and the Groupe pour l'Abolition des Mutilations Génitales Féminines*—at the time advocated settling criminal cases regarding FGM at the highest criminal level, that is, the *Cours d'Assises*, (instead of at the level of the single judge) in order to give the case the character of a public warning. A jury trial before the *Court d'Assises* (drawing a lot of attention) promoted public visibility of the issue (Kool et al., 2005; Guiné and Moreno Fuentes, 2007; Nijboer et al., 2010).

All in all, some 40 criminal cases have been settled in France thus far, the majority ending in a conviction (Nijboer et al., 2010). Frequently, appeals were made to the cultural background of the accused to justify the genital mutilation or to exclude individual punishability. In a number of cases, experts established circumstances beyond the defendant's control; however, this defense has never been admitted. In fact, the feminist quarter has criticized such defenses, as the women in question were portrayed as victims of their own culture without a will of their own (Winter, 1994). In other cases, the accused invoked error of law, arguing that as an immigrant they had not been aware of the fact that FGM was punishable in France. Nijboer et al. are of the opinion that these defenses were meant to influence the nature and scope of the sentence, not to effect an acquittal or an exemption from punishment. This effect appears to have been realized, that is, with regard to the parents. The cultural background of the accused and the wish not to disrupt family life have been listed as reasons for relatively light sentences (Kool et al., 2005; Nijboer et al., 2010). By contrast, the cutters were often sentenced to severe and unconditional imprisonment, especially if they had been involved in a series of circumcisions.

This French "success" later attracted the attention of other countries, especially of the Netherlands. In response to the (seemingly) successful French approach, the Dutch House of Representatives insisted on a comparative law study to examine whether the Netherlands should follow the French example. The Secretary of State also paid a working visit to the country (Nijboer et al., 2010). Nevertheless, Nijboer et al. point out that most French criminal cases resulted directly from the arrest of a cutter, and that French criminal law lacks the minimum evidence requirement; the "conviction intime" suffices (Kool et al., 2005; Nijboer et al., 2010). Moreover, there have been very few reports on any other basis (except some active PMI circles), and there is no integrated official approach (Nijboer et al., 2010). The nationwide familiarity with the punishability of FGM generated by the criminal cases has not opened up the issue any further, nor intensified the combat thereof.

Notwithstanding the aforementioned qualifications, the question arises whether, and to what extent, the characteristically French republican views on immigration and assimilation have con- tributed to the French "success." This does appear to be the case, albeit with the usual provisos. It was pointed out that in the French setting the acceptance of authority (as implied in the hierar- chical relations between citizen and government) is more self-evident. In France, the question of whether parents are obligated to participate in a routine examination of the genitals by a doctor and to make a relevant statement is not raised—it is simply accepted. In comparison, we refer to the resistance encountered in the Netherlands in this respect. A proposal for the introduction thereof by the then Member of Parliament Hirsi Ali resulted in strong resistance, as objections were raised from the privacy point of view. It should also be noted that the "French examinations" have a countereffect: circumcision is postponed until the moment at which the child is not subject to the obligatory medical examination anymore (Kool et al., 2005).

The readiness of the various authorities to cooperate—especially the readiness in specific regional medical circles—to report their findings directly to the criminal authorities also testifies to a centralist attitude that is lacking elsewhere. The fact that, due also to the NGOs' involvement, the message was phrased in terms of promoting the equality of the sexes and protecting human rights, furthermore, promotes public and political support (Guiné and Moreno Fuentes, 2007).

This attitude also explains the lack of specific penal provision. The women's movement was in favor hereof, but it was rejected in conformity with the French republican spirit of realizing one shared identity. The introduction of a specific penal provision would differentiate between citizens, and thus might lead to discrimination and stigmatization of minority groups (Guiné and Moreno Fuentes, 2007; Nijboer et al., 2010). The French legislator continues to adhere to this methodology. In order to meet the explicit demand for criminalization contained in Article 38 of the Istanbul Convention, a legislative proposal was nevertheless drafted with the aim of supple- menting the general provision on abuse (Article 222-9 *Code Penal*) by the element "*mutilation génital feminine.*" Another proposal was made that explicitly criminalizes the attempt and/or the furtherance of FGM. This proposal is still pending as it has been referred to the Committee on Legislation.[*]

By contrast, an agreement was reached on the need to extend extraterritorial jurisdiction, in view of FGM practiced on French citizens abroad. The original connecting factor, requiring either the

---

[*] See http://www.assemblee-nationale.fr/13/dossiers/mutilations_feminines.asp

suspect or the victim to be a French national at the time of the offense, was relinquished in 2006; France now has jurisdiction in case of an underage victim with a permanent resident status. It should be noted that his legislative amendment came into effect with retroactive force (Nijboer et al., 2010).

England: A Climate of Polarization toward Cultural Minorities?

The English approach to FGM must be viewed against the background of the "compounded character" of the British Empire and its long colonial history. For many years, English society underwent large-scale, and prolonged immigration, which (has) shaped English views on citizenship. Some say that this colonial past has left the British (including the English) with a multicultural outlook discerning them from other Europeans. This view has been formulated prominently in the influential Parekh-report, which discusses the development of the United Kingdom as a multicultural nation (Runnymede Trust, 2000; Guiné and Moreno Fuentes, 2007).

Fortier (2000), however, points to the polarizing tone of the Parekh report, and to the critical attitude adopted herein with regard to the designation "the English cultural identity". Others have also questioned this multicultural identity that is publicly adhered to by politicians. Young (1999) interprets the hostile tone by English toward newcomers as stemming from a certain conservatism that is driven by the desire to maintain "the English community." Other authors point to underlying racism and animosity toward immigrants, inspired by the fear of Muslim terrorism (Mirza, 2012; Sales, 2012). They conclude that the past years have seen a shift in political thinking toward assimilation and integration.

Nevertheless, the English views on citizenship still exemplify the multicultural model. Although the former policy of "equal opportunity, coupled with cultural diversity" (Poulter, 1986) has become a bit worn, it has not been abandoned completely yet. The political feelings of guilt as regards the "racist (colonial authors') past" are too deeply rooted, according to Mirza. In this context, Mirza speaks of "faith-based approach multi faithism" (Fortier, 2005; Mirza, 2012: 121–123). This is reflected in the political influence of the multicultural NGOs on English policy with regard to FGM. More than elsewhere, the English authorities take into account the opinions of (locally) organized minority groups and consult these when outlining policies on multicultural issues. An illustration hereof is the involvement and method of the UK All-Party Parliamentary Group on Population, Development and Reproductive Health (APPG) (All-Party Parliamentary Group, 2000). The APPG, consisting of a group of parliamentarians aiming for a dialogue between Parliament, the people in the field and ethnical minorities in recent years has actively and successfully called attention to the issue of female genital mutilation by organising hearings and Parliamentary questions (APPG, 2000; HMG, 2014; Guiné and Moreno Fuentes, 2007). This policy characteristic also applies to the area of national health care, an important area in the fight against FGM (Guiné and Moreno Fuentes, 2007).

However, the involvement of these NGOs also has a downside: when issues of criminalization and the criminal enforcement of cultural offenses such as FGM are concerned, this quarter is quick in raising suspicions of racism against government policy (Guiné and Moreno Fuentes, 2007). This undertone can be heard in Mirza's writings, and may also be found in opinions on the punishability of other cultural offenses such as forced marriages (Mirza, 2012). At the same time, there has been a growing awareness in England that violations of human rights are to be prevented. Fortier (2000) argues in this context that the approach advocated in the Parekh report and endorsed at the time by the English government comes down to a "pluralist model of managing cultural pluralism in a human rights framework" (Fortier, 2000).

In December 2014, the U.K. government firmly condemned the practice of FGM and qualified it an "extremely harmful form of violence" (Her Majesty's Government (HMG), 2014). It appears from this official statement that the U.K. authorities have chosen a twofold approach to eliminate FGM: aiming to create awareness about the consequences of this practice while also using criminal law to discourage people from performing FGM (HMG, 2014).

On balance, England appears to be in a transitional phase with regard to the approach to FGM (and other cultural offenses). On the one hand, a policy that enjoys wide support and does not clearly pursue a homogeneous national identity is aimed for. However, societal unrest regarding the consequences of globalization and recent lack of success for efforts to combat FGM has resulted in a stronger emphasis on repression. This indicates a shift toward an ethnocultural model (Dustin, 2010).

The question as to why English authorities thus far have not managed to prevent FGM and/or to fight it through criminal law is not an easy one to answer. With regard to prevention, we do not know if this has been effected. What we do know is that FGM occurs on a large scale in England. For lack of adequate registration we can only guess at the scope hereof; reasoned estimates come up with 20,000 high-risk cases (Dorkenoo et al., 2007). Later research by the Health Department, however, mentions 80,000 high-risk cases, that is, over a quarter of all girls originating from immigrant groups under the age of fifteen (The Independent On Sunday, 2013). The majority of the girls at risk is between seven and ten and originates from Kenya and Somalia.

However, in the European context England is leading with regard to legislation. Already, in 1985, the *Prohibition of Female Circumcision Act* was adopted with the main purpose of promoting awareness. In addition to a specific penal provision, this act allows for genital circumcision on medical grounds. Despite its lack of clarity on the precise conditions under which this is permitted, it is clear that a woman's conviction of the rightness of the circumcision, as prescribed by tradition, does not constitute a justification. It is also noteworthy that the penal provision covers the genital mutilation of adult women at their own request. Moreover, the 1985 Act was replaced by the *Female Genital Mutilation Act 2003*; under this act, a substantially increased maximum sentence (from five to 14 years of imprisonment) applies and extraterritorial jurisdiction is extended so that genital mutilations practiced abroad by and on English citizens can also be prosecuted. To promote consciousness of the punishability of FGM, a pilot was started recently with the issuance of a so called "health passport," especially in the relevant countries of origin. The objective is to protect English immigrant girls who travel to relatives in their countries of origin against genital mutilations practiced there (HMG, 2012).

In addition, the Crown Prosecution Service (CPS) has drafted instructions on fighting FGM adequately (*FGM Guidance*). Supplementary to the Guidance, operating instructions were formulated for assistance prosecutors: CPS Female Genital Mutilation Pack. One of the instructions reads that on suspecting FGM, one should contact a so called Violence Against Women Coordinator (VAWC) (cps.gov.uk, 2015). These instructions are part of the broader policy of the CPS on fighting violence against women (*Violence Against Women Strategy and FGM*), which in turn is incorporated in the coordinating policy on fighting violence against women (HMG, 2014; Home Office, 2013). It is also noteworthy that anyone suspecting child abuse (including FGM) is obligated to report this to the local social services or to the police (*Children Act 1989*, Section 47) (Black and Debelle, 1995; Home Office, 2011). This applies despite possible professional, confidential duties (Home Office, 2011).

The English government, pressured by growing criticism of the observed enforcement deficit, has announced its intention to intensify combating FGM. Questions were recently asked in the House of Commons in response to the observation that between November 2009 and 2011, 63 cases had been reported to the Metropolitan Police, whereas not once had a prosecution been instituted. This resulted in a call for action to the English government to tighten its approach of FGM by the House of Lords and a motion of the House of Commons, which was adopted unanimously (parliament.UK, 2010). In addition, both the adoption of the Draft Resolution Aimed at Intensifying Global Effort to Eliminate Female Genital Mutilation by the United Nations (United Nations, 2012), and the publication of the aforesaid critical journalist research report play a role (The Independent on Sunday, 2013). A matter of permanent concern is increasing the willingness to report. For this, an attempt is being made to open up the issue through a community-based multiagency approach and local authorities are entitled to take preventive measures necessary to protect a child's health (custodial placement, request of ban to leave the country). The Crown Prosecution Service recently stated that it intends to start implementing these child protection measures in fighting FGM. Thus far, this policy has not led to any concrete acts of prosecution. In 1993, two doctors were judged guilty of "serious professional misconduct" by a medical disciplinary tribunal. One doctor had genitally mutilated a woman, although he was aware of its punishability; the other had offered to perform the operation. The first doctor was deleted from the medical register.

While there is no clear answer to what extent the English views on citizenship influence (have influenced) the combating of FGM, it is possible to discern an "English signature" subject to the necessary provisos. Unlike the French ideology, there is no centralist approach based on a homogeneous cultural identity. On the contrary, in the English setting one traditionally feels very strongly about every person's claim to his or her own cultural identity. Beneath the surface of this multicultural model, however, a trace of ethnocentrism has been spreading—inspired by an unspoken but nevertheless strongly felt superiority of the "real" English identity. This trace has been picked up by minority groups and has led to accusations of racism, which in turn interferes with the identification of FGM as a (cultural) offense.

The Netherlands: Toward an Ethnocultural Model of Citizenship?

The Netherlands began combating FGM after the nineties of the last century. Incidentally, Parliamentary questions had been asked before, but specific attention for female genital mutilation started only as of 1993 (Appendix Parliamentary Papers, 1982/83). Around that time, the multicultural model of citizenship ("integrating while preserving one's own culture") that had prevailed in the Netherlands in the 1970s was already beginning to shift. According to the Dutch Scientific Council for Government Policy (WRR), this earlier "open" attitude is to be put into perspective. They point out that although Dutch culture was receptive to external influences for a long time, these were "often made invisible by strongly nationalizing them" (Koopmans et al., 2005; WRR, 2006). The impact of the surge of labor immigrants that had begun in the 1960s resulted in a political swing toward embracing Dutch identity at the end of the twentieth century. The political debate began around the year 2000, in particular by the leader of the Dutch Liberal Party (VVD), Frits Bolkestein. Critical reports appeared in the media such as the article by Paul Scheffer in the NRC of January 29, 2000, which described the "multicultural drama." As of 2004, parliamentary debates and government circles showed an official dissociation from "multiculturalism as a normative ideal." The immediate cause for this was the publication of the report "Building bridges" (by the Blok Committee); the subject of the report was Dutch integration policy (WRR, 2006). As of then, an ethnocultural model of citizenship became popular that was characterized by a homogeneously-presented Dutch identity (Ghorashi, 2006). Its roots may be found in the former "pillarization" (i.e., the compartmentalization of Dutch society along traditional religious and sociopolitical barriers) entailing the policy of sovereignty within one's own circle. Although this policy was abandoned in the middle of the past century, in the wake of the "depillarization" the inherent typical development of identities along the lines of group building stayed intact beneath the surface. According to the Dutch Scientific Council for Government Policy, the WRR, the Dutch identity has a somewhat "implicit and sunk character" that permits little reflection on the normative principles at its basis (WRR, 2006). The Dutch criminal law also bears the signs hereof, as 't Hart has argued ('t Hart, 2000).

In this political climate, a firm stand was made against FGM. Its punishability was stressed, and it was labeled as an "imported offense" (Parliamentary Papers, 2003/04). The seriousness of the consequences led to its qualification as child abuse, an issue for which criminal law enforcement was (also) deemed appropriate. In conformity with the system of Dutch criminal law, the common criminal provisions applied (article 300 ff of the Dutch Criminal Code: *Wetboek van Strafrecht*) (Raad voor de Volksgezondheid, 2005; Dutch Ministry of Welfare, Public Health and Culture, 1993). Nonetheless, these were not enforced actively initially. Due to the sensitivity of the issue, a criminal investigation was considered undesirable (Appendix Parliamentary Papers, 1990/91).

FGM now falls under the heading of domestic violence, which is one of the spearheads of present criminal law policy (Dutch Government Gazette, 2010). The view that criminal law intervention may be appropriate in cases of FGM is undisputed in the present policy. What is more, the Dutch government extended its extraterritorial jurisdiction in 2006 and 2013 with regard to genital mutilations of nationals or residents practiced elsewhere (Dutch Government Gazette, 2006, 2013). The provisions on the prescription of the right to prosecute were also extended.

Despite the fact that the criminal law currently is an integral part of the approach to FGM, preference is still given to prevention and the rendering of assistance. This is also true for the Dutch approach toward FGM on a global level (Parliamentary Papers, 2013/14). Support for criminal law enforcement has increased lately, but the medical and youth services still adopt a reticent attitude. They are often not prepared to report suspicions and observations on FGM to the criminal authorities. This attitude has been respected by the government thus far; however, a legal obligation for medical services to report suspicions to one of the Child Abuse Reporting Centres (*AMKs*) was introduced recently (Dutch Government Gazette, 2013). It may be noted that the Instruction investigation and prosecution child abuse prescribes prosecution in case there is sufficient proof (Dutch Government Gazette, 2010). However, since the introduction of the *Social Support Act* in 2010, policy responsibility for the prevention of FGM exists at the local level. As a rule, this local level does not opt for criminal intervention but focuses instead on opening up the issue via the communities involved through the interference of key figures. From a Dutch perspective, it is presumed that the minority groups involved should also carry responsibility for the problems within these groups (Parliamentary Papers, 2011/12).

The question of whether the Dutch approach has proven fruitful and what fruits it has borne is not an easy one to answer. In terms of the number of criminal cases, the result is meager: thus far, only one case was submitted to the criminal court, which ended in an acquittal for lack of evidence. Moreover, this case was only opened up to the criminal authorities following a report by the (Dutch) mother (District Court Haarlem, 2009; Court of Appeal Amsterdam, 2012). In both instances, (partial) acquittals were pronounced. It was an established fact that the five-year-old girl had been circumcised, but there was no conclusive evidence that the suspect (the father) had performed it. In January 2013, a second case was submitted to the District Court Dordrecht, but the judgment was deferred. Both normal child abuse and circumcision are suspected. It is expected that the latter will not be included in the final indictment.

Politicians, however, insist that combating FGM through criminal law should be intensified. The right-wing liberal Freedom Party (PVV) particularly insists on this. As of 2008, six motions were submitted in the name of the PVV, aimed at intensifying combating of FGM. The proposals included increasing the maximum penalty, but also halting the asylum procedure and/or withdrawing residence permits in case of suspected FGM. Insisting on tightening criminal repression mainly seems to serve the purpose of demonstrating to the public that FGM is absolutely forbidden in the Netherlands, in the hope of deterring potential perpetrators. The extension of extraterritorial jurisdiction, which was introduced a while ago and extended recently, also fits into this context.

This is in line with a general tightening of the criminal regime with regard to cultural offenses that is currently visible in the Netherlands (Dutch Government Gazette, 2013). The Dutch government clearly wishes to draw the line with regard to the impunity of cultural practices and is convinced of being in the right, both from human rights and from a cultural angle (van den Brink and Tigchelaar, 2012). Objections to extending penalties and extraterritorial jurisdiction were invariably rejected with the argument that the disputed actions violate "the views of civilized nations." These, in the prevailing policy view, render it foreseeable for everyone that both FGM and other cultural offenses constituting violations of human rights are punishable according to Western views. The Dutch approach to FGM thus shows ethnocultural features (Kool, 2012).

Comparison and Conclusion

The French, English, and Dutch societies are all, in their own manner, clearly struggling with the impact of globalization and the resulting influx of nontraditional cultural practices. Their approaches differ due to (legal) cultural differences and underlying views on citizenship, but these seem to be the differences of degree. The conviction that, measured by Western views, FGM is punishable and should be combated is beyond dispute in all three countries. Also, there is more or less agreement on the approach: the focus is on prevention and assistance, with criminal law functioning as the tailpiece.

It is this last issue, the use of the criminal law (or to be more precise, the overlap of assistance and criminal law) where the biggest differences occur. The readiness of national governments and practitioners to resort to criminal law diverges. The existence of a specific criminal law provision is not decisive in this respect, as is shown by the French practice. Not the law, but practice decides whether there is support for actual criminal law intervention. This practice, as it turns out, is determined by the degree of tolerance toward cultural practices that is implied in national ideas on citizenship.

Although it is not possible to draw hard conclusions in view of the limitations discussed, the French and Dutch societies seem to take a "harder" stand on FGM than the English society. The message that newcomers are expected to adjust to the standards of the new motherland and assimilate can be heard clearly in France and the Netherlands. Such a centralist approach fits into the relatively simple political-administrative structure of the Netherlands, as compared to France and England. The fact that the same message applies in France, despite the more complex political-administrative structure, provides an extra layer to the felt homogeneity of the French identity. The contrary, however, applies to England: having a "bad conscience" toward a colonial past, the English policy features as "faith-based" (Poulter, 1986; Fortier, 2005; Mirza, 2012). Minority groups being politically active, the English authorities felt "obliged" to champion multiculturalism. However, notwithstanding the recognition of various cultural identities, the English identity is still felt to be "superior." Moreover, recent developments show multiculturalism to be in decline in England. All these factors influence the criminal law approach to FGM in these countries.

However, these three countries (like all Western European countries) have a great attachment to human rights and expect to provide adequate protection against gendered cultural practices that are considered to be harmful. This justifies the use of criminal law, in the course of which the human rights claim to universality leads to an extension of jurisdiction. At the practical level, the actual role of criminal law appears to be defined by the complexity of the issue of FGM and the related multicultural aspects, with the need of weighing opposite interests. It may come as no surprise that to date not one of these countries—France included—has been able to fight FGM adequately. The search for the "correct approach" will continue for a while—both at home and abroad.

References

Ahmady, K. 2015. *A Comprehensive Research Study on Female Genital Mutilation/Cutting (FGM/C) in Iran*. http://kameelahmady.com/wp-content/uploads/Kameel%20-%20EN%20Final.pdf. Accessed on October 8, 2015.

All-Party Parliamentary Group (APPG) 2000. *Parliamentary Hearings on FGM Report*. London, UK.

Berkovitch, N. and Bradley, K. 1999. The globalization of women's status: Consensus/dissensus in the world polity, *Sociological Perspectives*, 42(3): 481–98.

Black, J. A. and Debelle, G. D. 1995. Female genital mutilation in Britain, *British Medical Journal*, 310: 1590–2.

Brems, E. 1997. Enemies or allies?: Feminism and cultural relativism as dissident voices in human rights discourse, *Human Rights Quarterly*, 19(1): 136–64.

Council of Europe 2011. Convention on Preventing and Combating Violence against Women and Domestic Violence.

Doe, N. 2011. *Law and Religion in Europe*. Oxford, UK: Oxford University Press.

Dorkenoo, E., Morison, L., and Macfarlane, A. 2007. *A Statistical Study to Estimate the Prevalence of Female Genital Mutilation in England and Wales*. London, UK: Forward.

Dustin, M. 2010. Female genital mutilation/cutting in the UK, *European Journal of Women's Studies*, 17(7): 1–31.

EIGE 2013a. Female genital mutilation in the European Union and Croatia.

EIGE 2013b. Current situation of female genital mutilation in Sweden.

EIGE 2013c. Current situation of female genital mutilation in Spain.

EIGE 2013d. Current situation of female genital mutilation in France.

European Parliament 2012. Resolution 2012/2684 (RSP).

Fortier, A. M. 2000. *Multiculturality and the New Face of Britain*, Lancaster, UK: Department of Sociology, Lancaster University, Lancaster, UK.

Fortier, A. M. 2005. Pride politics and multiculturalist citizenship, *Ethnic and Racial Studies*, 28(3): 559–78.

Ghorashi, H. 2006. Paradoxen van culturele erkenning ["Paradoxes of Cultural Recognition"], *Tijdschrift voor Genderstudies* [*Periodical for Gender Studies*], 9(4): 42–54.

Guiné, A. and Moreno Fuentes, F. J. 2007. Engendering redistribution, recognition, and representation: The case of female genital mutilation (FGM) in the United Kingdom and France, *Politics & Society*, 35(3): 477–519.

Gunning, I. R. 1992. Arrogant perception, world travelling, and multicultural feminism: The case of female genital surgeries, *Columbia Human Rights Law Review*, 23(2): 189–248

Henrion, R. 2003. Mutilation génitals feminine, marriages forcés et grossesses précoces, *Bulletin de l'Académie Nationale de Médecine*, 187(6): 1051–66.

HMG 2012. *A Statement Opposing Female Genital Mutilation*. London, UK.

HMG 2014. *Female Genital Mutilation: The Case for a National Action Plan*. London: HM Government.

Home Office 2011. *Female Genital Mutilation Multi Agency Practice Guidelines*. London, UK.

Home Office 2013. *Domestic Violence*. London, UK.

Jugé, T. S. and Perez, M. P. 2006. The modern colonial politics of citizenship and whiteness in France, *Social Identities*, 3: 187–212.

Kalev, H. D. 2004. Cultural rights or human rights: The case of female genital mutilation, *Sex Roles*, 51(5/6): 339–48.

Kool, R. S. B. 2005. Strafbaarstelling en handhaving van meisjesbesnijdenis [Criminalization and enforcement in the area of female genital mutilation], *Nederlands Juristenblad*, 40: 2092–2095.

Kool, R. S. B. 2010. The Dutch approach to female genital mutilation: The time for change has come, *Utrecht Law Review*, 1: 51–71.

Kool, R. S. B. 2012. Drassige gronden voor strafbaarstelling. Het wetsvoorstel ter verruiming van de strafrechtelijke aanpak van huwelijksdwang. ["Sloppy Grounds for Penalization. The bill for expanding the criminal prosecution of forced marriage."], *Delikt en Delinkwent*, 1: 21–35.

Kool, R. S. B. and Wahedi, S. 2014. Criminal enforcement in the area of female genital mutilation in France, England, and the Netherlands: A comparative law perspective, *International Law Research*, 3: 1–15.

Kool, R. S. B., Beijer, A., Eelman, J., and Knoops, G. 2005. Vrouwelijke genitale verminking in juridisch perspectief ["Female Genital Mutilation in a Legal Perspective"], Zoetermeer, Netherlands: Raad voor de Volksgezondheid [National Advisory Council for Public Health].

Koopmans, R., Statham, P., Giugni, M., and Passy, F. 2005. Contested Citizenship. The Contentious Politics of Immigration and Ethnic Relations in Germany, Britain, France, the Netherlands, and Switzerland, Minneapolis, MN: University of Minnesota Press.

Lewis, H. 1995. Between Irua and "female genital mutilation:" Feminist human rights discourse and the cultural divide, *Harvard Human Rights Journal*, 8: 1–55.

Leye, E., Deblonde, J., García-Añón, J., Johnsdotter, S., Kwateng-Kluvitse, A., Weil-Curiel, L., and Temmerman, M. 2007. An analysis of the implementation of laws with regard to female genital mutilation in Europe, *Crime, Law, and Social Change*, 47: 1–31.

Limborgh, W. M. 2011. *Culturele vrijheid en het strafrecht [Cultural freedom and criminal law] (doctorate dissertation Erasmus School of Law)*. Nijmegen: Wolf Legal Publishers.

McCormick, D. 2005. Multiculturalism and its discontents, *Human Rights Law Review*, 1: 27–56.

Mirza, H. S. 2012. Multiculturalism and the gender gap: The visibility and invisibility of Muslim women in Britain, in Ahmad, W. I. U. and Sardar, Z. (eds.), *Muslims in Britain: Making Social and Political Space*. London, UK: Routledge.

Nijboer, J. F., van der Aa, N. M. D., and Buruma, T. M. D. 2010. *Strafrechtelijke opsporing en vervolging van vrouwelijke genitale verminking: de franse praktijk* ["Criminal Law Investigation and Prosecution of Female Genital Mutilation: The French Fractice"], The Hague, Netherlands: Boom.

Otto, J. M. 2014. Besnijdenis en islam, het ligt ingewikkeld ["Circumcision and Islam, it is complicated"]. In: Trouw, February 27, 2014, Opinion, p. 21.

Poulter, S. 1986. Ethnic minority customs, English law, and human rights, *International and Comparative Law Quarterly*, 36(3): 589–615.

Raad voor de volksgezondheid (Council for Public Health and Care) 2005. *Bestrijding vrouwelijke genitale verminking: beleidsadvies ["The Fight against Female Genital Mutilation: Policy Advice"]*, Zoetermeer, Netherlands: Raad voor de Volksgezondheid.

Runnymede Trust 2000. The Future of Multi-ethnic Britain (Parekh report). London, UK: Runnymede.

Sales, R. 2012. Britain and Britishness: Place, belonging, and exclusion, in Ahmad, W. I. U. and Sardar, Z. (eds.), *Muslims in Britain: Making Social and Political Space*. London, UK: Routledge.

Shweder, R. A. 2002. What about female genital mutilation? And why understanding culture matters in the first place? in Shweder, R. A., Minow, M., and Markus, H. R. (eds.), *Engaging Cultural Differences: The Multicultural Challenge in Liberal Democracies*. New York, NY: Russell Sage Foundation.

Siesling, M. 2006. *Multiculturaliteit en verdediging in strafzaken [Multiculturalism and defense in criminal proceedings] (doctorate dissertation Utrecht University)*. Deventer: Kluwer.

Smith, C. 2011. Who defines "Mutilation?:" Challenging imperialism in the discourse of female genital cutting, *Feminist Formations*, 1: 25–46.

't Hart, A. C. 2000. *Hier gelden wetten! [Here the laws apply!]* Deventer, Netherlands: Gouda Quint.

UNFPA 2014. *Implementation of the International and Regional Human Rights Framework for the Elimination of Female Genital Mutilation*, New York, NY.

van Boven, T. and Puig, S. 2005. Domestic violence against women and torture, in Westendorp, I. and Wolleswinkel, R. (eds.), *Violence in the Domestic Sphere*. Antwerp, Netherlands and Oxford, UK: Intersentia.

van den Brink, M. and Tigchelaar, J. 2012. Shaping genitals, shaping perceptions: A frame analysis of male and female circumcision, *Netherlands Human Rights Quarterly*, 30(4): 417–45.

van der Burg, W. 2011. Law and ethics: The twin disciplines, in van Klink, B. and Taekema, S. (eds.), *Law and Method*. Tübingen, Germany: Gulde-Druck.

Voorde, J. T. 2007. *Cultuur als verweer [culture as a defense] (doctorate dissertation Erasmus School of Law)*. Nijmegen: Wolf Legal Publishers.

Wadi 2010. *Female Genital Mutilation in Iraqi-Kurdistan*. Frankfurt am Main, Germany: WADI e.V.

Wahedi, S. 2012. De wederrechtelijkheid van jongensbesnijdenis: een ethische uitdaging voor het strafrecht? ["The punishability of male circumcision: An ethical challenge for criminal law?"]. *Nederlands Juristenblad*, 44/45: 3097–105.

Wheeler, P. 2004. Eliminating FGM: The role of the law, *The International Journal of Children's Rights*, 11: 257–71.

Wihtol de Wenden, C. 2003. Assimilation and struggle of Maghrebi immigration and French political culture, *Culture & Society*, 2: 69–74.

Winter, B. 1994. Women, the law, and cultural relativism in France: The case of excision, *Journal of Women in Culture and Society*, 19(4): 939–73.

WHO 2011. An Update on WHO's Work on Female Genital Mutilation (FGM).

WRR 2001. *Immigratie en integratieregimes in vier Europese landen ["Immigration and Integration Regimes in Four European Countries"]*, The Hague, Netherlands: WRR.

WRR 2006. *Identificatie met Nederland ["Identification with the Netherlands"]*, Amsterdam, Netherlands: Amsterdam University Press.

Young, J. 1999. *The Exclusive Society*. London, UK: Sage.

Case Law

ECtHR (Sept. 20, 2011). Appl. No. 8969/10, (Omeredo/Austria).
ECtHR (May 17, 2011). Appl. No. 43408/08 (Izevbekhai CS/Ireland).
ECtHR (Mar. 8, 2007). Appl. No. 23944/05 (Collins & Akaziebie/Sweden).
Hof [Court of Appeal] (Dec. 23, 2012). Amsterdam, Netherlands, *LJN* BO8531
Rb [District Court] (Sept. 11, 2009). Haarlem, Netherlands *LJN* BJ7447

Parliamentary Papers

Tweede kamer der staten-generaal (2013/14). Parliamentary Papers II, 22 112, No. 1774: 2–4.
Tweede kamer der staten-generaal (2011/12). Parliamentary Papers II, 28 345, No. 117.
Tweede kamer der staten-generaal (2003/4). Parliamentary Papers II, 29 200, XVI, 231: 7.
Tweede kamer der staten-generaal (1990/91). Appendix Parliamentary Papers, No. 1125: 2.
Tweede kamer der staten-generaal (1982/83). Appendix Parliamentary Papers II, No. 964.
Assemblée Nationale (June 24, 2010). No. 2658.
Assemblée Nationale (November 13, 2012). No. 368.

Dutch Government Gazette

Stcrt. 2013, 8838.
Stbl. 2013, 95.
Stcrt. 2010, 19123.
Stbl. 2006, 11.

Chapter 20

"You Just Don't See Us": The Influence of Public Schema on Constructions of Sexuality by People with Cerebral Palsy*

Tinashe M. Dune

Contents

---

* This chapter is a revised version of the author's published article: Dune, T. M. 2014. "You Just Don't See Us": The Influence of Public Schema on Constructions of Sexuality by People with Cerebral Palsy," *World Journal of Social Science*, 1(1): 1–19.

Introduction

Constructions of sexuality by people with cerebral palsy (within contemporary contexts) are informed, in part, by historical constructions of impairment and sexual behavior. For instance, prior to the twentieth century sexual activity for pleasure had been ignored, vilified, and undermined through segregation, institutionalization, and eugenics (Ross and Rapp, 1981). As such, the acceptance and representation of sexuality for people with disabilities was largely absent. Constructing sexuality and disability in this way continues within contemporary settings and include a number of public factors worthy of special consideration. Open discourse about the public factors that influence constructions of sexuality for people with disabilities brings awareness of the barriers, which may inhibit sexual participation and prompt awareness and understanding. In doing so, sexual expression, pleasure, intimacy, and ultimately satisfaction are acknowledged as essential to the formation of inclusive public constructions of disability. As such, this chapter qualitatively explores public factors and public sexual schema that may influence contemporary constructions of sexuality and disability for people living with cerebral palsy.

Public Factors

For people with disabilities, the relationship between impairment and the construction of their own sexuality is mediated by sociocultural attitudes about disability and expectations of sexual activity. For example, the myth that people with disabilities are asexual or incapable of sexual expression is a widespread myth that in itself disables sociosexual access and opportunities for people in this group (see Brown, 1988; Joseph, 1991; Stevens et al., 1996; Earle, 1999; Chance, 2002; Taleporos and McCabe, 2005; Sanders, 2007; Wiwanitkit, 2008; Dune and Shuttleworth, 2009; Xenakis and Goldberg, 2010). Many of the misconceptions about sexuality and disability can be attributed to a lack of clarity, representation, and education about people with disabilities and their sexualities. On the basis of contemporary literature, which explored disability and sexuality, the following themes have been indicated as important to constructions of sexuality in people with disability: the myth of disability and asexuality, contemporary media and popular culture, normative movement and functioning, lack of accessibility, and lack of privacy.

Myth of Disability and Asexuality

While alternate constructions of disability and sexuality exist, the erroneous construction of people with disabilities as asexual is increasingly recognized as an important influence in how sexuality within this population is constructed (i.e., Majiet, 1996; Shakespeare, 2000; Shuttleworth, 2000; Milligan and Neufeldt, 2001; McCabe and Taleporos, 2003). This public misconception of disability and sexuality is what Milligan and Neufeldt (2001), among others, call the "myth of asexuality." This encompasses two lines of thinking depending on whether the person's impairments are physical or intellectual

> [f]irst, for people with physical disabilities, because of actual or presumed sexual dysfunction, gratification opportunities are considered so limited that sexual needs are either deemed to be absent or subjugated. Second, although their sexual function is typically intact, individuals with intellectual disabilities and/or psychiatric disorders are thought to have limited social judgment, and therefore, lack the capacity to engage in responsible sexual relationships (Milligan and Neufeldt, 2001: 92),

Here, mental disability is defined as "any disability or disorder of the mind or brain whether permanent or temporary which results in a disturbance or impairment of mental functioning" (Law Commission, 1995: 36). Physical disability is defined as a condition where a person experiences significant deviation or loss in their body function or structure resulting in limitations in physical activity (World Health Organization [WHO], 2011). The eugenics movement in North America, for example, was particularly aimed at eliminating such disabilities. However, little differentiation was made between mental and physical disability and the social privileges and human rights these individuals were entitled to. This lack of differentiation between mental and physical disability is maintained and portrayed in contemporary contexts (i.e., media and popular culture) through condescending and paternalistic behavior exhibited toward people with disabilities.

Contemporary Media

The media acts a public influence on the expression of sexuality. In the past few decades—particularly with the advent of the World Wide Web—the media has penetrated almost every aspect of social life in developed societies especially. Baudrillard (1983) argues that one of the consequences of the extent of media infiltration in contemporary life has to do with hyperreality. Hyperreality is experienced when media consumers cannot distinguish between reality and the simulated images used in advertising, movies, television shows, or pornography. Therefore, a considerable part of how disability (and sexuality) is conceptualized has to do with "the ubiquitous presence of the media in our everyday lives [which] has contributed to its potency as an important influence on attitude formation" (Milligan and Neufeldt, 2001: 37).

Within popular Western media, for example, satisfying sexual encounters, desirable sexual partners, appropriate expressions of sexuality, and constructions of sexuality are portrayed as biologically, physically, and economically determined (Hung, 2010). By excluding representations of people who do not fulfill the media's target population demographics, sex as an act of pleasure and reproduction is reserved for the "best" human specimens. Subsequently, people with disabilities are viewed as unacceptable candidates for reproduction or even capable of engaging in sexual activity for their own pleasure as well as that of potential partners.

The sexual scripts portrayed in the media as "normal" and "appropriate" minimize the actual spectrum of human experience and instead focuses on ideals of perfection. As such, the media has a great influence on the representation of people with disabilities (Goggin and Newell, 2002).

Expectations of Normative Movement and Functioning

Expectations of normative bodily functioning affect both people with disabilities and typical others. Owing to physical restrictions some people with physical disabilities deal with, they may find it difficult to move their limbs, may have issues with trunk control, or have issues with spasticity or moving without pain. Besides, there are many individuals who use devices to assist them in activities of daily life, which can become barriers to sexual negotiation, "[w]hen dealing with sexual expression there is only so much you can do in a wheelchair" (Taleporos and McCabe, 2001: 137).

Shuttleworth (2000: 95) explains that, "in a culture that emphasizes sex acts and performance, men and women [with disabilities] are often portrayed as axiomatically prohibited from participation in satisfying sexual relationships and destined to emotionally empty lives." Shuttleworth (2000: 263) explored the accounts of the search for sexual intimacy for 14 men with cerebral palsy, which revealed a range of impediments, issues "and a complex inter-subjective process(es) in their search for a lover." He discussed the social expectations of normative functioning and control, which the majority of the men in his study expressed as a cause for frustration in their efforts to negotiate sexual relationships. Some of the men in the study felt that the impairment often physically disqualified them from social and sexual interactions.

The physical barrier of not being able to move in a way that society expects the body to move may affect how a person with cerebral palsy or other physical impairment relates to others and themselves based on their body. Thus, expectations of normative movement and functioning are factors in the disablement of a person's chances to be considered a sexual partner. In addition, there are structural barriers to the access of built environments that deprive people with disabilities of the same number of opportunities to interact with others as their peers, and can thus restrict access to sexual relationships and therefore the pathway to a sense of fulfillment and happiness.

Lack of Accessibility

Access has an important sociostructural influence on sexual participation (see Oliver, 1996; Corker and French, 1999; Corker and Shakespeare, 2002; Barnes and Mercer, 2010). Sociostructural access is characterized by the relationship between environmental infrastructure and social opportunities and ultimately mediates access to social opportunities and sexual information.

Access to social opportunities may be limited for some people with disabilities due to infrastructure which does not facilitate easy access to build structures such as social venues (Corker and French, 1999; Corker and Shakespeare, 2002). Limited sociostructural access may thus exacerbate the social expectation of normative movement and functioning, which some people with disabilities encounter daily (Schillmeier, 2007). For example, appropriate ramps, wide walkways, large-enough bathroom facilities that can accommodate wheelchairs or Hoyer lifts, appropriate elevators, automatic doors, and accessible buttons with which people can operate these devices continue to be absent or difficult to operate in modern environments (Pendo, 2010). In addition, many of the places people commonly frequent to meet new people are not accessible to people with disabilities who rely on wheelchairs or who find it especially difficult to go up a flight of stairs.

Lack of accessibility may be a symptom of a larger social problem in which people with disabilities are excluded from opportunities for social and sexual interaction. As the provision of social opportunities is often a precursor for sexual opportunities the lack of resources to include and integrate disability may very well be the most restrictive barrier to sexual inclusion. Social and sexual integration, however, can be supported through unrestricted access to education and information about disability.

Often the barriers to sexual activity and relationships that people with physical disabilities experience are the result or ignorance caused by a collective lack of education and information. For example, Anderson and Kitchin (2000) examine access to family planning clinics for people with disabilities and reported that facilities for sexual health education and relationship information were not adequately informative or accessible. Accessible and relevant information and education for young people and adults with disabilities promotes their right to intimacy and relationships and can facilitate a more accepting and inclusive social environment (see Esibill, 1980; Rousso, 1993; Berman et al., 1999; Earle, 1999; Murphy et al., 2000). Information designed to foster sexual knowledge, positive sexual identity, and sexual agency is vital for people with disabilities in order to promote self-respect, pleasure, and safety.

Lack of Privacy

Personal care is often a part of life for people with moderate to severe disabilities (Winkler et al., 2007). According to ParaQuad (2010), personal or attendant care is defined as home-based support and plays a vital role in the lives of people with high-level physical disabilities by supporting them to maintain active lifestyles, achieve independence and dignity, and have control over their lives.

Owing to personal care requirements that can often be quite intimate (i.e., bowel and urine voiding regimens) it can be difficult to maintain the privacy, which can be necessary to express one's sexuality. Crewe (1979), who discussed the psychologist's role in sexual rehabilitations for people with disabilities, emphasized that there are many people with physical disabilities that require daily, and some even hourly personal care. During the author's time working as a personal care assistant for students (most of whom had cerebral palsy) at a university in Ottawa, Canada, clients indicated that in certain other facilities in which they lived, the residents were not permitted to lock their doors and in some cases even to close them. Although it seems that these types of rules are enforced so that personal care attendants or emergency services can reach the client in the event that they were in trouble, this lack of privacy makes sexual expression particularly difficult. Thus, rules against something as simple as door closing or locking can inadvertently reinforce the myth that people with physical disabilities do not have a need for privacy and sexual expression (Crewe, 1979).

Public Sexual Schema

These historical and contemporary constructions of sexuality and disability form the basis for public sexual schema, which define how and with whom individuals should engage sexually. Public sexual schema (also known as public sexual scripts) are created, influenced, and reinforced by attitudes and interpretations presented in popular culture and media (Simon and Gagnon, 1986, 1987, 2003). As such, people may be encouraged to engage in sexual activity only with those who are publicly prescribed as appropriate (Simon and Gagnon, 1986). The public construction of which is an appropriate sexual partner often excludes individuals with disabilities and their experiences of sexuality (Guildin, 2000). If people with disabilities are publicly (i.e., via mass media) excluded from situations involving sexual acts (as part of healthy social activity), they may not be considered viable sexual partners, which could in turn lead to a reduction in their opportunities and even social marginalization. Owing to the pervasiveness of public sexual schema that excludes people with cerebral palsy (or other disabilities) understanding the salience and influence of these schemata is of interest. This research builds on understandings of public sexual schema by allowing people with cerebral palsy to describe the influence (if at all) of the factors, which make up sexual schema on their constructions of their sexuality.

Methods

This chapter presents an excerpt of results from a doctoral research project that employed a hermeneutic phenomenological approach to investigate the salience of sexual scripts (public, interactional, and private) in constructions of sexuality by people with cerebral palsy. An indepth, semistructured interview guide was used for data collection and was composed of the following sections: demographics and severity of disability, private sexual scripts, interactional sexual scripts, public sexual scripts, and reflective summary. Interviews were conducted via email, telephone, and/or via face-to-face interaction (based on participant preference).

In the *public sexual scripts* section of the interview participants were asked questions which aimed to gather information about the effect public sexual scripts had on constructions of sexuality as experienced by people with cerebral palsy. To understand how people with cerebral palsy were taught to construct (their) sexuality they were asked: *Where did you learn about sex? What did you learn about sex?* Further, participants were asked to reflect on their conceptualization and opinion about the term sexual spontaneity in order to ascertain whether people with cerebral palsy described their sexuality as inclusive of popular constructions of sexual spontaneity: *How would you define or explain the term sexual spontaneity? How does your explanation of sexual spontaneity fit into your sexuality?* In addition, participants were asked to describe their perception of romance (*What is your idea of romance?*) and satisfying sexual experiences (*What factors have influenced how you experience your sexuality?*). These questions were used to identify any aspects of sexual spontaneity within individual experiences of sexuality as well as gain information about the participant's perception of what their sexual partner would be like and/or look like. The data were analyzed for content by identifying topics and substantive categories within participants' accounts in relation to the study's objectives.

Sample and Participant Recruitment

This study included seven participants; five men and two women. Four of the participants were from Australia and three from Canada (see Table 20.1). The study recruited from Canada and Australia in order to enhance the possibility of finding members of the target population to participate.

In Australia, participants were recruited through advertisements published in community newspapers, bulletins, through advocacy groups, and sexuality and/or disability-focused newsletters, and web pages. In addition, the snowballing technique was carried out at the end of participant interviews and required asking each participant if they knew someone who met the eligibility criteria and, if so, whether s/he would be willing to give that person a copy of the participant information sheet. The author did not know the identity of this person, and the interviewee did not know if that person agreed to participate in the project or not.

Table 20.1   Participant Summary

Participant (Pseudonym)	Sex	Type of Cerebral Palsy	Assistive Devices or Services	Socioeconomic Status, Education and Ethnicity	Medical Interventions	Living Arrangements	Sexual Profile
John	Male	Spastic quadriplegic cerebral palsy (severe)	Mechanized wheelchair, daily personal assistance from others	Upper-middle class, tertiary education, Caucasian Australian	Major musculoskeletal surgery during childhood and adolescence. Rehabilitative maintenance	Lived with his mother in his family's home	Heterosexual, sexually active, no history of long-term sexually intimate relationships
Mary	Female	Spastic paraplegic cerebral palsy (moderate)	Occasional use of crutches	Middle class, tertiary-educated, Caucasian Australian	Major musculoskeletal surgery during childhood and adolescence. Rehabilitative maintenance	Lived independently in an apartment with her partner	Heterosexual, in a long-term sexual relationship at time of interview
Brian	Male	Ataxic quadriplegic cerebral palsy (severe)	Mechanized wheelchair, daily personal assistance from others	Middle class, tertiary-educated, Caucasian Australian	Major musculoskeletal surgery during childhood and adolescence. Rehabilitative maintenance	Lived in an independent living facility	Heterosexual, sexually active, no history of long-term sexually intimate relationships
Leah	Female	Spastic paraplegic cerebral palsy (moderate)	Mechanized wheelchair, daily personal assistance from others	Lower-middle class, tertiary-educated, Caucasian Australian	Major musculoskeletal surgery during childhood and adolescence. Rehabilitative maintenance	Lived in an apartment with her boyfriend	Heterosexual, in a long-term sexual relationship at time of interview

(Continued)

Table 20.1 (*Continued*)   Participant Summary

Participant (Pseudonym)	Sex	Type of Cerebral Palsy	Assistive Devices or Services	Socioeconomic Status, Education and Ethnicity	Medical Interventions	Living Arrangements	Sexual Profile
Ian	Male	Ataxic quadriplegic cerebral palsy (severe)	Mechanized wheelchair, daily personal assistance from others	Lower-middle class, tertiary-educated, Caucasian Canadian	Major musculoskeletal surgery during childhood and adolescence. Rehabilitative maintenance	Lived in an independent living facility	Heterosexual, sexually active, no history of long-term sexually intimate relationships
Trevor	Male	Spastic quadriplegic cerebral palsy (severe)	Mechanized wheelchair, daily personal assistance from others	Upper-middle class, tertiary-educated, Caucasian Canadian	Major musculoskeletal surgery during childhood and adolescence. Rehabilitative maintenance	Lived in an independent living facility	Heterosexual, in a long-term sexually intimate relationship at time of the interview
Alex	Male	Spastic quadriplegic cerebral palsy (severe)	Mechanized wheelchair, daily personal assistance from others	Upper-middle class, tertiary-educated, Caucasian Canadian	Major musculoskeletal surgery during childhood and adolescence. Rehabilitative maintenance	Lived in an independent living facility	Homosexual, high frequency of casual sexual encounters, no history of long-term sexually intimate relationships

In Canada, participants were sought through the Attendant Care Program in Ottawa, Ontario. The Attendant Care Program services two of the major educational institutions in the city with round-the-clock provision of personal care for tertiary students with disabilities who live in the university residence buildings. The program, which has been running for more than 20 years, services approximately 50–60 students per year with numbers increasing every year. Owing to the client-directed style of the program, clients are provided with the resources they need to live independently through the provision of dignity-focused care and accessible living arrangements. As the author was formerly employed by the service, she forwarded the coordinator of the program the details of this project and was informally given permission to ask clients (the majority of whom had cerebral palsy) of the Attendant Care Program if they would like to participate.

The data were analyzed for content by identifying topics and substantive categories within participants' accounts in relation to the study's objectives. In addition, NVivo was used to ascertain topical responses and emergent substantive categories, coding particularly for word repetition, direct and emotional statements and discourse markers including intensifiers, connectives, and evaluative clauses. Owing to the rich and contextual nature of the data, participant's responses have been presented in their conceptual entirety.

Results and Discussion

Four subthemes characterized the perceived influence of public sexual schema on participant sexuality: (1) Contemporary Media and Popular Culture, (2) The Myth of Disability and Asexuality, (3) Expectations of Normative Movement and Functioning, and (4) Issues of Accessibility.

Contemporary Media and Popular Culture

Primarily, participants expressed that media (although skewed) was a source for sexual information. Of equal importance was the impact of public sexual scripts; respondents noted that normative gender role expectations influenced how they constructed their sexuality. As such, Contemporary Media and Popular Culture (see Figure 20.1) included three subthemes: Media as a Source for Sexual Information, The Impact of Public Sexual Scripts and Constructions of Masculinity and/or Femininity.

Media as a Source for Sexual Information

Participant responses indicate that contemporary media served as a source for sexual information. The data indicate two conceptualizations about sexual information which participants acquired from the media (1) how to experience, conceptualize, and construct sexual behavior (see Sanders, 2008) and (2) sexual information from media as skewed and/or unrealistic (see Brown et al., 2005). Responses from Alex, Ian, and Trevor indicated that contemporary media has informed how they experience, conceptualize, and construct sexual behavior:

Alex: I learned about sex and what to do from the media. I was watching pornography from when
    I was 12.
Ian: From TV, movies, from media I learned what to do? How to do it? From pornography,
    I thought "oh ya that's how it's done."

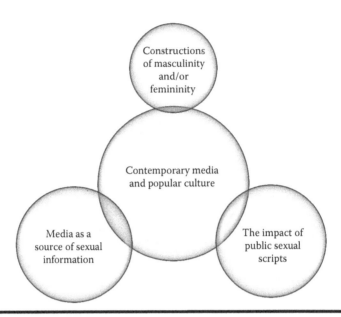

Figure 20.1 Contemporary media and popular culture theme and subthemes. (The size of each bubble represents its relative salience within the main theme.)

Trevor: I learned that sexuality and sex was an expression of intimacy between two (or more) partners for the purposes of enjoyment. I learned the mechanics of sex through sex education classes in school. I learned some of my own sexual barriers and desires, as well as what excites me. As a consumer of media, I learned a lot from television—although I recognized from an early age that a lot of it was a skewed reality.

Although all participants indicated that contemporary media and popular culture were sources of information, Trevor and John notably described the information as skewed or unrealistic. For John the process of learning about sexual experiences from the media was implicit but he ultimately thought of it as inaccurate:

John: You learn it by osmosis if the truth be told and you don't have to go far to find, it's all over the newspapers, all over the Internet. And I'm sort of matter-of-fact about it now that it doesn't even raise an eyebrow. It doesn't matter anymore. I mean particularly with the Internet. Everyone knows everything and everybody's seen just about everything. And you know, you can go back to the media, a lot of stars became very famous simply because they had some sort of extra, sexual exploit recorded on tape. And that tape ended up somewhere and somebody publicized it or gave it to a media outlet or put it online. I guess with my interest in media, current affairs and popular culture sexual information is always there whether in a polite or, most often, blunt way ... Equally though, I know it's not accurate either.

Through the intake (whether active or passive) of sexualized messages (accurate or otherwise) from contemporary media and popular culture, participants perceived public sexual scripts to have impressed upon them idealized portrayals of sexuality and disability.

Impact of Public Sexual Scripts

The impact of contemporary media and popular culture can be seen in participants' reiteration of popular public scripts about people with disabilities and their experiences of sexuality. Several types of impact described by participants included (1) the impact categorizations of disability in the media and popular culture have on sociosexual inclusion (see Hartnett, 2000), (2) the impact of representations of sexuality which lack inclusion of disability (see also Raynor and Hayward, 2009), (3) portrayals of disability which deny social and sexual agency (see also Duncan et al., 2010), and (4) public sexual scripts as the instigator of upward and downward social comparison (see Hammar et al., 2009). For instance, Brian and Alex explained that the ways in which disability is constructed and categorized by media made it difficult to be noticed:

Brian: One of my annoyances about the media is that disability tends to be constructed in two extremes. One is that we're terribly vulnerable or needy and totally reliable on a career (which holds a kernel of truth) or we exist as mountain climbers or paralympians conquering the world. And there is no middle ground but 99.99% of us live in this gray-area-middle-ground and you just don't see us.

Alex: I guess my idea [of romance] comes from media depictions and what I see played out at bars, but I have no real life experience to draw from. I honestly feel that romance is only in the movies and that because I am "different" I will not find it conventionally or long-term.

According to Brian and Alex, representations of sexuality and disability in the media may lack inclusivity. As such, participants felt that exclusive representations of sexuality and disability in the media restricted access to sexual opportunities. For instance, Leah and Mary felt that exclusive constructions of sexuality implied that they were socially and sexually inadequate:

Leah: And then when you've got someone who—the messages they are getting is that you're not sexually attractive, you're not going to get anyone to do that [have sex with you]. You're not going to have someone who is going to love you outside of your family. Because I think that's what a lot of people get because then it's going to affect your social development.

Mary: Yeah ... because part of me, I am a bit of a romantic and I think I like the idea of just that one person, but it's not always true or realistic. But thank goodness considering the amount of things I was willing to change in myself to try and make friends with people but doing that was not one of them. Because I could have [had sex] and I came close a couple of times.

Leah and Mary made an effort to conceptualize the salience of public sexual scripts within the construction of their sexuality. John, however, felt that media portrayals and discourse about impairment denied people with disabilities the right to sexuality. For instance, John explains that portrayals of disability within the media and disability advocacy groups exclude people with disabilities from experiences of sexuality and agency:

John: I suggest for example you look at some of the debates ... in the media, as to what you do with a severely mentally handicapped person ... And they are getting to the age that they'll have a period or something like that so it's probably best, to remove the sexual organs or turn them off in such a way so that a person won't have those "difficulties" because they won't understand what's going on. For my own part I take the view that it's actually quite a reasonable step to take when you are dealing with a person who is that disabled. And they can't deal with those sorts of problems. But there's a disability lobby that says "how dare you?"

Based on John's thoughts, discussions of sexuality in the media and advocacy groups seem exclusionary. However, Ian felt that public sexual scripts had a more balanced (neither wholly positive nor wholly negative) impact on the construction of his sexuality. As such, the construction of his sexuality involved both upward and downward social comparison. Ian explained:

Ian: Mass media and the sexually charged culture that we live in have also played a role in influencing my sexuality, both in the positive and negative. Positive because it has allowed me to place my sexuality in the context of the larger world and has slowly helped me build up my sexual confidence. In the negative, because it has at times, made it seem as though I need to look a certain way, or perform a certain act in order to be sexually desirable.

In this regard, Ian highlights the difficulty some people with cerebral palsy may have in the effort to feel positive about their sexuality while conforming to a variety of public sexual scripts. In particular, the implication of public ideals of masculinity or femininity as presented by contemporary media and popular culture was difficult to incorporate into the construction of participant's sexuality.

Constructions of Masculinity and/or Femininity

Contemporary media and popular culture produce many public sexual scripts, which influence human sexuality (see Brown et al., 2005). The participants believed that conforming to normative constructions of masculinity and femininity as portrayed by the media influenced the construction of their sexuality. Two issues were of relevance: (1) the traits a perfect male or female would have (see Lemish, 2010) and (2) acceptable and attractive female and male attributes and behaviors (see Jackson, 2005; Dune and Shuttleworth, 2009). Mary and Alex's description of "the" sexually attractive woman and man exemplifies this sentiment:

Mary: When you think of attractive people … They're the woman most women would hate, because they're perfect. The type of people who are good-looking, confident, and self-assured. They would just be able to put everybody at ease and there's something indefinably sexy about them. That's what I find sexy.

Alex: I always knew that I was "different" from other kids my age. I always found myself attracted to men. I had crushes on masculine TV characters (John Stamos aka Uncle Jesse from Full House). I liked how masculine he was in that role. I found myself attracted to that type even when I was young.

Although Mary indicated that the ideal of the "perfect man or woman" was sexy, she could comprehensively define why. From a young age, Alex internalized portrayals of masculinity from popular television shows, which influenced the "type" of man he presently finds attractive. Leah, however, perceived the normative construction of the perfect man as more difficult for males to deal with than the normative construction of the perfect woman for females:

Leah: I often wonder what it would be like to be a guy with CP because as a girl who is meant to be dainty and delicate and, you know, somewhat helpless for men, there's some ability for people to reconcile that with your physical weakness because you're a girl anyway.

On the one hand, Leah explained that her perception of the hegemonic construction of femininity involved women as dainty, delicate, and helpless. On the other hand, the men in this study indicated that part of their attempts to fulfill hegemonic constructions of masculinity involved conforming to what they were, or who they were supposed to find attractive. John's attraction to a popular female television personality exemplifies his acceptance of hegemonic constructions of femininity.

John: I think as a male you always maintain a certain amount of whatever the hormones ... which means you should respond positively when people or certain sights appear. Like, Jennifer Hawkins ... I'm the same sort of red-blooded male ... for any pretty face that smiles at you, particularly if they're long legged and absolutely gorgeous ... To add to the mixer, being hot for someone like that is really the first time you fall in love— although you don't really know it.

Being attracted to the type of woman that contemporary media validates as attractive contributed to how John constructed his idea of the ideal sexual partner. However, his thoughts imply through upward social comparison (see Hammar et al., 2009) that he would never be considered in return. Brian explained that proving oneself as a sexual contender is compromised by having a disability, while at the same time trying to conform to hegemonic constructions of masculinity:

Brian: Men have to do it and initiate. They can't get in there if they don't perform and ask the lady out and get things going. How are dudes expected to be negotiating sexual relationships when they have CP?

Brian's sentiments raise the important issue of incorporating one's sexuality into experiences of disability in an effort to consolidate one's identity. However, five participants indicated that positive constructions of sexuality while living with cerebral palsy were often undermined by the myth of disability and asexuality.

Myth of Disability and Asexuality

The data suggest that all the participants' constructions of their own sexuality were influenced by the pervasive myth that people with disabilities are not sexual beings. In this regard, five participants were concerned about the erroneous nature of the myth and how it affected the way that others perceived them. Four participants seemed to have internalized elements of the myth of disability and asexuality. In addition, they implied that asexuality was inevitable due to the pervasive nature of the myth. As such, participant data fell into two subthemes (see Figure 20.2).

Perceptions of how others Perceive Disability and Sexuality

Respondents indicated that they had several concerns about how others perceived disability and sexuality. Notably, participants articulated that public schema reinforced (1) the erroneous perception that people with disabilities were inherently asexual (see Milligan and Neufeldt, 2001), (2)

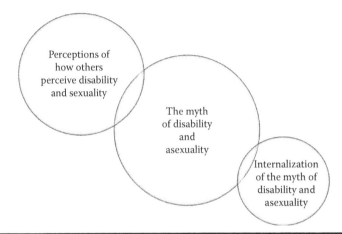

Figure 20.2   The myth of disability and asexuality theme and subthemes.

the erroneous perception that people with disabilities are destined to sexual dissatisfaction (see McCabe and Taleporos, 2003), (3) others' perceptions of disability and sexuality as detrimental to sociosexual development (see Dune, 2012a), (4) the presumption that people with physical disabilities also have mental disabilities (see Milligan and Neufeldt, 2001), and (5) the salience of a lack of public knowledge about sexuality and disability (see Cole and Cole, 1993; Shakespeare, 2000). Trevor and Ian, for example, explained how the erroneous perception from others that people with disabilities were inherently asexual manifested in their lives:

Trevor: I think that I am overlooked and not necessarily considered as a sexual partner.
Ian: As I say, I do not think that most able-bodied people will necessarily see disabled people as sexual. I think most people will remain to be quite disturbed with that concept.

The myth of disability and asexuality in this context implies that people with disabilities are destined to sexual dissatisfaction; destined to a life or celibacy, unsatisfactory sexual experiences, and negative constructions of their own sexuality due to social ignorance. Leah's response synthesized what she perceived the myth of disability and asexuality to imply:

Leah: The messages we are getting is that you're not sexually attractive; you're not going to get anyone to do that [have sex with you]. You're not going to have someone who is going to love you outside of your family … It's going to affect your social development.

Leah's description of the myth also indicated that these types of messages have an impact on how people with disabilities develop as social and sexual beings. As such, others' perceptions of disability and sexuality were detrimental to participants' sociosexual development. Of particular concern for Mary was how the myth of disability and asexuality seemed to stem from the misconception that people with physical disability are also intellectually challenged. For example, Mary explained how her transition from a wheelchair and onto crutches after major surgery made the public misunderstanding about disability quite clear:

Mary: Before my big surgery a lot of people would speak to me or to people around me as though they assumed I was intellectually retarded and when you're able enough to understand what's going on, you know, that's part of my issue when I went to school and trying to socialize because you're reticent to put much out there because you know that there's going to be people who are thinking those kind of things.

All the participants experienced the impact of the myth of disability and asexuality in some form. Notably, a lack of societal (public) knowledge about disability was cited as the cause of these experiences:

Leah: No one wants to talk about it because "people who are disabled don't have sex." They don't want to address it.
Alex: I think that people should know that being disabled doesn't stop any sexual urge; it doesn't mean that I am asexual.

In addition, Brian explained the impact that societal ignorance had on being considered by others as a sexual partner.

Brian: They just don't get it … it's really a taboo subject, disability and having sex. People with disabilities think that there is no chance for sexual contact with them [typical others]. They [typical others] would think that I'm just not sexually active. If they think I'm not sexy or sexual it makes it difficult to have a relationship with people like that.

As can be seen there are a multitude of messages integral to the myth of disability and asexuality. All participant responses indicated that although they may have wanted to construct their sexuality via other scripts, they had internalized the myth in some way, shape, or form.

Internalization of the Myth of Disability and Asexuality

The internalization of the myth of disability and asexuality was supported by evidence. The data suggest participants internalized the perception that people with disabilities were and would always be socially and sexually deprived (see Howland and Rintala, 2001). For instance, participants explained that satisfying sexual experiences were not going to be a part of the life of someone with a disability because of how sexuality and disability is publicly conceptualized. Mary explained how she has observed the myth impact her twin sister, who has a more severe form of cerebral palsy than herself:

Mary: When you look at someone like my sister, we're both about to turn 25, and the biggest thing in her head is that she will never live independently, she'll never partner, and she'll never be able to have sex or children. But no one talks about that with her. And I'm just saying I'm pretty sure that's what she thinks about—trying to find a partner.

While Mary highlighted the impact of the myth of disability and asexuality, she has distanced herself from it by highlighting its effects on others. Similarly, Ian also implied (in reference to his friend who also used a wheelchair) that people with disabilities are privy to fewer sexual options or consideration as sexual partners:

Ian: I mean thank god he was in a wheelchair, because if he wasn't he'd be running after anybody in a skirt, or not in a skirt.

John seemed to agree that sexual opportunities were limited and that his chances were slim, as he was never formally spoken to about sex or sexuality:

John: There was no great sitting down and telling me the facts of life because it wasn't really necessary. I mean, when am I going to end up in a situation where I need to be told? Well look, it's always put me along the lines of being asexual.

For Alex, the myth of disability and asexuality made him feel as though he must settle for unsatisfactory sexual encounters if he wanted to experience sexuality with others at all:

Alex: I now don't often equate sex with romance. As much as I have tried to do that in the past, and sometimes currently, I feel that it is not realistic … so now, I take what I can get. I am not happy this way, but I understand it to be the reality of my sexuality.

For these four participants, being considered asexual was integral to how they perceived and experienced sexuality with others. Furthermore, participant responses also indicated that having a physical disability went against what was publicly expected in order to be perceived as a sexual option for others.

Expectations of Normative Movement and Functioning

Expectations of normative movement and functioning seemed to influence how all the participants perceived themselves as potential sexual partners for others. Expectations of normative movement and functioning referred to the expectation that the body should move, function, and behave like that of typical bodies. Participants indicated that expectations of normative movement and functioning influenced who they would most be attracted to. As such, participant data fell into the following three subthemes (see Figure 20.3): Impact of Expectations of Normative Movement and Functioning on Sociosexual Development, The Ideal Partner and Perceptions of What is and is Not Physical Disability.

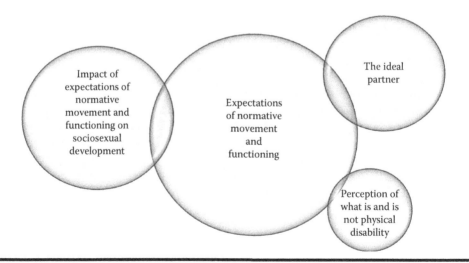

Figure 20.3 Expectations of normative movement and functioning subthemes.

Impact of Expectations of Normative Movement and Functioning on Sociosexual Development

Participants were of the view that being expected to physically move and function in the same ways as a typical individual created tension within the construction of their sexuality. Participants noted that expectations of normative movement and functioning (1) affected participation (see also Dune, 2012b), (2) affected sociosexual equality (see also Dovidio et al., 2011), and (3) implied that physical difference was a sociosexual "turn-off" to others (see also Dune and Shuttleworth, 2009). For instance, Alex and Trevor both indicated that living with a physical disability restricted their ability to participate in sociosexual activities and development:

Alex: My level of mobility also influences my sexuality because I can't perform all of the same functions as an able-bodied person so I often feel inadequate ... I feel like I won't find anything long term due to my disability.

Trevor: As I grew older, sexual thoughts developed from "playing house" into more sexual, or sexually charged, in nature. But due to my physical limitations, I was not able to fully explore those feelings as early as some people might.

Brian also explained the impact of having to use a wheelchair for mobility on sociosexual development. Primarily, he indicated that being in a wheelchair meant that he would not be considered as a social or sexual equal because he could not be at eye level with his peers:

Brian: Males are competitive, so I mean if I'm after one female and there are three other able-bodied males where is she going to go? I was talking to this girl and there were other guys who walked in and they didn't say "hello" or anything but they could stand and face her. I was in the room but I might as well not have been there.

The expectation that everyone can or should stand when conversing—particularly in the context of public social venues—made Brian feel that he could not be a social or sexual contender when physically typical men were in the room. John also articulated similar implications of the public expectation to move and function typically:

John: Even around professional colleagues, particularly when you go to a seminar and everybody breaks for morning tea, and usually how that works is everybody stands around a coffee table or a drinks table and has their cakes and biscuits and coffee. Because they're standing and you're sitting it is pretty hard to make it known that you're still there ... The problem is, and people don't do it deliberately, everybody has to stand up for conversation and you are immediately on the wrong level to get any tea, coffee, biscuits or a chance.

While John engaged in social activities in order to negotiate relationships, not being at eye level made him feel as though he were not and could not build relationships with his peers. Ultimately, some participants felt that living with a disability would be a complete "turn-off" to a potential partner. Ian and John described what they experienced as the realities of living with disability and the effect it would have on a potential partner and sexually intimate relationship:

Ian: ... in a world where we finally got over all our hang ups and we actually do the research and we actually make sure that we're not condemning people to disability just so someone can say that we can have a diverse society.

John: I mean the issue really is if you really claim that you really love someone and that you want to spend your life with them under what terms is that mediated ... The standard marriage vows go in sickness and in health and that's fine. But it doesn't go in sickness and in constant disease and in constant doctor's appointments and in constant co-morbidities.

The sentiment that impairment was unacceptable or unattractive to potential sexual partners was influenced to how expectations of normative movement and functioning were conceptualized. As such, Ian and John constructed the possibility of finding a suitable partner. As mentioned in the interactional theme Perception of Sexual Experiences with Others, participants' responses indicate that finding an individual to share in the realities of disability through understanding and openness was necessary. As such, finding a partner who accepted physical difference was both an interpersonal and public issue. Through the responses however, participants seem to allude to their ideal partner as a physically typical individual, who did not necessarily understand or have experience with impairment.

Ideal Partner

Interestingly, all the participants in this study discussed potential partners and previous partners as individuals who were physically typical. As such, participants' ideal partner would (1) meet public expectations of normative movement and functioning (see also Moin et al., 2009) and (2) be necessary to fulfill care needs and family sustainability (see also Wilder, 2006). For instance, Alex and Brian made it clear that a physically typical partner would be imperative:

Alex: My ideal partner would be able-bodied because I think that having sex with a disabled person is too much work. My ideal partner would be masculine, but extremely open-minded.

Alex blatantly indicated that being with someone who had a disability would not conform to his idea of the perfect partner as they would be *"too much work."*
Brian: They could walk ... yeah, definitely.

For John, a physically typical individual was indicated as necessary in order to fulfill care needs and family sustainability:

John: Well ... it would need to be a non-disabled person. Now I don't rule out the other but my concern would be that you're just mounting up the problems for yourselves ... I think 20 or 30 years down the track I'm going to be just as sick and just as disabled and just as cranky about all the things I can't do. And then you know somebody else is going to be doing even more.

Based on participant responses, the construction of the ideal sexual partner for an individual living with a severe physical disability conformed to expectations of normative movement and functioning. In particular, participants indicated that it would be difficult to navigate a satisfying sexual relationship with someone who also had a disability. Although Alex, Brian, and John indicated that their ideal partner would be physically typical, their choice may not have been founded on superficial reasons. As such, participant responses imply that an individual who was physically typical or did not have a moderate to severe impairment could serve as a sort of assistive medium for sexual expression and daily living requirements.

Perceptions of What Is and Is Not Physical Disability

Of the seven participants included in this study, Mary (whose twin sister has a severe form of cerebral palsy) was the only one who did not use a wheelchair for mobility (after major corrective surgery) but instead used crutches intermittently. Mary's experience with physical disability is of interest as she described that in certain situations others perceived her as physically typical. For Mary, this process of being what she perceived as partially typical was consolidated by both public perceptions about disability and interactional encounters with others. As such, Mary explained that living on both sides of the fence (physically typical and atypical) simultaneously proved to be challenging:

> I've got a disabled parking permit. But I always get people who shout at me for parking in the parks … I say I've got a sticker and then, you know, sometimes I drag my leg a bit more. Because they look at you! Old people are shocking for it. Like, I haven't been able to walk my entire life, these people end up on a stick at 70, get a parking permit. Get screwed!

For Mary being identified as both an individual with a mild and moderate impairment highlighted the confounding aspects the public scripts about physical impairment and public scripts about physical typicality. Mary's experience with disability brings to attention the many barriers that people with mild to moderate cerebral palsy face daily. Mary's dichotomous relationship with disability highlights public misunderstandings about atypicality, which limits access and therefore restricts social and sexual integration and inclusion.

Issues of Accessibility

Participants believed that access to services, resources, sexual opportunities, and the environment in which participants lived also influenced their construction of their sexuality. In this regard, four participants were concerned about the tedious and frustrating experience of trying to navigate structural environments in order to access sociosexual opportunities. However, three participants indicated that with the help of modern technology they were able to simulate courting and dating online. Finally, one participant indicated that without resources sexually intimate relationships with others were difficult to support for both parties. Participant view fell within three subthemes (see Figure 20.4): Structural Access Issues, Access to Sexual Opportunities, and Access to Resources that Support Sexually Intimate Relationships.

Structural Access Issues

Participants perceived that accessibility to infrastructure restricted sexual opportunities. Notably, participants perceived that (1) they spent more time than typical others in the preparation or negotiation of a social outing (see Yoshida, 1994), (2) infrastructure was generally as accessible as it was inaccessible (see Rummel, 2009), and (3) there were ways to bypass structural access issues (see Jang et al., 2010). For example, Brian perceived that he had to spend extra time and money when arranging social outings. For him this meant that he had to make more of an effort to access sexual opportunities than his peers:

Brian: It's really frustrating because like I said no one gets it. I think they don't understand what its like to want to do things like everyone else but I can't and I try but there are limits.

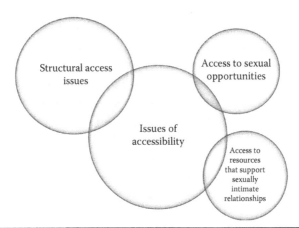

Figure 20.4 Issues of accessibility—theme and subthemes.

Wow! Just stuff like accessibility. I can't go where all the cute girls are going because I can't get in. The extra money I have to spend to do things. It's just difficult so I don't go to those places.

According to John the "extra time" and thought involved in order to organize a date reduced the opportunity to go out spontaneously with friends or a potential sexual partner:

John: Equally, I guess there's the practical point of view. How could I ask someone out? How can we go anywhere every time I go to a lunch? When I went to a lunch or dinner with the office I had to arrange taxis or get mum involved to get me there or to get me back or something like that. So there was always sort of an infrastructure or arrangements that had to be made, unmade or remade to make my attendance somewhere possible. The other factor, it has to be wheelchair accessible doesn't it? So there are immediate questions of, particularly about something being spontaneous, going through all those checkpoints there is nothing spontaneous.

Brian and John considered many social gathering places as difficult to access. However, the women acknowledged that there were places that did accommodate people with disabilities. For instance, while Leah felt that negotiating infrastructure (i.e., clubs, pubs, bars, restaurants, among other places) was difficult, it could be managed:

Leah: Where do people meet, in bars, restaurants, in cinemas? Again, a lot of those places are now accessible but equally a lot of them aren't.

For five of the respondents, feeling excluded from sexual opportunities was characterized by limited access to public spaces. However, Alex indicated that one does not necessarily need to "go out" to find a sexual partner:

Alex: My sexual history is mostly comprised of casual sexual encounters. I meet the men usually online, because it is difficult for me to get into bars. Most of the men I meet online aren't looking for anything serious though.

Although Alex felt that he might not have the chance to foster a long-term relationship from his interactions on the Internet, he highlights an innovative portal for access to sexual opportunities.

Access to Sexual Opportunities

For some participants, going online was a viable alternative to trying to navigate infrastructure, which was not guaranteed to be accessible. This was primarily exemplified through being virtually available via the Internet and being physically present at social venues and outings (see Holden, 2006). Sexual opportunities were also accessed through the employment of sex workers (see Sanders, 2007). For Mary, a conjunction of physically "getting out there" and using the Internet helped increase her chances when she met her boyfriend:

Mary: I think probably getting out there and going out to places and being seen and doing stuff. Maybe also the Internet. Seeing what's out there you know.

Brian also felt that navigating the virtual world of Internet dating proved to be less frustrating and more liberating than being out in the real world:

Brian: You just go online really. And I have several girls on my list and the virtual world gives me the chance to act out ideas or fantasies that I would like to experience. It's a lot of fun but it's frustrating … if someone doesn't like that. But I stay hopeful, like anyone else and just keep going.

For Ian the opportunity to be with someone sexually was all he really wanted:

Ian: In my experience it's probably just the opportunity to have sex, which makes it good. When I get an erection from someone touching my penis. Being able to experience my sexuality is the best part.

All participants perceived that it was difficult to access sexual opportunities due to structural restrictions or low levels of peer-receptiveness. To alleviate some of the social and structural issues, Brian (for instance) employed the services of a sex worker:

Investigator: Which was your best experience?
Brian: The one in Melbourne. It's called the "[name of Gentleman's Club]"
Investigator: … Why was that your best experience?
Brian: Well I got there and went to the room and it was a proper place. There was [*sic*] several rooms. And I had time with a dancer.
Investigator: So you got your own private dance? Anything else happen?
Brian: Oh yeah. I went to touch her and I thought I couldn't touch her. I spent quite a bit of money on her.
Investigator: Was it just dancing?
Brian: I spent a bit of money on her. So you can imagine.
Investigator: Have you been to any brothels?
Brian: No, not yet.

Investigator: Do you want to go?

Brian: At some stage, yeah.

Investigator: So your best sexual experience was someone who talked with you, danced for you and kinda [*sic*] just played with you and was cheeky.

Brian: Yeah.

Investigator: So there wasn't anything overtly sexual in terms of touching or anything …

Brian: Well you know …

Investigator: That's cool.

Brian: YEAH! IT WAS! [participant's emphasis]

Facilitation of sexual services (as provided by a sex worker in Australia) helped Brian bridge access to sexual encounters. In doing so, he may be privy to experiencing and constructing his own sexuality without the social or structural restrictions some of the other participants indicated. While Canadian participants could not legally have explored their sexuality through the employment of a sex worker, they did indicate that public access to resources which can support sexually intimate relationships was necessary.

Access to Resources That Support Sexually Intimate Relationships

The lack of resources that allow people with disabilities to enjoy long-term sexually intimate relationships was confounding to participants' construction of themselves as potential sexual partners (Kitchin, 2002). For instance, Ian felt by others not wanting to facilitate sexual activity between people with disabilities restricted his sexual expression:

Ian: I would have liked to [have sex] yeah but we just went to the bedroom and tried to get in there but we just ended up having a bit of a pash ["making out"] and a cuddle. I would have liked to [have sex] because at that time there was an attendant around they could have helped us but thought it was weird.

For John the practicalities of life with a disability made him feel skeptical about opportunities to access a long-term sexually intimate partner:

John: Let's just theorize for a moment. That other partner or person would end up with a great deal of the economic responsibility purely for the reason that employers will look at somebody with a disability and say "well yes we could tick a diversity box but we don't want all the red tape that goes along with it" and you know, that's a half reasonable economical decision to make. Particularly if you believe you are going to have to file a lot of forms, get a lot of approvals, and it's going to cost you to adjust the workplace, and if you're a small or even a medium or even sometimes a big business you wonder whether that is an appropriate use of your resources.

For all participants, accessibility proved to be an issue when trying to negotiate sexual opportunities. Not being able to engage in sexual activities or express one's sexuality had an impact on how people within the study constructed themselves and their bodies as sexual. In this regard, the consolidation of interactional and public sexual schema by the informants of this study was reinforced by private constructions of themselves and their sexuality.

Limitations

This study has some limitations (1) cultural homogeneity, (2) restrictions of qualitative methodology, and (3) constraints of script theory. First, all the participants in this study were Caucasian, from developed nations, had completed postsecondary education, and were within the spectrum of middle class socioeconomic status. Therefore, limited cultural and linguistic diversity (CALD) (Rao et al., 2006) may have skewed the findings. Research that includes a more culturally, ethnically, and financially diverse sample is needed in order to determine whether these diversification points would have an impact on the findings of this study.

Second, the qualitative methodology used within this study allowed for rich descriptive and contextual information. Interpretive inquiry allows for some data contours to be emphasized more than others (Mayoux, 2006). For instance, the data collected are mediated by the investigator's ability to ask questions or probe answers that enabled respondent's to comprehensively articulate their concepts, conceptualizations, and conceptions of sexuality with disability. In doing so, respondents may have found it easier to express some or certain sexual schema and not others due to their abstract nature or convolutions within the questions. Research that explores constructions of sexuality with cerebral palsy using different qualitative techniques (i.e., focus groups, case studies, and observations) would further clarify the findings of this study.

Third, sexual script theory was the theoretical basis for this research. Sexual script theory delineates sexual influences into public, interactional, and private sexual schema. However, the findings of this study emphasize that people with cerebral palsy are agents in the construction of their sexuality. Bandura's social cognitive theory (1986, 1997, 2006), which highlights people as social agents, may therefore be a better theory to apply to constructions of sexuality with cerebral palsy. Research that employs Bandura's social cognitive theory and constructions of sexual with disability would be beneficial to further understanding agency and sexuality with disability.

Conclusion

This study sought to investigate, understand, and develop existing knowledge and theory on how people with cerebral palsy construct their sexuality. Drawing attention to discussions on both sexual agency and being, this study found that constructions of sexuality with cerebral palsy are influenced by public sexual schema. It also highlights the role of people with cerebral palsy in the interpretation of those scripts and their manifestations. Ultimately, this study emphasizes that people with cerebral palsy are cognizant and intelligent about their sexuality the factors which influence its constructions. In particular, their conceptualizations and descriptions of their sexuality speak of their interest and awareness about key issues related to it.

In the recent past, constructions of sexuality were often defined by health care institutions and providers, educational institutions, religious organizations, parents, families, and peers' adoption of an "ignorance is bliss" attitude to discussing, educating, or advocating sexual activity for people with disabilities (Tepper, 2000). This lack of discussion concerning sexual expression and disability often stemmed from restrictions on the accessibility of comprehensive sexual information. Without inclusion in public discourses and popular culture, people with cerebral palsy and other disabilities may find it particularly difficult to accept themselves as complete sexual beings. While this may presently be the case, people with disabilities do experience and explore the many facets and potential faces of their sexuality. More about how they successfully do so requires exploration and dissemination amongst people with disabilities, disability advocates, and the general public in order to support sexual well-being and agency.

References

Anderson, P. and Kitchin, R. 2000. Disability, space, and sexuality: Access to family planning services, *Social Science and Medicine*, 51: 1163–74.

Bandura, A. 1986. *Social Foundations of Thought and Action: A Social Cognitive Theory*. Englewood Cliffs, NJ: Prentice-Hall.

Bandura, A. 1997. *Self-Efficacy: The Exercise of Control*. New York, NY: Worth.

Bandura, A. 2006. Guide for constructing self-efficacy scales, in Pajares, F. and Urdan, T. C. (eds.), *Self-Efficacy Beliefs of Adolescents*. Charlotte, NC: Information Age.

Barnes, C. and Mercer, G. 2010. *Exploring Disability*. Cambridge, UK: Polity.

Baudrillard, J. 1983. *Simulations*. New York, NY: Semiotext(e).

Berman, H., Harris, D., Enright, R., Gilpin, M., Cathers, T., and Bukovy, G. 1999. Sexuality and the adolescent with a physical disability: Understandings and misunderstandings, *Issues in Comprehensive Pediatric Nursing*, 22(4): 183–96.

Brown, D. E. 1988. Factors affecting psychosexual development of adults with congenital physical disabilities, *Physical and Occupational Therapy in Pediatrics*, 8(2–3): 43–58.

Brown, J. D., Halpern, C. T., and L'Engle, K. L. 2005. Mass media as a sexual super peer for early maturing girls, *Journal of Adolescent Health*, 36(5): 420–7.

Chance, R. S. 2002. To love and be loved: Sexuality and people with physical disabilities, *Journal of Psychology and Theology*, 30(3): 195–208.

Cole, S. S. and Cole, T. M. 1993. Sexuality, disability, and reproductive issues through the lifespan, *Sexuality and Disability*, 11(3): 189–205.

Corker, M. and French, S. 1999. *Disability Discourse*. New York, NY: Open University Press.

Corker, M. and Shakespeare, T. 2002. *Disability/Postmodernity: Embodying Disability Theory*. London, UK: Continuum.

Crewe, N. M. 1979. The psychologist's role in sexual rehabilitation of people with physical disabilities, *Sexuality and Disability*, 2(1): 16–22.

Dovidio, J. F., Pagotto, L., and Hebl, M. R. 2011. Implicit attitudes and discrimination against people with physical disabilities, in Dovidio, J. F., Pagotto, L., and Hebl, M. R. (eds.), *Disability and Aging Discrimination*. New York, NY: Springer.

Duncan, K., Goggin, G., and Newell, C. 2005. Don't talk about me … like I'm not here: Disability in Australian national cinema, *Metro Magazine: Media & Education Magazine*, 146/7: 152–9.

Dune, T. M. 2012a. *Constructions of Sexuality and Disability: Implications for People with Cerebral Palsy*. Saarbrücken, Germany: Lambert Academic Publishing.

Dune, T. M. 2012b. Sexual expression, fulfilment, and haemophilia: Reflections from the 16th Australian and New Zealand haemophilia conference, *Haemophilia*, 18(3): 138–9. US National Library of Medicine, National Institute of Health, Bethesda, MA.

Dune, T. M. and Shuttleworth, R. P. 2009. "It's just supposed to happen:" The myth of sexual spontaneity and the sexually marginalized, *Sexuality and Disability*, 27(2): 97–108.

Earle, S. 1999. Facilitated sex and the concept of sexual need: Disabled students and their personal assistants, *Disability and Society*, 14: 309–23.

Esibill, N. 1980. Sexuality and disability: A model for short term training, *Sexuality and Disability*, 3(2): 79–83.

Goggin, G. and Newell, C. 2002. *Digital Disability: The Social Construction of Disability in New Media (Critical Media Studies: Institutions, Politics, and Culture Series)*. Lanham, MD: Rowman & Littlefield.

Guildin, A. 2000. Self-claiming sexuality: Mobility impaired people and American culture, *Sexuality and Disability*, 18(4): 233–8.

Hammar, G. S., Ozolins, A., Idvall, E., and Rudebeck, C. E. 2009. Body image in adolescents with cerebral palsy, *Journal of Child Health Care*, 13(1): 19–29.

Hartnett, A. 2000. Escaping the "Evil Avenger" and the "Supercrip:" Images of disability in popular television, *Irish Communications Review*, 8: 21–9.

Holden, C. 2006. Just getting on with it: A record of service about relationships and disability, *Social Work with Groups*, 30(1): 29–44.

Howland, C. A. and Rintala, D. H. 2001. Dating behaviors of women with physical disabilities, *Sexuality and Disability*, 19(1): 41–70.

Jackson, S. 2005. "Dear girlfriend ...": Constructions of sexual health problems and sexual identities in letters to a teenage magazine, *Sexualities*, 8(3): 282–305.

Jang, M., Choi, J., and Lee, S. 2010. A customized mouse for people with physical disabilities, ASSETS 10 Proceedings of the 12th international ACM SIGACCESS conference on Computers and accessibility, New York, NY: ACM Digital Library.

Joseph, R. 1991. A case analysis in human sexuality: Counseling to a man with severe cerebral palsy, *Sexuality and Disability*, 9(2): 149–59.

Kitchin, R. 2002. *Towards emancipatory and empowering disability research: Reflections on three participatory action research projects*. Retrieved March 17, 2011, from http://sonify.psych.gatech.edu/~walkerb/classes/assisttech/pdf/Kitchin(2002).pdf.

Law Commission 1995. *Mental Incapacity: A Summary of the Law Commission's Recommendations (LC231)*. London, UK: Stationary Office.

Lemish, D. 2010. *Screening Gender on Children's Television: The Views of Producers Around the World*. London, UK: Taylor & Francis.

Majiet, S. 1996. Sexuality and disability, *Agenda*, 28: 77–80.

Mayoux, L. 2006. Quantitative, qualitative, or participatory? Which method, for what and when, in Desai, V. and Potter, R. B. (eds.), *Doing Development Research*. London, UK: Sage.

McCabe, M. and Taleporos, G. 2003. Sexual esteem, sexual satisfaction, and sexual behavior among people with physical disability, *Archives of Sexual Behavior*, 32: 359–69.

Milligan, M. S. and Neufeldt, A. H. 2001. The myth of asexuality: A survey of social and empirical evidence, *Sexuality and Disability*, 19(2): 91–109.

Moin, V., Duvdevany, I., and Mazor, D. 2009. Sexual identity, body image and life satisfaction among women with and without physical disability, *Sexuality and Disability*, 27(2): 83–95.

Murphy, K. P., Molnar, G. E., and Lankasky, K. 2000. Employment and social issues in adults with cerebral palsy, *Archives of Physical Medicine and Rehabilitation*, 81(6): 807–11.

Oliver, M. 1996. *Understanding Disability: From Theory to Practice*. Basingstoke, UK: Palgrave.

ParaQuad. 2010. *Personal care*. Retrieved October 26, 2010, from http://www.paraquad.org.au/CommunityServices/PersonalCare.aspx.

Pendo, E. 2010. A service learning project: Disability, access, and health care, *Journal of Law, Medicine, and Ethics*, 28: 2010–13.

Rao, D. V., Warburton, J., and Bartlett, H. 2006. Health and social needs of older Australians from culturally and linguistically diverse backgrounds: Issues and implications, *Australasian Journal on Ageing*, 25(4): 174–9.

Raynor, O. and Hayward, K. 2009. Breaking into the business: Experiences of actors with disabilities in the entertainment industry, *Journal of Research in Special Educational Needs*, 9(1): 39–47.

Ross, E. and Rapp, R. 1981. Sex and society: A research note from social history and anthropology, *Comparative Studies in Society and History*, 23(1): 51–72.

Rousso, H. 1993. Special considerations in counseling clients with cerebral palsy, *Sexuality and Disability*, 11(1): 99–108.

Rummel, A. M. 2008. *Travel by People with Physical Disabilities: A Diffusion Study Focused on Opinion Leadership*. Detroit, MI: Michigan State University.

Sanders, T. 2007. The politics of sexual citizenship: Commercial sex and disability, *Disability and Society*, 22(5): 439–55.

Sanders, T. 2008. Male sexual scripts: Intimacy, sexuality and pleasure in the purchase of commercial sex, *Sociology*, 42(3): 400–17.

Schillmeier, M. 2007. Dis/abling spaces of calculation: Blindness and money in everyday life, *Environment and Planning D: Society and Space*, 25(4), 594–609.

Shakespeare, T. 2000. Disabled sexuality: Toward rights and recognition, *Sexuality and Disability*, 18(3): 159–66.

Shuttleworth, R. P. 2000. The search for sexual intimacy for men with cerebral palsy. *Sexuality and Disability*, 18 (4): 263–282.

Simon, W. and Gagnon, J. H. 1986. Sexual scripts: Permanence and change, *Archives of Sexual Behavior*, 15(2): 97–120.

Simon, W. and Gagnon, J. H. 1987. A sexual scripts approach, in Geer, J. H. and O'Donohue, W. T. (eds.), *Theories of Human Sexuality*. London, UK: Plenum.

Simon, W. and Gagnon, J. H. 2003. Sexual scripts: Origins, influences, and changes, *Qualitative Sociology*, 26(4): 491–7.

Stevens, E., Steele, C. A., Jutai, J. W., Kalnins, I. V., Bortolussi, J. A., and Biggar, D. 1996. Adolescents with physical disabilities: Some psychosocial aspects of health, *Journal of Adolescent Health*, 19(2): 157–64.

Taleporos, G. and McCabe, M. 2001. Physical disability and sexual esteem, *Sexuality and Disability*, 19: 131–48.

Taleporos, G. and McCabe, M. 2005. The relationship between the severity and duration of physical disability and body esteem, *Psychology and Health*, 20(5): 637–50.

Tepper, M. S. 2000. Sexuality and disability: The missing discourse of pleasure, *Sexuality and Disability*, 18(4): 283–90.

Wilder, E. I. 2006. *Wheeling and Dealing: Living with Spinal Cord Injury*. Nashville, TN: Vanderbilt University Press.

Winkler, D., Sloan, S., and Callaway, L. 2007. *Younger People in Residential Aged Care: Support Needs, Preferences, and Future Directions*. Brentford Square, Australia: Summer Foundation.

Wiwanitkit, V. 2008. Sexuality and rehabilitation for individuals with cerebral palsy, *Sexuality and Disability*, 26(3): 175–7.

WHO 2011. Disabilitites.

Xenakis, N. and Goldberg, J. 2010. The young women's program: A health and wellness model to empower adolescents with physical disabilities, *Disability and Health Journal*, 3(2): 125–9.

Yoshida, K. K. 1994. Intimate and marital relationships: An insider's perspective, *Sexuality and Disabiltiy*, 12(3): 179–89.

Index

Note: Page numbers followed by "*fn*" indicate footnotes.